How We Became Middle-earth

A Collection of Essays on *The Lord of the Rings*

Edited by Adam Lam and Nataliya Oryshchuk

2007

Cormarë Series

No 13

Series Editors
Peter Buchs ● Thomas Honegger ● Andrew Moglestue

Editor responsible for this volume:
Peter Buchs

Library of Congress Cataloguing-in-Publication Data

Lam, Adam and Nataliya Oryshchuk (eds.)

How We Became Middle-earth

A Collection of Essays on The Lord of the Rings

ISBN 978-3-905703-07-8

Subject headings:

Cultural Studies—Globalization, ethnicity, modernity and postmodernity,
    postcolonial studies, consumerism
Fantasy fiction, English—History and criticism
Film—Adaptation, release, DVD release, audiences, national cinema, global cinema
Game—Internet, computer, video, role-play
Internet—Cyber space, virtual community, virtual space, game
Literature, Comparative
Middle-earth (Imaginary place)
New Zealand
Tolkien, J.R.R. (John Ronald Reuel), 1892-1973
Tolkien, J.R.R. (John Ronald Reuel), 1892-1973—Criticism and interpretation
Tourism

Photo of Hobbiton sign on the cover by Bill J. Jerome. All images in this book are photographed by Adam Lam, Nataliya Oryshchuk or Bill J. Jerome, as specified.

All rights reserved. No portion of this book may be reproduced, by any process or technique, without the express written consent of the publisher.

For my beloved children Nicholas and Annabelle

Adam Lam

To my New Zealand and Middle-earth friends:
Men, Elves and Hobbits, and to Professor Tolkien

Nataliya Oryshchuk

Contents

List of Abbreviations and Associated Terminology v

The Lord of the Rings Filmography vi

Foreword: Straddling the Date Line in *The Lord of the Rings*
Howard McNaughton... vii

Part One: The (Research) Fellowship of the Ring

1. Introduction: The Journey of the Ringbearers
   Adam Lam and Nataliya Oryshchuk.. 3
2. The (Research) Fellowship: Short Autobiographical Journals
   The Contributors 9
3. Creating Middle-earth: The Insiders' Views
   Anne Buchmann (Interviewer) 33
   Paul Brewer.. 35
   Erica Challis 38
   Carlene Cordova 41
   Warren Green 45
   Vic James 47
   Jean Johnston 50
   Peter Lyon 53
   Liz Mullane 55
   Daniel Reeve 58

PART TWO: A WORLD CONSUMED BY TWO TOWERS

SECTION I: Film Tours and New Zealand's Postcolonial Identity

4. POSTCARDS FROM THE SHIRE: Global Impressions of New Zealand after *The Lord of the Rings*
   LYNNETTE R. PORTER 67

5. THEME/FILM TOUR: The Disappearing of Illusion into Integral Reality
   LISA WONG 87

6. SEEING THE PROMISED LAND FROM AFAR: The Perception of New Zealand by Overseas *The Lord of the Rings* Audiences
   MARTIN BARKER AND ERNEST MATHIJS 107

7. WHOSE MIDDLE-EARTH IS IT? Reading *The Lord of the Rings* and New Zealand's New Identity from a Globalized, Post-Colonial Perspective
   DANIEL SMITH-ROWSEY 129

SECTION II: Modernity, Ecology, Space and Environmentalism

8. ONE WALL AND NO ROOF MAKE A HOUSE: The Illusion of Space and Place in Peter Jackson's *The Lord of the Rings*
   DAVID BUTLER 149

9. DIGITAL PERFECTION OR, WILL MIDDLE-EARTH BE THE DEATH OF NEW ZEALAND?
   LAURA CROSSLEY 169

10. BLOCKBUSTER PASTORAL: An Ecocritical Reading of Peter Jackson's *The Lord of the Rings* Films
    THOMAS MURRAY WILSON 185

11. MILLENNIALISM IN MIDDLE-EARTH: An Examination of the Relevance of *The Lord of the Rings*
    MICHAEL J. BRISBOIS 197

SECTION III: The Pilgrims in and beyond the Tale

12. ALL I REALLY NEED TO KNOW ABOUT NEW ZEALAND I LEARNED FROM PETER JACKSON
    BILL J. JEROME 215

13. TO SEX UP *THE LORD OF THE RINGS*: Jackson's Feminine Approach in His "Sub-creation"
    ELISE MCKENNA 229

14. IN LIGHT OF ZEN BUDDHISM: Reading Frodo Baggins' Journey to Rivendell
    LALIPA NILUBOL 239

15. THE WEIGHT OF EXISTENCE: A Camusian Analysis of Frodo's Journey
    GERALD A. POWELL 257

PART THREE: WHERE DOES THE KING RETURN TO?

SECTION IV: Interpretations Forever

16. SURPRISED BY JOY: Eucatastrophe in Tolkien's and Jackson's *The Lord of the Rings*
    CHRISTOPHER GARBOWSKI 271

17. J.R.R. TOLKIEN AND THE CHILD READER: Images of Inheritance and Resistance in *The Lord of the Rings* and J.K. Rowling's *Harry Potter*
    LORI M. CAMPBELL 291

18. ONE RING TO RULE THEM ALL: Power and Surveillance in the Film Adaptations of *The Lord of the Rings*
CHERYLYNN SILVIA 311

SECTION V: Tale after Tale

19. EXTENDING THE TALE: An Analysis of *The Lord of the Rings* Extended Editions
PAOLA VOCI 327

20. BREAKING OF THE FELLOWSHIP: Competing Discourses of Archives and Canons in *The Lord of the Rings* Internet Fandom
ROBIN ANNE REID 347

SECTION VI: The Lord of the Games

21. LORD OF THE GAMES? Father and Son Review *The Lord of the Rings* Video Games
KENNETH AND SIMON HENSHALL 373

22. WILL AN ONLINE VIRTUAL MIDDLE-EARTH STAND A CHANCE?
BILL J. JEROME 393

CONCLUSIONS

23. A ROAD TO EREWHON: Waiting for the King to Return
NATALIYA ORYSHCHUK 407

24. A JOURNEY TO EREWHON OR A JOURNEY TO NOWHERE?
ADAM LAM 415

INDEX 425

LIST OF ABBREVIATIONS AND ASSOCIATED TERMINOLOGIES

N.B. When reappeared in the same chapter, following abbreviations will be used and "novel" or "film(s)" might be omitted when context is clear.

FotR film	Peter Jackson's film adaptation of *The Fellowship of the Ring*; also written as **Peter Jackson's *FotR*** or **Jackson's *FotR***
FotR novel	J.R.R. Tolkien's novel of *The Fellowship of the Ring*; also written as **J.R.R. Tolkien's *FotR*** or **Tolkien's *FotR***
LotR	the tale of the Lord of the Rings (especially when used as a qualifying noun)
LotR film(s)	Peter Jackson's film adaptations of *The Lord of the Rings*; also written as **Peter Jackson's *LotR*** or **Jackson's *LotR***
LotR novel(s)	J.R.R. Tolkien's novel *The Lord of the Rings*; also written as **J.R.R. Tolkien's *LotR*** or **Tolkien's *LotR*** (see Bibliography section at the end of each chapter for the precise edition an author refers to)
RotK film	Peter Jackson's film adaptation of *The Return of the King*; also written as **Peter Jackson's *RotK*** or **Jackson's *RotK***
RotK novel	J.R.R. Tolkien's novel *The Return of the King*; also written as **J.R.R. Tolkien's *RotK*** or **Tolkien's *RotK***
TT film	Peter Jackson's film adaptation of *The Two Towers*; also written as **Peter Jackson's *TT*** or **Jackson's *TT***
TT novel	J.R.R. Tolkien's novel *The Two Towers*; also written as **J.R.R. Tolkien's *TT*** or **Tolkien's *TT***

THE LORD OF THE RINGS FILMOGRAPHY

N.B. This Filmography does not intend to give an account of all filmic/video adaptations of the *The Lord of the Rings*, but merely lists the film, video and DVD releases that are referred to in this book.

The Lord of the Rings
    Animated feature, dir. Ralph Bakshi, sc. Chris Conkling and Peter S. Beagle, Fantasy Films and Saul Zaentz Production Company
    a. Cinema release version 1978
    b. Home video release versions (Republic Pictures) 1995
    c. Home video/DVD release version (Warner Home Video) 2001

The Lord of the Rings: The Fellowship of the Ring
    Feature, dir. Peter Jackson, sc. Fran Walsh, Philippa Boyens and Peter Jackson, New Line Cinema and WingNut Films
    a. Cinema release version 2001
    b. Home video/DVD release version (New Line Home Entertainment, Inc.) 2002
    c. Home video/DVD release special extended version (New Line Home Entertainment, Inc.) 2002

The Lord of the Rings: The Two Towers
    Feature, dir. Peter Jackson, sc. Fran Walsh, Philippa Boyens, Stephen Sinclair and Peter Jackson, New Line Cinema and WingNut Films
    a. Cinema release version 2002
    b. Home video/DVD release version (New Line Home Entertainment, Inc.) 2003
    c. Home video/DVD release special extended version (New Line Home Entertainment, Inc.) 2003

The Lord of the Rings: The Return of the King
    Feature, dir. Peter Jackson, sc. Fran Walsh, Philippa Boyens and Peter Jackson, New Line Cinema and WingNut Films
    a. Cinema release version 2003
    b. Home video/DVD release version (New Line Home Entertainment, Inc.) 2004
    c. Home video/DVD release special extended version (New Line Home Entertainment, Inc.) 2004

Foreword
Straddling the Date Line in *The Lord of the Rings*

Howard McNaughton

Two young women, Liz and Prue, walk along a beach, paddling, and in a playful holiday mood. Their speech is New Zealand English. They are approached by a young German man.
Man: Excuse me. I wonder could you tell me is this where they make the film *The Piano*?
Liz: Aw no; that's the next-door beach, Karekare.
Man: Thank you. *He walks off.*

FILM LOCATION TOURISM was already well-established before it was parodied in the New Zealand postmodern film *Topless Women Talk about Their Lives* (dir. Harry Sinclair, 1997). The beach had become an international tourist destination within a few weeks of Jane Campion's success at Cannes, and was even used as the location for a music video by New Zealand's pioneer rap band, the Upper Hutt Posse, in a heavily politicized track (in Maori) addressing the pakeha as a pollutant of the land, *Whakakotahi*.

Similar contestations had surrounded other film projects as New Zealand was promoted as a location in the 1990s. But as well as these it may be noted that as filmmaking projects generated internal tensions over issues of cultural property rights and the politics of representation, externally there was a simultaneous refashioning of the visibility of the country and hence its cultural identity. At a conference in Chicago in 1996, the New Zealand film most familiar to participants was *Hercules: The Legendary Journeys* (TV series, 1995-1999), starring Kevin Sorbo, which in turn spawned *Xena: Warrior Princess* (TV series, 1995-2001). Both series included Danielle Cormack, Liz of *Topless Women*, but the feature that most confused the New Zealand eye was the sight of centaurs frolicking through tree ferns, cabbage trees, and other iconic elements of New Zealand vegetation that were not particularly prolific in pre-classical Greece. That the centaurs were played by Maori actors brought another layer of confusion, the tangata whenua being othered in their own land. A similar *trompe l'oeil* would be a recurrent motif in *The Last Samurai* (dir. Edward Zwick, 2003), filmed in Taranaki, and would be pervasive in the *LotR* trilogy.

Such a reading of *The Lord of the Rings*, through a post-colonial lens, is advanced in this book by Daniel Smith-Rowsey, who notes that Maori actors were often cast as "Uruk-hai—never as members of the race of Men", and suggestively relates this to Franz Fanon's writings on colour symbolism. Beside that, Laura Crossley cogently argues that "the very act of creating Middle-earth out of an existing landscape repeats the work of colonization: in the same way that colonial powers emptied a landscape of its original occupants and replaced their culture with their own settler history.... the barbarism and animal savagery of the autochthonous Uruk-hai is constructed and encoded" on the Maori body.

To the Chicago viewer, however, a Maoriland populated by Maori centaurs seemed unproblematic; after all, Marlon Brando's last film, *The Island of Doctor Moreau* (dir. John Frankenheimer, 1996), used Maori actors as animal-human composites. Internationally, the primary appeal of the New Zealand location was that it was cinematically untouched, a *tabula rasa* where anything might appear, a version of the 100% pure tourist promotional campaign to which President Clinton would contribute in 1999, playing golf in the shadow of Wakatipu's The Remarkables mountain range, the location of *Vertical Limit* (dir. Martin Campbell, 2000).[1] This was something the Australian film industry had gone through in the marketing of the desert (Murray, 1988), initially with Mel Gibson's *Mad Max* trilogy (dir. George Miller, 1979-1985) and features like *Walkabout* (dir. Nicolas Roeg, 1971), followed by *The Adventures of Priscilla, Queen of the Desert* (dir. Stephan Elliott, 1994) and *Rabbit Proof*

---

[1] The promotion, which is still active at http://www.newzealand.com/travel/, emerged in the late 1990s as "100% Pure New Zealand".

Fence (dir. Phillip Noyce, 2002). But the fundamental question is: Is this use of location production- or consumption-driven? Does the producer or the viewer determine the meaning that will brand the film?

The BBC used New Zealand locations for *Walking with Dinosaurs* (TV series, 1999) presumably because New Zealand's native flora is all evergreen, untouched by exotic deciduous trees especially in the virtually unpopulated Fiordland, where the terrain also contributes to a primordial ambience. An ambience, one could add, that might have had limited visibility if international film celebrities such as Sam Neill, of *Jurassic Park* (dir. Steven Spielberg, 1993) fame, did not live in the near vicinity. A similar explanation might lie behind the filming of Conan Doyle's *The Lost World* (TV film, dir. Stuart Orme, 2001),[2] originally located in Patagonia but filmed on the West Coast of the South Island, or in the 1999 screen version of *Journey to the Center of the Earth* (TV film, dir. George Miller) where Jules Verne's point of entry, Iceland, was ignored in favour of the off-shore volcano of White Island, relocated in the middle of Lake Taupo.

It's easy to explain this from a production point of view. Film New Zealand manager Jane Gilbert explained that in marketing "[w]e focus on New Zealand being a fantasy, surreal, alien, historical location." This remained Film New Zealand's position throughout the production of *LotR*:

> To truly create Middle-earth for *The Lord of the Rings*, the filmmakers had to find a location that could represent the earth as it might have appeared 7,000 years ago. In the South Pacific, across the International Date Line, they found their idyll in New Zealand, where a primal, untamed and unruly landscape still exists almost untouched by any blight of modern technology. "New Zealand has the essence of the old European countryside," says Peter Jackson. "Yet it also has an extraordinary quality that makes it perfect for *The Lord of the Rings*, as well as very experienced crew members." ... Adds John Rhys-Davies, who plays the Dwarf Gimli: "New Zealand is such a primitive land it can take you back to a primitive time in history. It's so breathtakingly beautiful that you believe that even in the twilight of doom there might still be humor, honor, courage and compassion." (Anon, 2007a)

---

[2] Filming of this was in 2000-2001; other versions were done at about the same time in Mongolia and in the Canadian Rockies.

Among many other similar statements, Jane Campion herself states that "New Zealand has a very deep sense of mystery in its landscape... There's a lot of sort of misty, foggy, primordial, deep looks to the New Zealand landscape."[3] For someone with an art school training, it's odd that these looks are not acknowledged as the constructions of the looker, that landscape is a cultural, not a natural, construction. This important point is emphasized by David Butler in this book, quoting Umberto Eco's assertion that landscape is "picked out, prepared, selected and hence *falsified* to some degree for the benefit of the shot".

But by the time our German tourist arrives on Campion's beach, it has been reclaimed and reinscribed in numerous ways—by no means the least being Maori repossession[4]—to the extent that Campion has already become an absence. As Dean MacCannell argues in his pioneer theorization of tourism, a tourist is a pilgrim who is drawn to a site which has been enhanced and signalled by "off-sight markers", a concept of pilgrimage nicely articulated in Lisa Wong's and Lynnette Porter's essays below. But what was Campion's beach has now been erased—let's say desemiotized—to the extent that our tourist, deprived of off-sight markers, has to approach the women on the beach for directions. And as he sets off, he carries with him his mental picture of what the beach should be like, a picture constructed from the film itself, from publicity material, and probably from necessarily out-of-date guidebooks. All of this prefigures how the dynamics of location tourism would function, albeit in a much more complex manner, in *LotR*, where, as Lisa Wong points out, Baudrillardian image-saturation has exploded to the point where the Te Papa exhibition actually *preceded* the release of the film. But it can also be asked if our German tourist is really a tourist, in MacCannell's sense of someone who temporarily leaves home in search of alienated leisure, or if he is rather a nomad, one who takes his home with him or travels in search of a home.

---

[3] This text, originally from a TV interview, is no longer on line, but is reported in *The New York Times*. (James, 2000)

[4] This was more carefully negotiated in *LotR*, where "Many of the locations were under the protection of the New Zealand Department of Conservation, but the filmmakers treated the land with the respect it deserved. The indigenous New Zealand people, the Maori, came to bless the production's soundstages before principal photography began." (Anon, 2007a)

Before addressing this question, we must note that the composition of Jane Campion's beach is not particularly well known. In pre-production, almost as important as Diana Rowan's role as casting director was Sally Sherratt's as location finder, whose job was checking out the numerous notionally "untouched" beaches within an hour of downtown Auckland to find the required features of black level sand, big surf, and so on. Her job of course was not to find a beach, or even to cast a beach, but to construct a beach, to assemble a set of signs of a beach. This process is well documented in the composition of *LotR*. No longer was a single location finder sufficient: now, scouts were followed by helicopter crews: "Jackson, along with Director of Photography Andrew Lesnie, first assistant director Carol Cunningham and a number of key crew set out on 'wreckeys' (helicopter scouting trips) to find their locations." (Anon, 2007b)

In this sense, as a syntagmatic assemblage, we may readily say that the screen seascape, the maritime montage of many cuts from many beaches, was Jane Campion's beach. In fact, when she refers to montage, as in her Lincoln Center interview, she talks about it in almost psychoanalytical terms, as linkages almost trying to find a syntax in the unconscious. This is what Kaja Silverman means when she writes of montage as indexical. (Silverman, 1983)

But such a structuralist understanding of location overlooks the postmodernism of *Topless Women* as well as the referentiality of *LotR*. When the German tourist walks off in search of the beach he can never find, Liz and Prue throw a filmscript into the surf:

> Liz: Aw, I forgot, I forgot. *Liz reaches into her satchel and pulls out a sheaf of typescript.* Check this out, it's Ant's screenplay. Read this, read that. *She hands the typescript to Prue, who hesitantly reads:*
> Prue: "Rebecca takes off her shirt, and then her bra. She looks at the camera, proud, defiant. 'When I was fourteen my family moved to Hamilton because my father had a job as the foreman on a construction site.'" That's weird!
> Liz: It's not weird, it's crap, that's what it is, it's crap. *She hurls the script into the surf.*
> Prue: You can't do that, it may be his only copy.

The metatheatricality of this situation, trashing a tabloid film within a film, is obvious. But we may also think they are playing out a scene of alienated leisure, literally leaving behind an emblem of metropolitan sleaze before they resume their paddle along the untouched beach. That, however, is to read the scene through the lens of tourism theory. To the untheorized eye of German tourism, the situation is quite different:

> *Cut to the women again paddling, singing. The German tourist reappears, walking back.*
> Man: Excuse me, I want a photo of... Ah, hello again. I want a photo of myself here. I don't have time to go to the other beach. I will just pretend.
> Liz: Sure.
> Prue: He's gorgeous. I haven't had sex since Ricky died.
> Liz: Honestly?
> Man: I'm ready now. *They photograph him.* How can people leave rubbish in this beautiful place? It's terrible. *He gropes in the surf.* Oh, it's a film script: "*Topless Women Talk about Their Lives*, by Anthony Bainbridge." Interesting. I have a friend who makes films in Germany. *They laugh.* Is funny. *To Prue.* I wonder, could I have a photo of you and me? Do you mind? *Liz takes a photo.*

So, in this early scene characters find in the surf the film they are actually in. This is a precise illustration in filmic terms of Deleuze and Guattari's concept of the nomad, and carries dynamics of deterritorialization, reterritorialization, and desemiotization that would be explored in much greater depth in *LotR*. The nomadic subjectivity that the German tourist brings is paradigmatic of the spatial manipulations that would govern *LotR*.

For Deleuze and Guattari, the essence of the nomad had been identified by Arnold Toynbee:

> ... the nomad is *he who does not move*. Whereas the migrant leaves behind a milieu that has become amorphous or hostile, the nomad is one who does not depart, does not want to depart.... It is in this sense that nomads have no points, paths, or land, even though they do by all appearances. If the nomad can be called the Deterritorialized par excellence, it is precisely because there is no reterritorialization *afterward* as with the migrant... With the nomad... it is deterritorialization that constitutes the relation to the earth, to such a degree that the nomad reterritorializes on deterritorialization itself. (Deleuze and Guattari, 1980: 381)

Such reterritorialization is subtly analyzed by Martin Barker and Ernest Mathijs in terms of "the transfer of meaning from landscape to film, and from film to landscape", where they observe that "[t]he *image* of the land could thence shift... to an *empty but fertile* set of imaginary spaces". As an illustration of this process, we may note Bill Jerome's epiphanic arrival at Mt. Sunday.

When the *LotR* trilogy was finally completed, Film New Zealand released an A0 two-sided map. One side showed *LotR* filming locations and production activity, medievalized so that the whole project was given a pre-industrial, if not exactly Neolithic, aura, with the workers identified as tanners, coopers, and the like, all floating in nomadic space; this may be seen as an instance of what Daniel Smith-Rowsey identifies as "the recovery of a legendary past through radical de-historicization and reconstruction of myths". The other side mapped the filming locations of about thirty well-known New Zealand feature films, making the point that films have been made in every part of the country, an argument supported by numerous boxes inviting us to "view 7000 more images at www.filmnz.com". Such a use of a pre-industrial veneer to camouflage what is essentially state-of-the-art production technology, is a commonplace trope of tourism, which MacCannell nicely terms "staged authenticity", and which is perhaps most commonly visible in the heritage site industry of reconstruction or restoration. Such projects often invoke the notion of an "original" which proves notoriously difficult to identify under close scrutiny. The museologist Tony Bennett goes so far as to argue that such a flirtation with the pre-industrial may be seen as

> ... materialising an idealised set of social relations which seems to flow from the past to the present in an unbroken continuity.... The past, as embodied in historic sites and museums, while existing in a frame which separates it from the present, is entirely the product of the present practices which organise and maintain that frame. (Bennett, 1993: 233)

So the past is only allowed an existence insofar as the present gives it a frame, as the present puts it on display.

Bennett's recurrent word is "idealised". The notion of an idealized past obviously fits in with the world of *LotR*, not just in terms of what Christopher Garbowski and others identify as "eucastastrophe", but also in terms of the social relations which Michael Brisbois related to the "shared fantasies" of "symbolic convergence theory". One way of constructing such relations is as a portal—Bennett would call it a frame of the present—through which the idealized alternative world may be accessed.

For nomadic subjectivity, however, there can be no singular portal any more than one singular alternative world. The filmmaking practice of Peter Jackson straddles both Mt. Ruapehu *and* the Weta Workshops, both of which are deeply implicated in Jackson's project of territorialization. That project eludes both spatial and temporal limits. The construction of Mt. Sunday and Ruapehu as markers of Middle-earth did not stop when Jackson's filming stopped. When Bill Jerome got to Mt. Sunday, someone was already there photographing it, potentially adding to Film New Zealand's stockpile of 7000 images. When the German tourist asks to be photographed playing the (wrong) Ada on the wrong beach, in the wrong *Piano*, he is constructing an alternative world, a possible sequel, queering Campion's beach.[5]

More than fifty years ago, Prague semiotics taught us that actors do not have to be animate: a block of wood can be an actor, an actor is simply a sign that refers to something else (often a character). Within the frame of Jackson's practice, Sunday and Ruapehu similarly become actors, generating a plasticity similar to the way that Jackson had morphed out buildings in *Heavenly Creatures* (dir. Peter Jackson, 1994) and *The Frighteners* (dir. Peter Jackson, 1996). Beside that, Cherylynn Silvia's Foucauldian reading of *LotR* unpacks complex mechanisms of power and surveillance that extend far beyond human agency or subjectivity. That Jackson also knows his Prague semiotics is clear from his comment: "Tolkien describes the locations very vividly in the book.... You can just imagine them in your mind's eye, so finding them was almost like casting an actor." (Anon, 2007b)

A similar malleability underpins Campion's beach, and she has in fact described her own attitude before making *The Piano* (dir, Jane Campion, 1993)

---

[5] *Topless Women* was released in two versions: as a tabloid television series of about forty three-minute episodes as a Friday serial on New Zealand's TV4, and later re-cut as a feature film. The passages quoted are from the tabloid version. Immediately after the last quotation in which the German is photographed with Prue, the script continues with a scene that was not included in the feature version:

Man: Thank you. I don't want my parents to know that I am homosexual. I want them to think that I meet nice girls.
Liz: Why don't you just tell them the truth?
Man: It would kill them.
Prue: The best guys are always gay.
Man: I agree. Yes. *They register the ironies, laugh, and dance in the surf.*

loosely in these terms, explaining in the Lincoln Center interview why she preferred working with friends rather than professional actors:

> I was like a control freak, an absolute maniac. I thought, "Actors, they're going to have ideas of their own—terrible, no way, forget it!" I'd have the detail of what everybody had to do down to the lift of the hand, you know. So I used friends, whose characteristics I liked, who were real and who could be real... But I didn't have to deal with them having too many ideas. [6]

We may note that Campion's perception of herself as a control freak is perhaps reflected in the object status of Ada, established on the first page by her statement that "today he married me" "a dumb creature" "to a man", and continuing until the last page when she expresses satisfaction with her prosthetic finger, the gift of a man to compensate for the act of another man.

In the *Topless Women* clip, the landscape loses its innocence as well as its mystery. The beach no longer has Campion's murky blue-green tinting, what the director of photography called the "bottom of the fish tank" effect, and which was supposed to make the bush and beach shots echo the underwater theme. Instead, it has a kind of public clarity. Its visibility is so great that it assumes the "artificial transparency" which Daniel Boorstin found characteristic of "pseudo-places" (Morris, 1993: 245), so that for the tourist any one of a chain of beaches or pseudo-beaches will do just as well. The idea of an original beach dissolves into a chain of undifferentiated coastal photo-opportunities. This of course was also true of Campion's beach-construction, except that it was camouflaged behind the shroud of what she called "mystery" and what Paul Fussell, following Boorstin, would term "opaqueness". (Morris, 1993: 245)

Peter Jackson's practice as a filmmaker had operated in these terms from the start. His manufacture of pseudo-places was central to *Forgotten Silver* (1995), the television hoax about a pioneer New Zealand filmmaker; Jackson himself was filmed discovering his abandoned epic sets in the South Island jungle. The model for such a media hoax was of course Orson Welles, who was also used by Jackson as an intertext in his psychosexual fantasy, *Heavenly Creatures*. Tara Brabazon has compared the use of Sam Neill as an actor with the use of filmic location in

---

[6] Same as Note 3 above.

Jackson's *The Frighteners*, where Christchurch's port of Lyttelton was given a daily makeover to serve as an American coastal town where Michael J. Fox practices a hoax exorcism business. As a local by-law requirement, the public set had to be struck every night, street and shop signs were regularly changed, traffic alternated between the left side of the road and the right, and so on. The town was caught up in a regular tidal drift between Americanization and New-Zealandization, Americanization and New-Zealandization, for day after day, between being a place and a pseudo-place or the sign of a place, an authentic lived place and an actor place. Tara Brabazon compares this with Sam Neill:

> For the knowing viewer, the specificity of place adds layers of interpretation to the film. Sam Neill is like a Lyttelton. He can be moulded by landscape and history to reveal a viewer's desire for authenticity, specificity or invisibility. (Brabazon, 2001: 171)

The "uncanny" dimensions of such a strategy of repeated desemiotization have been interestingly explored by those who have written on the Gothic substratum of *LotR*. Estella Tincknell had argued cogently for a Gothic reading of *The Piano*,[7] and it is scarcely surprising to find it extended to *LotR* in *Gothic NZ: The Darker Side of Kiwi Culture*, edited by Misha Kavka, Jennifer Lawn and Mary Paul. Specifically, Tincknell finds that *The Piano* draws on the tradition of the "Gothic 'dark wood'... dense, threatening, strangely claustrophobic", the antithesis of the prologue and epilogue set in "Scotland and Nelson, ... flooded with shimmering sunlight and brightly-lit, Technicolor hues", thus evoking the "pastoral paradise" of the book's title. In the same book, Andrea Wright would examine "Realms of Enchantment: New Zealand Landscape as Tolkienesque" to argue that

> New Zealand's affinity with Middle Earth is certainly connected with its abundance of unspoilt natural landscape but, more specifically, the concept of a primordial land... the film is a patchwork of locations used to create a sense of dis-location within an idyllic and complete fantasy space. (Kavka, 2006:55-56)

---

[7] Estella Tincknell, "New Zealand Gothic?: Jane Campion's *The Piano*". (Conrich and Woods, 2000: 107-119) A similar reading was also advanced by Kirsten Moana Thompson. (Thompson, 1999)

If this seems fairly self-evident, the uneasy juxtaposition of the pastoral and the Gothic is astutely analyzed in the present volume by Thomas Murray Wilson, who quotes Merry ("All that was once green and good in this world will be gone") to highlight the film's transition from a world of greenness and softness to one of rock and fire.

However, the very making of the film frequently invoked Freud's concept of the uncanny:

> "Middle-earth has a familiar feel to us, but as an audience you don't know exactly where it is. That is the beauty of New Zealand with fields that resemble England, mountains that could double as the Swiss Alps, or beautiful pristine lakes that you get in Italy—all this eclectic mix of locations in a small country where it is easy for a film crew to get from point A to point B," says co-producer Rick Porras. "It meant I didn't have to use my imagination because Hobbiton was there for Gandalf to feel at home in," notes Ian McKellen. (Anon, 2007a)

McKellen is clearly Jane Campion's ideal actor, untroubled by imagination or 'ideas'.

But it may also be argued that there is a heavily gendered edge to the uncanny in *LotR*. Following Tania Modleski, Estella Tincknell had analyzed *The Piano* on the basis that women's "sense of the uncanny may actually be stronger than men's": "This 'sense of the uncanny' is formalized in Gothic romance through the forebodings... as well as through anxiety about mothers and daughters." (Conrich and Woods, 2000: 111) In the present volume, we find Elise McKenna arguing that a "restoration of the feminine" pervades *LotR* from the moment *The Fellowship of the Ring* "opens with a woman's voice speaking Elvish". This of course has strong echoes of the opening of *The Piano*, as well as of the feminization of narrative in Lee Tamahori's *Once Were Warriors* (1994), but McKenna can extend the analysis to argue that Jackson gives his audience "a twenty-first century woman who is empowered to make a difference in the reconstructed mediaeval culture of Middle-earth".

Once Jackson's project is seen as one of "reconstruction", numerous parallel worlds emerge alongside Tolkien's text. As Lori Campbell notes, Tolkien "famously despised 'machines'... so one can only speculate about his response to websites and video games representing Middle-earth and its battle against evil." Paola Voci's description of Jackson's extended editions as a "self-reflective meta-text" is an attractive way of accounting for this parallelism, further extended into the sphere of alternative possible worlds in Bill Jerome's essay on virtual Middle-earths. Here the "original"—or even the possibility of an "original"—is left far behind, and even the concept of "the final integrity of the original work" is brought into question, as postmodernity processes Tolkien's master-text. But in the end even the concept of such a text is a simplification, as shown by Robin Anne Reid's account of the debates within fandom of the very idea of a Tolkien canon.

Of course, what is now at issue is the role of the reader—or rather the empowerment of the reader—as the response of the "interpretive communities" Paola Voci has written of means that reception analysis rewrites the text. This book demonstrates how different reading perspectives—from the Camusian to the Zen Buddhist to the child reader—generate radically different interpretations, each with a claim to its own legitimacy. In fact, it might even be seen to go beyond that, in the way that the video games discussed by Simon and Kenneth Henshall stimulate the players' world-creating energies, in this case leading to a proliferation of "cultural afterlives". Finally, it is the complexity of Tolkien's and Jackson's creation that accounts for its myriad groups of fandom and interpretive communities, but it is its richly heteroglossic texture alone that accommodates such a varied readership. A readership, one may add, that promises to expand dramatically if Nataliya Oryshchuk is successful in her current project of initiating Hobbits into the Dark Art of Cultural Studies.

Acknowledgement

Michael Daly of Film New Zealand has been extremely helpful in supplying information for this article.

Bibliography

Anon (2007a), "Middle-earth Down Under: The New Zealand Locations":
http://www.filmnz.org.nz/middleearth/press/notes/fellowship/10-nz.pdf

Anon (2007b), "Stylistic Harmony: Locations, Sets and Miniatures":
http://www.filmnz.org.nz/middleearth/press/notes/rokt/STYLISTICHARMONY.pdf

Bennett, Tony (1993), "History on the Rocks" in John Frow and Meaghan Morris (eds), *Australian Cultural Studies: A Reader*, University of Illinois Press, Urbana, pp. 222-240

Brabazon, Tara (2001), *Tracking the Jack: A Retracing of the Antipodes*, University of New South Wales, Sydney

Conrich, Ian and David Woods (eds) (2000), *New Zealand, A Pastoral Paradise?* Kakapo Books, Nottingham

Coombs, Felicity and Suzanne Gemmell (eds) (1999), *Piano Lessons: Approaches to* The Piano, John Libbey, Sydney

Deleuze, Gilles and Félix Guattari (1980), *Mille plateaux: Capitalisme et schizophrenie II*, Minuit, Paris

Film New Zealand, with Investment New Zealand (2005), *The New Zealand Screen Production Guide*. 2nd ed., Film New Zealand, Wellington; Investment New Zealand, Auckland

Gibson, Ross (1992), *South of the West: Postcolonialism and the Narrative Construction of Australia*, Indiana University Press, Bloomington

Gilbert, Jane and Desiree Keown (1999), *The Production Guide to the World in One Country*, Film New Zealand, Wellington

James, Caryn (2000), "Television Review; Why They Became Film Directors" *The New York Times* (17 February)

Kavka, Misha, Jennifer Lawn and Mary Paul (eds) (2006), *Gothic NZ: The Darker Side of Kiwi Culture*, University of Otago Press, Dunedin

MacCannell, Dean, (1976), *The Tourist: A New Theory of the Leisure Class*, Macmillan, London

Morris, Meaghan (1993), "At Henry Parkes Motel" in Frow, John, and Meaghan Morris (eds), *Australian Cultural Studies: A Reader*, University of Illinois Press, Urbana, pp. 241-275

Murray, Scott (ed.) (1988), *Back of Beyond: Discovering Australian Film and Television*, Australian Film Commission, Sydney [the proceedings of a Bicentenary project, a conference on Australian film held at UCLA]

Silverman, Kaja (1983), *The Subject of Semiotics*, Oxford University Press, New York

Thompson, Kirsten Moana (1999), "The Sickness unto Death: Dislocated Gothic in a Minor Key" in Felicity Coombs and Suzanne Gemmell (eds), *Piano Lessons*, John Libbey, Sydney, pp. 64-80

Reinvented geography: a place otherwise nameless is now called "LOR 6".
(photo by Nataliya Oryshchuk)

PART ONE

THE (RESEARCH) FELLOWSHIP OF THE RING

1

INTRODUCTION
The Journey of the Ringbearers

Adam Lam and Nataliya Oryshchuk

PERHAPS NOTHING defines our work here more clearly than the following passage, which we tagged "The Fellowship Manifesto" and attached to our call for contributions for this book:

> Scholars (at least those optimistic ones) have always acknowledged the value of humour, fun and play in their academic work. However, generally (if not always), they see these elements as enhancers—the icing on their academic cakes. As a matter of fact, the cakes are sometimes so dry, so plain and so tasteless, that only fellow scholars are able to appreciate their nutritional values.
>
> We are a group of serious scholars but we see knowledge as the icing on the cake—the enhancer of human lives—and something to be enjoyed. We make sure that our work is packed with humorous, funny and playful academic pursuits, yet we are, after all, playing a wonderful game.

So here is the cake—baked by all the contributors, many from very dissimilar fields and backgrounds. While we unanimously celebrate the fun and joy we experienced during the planning, writing and editing of this book, we also acknowledge the variety of viewpoints taken by each of us in our research careers, as well as in our lives. This diversity is evident from the very beginning, as you will see, in the Introduction—a split column effort, by both the editors.

We hope you will enjoy our cake... and appreciate the icing!

ADAM LAM
PhD
Programme Director for Cultural Studies
Senior Lecturer in Chinese
University of Canterbury
Christchurch
Aotearoa New Zealand

NATALIYA ORYSHCHUK
PhD
Tutor in Russian Studies
School of Languages and Cultures
University of Canterbury
Christchurch
Aotearoa New Zealand

I

Twelve years ago, in 1995, I migrated from Hong Kong to New Zealand (which, nowadays, is frequently referred as Middle-earth, as a result of the international triumph of Peter Jackson's cinematic adaptation of J.R.R. Tolkien's *The Lord of the Rings*). Although twelve years can be seen as a mere drop in the ocean, in terms of both human and Elvish history, this number still has some cultural significance. A number of events occurred in New Zealand's film and culture(s) during this short period which cannot be easily forgotten. First of all, twelve has frequently been expressed in different cultures as a set measurement of time—from the two twelve hour periods in a day to the twelve months in a year. Also, in the twelve years from 1993 to 2005, New Zealand experienced a change from

II

My journey to this collection started at the very beginning of the 1990s, when I read the first Russian translation of *The Hobbit*—a highly entertaining tale written by some Englishman. What was his surname? It sounded foreign but also Russian, at the same time. I soon learned that this Englishman was an Oxford professor and his name was J.R.R. Tolkien. I also learned that, as well as other tales, he had written an epic called *The Lord of the Rings*, which had recently been translated into Russian. The year of this discovery was mere international acknowledgement on the silver screen (through *The Piano*, dir. Jane Campion, 1993) to an established film location for Hollywood blockbusters, such as the *LotR* trilogy, *The Last Samurai* (dir. Edward Zwick, 2003), *King Kong* (dir. Peter Jackson, 2005) and *The Chronicles of Narnia: The Lion, the Witch and the Wardrobe* (dir. Andrew Adamson, 2005). The country now tops many tourists' lists of destinations for tracing fairy-tale fantasies or observing a down-to-the-earth, environmentally friendly and ecological location. In the global gaze, at the end of the twentieth century and the dawn of a new millennium, New Zealand emerged from a once isolated and colonial Middle-Ages and proudly stepped into the postcolonial world by branding itself as Middle-earth—a location in Tolkien's genre of the Fantastic, a hyperreal identity for this pacific nation. What have the cultural impact of Tolkien's original work and Jackson's adaptation of it brought to New Zealand and the rest of the world? How do we brand our national and cultural identities in the age of globalization? In searching for answers to these questions, we assembled a

1991; the place—the collapsing Soviet Union. Like many other Soviet teenagers enchanted by Tolkien's story, I was excitedly reading about the fall of Mordor and witnessing the historical fall of the USSR, simultaneously. Did we, standing on the ruins of the Soviet Empire (branded the "Empire of Evil" in the West), feel like the inhabitants of Middle-earth, at the dawn of the Fourth Age? Yes and no. Our Middle-earth was not to be found in the new post-Soviet (or post-Mordor?) reality, which (like most realities usually do) turned out to be harsh, chaotic and unwelcoming. But we did our best to become Middle-earth: speaking it, drawing it and role-playing it. And, exactly a decade after the rise of mass Tolkienism, the post-Soviet countries saw the "real" Middle-earth on the big screen, in movie-theatres. This illusionary yet very convincing Middle-earth was created by a New-Zealander: Peter Jackson. Did its convincing qualities mean that all New-Zealanders were true inhabitants of Tolkien's "promised land"? Was the Middle-earth identity a well-deserved reward or just an unexpected gift? Or was it a *gift* at all? To find out, I immigrated to New Zealand, where group of people with similar interests and, subsequently, collaborated on this volume of essays.

III

The birth of this book, as with many others (be they biographical, fictional or academic), was based on a coincidence or, to echo Christopher Garbowski's chapter title (which is borrowed from C.S. Lewis's book title), a "surprise by joy". Although Nataliya had been an MA student and then a PhD candidate at the University of Canterbury for a couple of years, we only really *met* in October 2004, at a postgraduate conference organized by the School of Languages and Cultures, where she gave a paper comparing the work of J.R.R. Tolkien and Russian writer, Alexander Grin. During the tea break, we chatted and I mentioned the coincidence that my wife, Lisa Wong, had written an essay on the *LotR* film tour in New Zealand (Chapter 5 in this collection). When we met again soon afterwards, we discovered that we shared the same dream of a book project. Three years later, this dream has come true. This is thanks firstly to Lisa, who brought the *LotR* films to my (serious) attention, and secondly to the quest for this collection awaited for me.

IV

I have always been fascinated by the topic of fairy-tales and heroic quests. When my plane landed in New Zealand, in January 2002, I felt like a little Hobbit on a quest for adventures. I marched straight to the walls of the enchanted castle (as I then imagined the University of Canterbury) and, with the battle cry "A Elbereth!", began fighting the dragon that is an MA in Literature. Possibly the Elvish magic of the cry worked because, a year later, I successfully graduated. But my real quest had barely begun, with the path of a PhD journey lying at my feet. I chose the Russian neo-Romantic writer Alexander Grin (still, alas, underestimated by the majority of critics) as my subject. While researching his enigmatic works and his influence on Soviet society, I discovered the connection between the fate of his and Tolkien's books: the creation of literary Romantic "cults"—"Tolkienism" and "Grinism", respectively. I was sharing my research findings at the postgraduate conference in October 2004 when I

Nataliya, whose enormous interest in and knowledge about Tolkien and the Fantastic genre has been the foundation of this project.

V

(It may sound as though I am a white-haired old man, from the Gandalf "affiliation" given to me by Nataliya, but no—I simply started to go grey when I was a teenager and, surprisingly, my hair is still only grey, not white!) There were three or four consecutive months when Nataliya and I worked together, on a daily basis (thanks to the convenience of being on the same campus and Internet technologies such as email), to establish the overall theme and style of this book. Our call for contributors was made early in 2005, and by the end of that year we had received chapter drafts from all the selected contributors. We were gratified by the responses, not only from scholars but also from Tolkien fans.

unexpectedly met Dr. Adam Lam (exactly as it *should* happen in a fairy-story!), who was also quite fascinated by the topic of imaginary lands and literary/film cults. "Why don't we co-edit a collection of works?" he asked, with a provocative, Gandalf-like intonation. And, like Bilbo Baggins, I couldn't bear the idea of being left behind when the others were going "to find a long-forgotten gold". Like him, I joined this exciting adventure.

VI

Our journey through this collection has had dangers hidden along the way (of course!). Most often, we had to face the monsters of Choice and Decision: selecting and refereeing essays, dividing the book into sections and, from time to time, adjusting previous decisions in keeping with new circumstances. For me personally, one of the most painful sacrifices was the necessity to "chop" the section on Russian/post-Soviet Tolkienism due to an insufficient number of chapters (one day I hope to embark on another journey and return to this topic!). Various other reasons prevented some potential authors from including their essays in this collection. Thus, our

Fellowship lost some of its members on the perilous road but the majority of us survived, fulfilling the quest and bringing twenty-four different chapters to our readers' attention.

The logic behind the arrangement of the chapters is self-explanatory and can be seen in the table of contents. We echo the volume titles Tolkien himself chose, quite arbitrarily, when his novel was first printed as a trilogy (at his publisher's request).

Most editors choose to include a thematic introduction of chapters at the beginning of a collection. However, whilst we felt it was important to express our appreciation of the richness and diversity of the chosen papers, we decided it would be more appropriate to let other contributors speak first. Consequently, we have left our own critiques and reflections for our concluding chapters.

We would like to thank all the people who responded to us and offered help with this wonderful project. In particular, we would like to thank all contributors to the book (the Research Fellowship). We also extend our gratitude to all those enthusiastic fans who wrote to us, at different stages of our research, offering assistance and inquiring about the date of the book's release. We very much appreciate the opportunity given to us by Walking Tree Publishers and owe special thanks to Thomas Honegger and Peter Buchs, at WTP, who provided valuable advice and continuous assistance. In addition, we wish to thank our colleagues at the University of Canterbury. Amongst them—Associate Professor Kenneth Henshall (Head of the School of Languages and Culture when this research began) gave us ongoing encouragement, and his support went further when he agreed to help us by completing the Index section of the book; Professor Howard McNaughton (former Head of the School of Culture, Literature and Society) advised us on various issues regarding publication; Pip Manley, a BA graduate currently completing her MA in Cultural Studies, helped by proofreading our earlier sample chapters and documents for the book contract; and last but not least, Colleen Borrie (Administrator of the School of Languages and Cultures), who undertook the heavy task of proofreading the final drafts of the book.

2

THE (RESEARCH) FELLOWSHIP
Short Autobiographical Journals

The Contributors

EACH CONTRIBUTOR to this book was invited by the editors to write a short bibliographical journal regarding her/his personal and/or academic background, engagements with *The Lord of the Ring* (books and/or films) and with this book project, and any opinions that they were not be able to include within the constrains of the "formal" chapter text. While we, as editors, have already utilized the space in the Introduction to give our accounts of the journey, the entries of the other contributors are arranged here in alphabetical order by name.

The Editors

MARTIN BARKER

PhD, Professor of Film and Television Studies, Head of the Centre for Audience and Reception Studies, University of Wales, Aberystwyth, U.K.

I have, for a long time, researched the history of censorship campaigns, the nature of controversial media forms, and the reactions of real, rather than assumed, audiences to these sorts of materials. Among my books are *A Haunt of Fears* (1984), *The Video Nasties: Freedom and Censorship in the Arts* (1984), *Comics: Ideology, Power and the Critics* (1989), (with Roger Sabin) *The Lasting of the Mohicans: History of an American Myth*

(1997), (with Jane Arthurs and Ramaswami Harindranath) *The Crash Controversy: Censorship Campaigns and Film Reception* (2001), and (with Julian Petley) *Ill Effects: The Media/Violence Debate* (1997/2001). I was Director of the 2003-2004 international project to study the launch and reception of the final part of the film trilogy of *The Lord of the Rings*.

Born in 1946, I first read Tolkien's work in the late 1950s—and then again and again across the 1960s. Although I probably couldn't have said it at the time, reading Tolkien was part of the development of my socialist political perspective on the world, because of the ways the books for me raised the issues of choices between right and wrong, the inexorable nature of evil, and the need for people to band together, even sometimes without hope, to challenge the wrongs of their world. Part of my motive for initiating the study of the film's audiences was because of my own reactions to the film adaptation. Enjoying the sheer drama and spectacle, and the films' bravura, I was nonetheless deeply bothered by a series of changes which to me reduced the processes of *reasoning* and *choosing* in the narrative. But no one else seemed to share my particular objections, so the researcher took over, and I wanted to know how others had responded. Such is the life of the convinced academic.

MICHAEL J. BRISBOIS

PhD candidate, University of Calgary, Canada

My lifelong involvement with Tolkien's work stems back to elementary school. Since being caught reading *The Lord of the Rings* during math class, I have let the interests in all things literary that the novel awakened lead me to a career in English Studies. My previous publications include "Tolkien's Imaginary Nature: An Analysis of the Structure of Middle-earth" (*Tolkien Studies* 2.1, 2005: 197-216). Currently I am involved in research projects related to International Modernism and Cultural Theory.

ANNE BUCHMANN

PhD (Lincoln University), Aotearoa New Zealand

I am currently completing a Doctor of Philosophy at Lincoln University, Aotearoa New Zealand. The thesis title is *In the Footsteps of the Fellowship: Understanding the Expectations and Experiences of Lord of the Rings Tourists on Guided Tours in New Zealand*. It is a qualitative research project that investigates the experience of tourists in guided film tours through a variety of methods including observations, participant journals, questionnaires and interviews. The study found that film tourists, especially *Lord of the Rings* tourists, undertake a meaningful and spiritually significant journey that is enhanced through the experience of embodiment and a (perceived) mythical landscape.

I have been working as guest lecturer, conference moderator, and referee for various publications and am now applying for academic jobs. My previous dissertation project was entitled *Gender and Sustainability: The Influence of the "Sex and Gender"-Debate within the Chilean Sustainability-Discourse* for a Master of Environmental Sciences degree at University of Lüneburg, Germany (1996-2003). I hold various Academic Awards, including Lincoln University Postgraduate Scholarship (2005-2006), McEwings Mountain Sports Macpac Wilderness Equipment Research Scholarship (2004) and Hans Böckler-Stiftung full academic scholarship through the German Foundation for the Highly Gifted (1998-2003).

My main research interests are tourism and myths, literature and film, medieval history and (of course) Tolkien. I am a member of a re-enactment sword fighting and horse jousting team with armour, helmet, mail and garb made in accordance with historical sources. I am an enthusiastic reader of *The History of Middle-earth* and avid hiker of Aotearoa New Zealand.

The Contributors

DAVID BUTLER

PhD, Lecturer in Screen Studies, University of Manchester, U.K.

The Lord of the Rings was daring me to read it from an early age. The book lurked on a shelf in our house, with a cover that promised adventure (a group of travellers standing at the head of a valley, gazing out toward distant peaks, with the borders of the cover a tangle of tree roots within which dwelt strange creatures with bulbous eyes. Not for the last time would I be challenged by those bulbous eyes). I don't know who had bought it or even if they'd read it—maybe it was part of a *Reader's Digest* offer my Dad had signed up for. But it sat there, on a bottom shelf in the living room, daring me to open it and read.

And I tried and gave up. I must have been four or five, but I had a go and couldn't get past chapter one. There was something about a dragon, which sounded promising, but a lot about the arrangements for a party, which sounded dull, and so the book was closed.

But Middle-earth wouldn't go away. In 1978 my Mum took me to see Ralph Bakshi's animated film and it terrified me. To this day, I'd still argue that, for all the film's flaws, there is a gothic monstrousness to Bakshi's Ringwraiths that makes them far more strange and disturbing than Peter Jackson's. A few years later, in 1981, I was listening to the BBC radio version, with the episode set in Moria making a great impression, but still not enough to return to the book.

Then the turning point. In 1983 we got a ZX Spectrum computer and, soon after, the adventure game based on *The Hobbit*. You got a free copy of the book too but I naively plunged into the game, convinced I didn't need to do any training by reading-up in advance. And I kept getting eaten by the trolls. I had no idea how to defeat them. In frustration I turned to the book and learnt that all I needed to do was... nothing. Wait for the sun to rise and the trolls turn to stone (they don't teach you important things like this at school). And *now* I wanted to read!

I've loved Tolkien's work ever since. Not unreservedly—there are idiosyncrasies and attitudes that, at differing times, I've found bemusing, perplexing or troubling. But exploring Middle-earth as a child gifted me two things that have remained with me ever since: a deep love and respect for the natural world (growing up around the Lake District meant that Middle-earth never seemed that far away and that impossible), and a joy in the creative act and expression of identity through culture, whether that was map-making, singing a song as we walked the fells or telling stories as we shared a meal. I've found far more in Middle-earth than I could have imagined since closing that first chapter all those years ago: perseverance not least!

LORI M. CAMPBELL

BA, MA, PhD, Visiting Lecturer, Department of English and Cultural Studies, University of Pittsburgh, U.S.A.

From about the time I learnt to read at two and a half (thanks Dad, wherever you are in the Undying Lands) to the present, I have had a deep love for the Fantastic. Yet, being of a generation or so beyond his original publication, I did not come to Tolkien until about nineteen, when I noticed an "Anniversary Edition" of *The Lord of the Rings* in a vintage bookshop. At the time I had just undergone a particularly painful break-up with a boy and found such comfort in Middle-earth. Superficially, of course, this was due to the lack of "sappy" romance in *LotR*. More profoundly—and I'm sure I didn't consciously realize this then—I responded to that elusive *something* in this volume that we, along with countless readers and scholars before us and assuredly in the future, have and will continue to explore and seek to unravel. To explain this *something* in what can only be an inadequate way, I will simply reiterate what so many have felt over time: Tolkien speaks to and about the essences of things in a way that is undeniably true and intimate for each reader, as well as for that weighty entity of "humanity" fraught with so many complexities, frailties, and paradoxes.

Since that first reading, I have reread, studied, and taught *LotR* many times. My graduate work in nineteenth- and twentieth-century British and American literature at Duquesne University included a special focus on the Fantastic. At University of Pittsburgh, I primarily teach courses in Fantasy, the Gothic,

Children's Literature and Childhood Studies, along with a range of courses in Romantic, Victorian and Twentieth-Century Literature, and in Composition. My publications are in these fields, dovetailing with my book project, *Portals of Power: Magical Agency in Literary Fantasy from the Victorian to the Contemporary*, which provides an in-depth study of the gateway between worlds. In 2005 I established The Fantasy Studies Fellowship, a social and intellectual discussion group for Pitt students dedicated to the study and appreciation of the Fantastic. The group continues to draw savvy, passionate members who, while coming to the genre for their own myriad reasons, continually illustrate to me in very moving ways the power and magic that in many ways begins with J.R.R. Tolkien.

LAURA CROSSLEY

MA, PhD candidate, University of Manchester, U.K.

I completed my MA in Screen Studies at the University of Manchester in 2004 and am currently in the third year of my PhD. My thesis focuses on how British national identity is constructed in contemporary screen myth, with Peter Jackson's *The Lord of the Rings* trilogy (2001-2003) forming the core of the case studies. My other research interests include the evolution of classic *film noir* into contemporary *neo noir*, the ideology of American politics on film, and Chinese cinema.

My main interest in *LotR* is in examining how it fulfils a similar function as that of the Arthurian myth cycle: namely, how it reflects cultural issues and anxieties largely centred on nationhood and identity.

CHRISTOPHER GARBOWSKI

PhD, Associate Professor, Department of English, Maria Curie-Sklodowska University, Poland

I am the author of *Recovery and Transcendence for the Contemporary Mythmaker: The Spiritual Dimension in the Works of J.R.R. Tolkien* (2000) and *Spiritual Values in Peter Jackson's* The Lord of the Rings (2005).

Before I outline my personal involvement with Tolkien scholarship, I'd like to point out that inadvertently or not, the editors of this volume have raised a timely issue by calling its contributors section "The Fellowship". Fellowship is a Tolkienian term evoking the theme of community. Tolkien himself taught at Oxford, one of the oldest "community of scholars". However, for some time research at a university has been undergoing a transformation into virtually an industrial affair. With its initial low status, the study of Tolkien partly avoided this process but is now quickly becoming integrated into the "knowledge factory": among other signs, a yearbook of the latest scholarship is currently published by a university press, while an encyclopaedia with contributions by well over a hundred scholars has recently been published by Routledge. This publishing and research activity has given Tolkien studies a modicum of respectability in literary studies and opened it up in new fields such as cultural studies and, now with Peter Jackson's adaptation of *The Lord of the Rings*, film studies as well. More disciplines are likely to follow. This is all very exciting in theory, and I have in my own way participated in the process, but it does put a strain on the practice of fellowship and sense of community which earlier scholars in the field could experience. I might add that it is in wonderful havens like Walking Tree Publishers that the original sense of community is largely maintained.

The title of this volume *How We Became Middle-earth* refers to New Zealand, but it can also pertain to the contributors. Certainly to the extent that my years of writing about Tolkien have had an impact on me—and they certainly have—I also carry some of Middle-earth within me. It is in drawing upon my accumulated body of reflections on that enchanted land that I have attempted to contribute to this Fellowship's journey there and back again. Aside from the normal course of academic research on Tolkien, my work has incorporated, at least indirectly, the experience of reading his works to my sons and watching their fascination branch off into related interests, such as fantasy role-playing games. It has likewise included the rich experience of speaking on Tolkien outside the regular academic venues at events organized by various Tolkien societies in different countries, with the chance to meet his readers from a variety of walks of life. There are a number of fields outside of Tolkien studies that I wish to explore, but the above reasons have made it particularly precious to me (Oops, that has a nasty Ring to it!).

Kenneth Henshall

PhD, Associate Professor of Japanese, University of Canterbury, Christchurch, Aotearoa New Zealand

More than four times the age of my son Simon, I am described by said son as completely uncool except for my ability to get gold in all the *Gran Turismo* licences and to score 1200 runs (the game's limit) in *Shane Warne Cricket*. I went to the same secondary school in England as Tolkien, and, swayed by its academic heritage, foolishly forsook a career in professional soccer (albeit in the days before mega-salaries) to become an academic. I have fourteen books to date in the field of Japanese Studies, and one on early British history appearing shortly (a personal interest). I have been fortunate in that my books on Japanese history and Japanese characters have proved particularly popular. I list my top five books as:

- *A History of Japan: From Stone Age to Superpower* (Macmillan, London, 1999; second edition PalgraveMacmillan, London, 2004; also translated into a variety of languages including Chinese);
- *A Guide to Remembering Japanese Characters* (Tuttle, Tokyo, 1988);
- *The Last War of Empires: Japan and the Pacific War, 1941-1945* (with Laurie Barber: Bateman, Auckland, 1999);
- *A Guide to Reading and Writing Japanese* (chief editor, with Chris Seeley and Henk de Groot: Tuttle, Tokyo, 2003);

- *Dimensions of Japanese Society: Gender, Margins and Mainstream* (Macmillan, London, 1999).

SIMON HENSHALL

Student, Darfield High School, Aotearoa New Zealand

Simon Henshall was thirteen years old at the time of writing and a Year Nine Student at Darfield High near Christchurch. He has been an avid video game enthusiast ever since getting a Nintendo 64 for his sixth birthday, and is familiar with all platforms and formats. In 2003 he came top in the country with 100% in the University of New South Wales Computer Science Test, and has achieved world record times for fastest completion in a number of video games. In 2005 he attended a week-long workshop on game programming. He has already produced his own basic video game and is considering a career in this field. His favourite game at the moment is *Halo 2*, and his online favourite is *Runescape*. His other likes include cats, word games, chess (he's the youngest member of his school team), and gangsta rap music; his hates include garden centres, homework, tidying his bedroom, and being seen by his friends while out with his parents.

BILL J. JEROME

BS, MHCI, Research Programming Project Director, Carnegie Mellon University, U.S.A.

I am a Research Programming Project Director at Carnegie Mellon University (Pittsburgh, Pennsylvania, USA) working for the Open Learning Initiative. Having previously obtained a BS in Computer Science and a Masters in Human Computer Interaction from CMU, I am currently employed using both sets of skills to produce and evaluate software infrastructures for creating online courses that represent the enactment of teaching, rather than simple presentation of static course material. My research interests also include user community development via online tools in online gaming environments, as well as observing the interaction of software engineering and usability expert techniques in the non-academic world in an effort to guide research results into corporate practice more effectively.

A graduate of Guilderland High School in Guilderland, NY, I spent a lot of time working at the school's television studio, both as an anchor/reporter and as a technician. My favourite interviews included candidate and mogul Steve Forbes, Senator Bob Dole, and Mike Pinder of the Moody Blues. I also worked for a local network affiliate for a number of years. These experiences have helped to give me a partial appreciation of the difficulty involved in producing the *The Lord of the Rings* films, and my computer expertise gives me an even better one.

My hobbies include home audio and theatre, reading, enjoying music and camping. Recently, figuring out how to get back to New Zealand has also been a preoccupation.

Ernest Mathijs

PhD (Brussels), Assistant Professor in Film and Theatre Studies, University of British Columbia, Vancouver, Canada

Such are my professional affiliations. On a personal level, *The Lord of the Rings* research has brought me closer to my family, whose enthusiasm for the stories I can now share. It has also forged a bond with colleagues and *companions de route* which will never fade.

The *LotR*'s appeal always posed a mystery to me, and it is perhaps because of the need to understand others' never-fledgling passion for it that I felt the urge to embark upon a research project to investigate its worldwide reception. Next to that, the challenge to study the anticipation with which a Hollywood blockbuster is prepared for an audience was one I did not want to miss out on. My co-author here, and the director of the project, Martin Barker, pulled me into the research with the cunning philosophical wit of a Wizard, and managed our collaboration with the sense of practicality of a Hobbit. It has been a most wonderful ride, and we became close friends. Administratively speaking, most of the research for this contribution was conducted at the University of Wales, Aberystwyth, and funded by the ESRC (project number: 000-22-0323). Its core results are published in *Watching the Lord of the Rings* (edited, with Martin Barker, Peter Lang, 2007). Other results appear in *The Lord of the Rings: Popular Culture in Global Context* (Wallflower Press, 2006), and *From Hobbits to Hollywood* (with Murray Pomerance, Editions Rodopi, 2006). Additional materials were published in the *Tijdschrift voor Media and Communicatiewetenschap* (2006), and presented at ICA, IAMCR and SCMS conferences.

My other academic efforts concern the receptions of alternative and cult cinema, and of film and stage performance. These were published in *Film International, Screen, Cinema Journal, Social Semiotics, Literature/Film Quarterly*, and *History of Political Economy*. I have also edited the books *The Cinema of the Low Countries* (Wallflower Press, 2004), *Alternative Europe* (with Xavier Mendik, Wallflower Press, 2004), *Big Brother International* (with Janet Jones, Wallflower Press, 2004). Currently, I am editing *The Cult Film Reader*, and finishing the monograph *The Cinema of David Cronenberg*. I coordinate the series *Contemporary Cinema* (with Steven Schneider) and *Cultographies* (with Jamie Sexton and Xavier Mendik), and chair the editorial board of the online journal *Particip@tions* (www.participations.org).

ELIZABETH (ELISE) CAEMASACHE MCKENNA

MA, Creative Writing and Composition Instructor, University of Central Florida and Valencia Community College, Florida, U.S.A.

I have been a fan of J.R.R. Tolkien for nearly thirty years and am honoured to be a part of the *How We Became Middle-earth* project. I am a member of the Tolkien Society, the Joseph Campbell Foundation, the Daytona Beach Paranormal Research Group, and the International Thespian Society. With over twenty years of experience in education and as a recipient of local awards and grants, I have been teaching literature and creative writing, using myth as a basis, at the college and university level for six years. My first scholarly essay on J.R.R. Tolkien titled, "Peter Jackson's *Phantasia*: The Fellowship of the Ring" was published in the July 2004 issue of *Eclectica*. I am slated to teach a Tolkien class at Valencia Community College in January 2007. I have conducted workshops and symposiums as well as a presentation entitled as "Sound and Element: Feminine Magic in J.R.R. Tolkien's *The Silmarillion*" at the Tolkien Down Under conference: "The Art & Science of Magic in Middle Earth" in August 2007.

I have always been fascinated by the fantasy genre and have several short stories of that nature published. My Master's thesis, *A Sense of Other*, also dealt with this topic, relying on myth partly inspired by Tolkien's creative and academic works. I started my own critical work on the Tolkien writings in an American high school, where I read and analysed *The Hobbit*. From there, my fascination and appreciation of the other works of Tolkien continued, contributing immensely to my bookshelf. My favourite short story is "Leaf by Niggle"—however, my first love is *The Silmarillion*, and I am currently working on an article analysing the journey/quest theme in the tale of Beren and Lúthien. The story is both touching and unique because a male and a female character are working in unison as heroes. Knowing that Tolkien's inspiration was his sweetheart and wife, Edith, deepens the passionate story of the two characters, something that I aspire to in my writing. In my own life, I was fortunate enough to find my Beren, Thomas Allen Begley, Jr., my husband of thirteen years. We have been constant companions since the day we first laid eyes upon one another. Thomas' unconditional love, never-ending support, and foolish willingness to brave the raging North Sea at Scarborough for a vial of living water were miracles in my life. In memory of Thomas, whose life was tragically cut short in November 2006, I dedicate this poem:

Mo leannan àlainn

Mo chroí,
Mo cairde,
Anamchara a duine eile,
mo chuisle,

táim i ngrá leat
Gráim thú
cronaím thú
Tá tú go h-álainn
grá mo chroí
le grá go deo
go síoraí,
go deo na ndeor.

Howard McNaughton

PhD, LittD, Professor of English and Cultural Studies, University of Canterbury, Aotearoa New Zealand

My first MA was in Classics, at a time when Comparative Philology was still hot: Linear B had recently been deciphered, and we were queuing up to crack Linear A. So when I switched to English for my second MA, J.R.R. Tolkien immediately seemed like a kindred spirit: a distinguished scholar of Old English and the alliterative tradition, who was rumoured to have a secret life in the non-canonical world as well.

We, of course, didn't consider reading *The Lord of the Rings* at the time, probably dismissing it as one of those eccentricities that went with an Oxford chair. It was only in the 1980s when, stimulated or challenged by the growth of Cultural Studies, English Literary Studies started relaxing its barricades and looking at texts other than poetry, drama and the novel, that we were surprised to discover that scholars of Tolkien's generation were often untroubled by such narrow thinking. We introduced *LotR* as a set text for our Introduction to Literary Study course, and followed it up with *The War of the Worlds* and *The Hunting of the Snark*.

Cultural Studies also brought new perspectives on visual culture, including film, and after a predictable amount of academic debate it became acceptable to include films as texts in courses such as New Zealand and Australian Literature. Literary and Cultural Studies began to merge in ways that clearly enriched the curriculum, and the emergent New Zealand film industry offered a parallel growth pattern which has always been very supportive of our course development. The interdisciplinarity of Cultural Studies—which I find among its most attractive features—means that this is the third very interesting book project I have worked on with Adam Lam. My ambition for the moment is to find time to go back to read Tolkien on *Beowulf* and *Gawain*, through the lens of *LotR*.

LALIPA NILUBOL

MA, Independent Scholar, Wellington, Aotearoa New Zealand

I certainly wasn't a Tolkien fan as a child. When I was about six or seven, my Mum bought me one of those *The Lord of the Rings* cartoons, and I found that the Black Riders were far too scary for me. So I think that put me off *LotR*—somewhat. Then, around fifteen years sailed past, and Christmas 2001 came along. The first screening of *The Fellowship of the Ring* was about to hit Wellington. And, needless to say, Wellington was "over-heated" with anticipation. Then came the day of the *FotR* premiere—the day when Wellington literally became Middle-earth. Just for the day of the premiere, the name of our capital was changed to Middle-earth; Wellington City Council became Middle-earth City Council; *The Dominion Post* became *Middle-earth Post*; and Wellington Town Hall became Middle-earth Town Hall, to name only a few these transformations. But since it was announced that Cate Blanchett (one of my most beloved actresses) wasn't coming, I did not plan to go to the premiere.

Five p.m., 18 December 2001—the day of the premiere of *FotR*: I went downtown, intending to buy some groceries. But, alas, that was not meant to be, as Courtenay Place was overflowing with crowds waiting to welcome the cast and crew. So I decided to wind my way through the crowds. "I might as well stay," I thought to myself, "I'm here now." I managed to make my way to the Deluxe Café which is right next to the Embassy Theatre where the film would be screening. I sat myself comfortably next to the window of the café—the window that would provide me with golden views throughout the whole event.

Finally, the cast and crew arrived, and everyone was screaming, needless to say—I mean, *I* was screaming! I didn't even know who half of them were: who was Dominic Monaghan? Who was Billy Boyd? Who was Orlando Bloom? (Boy, can you *imagine* not knowing who Orlando Bloom is *by now*?!) The earth shook when Peter Jackson arrived! And then I spontaneously understood what "stardom" meant, and moreover, what it meant to be gazing at "stars" in the flesh, especially when they are completely immersed in their moment of stardom. And it was then that I came to a realization that *LotR* film trilogy was to become a source of national pride, obsession, and poetic fantasies. The spirit of the fan had possessed me I'm afraid, even before I saw the first of the film trilogy, and even before I started seriously reading Tolkien's works.

I hope that my article "In Light of Zen Buddhism: Reading Frodo Baggins' Journey to Rivendell" manages to convey that the quest for a spiritual source is indeed a universal one, and that works of supreme romantic imagination such as Tolkien's writings and Peter Jackson's film trilogy have shown this universality most skilfully.

LYNNETTE R. PORTER

PhD, Associate Professor, Department of Humanities and Social Sciences, Embry-Riddle Aeronautical University, U.S.A.

J.R.R. Tolkien and, much later, Peter Jackson have Bilbo Baggins warn Frodo about being swept off his feet if he steps out on to the road outside his door, because there is no telling where he might end up. Creatively, professionally, and geographically, this advice certainly has been prophetic for me. Travelling the Tolkien road is an adventure. I enjoy the places where I have been swept, but the journey is not over yet, I'm sure. My long association with and affection for Tolkien and *The Lord of the Rings* began at fourteen, when I first read the book. Since then I have reread it many times and seen and heard numerous adaptations, from the BBC radio version to stage productions to Peter Jackson's cinematic trilogy. When Jackson's first *LotR* film arrived fresh from New Zealand, with the result that my students developed a keen interest in Tolkien and *LotR*, I incorporated studies of the book and films in Honours classes at Embry-Riddle. The films renewed my interest in all things Tolkien, which sparked my scholarly creativity and motivated me to write. The result, so far, has been *Unsung Heroes of* The Lord of the Rings: *From the Page to the Screen* (Greenwood, 2005); two essays in *Lembas for the Soul* (2005), White Tree Press's initial publication; scholarly presentations before the Popular Culture Association, Popular Culture Association in the South, Tolkien Society gatherings, and fan-oriented conventions such as the UK's Fellowship Festival and the US' ORC and ELF; and public presentations at universities and libraries about a variety of Tolkien-related topics.

The *LotR* road is full of surprising twists, one being this book. I first learned of the New Zealand-based project through a notice posted on TheOneRingNet, and now, months after an initial inquiry about that post, I have new friends at The University of Canterbury and a chapter in this book. During a sabbatical in 2007, I once more visited New Zealand, this time to gather information for another *LotR*-themed book. My research at the Tolkien Archives at Marquette University in 2006 undoubtedly will provide me with information for yet another book about Tolkien's works. Because Tolkien's characters and themes always inspire me, I envision writing about them for a long time to come. In the past few years, largely because of a globally shared interest in *LotR*, my research and presentations took me to England and New Zealand, which have now become favourite haunts. But the best part is talking with people whose lives are changed for the better because Tolkien wrote *LotR*, from Tolkien family members to revered scholars to film actors and artists to diehard fans. I am honoured and blessed to be a part of this community.

GERALD A. POWELL, JR.

PhD, Assistant Professor of Philosophy of Rhetoric, Department of Communication Studies, George Mason University, Washington, D.C., U.S.A.

I have an interdisciplinary range of written publications and expertise within the fields of Rhetorical Theory, Semiotics, Philosophy, Multiculturalism and Interpersonal Communication. My research focuses on the works of Friedrich Nietzsche and Emile Cioran and their contributions to the topics of Ennui and the Architectonics of knowledge.

The *How We Became Middle-earth* project has probed me to move in several directions and has encouraged a number of insights concerning humanities' general state of affairs, a few of which I will briefly share.

Absurdity, hope, cultural sensitivity, and compassion were obvious Camusian themes I wrote about in this book, but layered within and interwoven among the intricate plots and characters is Tolkien's simplest yet most difficult plea to humanity—*love each other or die*. I have taken to heart Tolkien's keen proverbial request, but I am afraid that ruminating and talking about Tolkien's insight is a comfortable luxury that humankind no longer has; peaceful and thoughtful praxis is needed. Nevertheless, war seems to be the native and preferred praxis of humanity. A kind gentleman, Bernard den Ouden, asked me last July at a humanities conference in Tunis, Tunisia *"Are freedom and dignity possible?"* I do not have the answer to this question, but we as human beings—like Frodo, Treebeard, and Sisyphus—have no choice but to stand committed and fight for the equality of *all*. In closing, if the pages to come in any way transform perspective to peaceful humanitarian praxis, then my effort is not a vain one.

Robin Anne Reid

PhD, Professor, Department of Literature and Languages, Texas A&M University-Commerce, U.S.A.

In third grade, a librarian told me I would like *The Hobbit* because I liked Oz. I disliked the book. Later, reading Tolkien's discussion of narrators talking down to child readers, I came to believe that was a possible reason. In 1965, when a family friend I adored told me I would like *The Lord of the Rings*, I read the trilogy and fell immediately in love. I immediately reread, logging 100 readings between the ages of ten and seventeen, then settled down to an annual reading for years. I first read the books on the western Washington coast, perfect for Tolkien since we camped in the woods and spent hours on the beach which faced west. Although I did not become a medievalist, I went on to become a nature poet, a writer, an English teacher, and to have a life-long interest in linguistics and the history of the English language.

However, Tolkien's work did more than inspire me to choose a field of study. Because "science fiction" (a catch-all term) was disdained where and when I grew up, especially for girls, I developed early a contrarian streak with regard to the social forces that try to canonize "literature", as well as an attitude about the social construction of gender. To say that Tolkien caused me to become a feminist is overstating, but his work was an influence.

I was a girl, and I loved *LotR*. No academic or critic could convince me the work was trash. My attitude served me well in later years as I moved to study other marginalized literatures: women writers, multicultural literature. Since I knew from experience that the marginalized literatures of SciFi and fantasy were worth reading, I was prepared to assume that works by "women" and "minority" writers were also worth reading, especially when I found their fantasy and SciFi!

I stopped reading Tolkien during my angry young feminist period because I did not want to "lose" my perfect memories of the text. However, despite many moves which required reducing my library, I never discarded my books. I kept and carefully packed first both the paperback (pink flamingo version, the third copy I'd owned since I read the first two to death), and the red and green bound hardback editions I bought with my first paycheck in 1973. I went on to complete a PhD and started teaching in Texas. Years later, when rumours of a live-action film surfaced, I was unimpressed. However, when I saw a preview in a theatre the summer before *The Fellowship of the Ring* was released, I recognized Moria. The sense of recognition, for a place in a book I had not read for about fifteen years, was so strong I had to see the film; before I saw the film, I had to reread the book.

The book held up well. Unlike other works by authors I'd loved in childhood and could not read as an adult, I still enjoyed the book. And, unlike many book fans, I fell in love with the film as well. I saw *FotR* forty-five times before it left the theatre, a number that shocks many, but, as I continue to point out, not unusual given my history of reading the book. (I can no longer keep track of how many times I've read the book or seen the films because I've been more or less continuously working with them since, both in my teaching and my scholarship.)

The film led me back into active fandom which I'd left when I began writing my dissertation, and by unknown paths, into new areas of scholarship: film theory and fan studies. My chapter in this book comes directly out of my interest in Tolkien's work, Peter Jackson's film, and the issues of canonization and literary debates over "writing" as shown in Internet *LotR* fandom.

CHERYLYNN SILVIA

BA, MA candidate in Critical and Cultural Theory, Cardiff University, Wales, U.K.

When I was fourteen I donned a monkey suit reused from *The Wizard of Oz* to play a goblin in a community production of *The Hobbit*. The director of that production, who told us *The Hobbit* was her favourite story, later became a close friend and encouraged me to read *The Lord of the Rings*. The rest, as they say with the clarity of hindsight, is history. While she is no longer with us, her influence lives on, most palpably (although not most importantly) in my contribution to this book.

---

28   **The Contributors**

Daniel Smith-Rowsey

BA, MA, PhD candidate, Institute of Film and TV Studies, University of Nottingham, U.K.

I acquired a double-Bachelor of Arts degree in Politics and Film from the University of California at Santa Cruz. I went on to obtain a Master of Arts in Critical Studies at University of Southern California's School of Cinema and Television. I am scheduled to receive my doctorate in Film and Television Studies from the University of Nottingham in June 2008. I have spoken at several conferences and have been published in *Newsweek, Eonline,* and *Film International magazine,* and I am the film reviews editor for *Scope* magazine.

Before all that, I was yet another role-playing geek; I owe a world of childhood fantasy to J.R.R. Tolkien. Years later, I took a long informal driving tour of New Zealand, and still find it difficult to believe that Peter Jackson managed to afford enough CG (computer graphic) to remove all the sheep from the footage that became *The Lord of the Rings* films. I recently managed to convince my father to watch all three films for his first time; his only complaint was that they seemed a bit long; only when Sam and Frodo arrived at Mount Doom did I admit to my father that we had been watching the extended versions.

Paola Voci

PhD, Lecturer in Chinese Languages and Cultures, University of Otago, Dunedin, Aotearoa New Zealand

I have an insane passion for Tolkien's trilogy which I have read multiple times not only in its original version, but also in Italian (when I still did not know English), French and Chinese (when the English version was not available). I have an equally insane addiction for the movies that I have also watched numerous times.

During the little time left when I was not reading or watching the *LotR,* I completed a BA in Chinese Language and Literature (Venice University, 1991), a Diploma in Film Theory and Practice (Beijing Film Academy, 1991), an MA in East

Asian Studies (Indiana University, 1997), and a PhD in Chinese (Indiana University, 2002). My area of study combines East Asian Studies (especially Chinese language and culture), film and media studies, and visual culture. In particular, my recent research has been focused on documentary film/video making in contemporary China and the media of the Chinese diaspora. I have been published in *Modern Chinese Literature and Culture* and *Senses of Cinema* and I have contributed to the *Encyclopedia of Chinese Cinema*. My works were also included into several edited collections of essays, such as *Lingyan xiangkan: haiwai xuezhe ping dangdai Zhongguo jilupian (Reel China: A New Look at Contemporary Chinese Documentary*, Shanghai Wenhui Publishing House, 2006), *Ombre Elettriche. Cento anni di cinema cinese 1905-2005 (Electric Shadows: 100 Years of Chinese Cinema 1905-2005*, Fondazione La Biennale di Venezia, 2005), *Asia in the Making of New Zealand* (Auckland University Press, 2006) and *Handbook of Film Studies* (Sage, forthcoming in 2007). I am currently writing *China on Video* (working title), a book that analyses movies made and viewed on smaller screens (i.e., the DV camera, the computer monitor—and, within it, the Internet window—and the cellphone display).

THOMAS MURRAY WILSON

PhD, Independent scholar, Perth, Western Australia

At the end of 2004 John Howard won a federal election in Australia, and George Bush won a federal election in America. As expected, both men have since refused to take actions to seriously curb their nation's disastrously large emissions of carbon dioxide. A few weeks after these events, I flew from Melbourne, Australia, to Christchurch in New Zealand.

A day later and here I was, at Lake Pukaki, the most azure body of water I'd ever seen, with Mount Cook standing indomitable at its head, laden with white powder. Walking down the bank through the pines to the shore of the lake I felt shadows flicker across my shoulders, and smelt the resin of the trees: tart, fresh and gratifying in my nose. I wasn't just looking at a lake, I was engaging in sensual interchanges with the ecology of a wild place. Like Aragorn running into hiding in a copse of pines on the lake shore, I felt engaged.

As I discovered on this trip to New Zealand, the Southern Alps, approached by undulating green swathes of grassy foot hills with startled deer standing on their sides, are truly grand, and perhaps a little mystical. And yet I had recently watched Peter Jackson's *The Lord of the Rings* films. Whose overtones of other-worldliness were working in my imagination to free the aesthetics of this place from being simply Kiwi foot hills? Were they Peter Jackson's? I think the natural environment of New Zealand would make even the most jaded urban denizen gasp, but I noticed that in remembering the recent filmic Middle-earth my imagination was also being freed to enjoy a more mythical realm.

My trip to New Zealand was enframed by political events which boded ill for the natural world I was admiring. Had I been running away from the reality of an environmentally destructive government when I flew from Australia to New Zealand in late 2004? Was an absorption in the environmental aesthetics of *LotR* also a kind of escapism? Writing my contribution to the present book helped me to resolve all kinds of aporias circulating around these questions.

When I'm not fondly remembering that trip to the South Island, I'm writing environmentally-valenced literary criticism where I live in the port city of Fremantle, Western Australia. My book *The Recurrent Green Universe of John Fowles* (Rodopi, Amsterdam/New York, 2006) is the first ever study of the writings of John Fowles from an ecocritical perspective. More information about myself, including a selection of my environmental photo-journalism, is available at www.tmwilson.org.

LISA WONG

BA (Hons) in Cultural Studies, University of Canterbury, Real Estate Consultant, Christchurch, Aotearoa New Zealand

10 February 2007

My chapter in this book was among the essays I wrote for the completion of my BA (Hons) in Cultural Studies at Canterbury University in New Zealand. I finished my studies in 2003 and decided I would not go any further. Then the editors asked me to write an auto-biopic. The word "auto" reminds me of confession. OK, let me think: I haven't got a PhD or held a relevant academic position at a university. Neither am I a *The Lord of the Rings* fan (book or films). My career as a real estate consultant and the incongruence between real estate and academia almost make me suspect that my very presence in this book may contaminate the whole project. Should I keep on?

OK, let me start again. I am a mother of two. Annabelle, my five year old daughter, started school this week. She borrowed a book from the school library on her second day at school. The book is called *Polar the Titanic Bear*. The cover emphasizes that it is "A True Story". Daisy Corning Stone Spedden wrote a book from the eyes of a Polar Bear about the adventures of the family, printed the cover illustration and gave it to her eight year old son in 1913, a year after the disaster of Titanic. The Spedden family survived the Titanic tragedy. Daisy's son's favourite Polar Bear toy survived too. Eighty years later, Leighton H. Coleman III discovered the book among other belongings of Daisy Spedden. Leighton reproduced the book by incorporating lots of Spedden family portraits as well as other Titanic related paintings and photos. The book illustrator, Laurie McGaw, found models to pose as Daisy, her son Douglas and other family members. The bonding between the Polar Bear and the six year old boy, and the adventures they experienced fascinate my daughter. The reproduction process of the book and the reconstruction of the past fascinate me. The valuable historic photos alongside the immaculate illustrations *almost* took me back to observe the events happened in 1913.

I started wondering whether we should start to recollect and recover the *historic relics* of the Middle Kingdom. If the photos and diary of a real person brought us a "true story" of the past, can film and simulacra bring us a hyperreal story of the *past*? Our next *LotR* related project?

Auto-biopic is a funny word. I am glad that I have the "auto" power to picture the parts of myself which I think are relevant to my book chapter. Who I am is not important. The way I describe myself is more important, I believe.

3

CREATING MIDDLE-EARTH
The Insiders' Views

Anne Buchmann (interviewer)

THE "greatest book ever written" led to the "greatest film project yet undertaken" and also created an impressive influx of Lord of the Rings tourists seeking Middle-earth.

While conducting field research for my Doctor of Philosophy into *LotR* film tourism, I repeatedly travelled the country and met literally hundreds of people whose lives had been transformed because of *LotR*. Many of these people worked in the tourism industry, while others were from the film industry or other related occupations. Their stories offered unique insights into how *LotR* films have influenced the world: a perfect inclusion in this collection on *LotR*.

For this book, I conducted a dozen interviews with professionals whose work related directly or indirectly to the *LotR* films, and eventually selected nine for publication. Of those interviewees, some were veterans of the film industry (casting director and film officer), others were artists (armoursmith, swordsmith and calligrapher), as well as professionals involved in *LotR*-related projects (exhibition coordinator, tour operator and webmaster). As some of the interviewees were very busy, finding interview time was often a challenge. Consequently, although I always sought to meet the interviewees in person if possible, some interviews were conducted by email or phone. We met in either public or private spaces, and I would record and later transcribe these interviews. Each interviewee was asked the same nine questions, though the sequence was adapted to the flow of the conversation. The questions focused on the interviewees' involvement with *LotR* films and the range of their individual experiences, and asked their opinions about the impact of the movies on New Zealand. Most interview transcripts were rearranged for publication in order to produce a homogenous appearance in which the questions were addressed in the same order.

In general, I learnt from the interviewees that the LotR tale produced a myriad of meaning and opportunities for the individual. All interviewees said that their lives had been positively transformed through their involvement with the *LotR* films. They also described a feeling that their experience had made them part of "something bigger". Many mentioned a newfound pride in the country that had produced the project. There were points where the interviewees' experiences differed: some people found themselves in the limelight while others found new occupations and meaningful relationships.

The interviews allow an insight into the power of creation and how those creating fantasy face very real challenges. They present a mosaic of experiences, ranging from the revival of ancient handicrafts to modern management and networking. Their experiences demonstrate how individuals created a project and how the project in turn influenced those individuals' lives. The *LotR* film project became a test of people's imaginations and abilities, and ultimately exceeded expectations with its success. The film project also connected people and acted as a catalyst. For all interviewees, it was an ultimately rewarding and meaningful journey that would live on in hundreds of stories. Some of those stories can be read in this book.

I would like to thank all the interviewees who took the time to answer questions, and especially the fellowship of the nine who were selected for publication. Thank you Paul Brewer, Erica Challis, Carlene Cordova, Warren Green, Vic James, Jean Johnston, Peter Lyon, Liz Mullane, and Daniel Reeve for sharing your stories!

Anne Buchmann, March 2007

Paul Brewer

Director of Marketing and Communication at Te Papa Tongarewa and a key person in the realization of the Lord of the Rings the Motion Picture Trilogy: The Exhibition *that travelled around the world*

My involvement with *LotR*:

I was involved in the conceptualisation of the *Lord of the Rings the Motion Picture Trilogy: The Exhibition* at Te Papa Tongarewa. This exhibition became the most successful in New Zealand history with over 300,000 visitors. More than a million people throughout the world have now seen the exhibition and it has broken many records since it began travelling to science museums overseas. We still receive requests from science museums asking to host the exhibition—even department stores are interested! Without doubt, we could keep it running for years.

How I became involved in the *LotR* movie project:

I am Director of Marketing and Communication at Te Papa. Even several years before the release of *The Fellowship of the Ring* we saw an opportunity. This movie project caught our interest on many levels. We realized that it would be something good and rather special. The story of its making highlighted the development and application of new technology and also demonstrated new ways of solving technical and filming problems. Once Te Papa committed itself to the exhibition, we began to conceptualise it, and Story Inc. developed the final product.

My experience of working on the project:

It has been an incredible journey, from the first idea—convincing stakeholders and developing the exhibition—to the day it opened amid incredible media and public interest. Even now I still travel to science museums around the world to open the exhibition to new audiences.

Anne Buchmann (interviewer)

The most rewarding aspect of my job:

The period of working for the *Lord of the Rings the Motion Picture Trilogy: The Exhibition* has been amazing. I was fortunate to meet and work with extremely gifted people. I remember Richard Taylor as a wonderful and very helpful man. Then, of course, there was the rush of interest when the exhibition was opened. Te Papa held a press conference with the entire cast just before the world premiere of *The Return of the King* in Wellington. I also regarded it as a reward to take Peter Jackson around the exhibition myself.

We now know that we were able to provide a wonderful experience for people by creating one of the most successful popular science exhibitions ever. This exhibition has exceeded the combined visitation numbers of both the *James Bond* and *Titanic* exhibitions in London! We continue to see people returning, for example, to shop at the Te Papa Exhibition Store, which still sells *LotR* merchandise.

The most challenging aspect of my job:

The process of planning the exhibition took more than two years, and was very challenging. The negotiations with New Line Cinema were very complex as contracts detailing copyright issues had to be drafted and signed. This meant that I travelled, alone or in a team, to the production company offices in both L.A. and New York, where I would introduce our plan to the person in charge. Of course these people do not do exhibitions—they are into filmmaking—and I had to explain the idea over and over again, meeting more vice-presidents of the *LotR* film production companies than I can count. But it all ended well and we now have a fantastic relationship.

The most unexpected aspect of my job:

No one could have predicted the interest we would experience with this exhibition. Now I have an opportunity to travel to exotic places all over the world as the keynote speaker when the exhibition yet again opens in another city. I have been to Houston, Singapore, Sydney, London, and many other places. I am responsible for dealing with the media, which includes TV interviews for local media overseas and New Zealand media.

The impact of the *LotR* movies on New Zealand:

LotR is a great story and the movie trilogy was also about New Zealand. Our incredible landscape proved to be an intrinsic fit for the story and showcased New Zealand to the world. Now people are proud; everybody feels this was huge and exciting. This trilogy turned Wellington into the vibrant film capital of New Zealand and changed it forever.

And of course, tourism has benefited enormously. Even Te Papa experienced an increase in overseas groups, including a memorable one when a group of Japanese fans dressed up as Hobbits!

How involvement in the *LotR* project changed me:

Te Papa proved that it is able to develop a world-class exhibition, and even better, an exhibition that showcased New Zealand expertise, creativity, innovation and teamwork. I feel immense amount of pride when I travel nowadays and see huge billboards advertising the exhibition, with the lines "Produced by Te Papa" and our characteristic thumbprint logo.

Is New Zealand Middle-earth?

It is interesting: Peter Jackson reinterpreted the New Zealand landscape as a holistic Middle-earth, but as Kiwis we recognize our home country. I remember an incident when I took my nephew to Kaitoke Regional Park and British tourists approached us, asking about the location of the Elven dwelling of Rivendell. I had to tell them honestly that none of the set was left and this had been an ancient forest all along. But I have no doubt that the slogan "New Zealand is Middle-earth" is quite clever and will remain a successful marketing tool.

Anne Buchmann (interviewer)

Erica Challis

Co-founder and New Zealand representative of TheOneRing.net, one of the biggest sites online made by and for LotR *fans*

My involvement with *LotR*:

It started in 1999 when I began communicating online with other enthusiasts about the *LotR* movie project that was being developed in New Zealand. I reported on the progress of the films, as well as helped develop our website TheOneRing.net in various ways, for example writing articles about Tolkien, posting photos of places in New Zealand that seemed suitable locations or that were rumoured to have been chosen as film locations. Being a New Zealander gave me incredible opportunities and allowed me to source information at an early stage.

How I became involved in the *LotR* movie project:

During an online discussion about new happenings regarding fantasy and science fiction films and books, I happened to mention to a contact on the Net in Montreal, Mike Regina, that *LotR* was being made in New Zealand. He suggested that we start a webpage to report on the films, and I started looking around for gossip and information I could send him from New Zealand. We got enough good news and stories to attract the attention of AICN, an online film news and gossip site. Because of that, we were contacted by Bill Thomas and Chris Pirrotta, who joined the website and helped develop it into a more professional-looking venture.

Consequently we attracted a lot of worldwide interest and grew quickly to become one of the biggest fan-made online sites for *LotR* and Tolkien. We even have our own merchandise store, though that happened by accident: we were seeking more funding and found this to be an effective method. But it really all started in the first place with people inquiring about merchandise.

My experience of running the website:

It was tremendous fun. I met great variety of people from around the world and became part of a large online community of many like-minded souls. Finding news about the films was challenging, and trying to get the best, most accurate stories and be the first in the world to post them online was very exciting. Acting as a go-between in passing information on to people who wanted it was a great feeling. We ended up knowing a lot about what was going on in the world of Tolkien fandom, and there were many occasions when we were able to help out someone who needed specific information or help. I met some of the smartest, funniest people and enjoyed people's common love of the books and their love of creativity, imagination and fantasy.

The downside of the experience was learning that the film world in Hollywood seems completely corrupt. The filmmakers themselves were good people but the further one was from the creative aspect of the films, the more things became mired in weird Hollywood politics and paranoia.

One of the most entertaining incidents happened when the film company, New Line Cinema, decided to issue a trespass order to keep me from visiting the Minas Tirith set. This order was issued before I had even been to the set and was thus most unusual. It attracted a lot of attention in the New Zealand media and put me and our webpage in the headlines. It was rather fun to get so much attention, while the film company was made to look rather lame for overreacting. Peter Jackson and Barrie Osbourne then decided to make up for this and invited me to visit various sets, an experience that meant a lot to me and other fans worldwide.

The most rewarding aspect of my job:

This is the people I met, and the work we did together creating the website. I already mentioned that I encountered all sorts of people from all over the world, each with their own unique story. I think reading *LotR* can empower people and even serve as a moral compass; it has a strong appeal especially in modern times. I have a quite deep personal connection to the books myself, and over the years I heard many more stories about how other peoples' lives had been touched by *LotR*. This has given me invaluable and treasured memories.

Anne Buchmann (interviewer)

The most challenging aspect of my job:

One of the most challenging aspects of my job was definitely dealing with the film company personnel, especially public relations people and so on. After all, this was a huge commercial production, and people had to deal with many worldwide interests very intensively. Under such circumstances the film industry tends to become paranoid. I dealt with hierarchy and management matters and did not enjoy this more bureaucratic aspect of filmmaking and reporting. Sometimes I found it impossible to deal with these issues.

The most unexpected aspect of my job:

I never imagined that I would meet my husband-to-be this way—now he has come to live with me in New Zealand. I also published two books. And I became known to millions of people—something that strangely a fortune-teller predicted fifteen years ago. I would not have thought that this would happen when we started the webpage.

The impact of the movies on New Zealand:

It's given our country a sense of identity and self-confidence that does not depend on sport or war. We have not had this before. I think the *LotR* films created a wave of optimism and pride in what New Zealand could do, because we put our creative talents on to the world stage and received approval from millions of people. Many of those people didn't know anything about New Zealand, let alone that we were capable of something like *LotR*. I reckon people now dare to follow their dreams—it proved that there is a way if one simply works at it. And it will surely get a lot more people into the film industry!

How involvement in the *LotR* project changed me:

I became a professional writer and realized that I loved finding and reporting news and writing articles. I decided to pursue this by completing a diploma in journalism, though following my personal experience I do not intent to pursue entertainment journalism. People seem to like reading what I write. I wrote my first full-page article in *The Dominion Post* recently and received strong feedback.

Is New Zealand Middle-earth?

Sometimes! I can see a lot of Tolkien's raw nature and Englishness in present-day New Zealand. There are still places that are untouched. You can dream you are seeing something that Tolkien imagined when he thought of the Elves waking in Middle-earth for the first time. And there are Kiwis with Hobbit qualities, both good and bad. Even this strange country, insular and yet open, evokes memories of the Shire and Middle-earth.

CARLENE CORDOVA

Director of Ringers: Lord of the Fans (2005), *an award-winning documentary that explores how LotR has influenced Western popular culture for over fifty years*

My involvement with *LotR*:

First of all I am a Tolkienist. *LotR* has been my favourite book since I first read it at the age of fifteen. Thus, the idea of making a documentary about how this book has affected people from rock stars to filmmakers to ordinary people like me, developed a great appeal. And as a firm believer in books and reading and anything to help the cause of literature, it was worth the three plus years of my life to make *Ringers: Lord of the Fans*.

How I became involved in the *Ringers: Lord of the Fans* project:

It had a lot do with meeting other enthusiasts. I met Cliff Broadway, who writes as Quickbeam on TheOneRing.net, by pure chance at an Ian McKellen book signing that was held a few weeks after the release of *FotR*. We started chatting and he invited me to attend a Golden Globes party for *FotR* held by TheOneRing.net. There

I met TheOneRing.net founder Chris Pirrotta, who writes as Calisuri on TheOneRing.net and encouraged me to join the staff. There were no financial rewards as everyone on TheOneRing.net worked as a volunteer. At the time, I was a Senior Producer at Sony Pictures Digital Entertainment, developing and producing original online shows for the Internet. It was a perfect time to become more active within the fan community.

One day, Cliff and I covered a signing event at an L.A. bookstore attended by Peter Jackson, Fran Walsh, Phillippa Boyens and Sean Astin. I was surprised to see that hundreds of people had turned up for the event. We began talking to people and it transpired that some had been waiting since 3 a.m., while others had driven all night from Las Vegas to attend. We continued to interview the fans and I was fascinated by their stories of how *LotR* had touched their lives.

After a similar event I remember saying to Cliff: "Someone should document this phenomenon." That's when we realized that someone should be us. After all, we were in the unique position as TheOneRing.net staff of having access to the filmmakers, stars and fans of *LotR*. We decided that I would direct the film and co-write and produce it with Cliff and the other talented people that we had brought onboard.

My experience of making *Ringers: Lord of the Fans*:

Ringers: Lord of the Fans has been an education for us all in what can be achieved with persistence and perspiration and very little money. And mostly it's been a great experience to travel the world, meet interesting and wonderful people, and essentially reinforce our notions of how the power of goodwill and a good book can change the world.

The most rewarding aspect of my job:

In common with most film directors, I'd say that it's the experience of seeing something that you dreamed up become a reality. And then, to watch an audience take your film and make it their own and enjoy it! I'm thrilled at the overwhelmingly positive reaction that audiences have had to *Ringers: Lord of the Fans*.

The most challenging aspect of my job:

It was very challenging to create a film with no real funding at backing. I guess it's a challenge that every independent filmmaker faces but it was hard at times. Though we were able to find some private investors to get us started, we never had quite enough money. Luckily we attracted the attention of Tom DeSanto (executive producer of *X-Men*, 2000 and *X2: X-Men United*, 2003; producer of *Transformers*, 2007) who joined us as executive producer. He was able to obtain the funding we needed to finish the film. Still, this didn't include salaries for the filmmakers and most of us have survived on peanut-butter and jelly sandwiches for the past three years. We even had to sell most of our *LotR* collectibles on eBay to pay our bills. The rewards have been good career-wise, but not so good financially.

The most unexpected aspect of my job:

I knew there was a large audience for this yet I am still surprised at the huge international reach of *LotR*, which seems to cross culture and language barriers with ease. However, I wasn't expecting the seeming bias from the arty indie-film* community and Hollywood types against genre fans or "geeks", for lack of a better word. It's the same situation that Professor Tolkien faced upon publication of *LotR*: the literati looked down their noses at his work and called it "childish". But I consider Hollywood's perspective outrageous as those projects that appeal to genre fan audiences are taking the lion's share of the box office these days. I think that the Hollywood and independent film elite are out-of-touch with the kinds of films most people want to see. For us, it was an extremely rewarding experience to be at our TheOneRing.net Oscar party with 1,200 other fans, watching *RotK* sweep the Academy Awards!

I am also extremely proud of *Ringers: Lord of the Fans*! It turned out much better than I hoped and most importantly, it is being well received by the Ringers, as we call the Tolkien fan community.

---

* *Editors*: "indie" refers to independent.

Anne Buchmann (interviewer)

The impact of the *LotR* movies on New Zealand:

We travelled to New Zealand to cover the world premiere of Peter Jackson's *RotK* for *Ringers: Lord of the Fans*. I remember the world premiere as an incredible day when about 125,000 people lined the streets of Wellington to celebrate with Peter Jackson and the cast and crew of the movie. The Prime Minister of New Zealand spoke to the crowd and the Mayor of Wellington and Members of Parliament were there. I couldn't have imagined an entire country turning out for a movie premiere and I actually don't think that's ever happened before. It seemed to illustrate just how important the *LotR* trilogy was to New Zealand.

How involvement in the *LotR* project changed me:

I was involved in Peter Jackson's *LotR* project through my status as a staff member of TheOneRing.net; I produced all three of TheOneRing.net's Oscar parties held in Los Angeles. I also shot and produced short interview segments for TheOneRing.net Digital to be streamed online. These activities eventually led to us meeting the stars and filmmakers of *LotR*, which of course later helped us in producing *Ringers: Lord of the Fans*. Three years later our work was honoured when Sony Pictures Home Entertainment selected the documentary for worldwide distribution.

Is New Zealand Middle-earth?

Most definitely! We had the luck to be included on a tour of the *LotR* locations in the South Island, and the locations we visited captured Tolkien's Middle-earth perfectly. I have never been to a more beautiful country in my life!

Warren Green

Armoursmith for the medieval re-enactment scene in New Zealand and for Weta Workshop during the making of the LotR movies

My involvement with *LotR*:

I was the armoursmith for the three *LotR* movies. I needed to draw on all my experience to fulfil this role. Many years before this project started, I had my first practical experience of making historically accurate and functional armour. Armouring is a combination of design, pattern cutting, and panel beating, together with its own unique blend of skills. It requires a number of associated soft-cloth and metal disciplines to produce a practical finished product from either illustration or an existing item.

Over time my armouring has placed me in some unusual areas, including lecturing at schools, universities and polytechnics, producing various objects and equipment for a range of TV commercials and films, and providing commissioned items for collectors and re-enactors both here and in Australia, USA, and Europe. Ultimately, my knowledge of armouring and the film industry increased to the point where I could actively contribute to the *LotR* movie project.

How I became involved in the *LotR* movie project:

In 1999 I was recruited by Richard Taylor to work for Weta Workshop as the specialist armourer on their forthcoming *LotR* project, on recommendation of Peter Lyon who later became Weta's master swordsmith.

During the final interview I was shown concept drawings and samples of completed armour. These items were of such inspiring excellence that I realized this project could make New Zealand and world movie history. As a Tolkien addict of long standing, I couldn't resist this opportunity to become part of the *LotR* project.

My experience of working on the project:

My involvement in *LotR* covered almost two years, with my work featuring in the armour, jewellery and various accoutrements for Aragorn, the Ringwraiths,

Gondorian royalty, and others, as well as some miniature modelling for the citadel of Minis Tirith. I provided technical advice and research materials when required, and also scored a background bit part as an Orc armourer in the hellpits of Isengard.

The most rewarding aspect of my job:

The experience has added much to my life. As well as forging strong friendships and acquiring new skills I had the chance to meet many incredibly skilled and talented people with whom I bonded on a fantastic project. This made it an unforgettable experience. The most rewarding aspect was not financial, but the interaction with creative, good people, and being free to produce, share, show, touch and teach the things I enjoy.

The impact of the *LotR* movies on New Zealand:

I feel that movies such as in *LotR* and *The Last Samurai* (dir. Edward Zwick, 2003) have demonstrated that Kiwi creativity is world-class. There was also the revelation of the mind-blowing and accessible scenery. I hope the *LotR*-legacy makes us mindful of those resources that need preserving and nurturing at all costs.

Is New Zealand Middle-earth?

In old Norse the world was known as Midhgardhr—in other words "Middle-earth". But in my view New Zealand is actually more like Hobbiton—a small rural farming land, where in times of need people are able to pull together and create history and world acclaim.

VIC JAMES

Owner of Red Carpet Tours, New Zealand, which offers LotR *location tours*

My involvement with *LotR*:

A few years ago, just after the release of *FotR*, I decided to start a company to provide monthly twelve-day tours of selected *LotR* sites, as well as day tours to Hobbiton. Our participants are mainly from the United States, United Kingdom and Australia, but also elsewhere—so far we have met people from over twenty-four countries.

How I became involved in the *LotR* movie-related business:

My wife and I love to travel and welcome any opportunity to show people more of our own country. When we first heard rumours of the *LotR* project, we soon began to consider the possibility of sharing our excitement with like-minded people from all over the world. When we met another dedicated New Zealander, Erica Challis of TheOneRing.net, with the necessary knowledge of the film production and its locations, we knew we had found a way and Red Carpet Tours was born!

My experience of running the *LotR* tours:

Our experience with *LotR* location tourism has exceeded all our expectations. Initially we were uncertain about how our tours would be received, but we were soon reassured. The movies have sparked a greater interest in the books and in New Zealand. People find something meaningful in them—and it also makes them interested in visiting the film locations in person. The chance to see my own country with new eyes has proven to be very special.

The most rewarding aspect of my job:

It is extremely rewarding to witness the enjoyment shown by our participants. Being on location, especially such outstanding ones as Hobbiton and Edoras, seems to be an almost spiritual experience for everyone. It is like a pilgrimage to a place where their heroes have been. There are so many emotions involved, for example, many people shed tears of joy when flying over the mountains where the Lighting of Beacons took place—a powerful scene both in the movie and in real life.

In general, many of our clients are professionals who worry about their own as well as our common future. They strongly connect to the various themes in *LotR*, like the discussions about war, the nature of good and evil, and the influence one person can have in the world. I am often included in such discussions and it makes me realize how meaningful this journey is to people. I certainly enjoy sharing such discussions.

The most challenging aspect of my job:

In the beginning, our greatest challenge was to set up and establish such a specialised business. For this, we had to find effective ways to reach potential clients. Now that we are fully operative; we try to keep adding value to our tours by identifying and incorporating new attractions. There is also the occasional challenge of dealing with anxious inquiries from partners who accompany real *LotR* fans; many of them wonder if they will be bored. Luckily our experience has shown quite the opposite. They become very interested in it all themselves!

The most unexpected aspect of my job:

We really did not expect the vast interest from people from all corners of the globe. There were literally hundreds of inquiries from everywhere. We were also surprised by how many of our participants claimed the tour was too short: some people have returned to take the tour three times!

The impact of the *LotR* movies on New Zealand:

The *LotR* movies and their media coverage have provided New Zealand with the kind of publicity which the government could never have afforded. We will see the benefits of that exposure over the coming years. It seems like a paradox that many Kiwis think of *LotR* as just another movie, while the worldwide audience is still in awe of it. I do not think that New Zealanders realize the extent of the interest throughout the world.

An increasing number of people have begun to recall previous films shot here; there is revived interest in movies such as *Braindead* (dir. Peter Jackson, 1992) and other Peter Jackson movies, as well as film projects like *Whale Rider* (dir. Niki Caro, 2002) and *The Lion, the Witch and the Wardrobe* (dir. Andrew Adamson, 2005).

How involvement in the *LotR* tours changed me:

Our lives have been truly transformed. I said earlier how much my wife and I enjoy travelling in our own country and that we are also fans of Tolkien's writings. Being able to combine these interests as an occupation is beyond what we had hoped for. We meet so many wonderful people, both our participants and fellow New Zealanders. There is so much laughter and enjoyment involved. We are very happy with what we have accomplished so far.

Is New Zealand Middle-earth?

Many people who visit New Zealand look for something physical like a film location. But what they end up enjoying most is their encounters with people here who seem to live their dream life. These travellers find that qualities like a decent attitude and respect towards others are still common characteristics in New Zealand. We Kiwis are still comfortable in our lives and this seems quite different from other places in the world. All this makes it easy for seekers to believe that New Zealand could be Middle-earth indeed. For us, it is!

Anne Buchmann (interviewer)

JEAN JOHNSTON

Manager of Film Wellington, the first Film Office in New Zealand set up by the Wellington City Council

My involvement with *LotR*:

I was involved in the *LotR* project from the beginning, even before it went public. It all started when Camperdown Studios purchased an old paint factory and began turning it into a studio. This involved various necessary changes relating to water supply, drainage and parking, and Film Wellington helped to resolve these issues before filming began.

How I became involved in the *LotR* movie project:

Film Wellington is the capital's film office and deals with all the logistics of filming—sourcing locations, arranging parking for the crew, closing roads, drafting location agreements, organizing film permits, fire permits, helping with building consents, etc., as well as marketing the region to international filmmakers. We are known for being a "one stop shop". Having previously worked successfully with Peter Jackson on *The Frighteners* (dir. Peter Jackson, 1996), Film Wellington found itself once more involved in a major movie production.

My experience of working on the project:

Amazing, exciting, tiring, stressful. The *LotR* project became a milestone in so many respects: this was the first time in the world that someone had shot three movies at once. It was New Zealand's first epic-style production. This was also the first time the Film Office had to sign papers binding itself to secrecy about the entire project, which made media contacts quite difficult to deal with.

The most rewarding aspect of my job:

It was extremely rewarding to see the final result on screen and I felt very privileged to have been a part of it. And of course, I could attend the world premiere that was held in our capital. It was a perfect day and seeing all the people lining the streets in celebration was an overwhelming sight. Like everyone else we watched in awe when *LotR* received all those Bafta and Academy Awards. There were other, smaller occasions that are vivid in my memory too, like being asked to take some of the stars to a Bledisloe Cup game. But the most rewarding aspect was seeing a united New Zealand coming together.

The most challenging aspect of my job:

I found it challenging to deal with the constant phone calls and media enquiries while *LotR* was being filmed. The phones were very busy and I also had to stay in contact with the production company and of course Wellington City Council. It proved a blessing that we had established communication channels so early on, plus I was allowed to make small decisions independently which sped up the process. I also found it very challenging to obtain my personal invitation to the world premiere of *RotK*.

The most unexpected aspect of my job:

One day, I was going to a meeting at Stone Street Studios and suddenly bumped into Liv Tyler. I did not expect to meet one of the stars in person.

I have just been invited to walk around the New York City set of *King Kong* (dir. Peter Jackson, 2005). It looks so realistic! But every film set has that effect on me: I really enjoy the artistic atmosphere. I feel energized when I am behind the scenes and very lucky to have my job.

The impact of the *LotR* movies on New Zealand:

They have had a huge impact economically. It has boosted our tourism and will continue to do so for some time. It has also brought work to our own film industry and given them experience of working on a big budget movie. The spin-offs have also been significant for local business. There is a strong sense of national pride when people talk about *LotR*. It has created more jobs. Anyone you speak to in Wellington seems to have either been involved or know someone who was involved in some way with the films. And now other production companies are taking an interest in New Zealand and looking to bring their productions here.

We now have the big budget screen grant established by the government, which brings us in line with other big players in the world. We also have a brand new international sound stage and a state-of-the-art post production house, complete with a laboratory. Weta Workshop now expanded and renovated their old premises, and of course we have Weta Digital. Only a few years ago, such massive positive changes would have been considered impossible.

How involvement in the *LotR* project changed me:

Recognition at last of the work we do at Film Wellington. People do not realize the huge amount of behind the scenes work done here. The Film Office is busier nowadays and I have finally got an assistant. In the long-term I would like to see at least six people working here to manage the negotiations between film companies, businesses, the council and the public, that characterize our job.

Is New Zealand Middle-earth?

Many years ago I approached Tourism New Zealand about the possibility of using film projects to encourage tourism, citing successful examples like *Field of Dreams* (dir. Phil Alden Robinson, 1989) in the United States and *Braveheart* (dir. Mel Gibson, 1995) in Scotland. But back then no one was interested. Now, of course, everything has changed and the slogan "New Zealand is Middle-earth" is everywhere. For me, personally, Middle-earth is a mythical place, although I can see its origins in Britain. But a lot of Kiwis became quite close to Middle-earth. There are places like the location of Hobbiton, where many locals proudly relate to the *LotR* project. In some ways it is as though the Middle-earth theme has brought us all together. And the international audience never had a doubt anyway. In this sense, yes, New Zealand is Middle-earth.

Peter Lyon

Swordsmith for the medieval re-enactment scene in New Zealand and for Weta Workshop during the making of the LotR *movies*

How I became involved in the *LotR* movie project:

I have always been interested in historical and medieval re-enactments and introduced myself to Richard Taylor in 1994. I showed him a selection of my work as a swordsmith and he loved it. Several years later, the right project came along and he offered me the position of sword-smith on what turned out to be *LotR*.

My experience of working in the project:

I joined the Weta Workshop team in the early stages of pre-production. This was when Peter Jackson was still trying to establish what could be done—what would be possible. It was an interesting time and we experimented with many different weapon designs. Eventually our initial team of twenty people began to grow as we moved towards full production scale. I have now worked in my position for many years and my experience has been mostly very good. Even though I didn't initially know much about the film industry, my sword making skills and historical knowledge were valued and I was given a lot of autonomy in turning designs into finished weapons.

The most rewarding aspect of my job:

This was my involvement in the execution of complex designs. I enjoyed this because I like to learn new procedures and push my personal boundaries. In the process I learned a lot about creating good design, and how to make the final pieces "work" for the camera. For example, a sword can be distracting if it catches the rays of the sun in certain scenes. This meant I had to take care not to polish that particular sword too much.

The most challenging aspect of my job:

Learning how the film industry worked. Also, there were sometimes almost contradictory requirements for on-set use, concerning safety, appearance, stunt requirements, lighting effects and so on. We had to balance such aspects. It was a steep learning curve, and showed me how little I had understood the film industry when I started.

The most unexpected aspect of my job:

I still marvel at the reality of filmmaking: the degree of preparation needed for each shot is immense! It makes me try to give the director as many options as possible and not limit his freedom to set up shots. This might involve, for example, making a sword to a better finish than the shot requires, in case the sword ends up close to camera, or making a sword with a blade that can be drawn from its scabbard, even if it is not scheduled to be drawn in any shot, just in case the shot is changed on the day. In a wider context, I learnt to analyze everything that might be needed on the day, to make sure that it was available, and tried to anticipate and solve any potential problems.

I also did not expect to be working in the merchandising industry. I am responsible for producing weapons—everything from Aragorn's sword to Sam's sword—on a scale of 1:6. I find this challenging; it is necessary to work very precisely as every detail will show up in the mould.

The impact of the *LotR* movies on New Zealand:

The movies have had a major positive impact on tourism and immigration. For example, I have been personally contacted by people inquiring about New Zealand because they were considering moving here. This began even before *FotR* was released! Overall, *LotR* has been a showpiece for the attractions of New Zealand. It did not only show our scenery but also our craftsmanship and general abilities as a filmmaking nation.

How involvement in the *LotR* project changed me:

Working on *LotR* has been a life-changing experience. It gave me the inspiration and means to take my interest in medieval history and its re-creation to a new level. Since starting on *LotR*, I have become involved in jousting and medieval equestrianism, and returned to university extramurally to finish my degree—a BA in History specialising in medieval Europe. This also feeds back into my work, helping with historical and equestrian questions. And of course my name and work is now known worldwide. Movie fans, re-enactors and sword collectors are all trying to commission me for private works. Even if I had a clone, we would both be busy for years!

Is New Zealand Middle-earth?

Not quite, but it is as near as anywhere on Earth can be to Middle-earth. Altogether I see a very universal theme in the *LotR*; the theme of unavoidable change and the decline of once great civilizations. We see the characters walking through the remains of older cities, now abandoned, and realize that even if humans are careful, the world they know will disappear. This makes me wonder if we will see fundamental changes in our world soon, too. What will New Zealand be like in the future?

LIZ MULLANE

Casting Director for the LotR movies in New Zealand

My involvement with *LotR*:

I was hired towards the end of 1998 to be the New Zealand Casting Director. This meant I was responsible for auditioning New Zealand actors for speaking parts, and heading a casting department of ten people to find, cast, and coordinate all the New Zealand actors, extras, doubles and stand-ins.

Anne Buchmann (interviewer)

How I became involved in the *LotR* movie project:

I have worked with Peter Jackson and Fran Walsh on a number of their films, for example *The Frighteners* and *Heavenly Creatures* (dir. Peter Jackson, 1994). Over the years we developed a very good working relationship and I became one of the most experienced casting directors in the country. Then I was invited to participate in the *LotR* project.

My experience of working on the project:

The experience was amazing. It was the hardest thing I have ever done and ultimately the most satisfying. The sheer size of the production was overwhelming, with up to five units operating in parallel, and all of them demanding people. We found it necessary to develop a healthy form of black humour to try the impossible—staying ahead of production—each day. It was very confusing at times, with three movies being made out of order and working all over the country.

The most rewarding aspect of my job:

Quite early in production it was decided to make the *LotR* movies a true Kiwi project. Thus I could concentrate on sourcing and casting local people. This was one of the most rewarding aspects of the job: being able to supply suitable looking and talented New Zealanders to play a wide variety of roles. In the process of doing this, I contacted virtually all known New Zealand actors, living here or overseas, and managed to fill the speaking roles quite quickly. Once filming began we took great satisfaction in the fact that our department had delivered. This was often done under immense time pressures, and in remote and difficult locations.

The most challenging aspect of my job:

I quickly came to see our work as one big logistical problem-solving exercise. Finding and casting roles for sometimes five units at a time, often at very short notice, and often in several remote locations at once. I was controlling a department and managing the demands of night and day shooting. I also had to find people who not only looked right for the many different creature types, but also had the right personalities to withstand the difficult and challenging costumes and make-up, and of course, to perform as required. And throughout the project I was dealing with literally boxes and boxes of applications sent by hopeful enthusiasts from all over the world. The interest in *LotR* proved much bigger than expected, and there was worldwide interest from the start in becoming part of it.

The most unexpected aspect of my job:

At first I did not realize the extreme challenge of having to find extreme physicalities. Production needed both extremely tall and extremely small people to play the scale doubles: for example, for all the scenes shared by Hobbits and Humans. This meant searching many countries to find adults around three foot six (1.07m) to four foot three (1.30m), of even proportions, with hopefully some performance ability, and who could speak or understand some English. Also unexpected was the added difficulty of coping with the huge international and somewhat fanatical interest in the project, while protecting the confidentiality of the creative development.

Just when I thought we had the hang of it, the seasons played a cruel joke on us. Despite my early warnings, the Battle of the Pelennor Fields was shot when the rural men worked as sheep shearers. As a result, many of the fierce Rohirrim Riders were actually women with beards. So we even found a way to deal with this shortage of suitable male extras. And it worked out just fine.

The impact of the *LotR* movies on New Zealand:

I believe that the movies have had several impacts. First and foremost is a growing belief and respect for our ability as a country. For many years Kiwis have had a bit of an inferiority complex in terms of our reputation on the international stage. These movies have strengthened our belief in ourselves and provided a form of "nationalism" that was not there before. We believed in ourselves as a sporting nation but the *LotR* project has broadened the arena. There have also been obvious economic benefits, and many small businesses have been able to develop because of it.

How involvement in the *LotR* project changed me:

Being part of *LotR* has meant a lot to me. It has further "upped" my organizational and problem solving skills. It has also given me immense confidence in New Zealand's ability to provide great talent with incredible versatility and strength of character. As well, it has proved to me that collaboration and communication is the key to success, and further cemented my belief that if you hire the right people you can do anything (I am referring to my ability to hire great assistants). Our casting department developed a wonderful team spirit, and through our experience of working and living so closely together, we became something like a family. Despite all the challenges and tears, we would all do it again!

Is New Zealand Middle-earth?

While working as a casting director, I had many opportunities to visit outdoor sets. I have many good memories, but being in the mountains and seeing the sunrise made me feel extremely privileged. It was almost a shock to go there, and to realize that this landscape was real. Working in areas like that proved uplifting to everybody and, yes, in moments like that we all felt as though we were walking on Middle-earth.

And there is another side to it: we as New Zealanders were able to prove that we have everything that any story could want—beautiful locations, technical expertise, determination and incredible spirit. Though we are small we think big. This makes us unique, like Middle-earth.

DANIEL REEVE

Calligrapher and cartographer for the LotR *movies*

My involvement with *LotR*:

I did all the calligraphy—books, maps and background inscriptions—for the *LotR* movies. This included creating the Red Book of Westmarch, Bilbo Baggins' travel journal, and even whole libraries like those in Rivendell and Minas Tirith. I worked on the *LotR* movie project for several years, and I later also worked on other productions made in New Zealand such as *King Kong* and *The Chronicles of Narnia: The Lion, the Witch and the Wardrobe*.

How I became involved in the *LotR* movie project:

I read the *LotR* books when I was about thirteen and loved them at once. I was also quite intrigued with the Elvish language and writings and this became a lifelong interest. When I heard about *LotR* being made in Wellington, I wrote a few documents in Elvish letters and showed them to Peter Jackson's film company. They loved them and immediately created my position in which I did all the calligraphy and maps for the movies.

My experience of working on the project:

It has been an amazing experience. For me, the calligraphy and maps of the movies play a vital role in the creation of a believable Middle-earth. Even if many of my works are only background props they still add to the look and flavour of this created world. Like other craft people at Weta, I felt as though I was part of something big and meaningful and I enjoyed the time when there was such a great team around me. It was seen more like a home project to most of us rather than the huge commercial operation it actually was. It was just us, a bunch of people who became a big family, who first and foremost wanted to see these movies done well. This meant a great attention to detail in all the craftsmanship. I was constantly astonished by the stuff the others made! Like many others, I worked hard and eventually full-time on the *LotR* films. It was a labour of love which comes through in the movies. All the love, time, effort and craftsmanship involved contributed to creating the Middle-earth that we are now so familiar with.

The most rewarding aspect of my job:

I am one of those fortunate artists who is experiencing good feedback in his lifetime, and even the reward of seeing my work shown on big screens worldwide. I also see my inscriptions on the One Ring everywhere, both in shops and worn by people. The same is true for the Middle-earth map, which has been distributed so widely. I still stare at them and marvel—after all, these are pieces of work I created in my garage!

The most challenging aspect of my job:

I expected from the beginning that some people would freeze-frame this movie while watching it, and realized that I would not be able to take shortcuts. Thus I took great care to write in such a way as to fit into Tolkien's world. Although most people will never trouble themselves to translate my works, those who do will read about adventures and tales mentioned or inspired by Tolkien himself.

Also, working in the film industry meant that I had to work to deadlines. These dates could be daunting at times, especially when a script change or a rearrangement of the shooting schedule occurred. I remember being given a few days to complete a rather complex piece of art. But it turned out to be something else completely from what I expected and I had to do it all over again with Alan Lee in two days. Then again, I remember writing more than thirty pages for a book of which only about six pages were shown on screen. Such is the fate.

The most unexpected aspect of my job:

I never quite expected the interest in *LotR* to last this long. But even years down the track there is still a strong interest. It is a bit like the *Star Wars* series (dir. George Lukas et al, 1977, 1980, 1983, 1999, 2002, 2005) I guess; there will always be a solid fan base. Also, I never pictured myself involved in film tourism, but a while ago a tour operator approached me asking if I could meet his tours on a regular basis. I took great pleasure in talking to people about my art and experiences in making these movies and agreed to meet these tourists. I showed them examples of my art and so far it's been a great experience for both sides.

The impact of the *LotR* movies on New Zealand:

They certainly put New Zealand on the map and introduced the world not only to the scenery we have but also the level of professionalism that moviemakers here can offer. I am referring to Weta Workshop, Weta Digital and also the general crew that has now worked together on many Peter Jackson movies.

How involvement in the *LotR* project changed me:

I mentioned the long journey this has been for me personally. And while I have always pursued an art career, my involvement in the movies sped up the whole process. I have developed a new direction in my life and that is what I have taken out of this project.

Is New Zealand Middle-earth?

Of course it is! Seriously, in retrospect it is easy to see, how the decision to make this film here in New Zealand impacted on how we imagine Middle-earth. But there is also another truth and that is, while many landscapes can be found worldwide, this country is the place that houses them all. We have bushland, forests, mountains, rivers and plains all in close proximity, which makes it a perfect match for epic filming projects of this kind. And I honestly believe that J.R.R. Tolkien himself would approve of our interpretation of Middle-earth. So yes, I believe that New Zealand is Middle-earth.

Peter Jackson is so hot and gets toasted: a portrayal of Jackson displayed in Wellington Airport using toasted bread of various degrees of darkness.
(photo by Adam Lam)

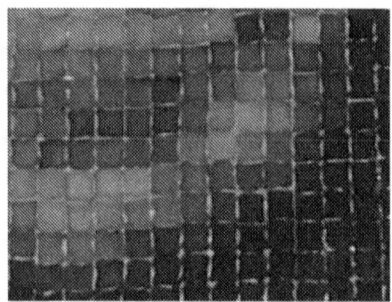

PART TWO

A WORLD CONSUMED BY TWO TOWERS

Section I

Film Tours and New Zealand's Postcolonial Identity

4

POSTCARDS FROM THE SHIRE
Global Impressions of New Zealand
after *The Lord of the Rings*

Lynnette R. Porter

In July 2004 I made a pilgrimage, not to any religious site or national monument, but to a deserted hilltop set midway between the plains and the mountains. The experience moved me deeply and remains a favourite life memory. As a patron of Hassle-Free Tours in the South Island of New Zealand,[1] I travelled to Mount Sunday, a small outcrop not far from Methven, which is a small town better known to local skiers than outsiders—except those well versed in Peter Jackson's *Lord of the Rings* lore, who know that the cast and crew stayed in Methven during location shoots. Mount Sunday is better known to film fans as Edoras, and on an unseasonably warm July morning, I stood on the site of the Golden Hall of Meduseld. As I gazed across the plains to the east, in my mind I, like Éowyn, watched Legolas and Gimli, Gandalf, and most importantly, Aragorn ride into Rohan. Turning to the west, I envisioned myself standing beside Merry and

---

[1] I was fortunate to have a private tour in mid-July 2004, although most tours involve small groups; Nikki Marsh graciously helped me arrange a special tour. The tour originated in Christchurch and featured a few stops along the way where guides Mark Gilbert and John Belcher explained unique geographical features and related stories about *LotR* and visitors' reactions to New Zealand. I had specifically looked for a day trip out of Christchurch and was well pleased with Hassle-Free Tours, whose guides know the area and their *Ring*-lore well. As well, this company has special access with the landowners whose grazing areas include and surround Mount Sunday; for me, this special access and the knowledgeable guides were selling points in selecting this company. They were also friendly and helpful, making my trip to "Edoras" everything I hoped it would be. Their website provides information about current tours. (Anon, 2005a)

Aragorn as they watched Shadowfax dwindle to a mere shadow across the land on his way to what is now private property inhabited only by sheep and goats.

Why is this spot so important? Why has it moved so many visitors, not only tourists but those who worked on the films? Alan Lee who, with John Howe, designed the *LotR* sets, props, and artistic themes that were brought to life by numerous craftspeople, told audiences at Tolkien 2005 and the Fellowship Festival[2] that the Mount Sunday set was a favourite location. He sometimes took time after the day's shooting to walk through the Golden Hall or survey the domain of the Rohirrim. The detailed construction and the quality of the work, behind as well as in front of the cameras, made these spots particularly appealing. This realism is possibly one reason why filmgoers also seem to love this place where the sets once stood.

Perhaps another reason is that so much information about filmmaking has been made available to audiences. Not only are the films memorable, and the scenes shot in under a fortnight near Mount Sunday beautifully wrought, but much has been said and written about this tiny part of New Zealand. The film lore surrounding the shooting has been presented in numerous television "making of" specials, as well as interviews with cast and crew when the films debuted and in the years following the production and premieres, not to mention DVDs with bonus features and commentaries, and a book or two written by insiders. This amazing amount of information provides fans, who never seem to get enough of Jackson's adaptation of *LotR*, with yet more personal stories of how the Rohan sets were created and what actors, directors, producers, artists, and others in the production fondly remember about this site.

What happens when *LotR* fades into a pleasant cinematic memory, and the actors, directors, and other artists, now busy with more recent projects to promote,

---

[2] Alan Lee made similar comments discussing his special fondness for the Edoras sets, including Meduseld, during Q&A sessions in his presentations at Tolkien 2005, Birmingham, England, on 13 August 2005, and a Q&A session at the Fellowship Festival in Wembley, England, on 28 August 2005. (During the latter Q&A session I asked both Alan Lee and John Howe about their favourite locations in New Zealand; Lee again described the Rohan set as a favourite.)

have nothing new to say about their filming experiences? Will Mount Sunday, as well as other *LotR* shooting locations, fall off the tourist map?

Somehow I doubt that will happen. Although new shooting sites may be added to tour companies' itineraries, *LotR* sites are sure to be kept in the mix. Books like Ian Brodie's guides[3] to the filming locations have been inordinately popular, and individuals who want to travel off the beaten, or filmed, path themselves can usually get close to what was once Rivendell or the Shire. As well, New Zealand cinema has become renowned for many companies' and individuals' work, such as the special effects and "creature" comforts provided by Weta Workshop, helmed by multiple award-winning Richard Taylor and Tania Rodger. Writer/director/producer Peter Jackson's ever-expanding Wellington studio is home to many in-production and projected films. In late 2005, two widely released films—*King Kong* (dir. Peter Jackson, 2005) and *The Chronicles of Narnia: The Lion, the Witch, and the Wardrobe* (dir. Andrew Adamson, 2005)—proudly bore the Made in New Zealand label. With such a pedigree, cinematic tourism should become a staple of the New Zealand economy for many years to come.

But cinetourism is only one part of the reason why many people worldwide consider New Zealand to be the new Middle-earth. The country's geographic diversity accords with the vision of a legion of readers who love Tolkien's book (although complaints that New Zealand appropriated an essentially English story continue to divide groups of book and film aficionados). To those with no prior experience of Tolkien's masterwork, New Zealand's rich landscapes create a memorable sensory experience. The lushness of the area close to Matamata replicates the near-idyllic Shire of Frodo's young hobbithood. The breathtaking glory of the Southern Alps presents a formidable winter challenge, not only for Hobbits but drivers, hikers, and skiers. The lonely silence complementing the view of plains and mountains from Mount Sunday echoes Éowyn's inner fears and longings. So many individual places within the country resemble Tolkien's description that audiences who fell in love with the Middle-earth shown on screen decided that they wanted to visit the country where filming occurred. New Zealand

---

[3] Ian Brodie wrote and revised location guidebooks, which continue to sell well internationally since its first edition in 2002. (Brodie, 2004)

may not be Middle-earth to everyone; however, it can represent a time and place that global audiences visit not only for wish fulfilment or nostalgia for the fresh, clean land that is vanishing from our planet, but to partake in the *LotR* legend. New Zealand is a wonder in itself, a country vastly different from any other, and it attracts visitors who begin as *LotR* film fans but soon realize that they are smitten with New Zealand itself.

Jackson's *LotR* has had a powerful effect on New Zealand, and the country, in turn, has provided a somewhat controversial point of contention between fans of the book and Jackson's adaptation. For good or ill, New Zealand is now part of LotR history, and it will continue to influence the story's readers and film audiences.

New Zealand and the LotR tale are now inextricably bound and their futures forever altered because of the connection, even if New Zealand is not *Tolkien's* vision of Middle-earth. Jackson's vision of Middle-earth invites virtual and real-life travellers to discard their preconceptions about the world and lets them (us) enter a land of possibilities. The following "postcards" from the Shire, sent from around the world over the past few years, illustrate my impressions of this "new" Middle-earth as well as the perceptions of others in the United States, England, and New Zealand who feel they have a special connection with Tolkien's *LotR* and now, to New Zealand.

Postcards from the Shire

For many people whose primary exposure to Tolkien's *LotR* is Peter Jackson's recent film adaptation, New Zealand is Middle-earth. The magical beauty and diversity shown throughout the films translate into a sense of awe for those from other countries. I enjoy Tolkien's *LotR* on many levels, and I have read the books many times during the past thirty-five years. However, New Zealand will always have a special place in my heart because of Jackson's adaptation; it complements, rather than replaces, my initial mental images of Middle-earth. As I travel to numerous conferences and fan gatherings, I discover that I am not alone either in my LotR fandom or my appreciation for New Zealand.

Auckland, New Zealand, December 2002

My first trip to New Zealand took place in December 2002, just a few weeks prior to the release of *The Two Towers*. Even if I hadn't been a *LotR* fan eagerly awaiting the next instalment of the cinematic trilogy, it would have been impossible to miss the excitement and national pride concerning the films.

A billboard featuring the film's main characters greeted me every morning as I took a shuttle to my academic conference—the real reason for my visit to New Zealand. The cast looked larger than life as they gazed solemnly onto the street; traffic in downtown Auckland on a busy morning seemed far removed from the quaintness of the Shire.

On a day off between conference meetings, I wandered down the street, searching for a trolley stop. Noticing my obvious lack of direction, a young woman guided me to the proper point on the pavement. She looked surprised when I thanked her in a prominent "American" accent. "Do you like *The Lord of the Rings*?" she asked. I assured her that I did, and in fact, I hoped to take a side trip to Matamata. "Hobbiton," she nodded approvingly.

The next morning saw me popping my head out my hotel room door as soon as the staff dropped the newspaper. All week I'd looked forward to *The New Zealand Herald*'s highly promoted *TT* feature. The insert included interviews with cast and crew, and I was especially pleased to find that Miranda Otto (who portrayed one of my favourite characters, Éowyn) had been interviewed for this edition. (Anon, 2002) As I found out later in the lift to the lobby, several guests had read the insert about *TT*, and whether from Japan, Australia, or the States, we all highly anticipated the movie. Everyone seemed to be caught up in the excitement of the films.

In fact, that enthusiasm was often hard to miss. When I finally found time to tour not only Matamata but also farther north to the Bay of Islands, I saw that New Zealand was everything that I had dreamed, and more importantly, as truthfully as Peter Jackson advertised in *The Fellowship of the Ring*. One word came to mind: lush.

Deceptively high hills caressed the sea; tropical vegetation gave way to well-tended farms and horse country; even a waterfall's gushing could be seen from a distant motorway. If the Shire truly looked as green as the land around Matamata on a warm December afternoon, I can understand why the Hobbits so seldom ventured far from home.

Ormond Beach, Florida, U.S.A., December 2002

A few days after my return from Auckland, I attended the midnight premiere of *TT* at my neighbourhood cinema. For all its local charm and tropical similarity to parts of New Zealand, Ormond Beach is psychologically and geographically about as far from the Shire as possible.

Of course, the lobby was packed with fans who arrived hours early for a good seat, and, just as expectedly, fans tended to chat to each other in line during the wait. The couple in front of me confessed that they never made it through the books (too long, too many pages), although the middle-aged woman assured me that she valiantly tried several times. However, the couple loved *FotR* on film. She proudly explained that they often played the film even when she or her husband were doing other tasks. They ran into the room to watch a favourite scene or spoke the actors' lines when they returned to their chores. The pair were saving money to go to New Zealand some day, and they had eagerly awaited this film for months.

My theatre buddies were, appropriately to my mind, duly impressed that I had just returned from New Zealand. Of course, I was fairly conspicuous in my bright purple Aotearoa T-shirt and greenstone necklace. News along the gossip grapevine travelled quickly among a caffeine-high crowd waiting impatiently for their movie to begin. Soon the ten people in front of me and about as many behind got the word that I actually visited New Zealand. Granted, my twelve-day trip, much of it spent in conference rooms on Auckland campuses, failed to make me an expert on everything Kiwi, but to at least part of the crowd at the local Regal I was the closest thing. I embraced my fifteen minutes of fame by answering questions about what I saw and did. Most questions centred on the accuracy of what was shown on film— Is the country really that beautiful? Are there wide open areas, or was that just movie magic? Is there really a Party Tree? Although I had briefly toured about half of the North Island and visited one area where only a few scenes in the entirety of the trilogy had been filmed a couple of years earlier, my lack of comprehensive information was unimportant. Any titbit about the promised land, whether called

New Zealand, the Shire, or Lothlórien, gave the audience more proof that Peter Jackson was right—New Zealand is a special place, and Hobbits and elves, as well as modern citizens, do right to preserve it.

The theatre lights darkened, and everyone quieted in expectation. When the film opened with the striking majesty of the Southern Alps, I vowed that my next trip would be to the South Island.

Dallas, Texas, U.S.A., May 2003

A technical communication conference in downtown Dallas, Texas, is probably one of the least likely places to learn more about New Zealand or make a *LotR* connection, but in spring 2003 that is exactly what happened. Dr. Richard Draper, a faculty member from Christchurch Polytechnic Institute of Technology, was primarily participating in the conference to promote CPIT's online technical communication program and to present a paper, but he quickly became an ambassador for New Zealand. When I visited the CPIT booth, I was both amused and horrified to hear conference-goers ask if Dr. Draper hailed from Australia, or wonder where in Australia Christchurch was located. With good humour, he gently corrected visitors' geographical blunders, and during his conference presentation, he readily noted that New Zealand was where *LotR* was filmed. People in the audience nodded and smiled; here was a geographic reference they understood.

Not guilty of shyness, I approached Dr. Draper after his presentation. We chatted about our mutual interest in *LotR*; he had even attended an audition for the films. For many people, including those professionals at the conference, New Zealand is most easily identified with the *LotR* films, and even Kiwis travelling abroad on business far removed from filmmaking or tourism may find themselves called upon as cultural representatives. Since 2000, anyone claiming to hail from New Zealand is likely to be asked about *LotR*.

Orlando, Florida, U.S.A., March 2004

Florida in winter hosts a variety of festivals and conventions that attract thousands seeking others with similar interests and the warmth of the southern sun. Megacon is one of the largest gatherings for fans of television series and films, animé and gaming, science fiction and fantasy. Standing in a line of revellers eager to storm the gates on opening day, I was amazed at the intricate costumes created by convention-goers. Although a large number of animated characters came to life, I, of course, was enthralled by Pippin and his family. The parents and both young children obviously learned about the latest in Shirewear from Jackson's films. Father Pippin wore a blue travelling coat with trademark scarf and, far away from the fire marshals, lighted a pipe half as tall as himself. Mother Hobbit (Diamond, perhaps?) seemed to take her fashion cues from pre-marriage Rosie Cotton. The children mirrored their parents' fashions. From pointed ears to curly haired toes, this Hobbit family was dressed for success, which they had in abundance at Megacon. Throughout the day, whether standing in line with other patrons or meandering among convention booths, the little family graciously smiled for photographers and posed with fans eager to have their picture taken with real-life Hobbits.

Although not all fans glue realistic fur on their (or their children's) feet, the level of commitment and interest in detail often stem not from Tolkien's descriptions, but Jackson's interpretation. In fact, the tendency to "know" what Hobbits, for example, would wear to a public event is often a point of contention between fans of book and films. At a recent LotR-related conference in England, I heard grumbling from observers who noted that at costume contests, film-inspired (or blatantly copied) attire and makeup win more often than designs based on Tolkien's textual depictions. Whether the cinematic vision some day becomes *the* interpretation of all settings and characters from LotR remains to be seen, but it is a concern for those interested in Tolkien's *LotR* but unimpressed by the films. Jackson's adaptations, often because of their highly refined details and careful attention to even minute aspects of set, prop, or costume, leave little room for individual interpretation. Jackson's imagery often seems to have "filled up the corners" of enthusiasts' imagination, with the result being a series of intricately and lovingly reproduced details that parrot those shown on film.

Caradhras from the Air, Over South Island, New Zealand, July 2004

My flight from Sydney to Christchurch took me over the Southern Alps. Impressive at any time, in the pink-purple twilight, the deep snows sparkled and bathed the mountains in serenely beautiful pastels. The young woman in the coveted window seat next to me quickly retrieved her digital camera and began snapping the view. Despite her enthusiasm and expertise, the little camera failed to capture the luminescent scene. Disappointed, she sat back so I could have a better look before night, and our flight path, hid the snowy heights.

"Do you remember the first scene in *The Two Towers* when they show the mountains?" she whispered. I nodded. "It looks exactly like that."

Indeed it did, and she and I both smiled at the shared cinematic, and now real-life, memory. My companion did not need to explain the setting or the film; we were both familiar with it. What vied for importance was the astonishing beauty of the scenery, made even more remarkable by our aerial vantage point and the lighting conditions on the one hand, and on the other, we had seen a view very similar to that seen by film crews as they focused their lenses for the second film's opening shots. At once, the tallest mountain in sight was both Mount Cook[4] and Caradhras for us. In an interesting study of the implications of tourism and culture, especially popular culture based on films as globally embraced as *LotR*, author/researcher Rodanthi Tzanelli noted that "from its inception, the LOTR cinematic saga had started taking on a life of its own, blurring the boundaries between imaginary and real worlds." (Tzanelli, 2004) This surreal juxtaposition of reality and fictional worlds is becoming more common among New Zealand tourists who are also *LotR* fans, as I can attest.

---

[4] In New Zealand, places are commonly listed with two names, Maori and non-Maori (English). In this chapter I have listed only the English version, Mount Cook, for example, although Aoraki is also this mountain's name. Unlike many other nations, New Zealand has been recognizing locations' original indigenous names and does not merely rename landmarks with English variants.

Mount Sunday, not too far from Methven, South Island, New Zealand, July 2004

Everyone associated with *LotR* praises the high level of dedication of the crew, as well as the cast. Care and pride are keywords, and Kiwis are a hardworking lot. That reputation has got around. Perhaps New Zealanders were willing to embrace the director's vision in part because Peter Jackson, the cast, and the crew all respected the country and its people. During a visit to the location formerly known as Edoras, my Hassle-Free Tours guide, Mark Gilbert, explained that the Golden Hall of Meduseld had been built on private land, but that care was taken to close the road to local traffic for only a short time. The scenes were filmed during a scant few days, where upon the landscape was returned to its original condition.[5] Today no telltale signs remain to show where the Rohirrim lived and worked; the land is back to its former natural glory, although the cinematic splendour of Rohan is preserved forever on film. Jackson's production teams respected New Zealand's natural beauty and its people, and even several years after filming, the goodwill continues.

Altamonte Springs, Florida, U.S.A., February 2005

To lure even more people to central Florida, Vulkon attracts film and television actors each year. Science fiction and fantasy find a welcome home in this part of the South, and February brought together hundreds of U.S. fans to chat with, among others, John Noble (Denethor). Although I have met several actors in a wide variety of convention venues, I was especially impressed with Mr. Noble. He not only pleasantly posed for photographs but took the time to chat with each fan in the long queue outside.

    A little girl, about six years old, and her father nervously awaited their turn in front of me. The chatty child became suddenly quiet when introduced to John Noble, who, in Saturday casual of jeans and button-down shirt, seemed more than a half a world away from Denethor, Steward of Gondor. Noble smiled and signed a

---

[5] Hassle-Free Tours. Tour to Mount Sunday. July 2004. (See also Note 1 for more information about Hassle-Free Tours.)

photo; he gently asked her a few questions. When prompted yet again by her father, the girl hesitantly asked what Billy Boyd was like; Pippin is her favourite character. Noble confided in her that he was a very nice man and a pleasure to work with. The little girl beamed, the father beamed, and another pair of fans walked away happy.

Of course, that's what actors do: they promote films, and themselves. However, Noble excelled in making each fan feel special and in really listening to what each person had to say. My experience was no less special, and I, too, walked away happy. As an ongoing ambassador for the films, Noble is well named. He maintains an actor's presence, but he is also a friendly guy who can easily converse with fans and their wide range of questions. He chatted knowledgably not only about the films and New Zealand, but Tolkien's and Jackson's genius.

During my few minutes at the autograph table, he took the time to talk about my favorite subject, New Zealand. He even agreed to continue the conversation via email to help me write this chapter. Like most *LotR* actors I have met over the years, Noble praised the director, cast, and crew of the film and confessed to a fondness for New Zealand. When I asked if *LotR* would have been as successful if Peter Jackson had chosen another country, or a series of global locations, as George Lucas did with the *Star Wars* films, John Noble replied that New Zealand

> is geographically unique. In the space of a few hundred miles the diversity is breathtaking. The glory of the South Island Mountains, and the sweeping scope of its high plains provided Peter Jackson with an accessible Middle-earth that could not be found in most places. [New Zealand] seems timeless and remote and yet was easily available. New Zealand embraced the project and barriers that inhibit so many projects did not hinder *LotR*.[6]

Noble further revealed his respect and admiration for Jackson, who made a seemingly overwhelming amount of work not only possible but a cherished memory. The actor explained that

> [t]he genius of Jackson to envisage such a project and to gather together such an extraordinary group of committed artists in a far flung corner of the world for so long is the stuff of legend.... I had the sense that the bar had been set very high,

---

[6] John Noble, personal email correspondence, 7 April 2005. I also talked with Mr. Noble during the One Ring Celebration, Pasadena, CA, U.S.A., on 21 January 2006, to discuss this chapter; he reiterated these comments.

and that anything less than my very best would not be good enough. It was challenging, exhausting, and thrilling. Bonds of friendship were forged that I think will last a lifetime.... Perhaps the greatest insight I gained was that people can respond magnificently if well led and inspired. Too often we underestimate ourselves and others. Cynicism and fear inhibit us from achieving our potential. *LotR* is a testament to J.R.R. Tolkien and Peter Jackson. Men of great vision, fearless determination, total lack of defeatism. Both faced scorn and criticism from lesser mortals, but were undeterred.[7]

What is surprising is that the sentiment behind Noble's eloquent comments is not unique. Other actors echo these types of comments, not only during interviews or on press junkets during each of the three films' premieres. Even after the premieres are over and the job no longer requires them to answer yet another question about *LotR*, John Noble and other cast members continue to share fond memories of New Zealand and *LotR*. Actors and fans worldwide share a genuine interest in what not only makes Jackson's trilogy special, but a belief that New Zealand serves as a wonderful Middle-earth.

Birmingham, England, August 2005

England is Tolkien's Middle-earth. A Tolkien Society-sponsored tour of Birmingham and nearby Oxford clearly pointed out several possible inspirations for aspects of Tolkien's story. Sarehole Mill is closely associated with the mill, as well as the miller and his son, described in *Farmer Giles of Ham*. The Shire boasts its own mill, which Ted Sandyman assists in "modernizing" almost to its, and the Shire's, destruction. Moseley Bog provides aspects of the Old Forest, and the hazy hills viewed from outside Birmingham may have served as the misty mountains. As a traveller among the checkerboard fields in Tolkien's Worcestershire, with their hedgerow borders and still-small villages among the industrial growth of larger Midlands' cities, I could easily see how England is Middle-earth from Tolkien's book. The myriad towers around Oxford make me compare them with the Barad Dûr and Minas Tirith of my imagination; Oxford's flower gardens bring to mind Sam Gamgee's careful tending of Bag End. So much of Tolkien's life and work

---

[7] Ibid.

remains in England; the sheer emotional weight of walking among so much history, with buildings and statued architecture dating back hundreds of years and Roman ruins not far away, bring to mind the nearly lost Númenorian history that presages the War of the Ring. Although New Zealand's Maori culture is vibrant with its own important past, it is vastly different from English history. Tolkien's England, and *LotR*'s Middle-earth, offer a sense of what came before them; Tolkien's English Middle-earth is an old land whose ties seem closer to those of Aragorn's ancestors.

Perhaps that is a large part of the reason why book and Tolkien defenders take such umbrage with the concept of New Zealand as Middle-earth. Between conference sessions at Tolkien 2005, I browsed book stands. A dignified older woman picked up a book about Middle-earth. Its cover featured a snow-capped mountain against a perfect blue sky. "Does this look like England to you?" she demanded of the startled bookseller. "I think it's supposed to be New Zealand," he suggested. "Exactly!" she frowned as she dropped the book back on the table. Her reaction might have been more extreme than some I encountered during this trip, but the sentiment that England is the rightful location of Middle-earth is alive and well and likely to further the global argument with New Zealand over the title.

Wembley, England, August 2005

The international crowd at the Fellowship Festival, hailing mostly from Europe with a contingent or two from the U.S., was obviously oriented more toward the film adaptation than the book. A group of speakers and workshop leaders from The Tolkien Society, led by Publicity Manager Ian Collier, provided an educational track of programming throughout the three-day event. The Tolkien Society participants emphasized Tolkien the author, book-related themes and characters, Hobbit-style dancing, and Elvish language. Although the sessions were well attended and brought forth more serious scholars or fans who wanted to learn more about Tolkien's world, the majority of attendees stayed near the main auditorium. There actors, stunt men (doubling as actors in several roles), artists (the illustrious Alan Lee and John Howe), and designers Richard Taylor and Tania Rodger from famed Weta Workshop answered questions from the crowds and showcased examples of their work. Fans have their personal favourites, of course, and most came away satisfied that they had met Orcs and Elves, a wraith or two, the King of the Dead, a Hobbit double, and a member of the Fellowship—or at least the actors who portrayed them in Jackson's adaptation.

Tolkien Society membership has grown with the recent popularity of the films. Fans of both book and films are welcome, and the Society plans more frequent activities, such as Oxonmoot, as well as special events like Tolkien 2005. Although some members clearly don't care for Jackson's adaptation, or other adaptations, many new members enjoy both book and films. Some Tolkien Society members initially became engrossed by the story because of the recent films, but the Society's activities and publications emphasize Tolkien the author and his works. The films are, necessarily, secondary. By providing programming at the Fellowship Festival and other events where film fans congregate, The Tolkien Society provides a counter-balance to purely film-related discussions of *LotR*.

For the crowd at the 2005 Fellowship Festival, many who asked questions about New Zealand and about the cast's and crew's experiences on set or more recent projects, Jackson's film clearly represents Middle-earth. If you could live in Middle-earth, where would you live? arose several times in the Q&A sessions, and many actors, as well as audience members when the question was returned to them, answered either the Shire or Rohan. When this group thought of Middle-earth, their vision clearly was of the New Zealand locations immortalized on film.

Of course, many actors attending the Festival were born and raised New Zealanders—such as emcees Craig Parker (Haldir) and Mark Ferguson (Gil-galad), Bruce Hopkins (Gamling), Joel Tobeck (Orc lieutenant best known for berating the pirates as they arrive for battle), Jed Brophy (Sharku/Snaga), Peter Tait (Shagrat/Corsair captain), Sandro Kopp (Gildor), Shane Rangi (White Witch, ring wraith, Witch King, and others), Jonathan Harding (Erestor), and stuntman Mana Hira Davis. It is only natural that they speak with pride about their homeland and help spread the word that New Zealand is uniquely beautiful and worthy of preservation on film.

Chief Executives of Weta Workshop, Richard Taylor and Tania Rodger, grew up in New Zealand and base their highly successful business there. They celebrate Kiwi creativity and ingenuity, especially important when they need dedicated professionals down to earth enough to get a job done right but with lofty dreams to create something that has never before been seen.[8]

Even actors born far from New Zealand have a lingering connection not only to *LotR* but to the country itself. Thomas Robins (Deagol) may have an English birthright but grew up in New Zealand. Stephen Ure (Grishnakh/Gorbag) has worked extensively in Australia and New Zealand. King of the Dead, Paul Norell, was London born but has worked often in New Zealand. Even Billy Boyd (Pippin), with no other New Zealand connection beyond the films, quickly answered "New Zealand, of course,"[9] when I asked during the Q&A session about his favourite worldwide filming locations. Although he also described the Mexican location of *Master and Commander* (dir. Peter Weir, 2003), New Zealand was his first reply, and he has said, both at this Festival and in press interviews, that he knows he will return. No matter their country of origin, those involved with Jackson's production have found an emotional touchstone in New Zealand, and they gladly share their positive impressions with anyone who asks.

Actor Bruce Hopkins commented with pride that New Zealand's workers should be given their due for helping make the films a success. He explained that the New Zealand film crews display "an incredible work ethic", and New Zealanders in general are

> renowned for their ability to solve problems on the spot using whatever resources are available, and this facet of how *LotR* was made should not be underestimated. The spirit and heart that permeated the production was incredibly supportive and generous. It really was a community that evolved with the project, and I am not sure if it would have occurred like this had the filming been done in another cultural setting.[10]

This sentiment is often heard in discussion among actors, and it has rubbed off on fans. Everyone with whom I have talked thinks highly of the New Zealand work ethic and creativity, not only in problem solving but in attention to the fine details

---

[8] Richard Taylor and Tania Rodger, Q&A session, Fellowship Festival, Wembley, England, 28 August 2005. Similar comments can be read in an article about Weta Workshop (White, 2005, 110-117).

[9] Billy Boyd, Q&A session, Fellowship Festival, Wembley, England, 29 August 2005.

[10] Bruce Hopkins, personal email correspondence, 27 July 2005.

so that a high-quality product—in whatever area of production—is guaranteed. Not only is New Zealand considered Middle-earth, but filmmakers and backers are considering the country's wealth of talent as something of a promised land of creativity as well as beauteous locations.

Especially at fan-based conferences, the connection between New Zealand and *LotR* continues to be strengthened. As long as fans line up to see their favourite actors from this adaptation, New Zealand will continue to be their Middle-earth.

Indianapolis, Indiana, U.S.A., October 2005

By late July 2005, the staff at the Indiana State Museum had been at work for more than a year to bring the travelling *LotR* exhibit to Indianapolis. Discussions between this museum and the Museum of New Zealand Te Papa Tangarewa began in autumn (in North America) 2003, and contracts were signed during summer 2004 for a 3 October 2005-6 January 2006 run. Jeff Matsuoka, Operating Manager at the Museum, had his hands full when tickets went on sale, first to museum members, and then to the general public beginning on 1 August. However, ticket sales were only one part of the production.

Special events held during the exhibit's run included two Taste of New Zealand dinners, featuring a five-course sampler of Kiwi cuisine and wines. (Anon, 2005b)[11] Of course, lamb was on the menu, but so were green lip mussels, grouper (hapuka), and lobster medallions. Although everyone expected certain dishes—such as lamb—Crystal Food Service, who prepared the menu, made certain that the meal went beyond cultural stereotypes. (For example, how many times have *LotR* fans heard about the number of sheep versus the number of people in New Zealand?) Adding a wide range of local New Zealand specialties to the menu, and showcasing the country's wine industry with an accompanying wine selection for each course, balanced the expected choices.

Other events included slide shows and discussions about New Zealand's diverse culture and travel destinations, as well as IMAX showings of all three films,

---

[11] The menu was listed on the museum webpage as on 15 September 2005: http://www.in.gov/ism/MuseumExhibits/lotr_prog.asp#Taste.

fan-related events, and educational programmes. Because the exhibit showcases Jackson's *LotR* artefacts, the New Zealand connection is prominent in attendees' minds. What is especially interesting is that the settings for this travelling exhibit have been well-known (and carefully selected) museums. Middle-earth artefacts—clothing, weapons, jewellery—have been displayed just like "real" museum artefacts from historically documented cultures. New Zealand's Middle-earth culture has been recorded in the manner of any cultural or historic artefact—a strange blend of "real" and "fake" history. Of course, the historiography of Jackson's films *is* real and worth study on its own. However, Middle-earth, as well as the filming of *LotR*, is the subject of many exhibits, certainly strengthening the veracity of the claim that New Zealand is Middle-earth. Perhaps that is why the buzz preceding the exhibit's opening in Indianapolis was greater than that for previous exhibits.

As a native Hoosier, I had a special interest in the *LotR* exhibit which travelled from Wellington to cities around the world, including London, Singapore, Sydney, Boston, Houston, and finally Indianapolis. Bringing *LotR* memorabilia to the U.S. Midwest is impressive in itself. Inviting locals, as well as visitors from as far away as Germany and Peru, to sample New Zealand's culture provided another challenge for the museum and a benefit for exhibit-goers. The people who called the museum months in advance to reserve tickets and made plans to travel across the United States or from other continents were certainly interested in *LotR*, but they also craved more information about New Zealand. The two are intricately linked in many fans' minds, and the Indiana State Museum staff worked hard to provide not only a fulfilling *LotR* experience but an introduction to New Zealand's cuisine and geography.

Indianapolis, Indiana, U.S.A., December 2005

Of course, I love to visit my family in Ohio any time, but the timing of my December visit was carefully coordinated with the end of my teaching semester and the first weekend available to visit the *LotR* travelling exhibit in Indianapolis, about a two-hour drive from my brother's home. Because the exhibit would close in early January

2006, the number of "available weekends" was dwindling, and my brother Bart agreed to make the pilgrimage with me amid a flurry of holiday preparations.

Despite having run for months, the exhibit continued to attract visitors. The Indiana State Museum was packed with fans (and their good-natured if bemused relatives tagging along), many on their second, third, or more visits to the special exhibit. Bart, whose height and friendly smile made him the ideal volunteer to reach swords stacked high on a wall, shared a bond with the husbands, brothers, and boyfriends helping with legions of female fans' last-minute holiday shopping. The museum's gift shop, well stocked with everything from books to key chains, weapons to jewellery, and, of course, T-shirts, did a brisk business while fans waited their turn to view the exhibit.

In the early afternoon, my turn finally arrived. Although the crowds sometimes made viewing video clips difficult, I slowly made my way to the front of the screen to learn more about how horses were used by the Rohirrim, as well as film crews, in key battle scenes. I saw the intricacies of animatronic Treebeard and gazed up in awe at the Ent's amber-eyed visage. Although Bart much preferred models of the Two Towers, which truly towered over the exhibit, he indulged my desire to stare (sometimes for long minutes) at the actual costumes that Liv Tyler and Viggo Mortensen wore on set.

As a final postcard, this experience was fulfilling. Not only did I hear and see how so many people from New Zealand and around the world came together for this special filmmaking effort, but I "bonded" with my brother and hundreds of fans who pointed out highlights as they reverently viewed the exhibit. We share a common respect for *LotR* and New Zealand; it links us, however peripherally, with every member of the many creative teams who made *LotR* a moving cinematic experience. We share common knowledge of the films and the places where scenes were immortalized.

In a similar way, fans who visited the travelling exhibit, not only in Indianapolis but on its many stops globally, share "memories" of New Zealand. What may have begun as Peter Jackson's monumental cinematic undertaking has taken on a life of its own, a multilayered cultural experience that unites fans more often than it separates them. New Zealand is at the heart of this experience, which, if these postcards are any indication, means that the new Middle-earth will be a virtual and real-life destination for many years to come.

Acknowledgments

I sincerely thank the members of The Tolkien Society, especially Ian and Anke Collier, for their guidance and support at Tolkien 2005 and the Fellowship Festival; John Noble for graciously talking with me in person as well as via email; Bruce Hopkins for his generosity in talking with me several times during the Fellowship Festival as well as corresponding by email; Nikki Marsh, Mark Gilbert, and John Belcher, at Hassle-Free Tours, for their ongoing assistance in my personal and professional exploration of New Zealand; and Richard Draper, for his friendship and goodwill in discussing everything New Zealand.

I also thank the many creative artists at the Fellowship Festival, including Billy Boyd, Mark Ferguson, Bruce Hopkins, John Howe, Alan Lee, Paul Norell, Craig Parker, Thomas Robins, Tania Rodger, Richard Taylor, and Joel Tobeck, who graciously, thoroughly, professionally, and pleasantly answered my many questions during their Q&A sessions at the Fellowship Festival. Thank you for giving me insights into your work and experiences making the *LotR* trilogy.

Bibliography

Anon (2002), "*The Lord of the Rings: The Two Towers*" *The New Zealand Herald* souvenir ed., 10 December

Anon (2005a), Hassle-Free Tours website: http://www.hasslefree.co.nz

Anon (2005b), "*Lord of the Rings* Exhibit" Indiana State Museum website: http://www.in.gov/ism/MuseumExhibits

Brodie, Ian (2004), *The Lord of the Rings: A Location Guidebook* rev. ed., HarperCollins, Sydney

Tolkien, J.R.R. (1999), *Farmer Giles of Ham* 50th anniversary ed., eds Christina Scull and Wayne G. Hammond, HarperCollins, New York

Tzanelli, Rodanthi (2004), "Constructing the 'Cinematic Tourist'" *Tourist Studies* 4.1, pp. 23-43

White, Paul (2005), "Wonders of Weta" *New Zealand Magazine* 1.1 (October/November), pp. 110-117

5

THEME/FILM TOUR
The Disappearing of Illusion into Integral Reality

Lisa Wong

$\mathscr{I}$N MAY 2003, the Nippon Travel Agency, a leading Japanese tourist company, launched a New Zealand package consisting of selected film locations from the popular *The Lord of the Rings* trilogy (2001-2003) which sold out in three days. After the success of this initial theme tour package, in July 2003 the Nippon Travel marketed three more. The first tour, which included attendance at the star-studded Emmy awards ceremony in Los Angeles in September 2003, targeted fans of the television series *Sex and the City* (dir. Allison Anders et al, 1998-2004). The theme of the second package, to Germany and Poland, was Roman Polanski's Holocaust drama *The Pianist* (dir. Roman Polanski, 2002). The third, a South Korean package, included Seoul and Chunchon, and was based on a Korean television drama, *Winter Sonata* (*Gyeoul yeonga*, dir. Seok-ho Yun, 2002). (Anon, 2003b) If you are a tourist who has been to New Zealand, Warsaw, Seoul and Chunchon, are you sure you have *really* been there? We are now referring to *LotR*'s New Zealand, *The Pianist*'s Germany and Poland, *Winter Sonata*'s South Korea.

To a certain extent, these newly *released* tourist destinations are somewhat like Disneyland theme parks. In "Disneyworld Company", Jean Baudrillard declares that "there is no real world anymore":

> Disney, the precursor, the grand initiator of the imaginary as virtual reality, is now in the process of capturing all the real world to integrate it into its synthetic universe, in the form of a vast "reality show" where reality itself becomes a

spectacle [*vient se donner en spectacle*], where the real becomes a theme park. The transfusion of the real is like a blood transfusion, except that here it is a transfusion of real blood into the exsanguine universe of virtuality. After the prostitution of the imaginary, here is now the hallucination of the real in its ideal and simplified version. (Baudrillard, 2003)

The media, including TV drama and films with their powerful imagery transformed the natural landscapes of different countries into "spectacle [*vient se donner en spectacle*], where the real becomes a theme park". While Disneyland Theme Parks have their fixed sites, anywhere in the world is vulnerable to transformation into a "mediated" theme park; thus "the real world" is about to be integrated into a "synthetic universe". What we gaze at is no longer what is, but images imposed on us by the mass media. It is slightly ridiculous to say that Peter Jackson brought Middle-earth to life and turned New Zealand into the past. However, we can probably declare the "death" of New Zealand when it declares itself the "Best Supporting Country in a Motion Picture".[1] Alternatively, we can add a "Post-" in front of "New Zealand".[2] If "Post-New Zealand" is not the "New Zealand" that tourists *used to* know, what is it? This question is probably easier to answer than "What is New Zealand in the eyes of tourists?" because if we follow Baudrillard's thought "Post-New Zealand" is supposed to be more "ideal and simplified" than the "real" New Zealand.

In this chapter, I attempt to investigate the cultural phenomenon of theme tours by investigating the effects generated by *LotR* film trilogy on New Zealand tourism. The first section will trace the change of tourist gazes from "negotiated reality" to "virtual reality". I argue that by reorganizing the real and the simulations, a new culture which de-differentiates media and other cultural practices, such as touring, is created. In the second section, by comparing the similar operational

---

[1] A full page advertisement placed by Tourism New Zealand stating "Best Supporting Country in a Motion Picture" appeared in the *LA Times* on 25 March 2002, the morning after the Academy Awards. The advertisement also appeared in the *New Yorker* in the United States, the *Empire* magazine in the United Kingdom, *Today* newspaper in Singapore and *Who Weekly* in Australia. (Tourism New Zealand, 2002a)

[2] I struggled to decide whether to call it "Post-New Zealand" or "Pre-New Zealand". I think I was a bit confused about the real and the simulation!

strategies of Disneyworld Company and "*The Lord of the Rings* Empire", I endeavour to highlight the gravitational force of consumption in postmodern society.

From negotiated reality to virtual reality

The theme tour is not new terrain in the tourist industry. What is surprising is the readiness of tourists to embrace simulations mediated by the mass media?[3] Not long ago (even nowadays), many tourists were satisfied with the live cultural performances by local people (preferably natives) in the host country. Does the Maori haka performed by Maori represent New Zealand's culture? Why does what is taken for granted in the tourist industry become a daily struggle for the natives in everyday life? These questions would not bother general tourists. Their concern is whether they are experiencing the *real* New Zealand as portrayed in the advertisements.[4] Tourists want to taste the authenticity of a country, but do not want to let the complexity of reality ruin their holiday mood. As Jennifer Craik points out, most tourists "want some degree of negotiated experiences which provide a tourist 'bubble' (a safe, controlled environment) out of which they can selectively step to 'sample' predictable forms of experiences." (Craik, 1997: 115) What is experienced as real by the tourists is a negotiated reality accommodating the pleasure of the tourists. In this sense, the readiness of people to embrace simulations mediated by film or TV drama is not surprising. From negotiated reality to virtual reality is not a tremendous step. To a certain extent, the New Zealand signified by Maori dance is not necessarily more real than Middle-earth's New Zealand created by *LotR*. It is especially the case if one agrees with M. Crick that all cultures are "staged" and inauthentic. (cited in Urry, 2002: 9) From tourist to "post-tourist"[5] is only a change of name if one agrees with Daniel J. Boorstin that tourists' experiences are "pseudo-events". (Boorstin 1961: 80)

---

[3] This is what John Urry calls "the *mediated* gaze". (Urry, 2002: 151)

[4] In tourist publicity, narratives about New Zealand describe it as a nation innocent, frank and free of ethnic tensions, in a sense, the country is presented almost as simple as Disneyland.

[5] Maxine Feifer uses the term "post-tourists" to refer to those tourists who almost delight in the inauthenticity of the normal tourist experience. They treat touring as a series of games or texts to be played. (cited in Urry, 2002: 12)

At stake here is the notion of real. If the allegory of simulation in the Borges tale cited by Baudrillard is too ancient to imagine, there is a more "recent" example. A popular nineteenth-century tourist attraction in New Zealand were the pink and white terraces rising above Lake Rotomahana. These were destroyed by the volcanic eruption of Mt. Tarawera at 3a.m. on the 10 June 1886, but photographs of them have remained popular. (see for example Anon, 2003g; Anon, 2007c) The physical attraction has been recreated by flowing geothermal water over artificially built terraces in a different location, close to existing tourist facilities.[6] The simulation remains after the real has been destroyed. What we now view as real are simulations of the images. That is the simulation of the simulation. In Baudrillard's words, "Simulation is no longer that of a territory, a referential being or a substance. It is the generation by models of a real without origin or reality: a hyperreal." (Baudrillard, 1988: 166)

Let us look back (or forward) to how we gaze at the hyperreal of *LotR*'s New Zealand. In the "Acknowledgements" in his *The Lord of the Rings Location Guidebook* Ian Brodie says, "This book is dedicated to J.R.R. Tolkien for his vision and Peter Jackson for making this vision three-dimensional." (Brodie, 2002: 5) What we see as "*LotR*'s New Zealand" is mediated by the vision of Peter Jackson of the vision of Tolkien's imagined Middle-earth. While years ago we actively visualised scenery described in books through our own imagination,[7] nowadays, we passively receive different signified sights from images provided by the media. Tourists no longer have their own vision, but consuming visions of powerful others. The visions of

---

[6] The "artificially built terraces" Urry refers to are the Wairakei Terraces in Taupo. Instead of copying the famous pink and white terraces, it is actually a replica of the destroyed Wairakei Terraces. The original Wairakei Terraces and geysers disappeared in 1950s due to development of the geothermal power station. However, people frequently refer to its resemblance to the pink and white terraces. It has become the simulacrum of the pink and white terraces. (Urry, 2002: 131)

[7] Prior to his travels in Italy, Goethe "read voraciously on all things Roman he pored over the history and street plans of the city; he studied engravings of the significant buildings, and he collected woodcuts, plaster casts, etchings and cork models. Goethe's imagination immersed itself in the city, so that upon arrival he remarks that 'everything is just as I imagined it, yet everything is new ... my old ideas have become so much more firm, vital and coherent'." (Rojek and Urry, 1997: 6)

powerful others are further supported by experts in the tourist industry. Let us look at the introduction of Nomad Safaris Rings tour on its website:

> When JRR Tolkien created Middle-Earth little did he know the magical landscapes of his imagination actually existed, 12,000 miles away from his homeland. It took Peter Jackson 10 years and millions of dollars to bring *The Lord of the Rings* to life on the big screen. Nomad Safaris have been taking people there every day for the past 12 years. Indeed, when David Gatward-Ferguson, owner of Nomad Safaris, first gazed across Skippers Canyon all those years ago, he instantly felt he was looking at "The Road to Mordor". (Anon, 2003d)

Or the one on Red Carpet Tours' website:

> Since Peter Jackson made his film trilogy, there is a place that millions recognise as the living reflection of Tolkien's imaginary world, and that place is New Zealand. You will come as strangers to a distant land and part as a band of companions who have shared a unique experience, exploring the length and breadth of the country that became Middle-earth. (Anon, 2003e)

The tourism experts tell us that Tolkien's imaginary realm "actually existed". It is only after Peter Jackson's *LotR* that million of audiences "recognised" New Zealand as the "living reflection of Tolkien's imaginary world" and it "became" Middle-earth. Thus the real is the living reflection of the simulacrum and the real has become hyperreal.

There are no differences between travelling and attending a movie in the sense that we are gazing at the very same signs. We take pictures in a "post-country" and try our best to ensure that the pictures we take are the same as the *pictures* we watched in the cinema.[8] If you join the "*Lord of the Rings* tour" run by Red Carpet Tours, your shots will probably included the following, as advertised on their website: stand beneath the "Party Tree"; clamber over volcanic rocks as the "Fellowship" did; meet the lead "Black Rider"; stand on the site of Edoras; visit the Pelennor battlefield; follow the escape route of Arwen and Frodo; soak up the

---

[8] Asserting that taking photographs is "a socially constructed way of seeing and recording", Urry outlines and develops eight characteristics of this. He uses the term "hermeneutic circle" to describe the way tourists track down and capture the images they have formerly seen in tour company brochures or TV programme. By making their version of the images, they are demonstrating that they really have been there. And since the "camera does not lie", it can prove that something is really there. (Urry, 2002: 127-129)

atmosphere of Lothlórien; visit Gollum's fishing pool; stand on the Warg's lookout rock.⁹

These tourists are not duplicating the real but the hyperreal. According to Baudrillard,

> [i]n this passage to a space whose curvature is no longer that of the real, nor of truth, the age of simulation thus begins with a liquidation of all referentials... It is no longer a question of imitation, nor of reduplication, nor even of parody. It is rather a question of substituting signs of the real for the real itself. (Baudrillard, 1988: 167)

When culture is dominated by simulation, the signs of the real no longer have firm references. Brodie's *The Lord of the Rings Location Guidebook* gives a good illustration of Crick's notion that "[c]ultures are invented, remade and the elements reorganised," (cited in Urry, 2002: 9) since cultures (the real) are now substituted by the imagination (the signs of the real). In discussing the idea of writing the *Guidebook*, Brodie says, "I imagined a blend of Middle Earth, a bit of Maori mythology and all the other things that are part of New Zealand." (Tourism New Zealand, 2003e) By juxtaposing Chris Winitana's account of the Maori myths in the "Introduction to New Zealand's Mythology" (Brodie, 2002: 10-11) and Alan Lee's description of the journey taken by the crew of *LotR* in their search for sites which fit into Tolkien's imagined Middle-earth in New Zealand, (Brodie, 2002: 12-16) we can trace Brodie's attempt to organically combine Maori myths with *LotR*'s myth and make the "reorganised" cultures of "Post-New Zealand" consumable.

Wellington, the capital of New Zealand, changed its name to Middle-earth for only one week. (Anon: 2003i) Hobbiton burgers were on sale in Matamata during the short time when the town changed its name to Hobbiton. (Anon, 2003a) The spaces *marked* by *LotR*, however, were forever double named in Brodie's *Guidebook* (probably in some of the tourists' minds too): Matamata-*Hobbiton*, Ohakune-*Ithilien Camp*, Rangitikei River Gorge-*River Anduin*, Takaka Hill-*Chetwood Forest*, Mararoa River-*Silverlode River*, Takaro Road-*Fangorn Forest*, to name only just a few. (Brodie, 2002: 8-9) I found myself deliberately noting the spaces with Maori names in the table of contents of Brodie's *Guidebook*. I do not intend to hide the colonial colour of

---

⁹ A number of sample shots can be found on the Red Carpet Tours site. (Anon, 2003d)

New Zealand by not listing Fernside-*Lothlorien and the Gladden Fields*, Harcourt Park-*Isengard Gardens and the Orc Tree*, Hutt River-*River Anduin*, Mt Olympus-*south of Rivendell*, Arrowtown-*The Ford of Bruinen*, etc. (Brodie, 2002: 8-9) What's in a name? It is interesting to look at names in New Zealand to find its identity. The "Post" in "Post-New Zealand" also marked the new role New Zealand plays in the world in this Post-modern era. There is not only "Matamata" in Maori and "Arrowtown" in English, but "Lothlórien" in Middle-earth signage. It is not bicultural, but multicultural and the multi-culture can be multiplied endlessly into a labyrinth of signs. Culture (or cultures) itself becomes hyperreal. I consider this an important historical moment for New Zealand.

New Zealand's Prime Minister, Helen Clark, who is also Minister for Arts and Culture, spoke at a film reception in Seoul on 26 July 2003. In her speech, she recognizes the role films play in constructing "national identity and culture". Meanwhile, she regards the achievement of *LotR* highly and refers to New Zealand as a "compact country" with "a wide variety of fresh and exciting locations" for film making. Clark declares that the government has "a new grant scheme to attract filmmakers to New Zealand". (Clark, 2003) If the scheme is successful, it is not hard to imagine the double, or even multiple naming of New Zealand locations. The very same *picture* can have totally different meanings depending on what is prescribed by the films. New Zealand, like an actor, can be nominated many times as "Best Supporting Country" as long as the directors, preferably financially supported by Hollywood investors, still consider New Zealand a versatile site. Then, there will be more and more simulation for us to have "reorganised" in our "national identity and culture".

By viewing simulation as a commodity, Baudrillard says,

> A simulation which can go on indefinitely, since—unlike "true" power which is, or was, a structure, a strategy, a relation of force, a stake—this is nothing but the object of a social *demand*, and hence subject to the law of supply and demand, rather than to violence and death. Completely expunged from the *political* dimension, it is dependent, like any other commodity, on production and mass consumption. Its spark has disappeared; only the fiction of a political universe is saved. (Baudrillard, 1988: 181)

If *whatever*'s New Zealand, like any other commodity, depends on production and mass consumption, does it have the potential to become an "Empire" like "Disneyworld Company"?

"*The Lord of the Rings* Empire"

Tourism is now the world's largest industry, as estimated by The World Tourism Organisation to be increasing by 3% annually. The Organisation predicts that there will be 1.6 billion travellers world-wide by 2010, generating US$8,454 billion in economic activity. (Tourism New Zealand, 2003a) Tourism generates 10% of New Zealand GDP, is directly and indirectly responsible for one in eleven jobs, supports over 15,000 businesses, and is one of the largest earners of foreign exchange. (Burton, 2003) It is not hard to tell from these figures why New Zealand strives to raise its profile as the world's most desirable tourist destination. Its performance in this regard is not bad at all. International visitor arrivals to New Zealand increased by 7% in 2002, more than the 3% provisional global tourism growth. (Tourism New Zealand, 2003f) The extensive coverage of New Zealand's connection with *LotR* film trilogy was among factors which raised New Zealand's profile.[10] I probably should not use the word "factor" here because nowadays factors are so intertwined that we can hardly separate them as individual entities.

Here is a quick glance at the whirlpool of *LotR* film trilogy:

On 19 December 2001, *The Lord of the Rings: The Fellowship of the Ring* was released in the cinema. Thousands of spectators attended an enormous street party prior to the Australasian premiere in Wellington and, in the spirit of the event, Wellington officially renamed itself "Middle-earth" for a week, renaming road signs and changing the name of the capital's evening newspaper to *The Middle-earth Post*. (Anon, 2003i) The film scored four Academy Awards on 24 March 2002. The next morning,

---

[10] Different international events such as the Americas Cup also helped promote New Zealand. Meanwhile, in 2002 Tourism New Zealand signed an agreement with the Discovery Channel, the most watched cable television channel in the world (launched in the United States in 1985), enabling coverage of New Zealand to reach audiences in North America. (Tourism New Zealand, 2003d)

the "Best Supporting Country in a Motion Picture" advertisement appeared in the *LA Times*.

On 05 December 2002, an Air New Zealand Boeing 747-400 featuring Frodo and Samwise Gamgee brought Elijah Wood to *The Lord of the Rings: The Two Towers* premiere, again in Wellington. Prior to the worldwide release of *TT* on 18 December 2002, there was a "New Zealand Night" on the Travel Channel (part of the Discovery Networks U.S.) on 15 December 2002 targeting 67 million homes in North America. The programme was hosted by Karl Urban, the New Zealand actor who portrays Éomer in the film. (Tourism New Zealand, 2002c)[11] This time, the "Best Supporting Country" was given a clearer identity as "Home of Middle-earth". On the "New Zealand Home of Middle-earth" website, launched in December 2002, one can find the video-stream interviews with actors such as Sean Astin, Elijah Wood, Karl Urban, and production crew as well as an interactive map, behind-the scenes stories, film locations, etc. (Anon, 2007a)[12]

The release of *The Lord of the Rings: The Return of the King* and the related events beforehand will certainly create some spectacles.* The "Return of the Ringers" party at the Skyline Restaurant on 30 November 2003 had sold all 350 tickets at the time of writing. Half the party-goers will be from overseas, including 170 organized by Rings tour company Red Carpet Tours[13]. There will be guests from Germany, the United States, Japan, Britain, the Netherlands, Poland and Australia. When Erica

---

[11] The United States is the largest outbound travel market in the world with 34 million people taking international holidays each year. The travel market in the States has grown by 7% since 1990; however New Zealand's visitor arrivals have increased by only 4%. That is why Tourism New Zealand has paid so much attention to the American market. (Tourism New Zealand, 2003b)

[12] Using the Internet as a powerful marketing tool is fully realized by the different tourist boards. Korea National Tourism Organization also has a website focus on Korean drama and movie theme tours. (see Anon, 2007b)

* *Editors*: The film was released in December 2003. Since the timing of this chapter (26 October 2003) adds some ingenuity to the writing, the tense has been retained so as it is to reflect this.

[13] Information given by Vic James, Managing Director of Red Carpet Tours, who I contacted by email on 21 October 2003. Red Carpet Tours was the "local expert" for the Nippon Travel Agency through which the Japanese travel agent organized their *Lord of the Rings* Tour to New Zealand in May 2003.

Challis,[14] the Auckland-based organizer, announced on the popular Rings fan website (www.theonering.net) on 3 October 2003 that she hoped to expand the party so that at least another 250 people could attend, she received requests for sixty more tickets within forty-eight hours. She was also contacted by a Japanese tour company which had 200 clients wanting to attend. (*The Dominion Post*, 2003e) The organizers finally decided to expand the party to 800 people and attach a large marquee to the restaurant building. In total 700 tickets have been sold for the Return of the Ringers party, including 200 for the Japanese tour group. (*The Dominion Post*, 2003c)

On 1 December 2003, the climax of these events—the world premiere of *RotK*—will be held in the Embassy theatre, Wellington. According to Vic James, Managing Director of Red Carpet Tours, 160 tourists from sixteen different countries will come to Wellington for their Premiere Tour. It has been estimated the world premiere of *RotK* will inject NZ$10 million into Wellington's economy. (*The Dominion Post*, 2003c)

Nothing has been left to chance in the campaigns for "The Lord of the Rings Empire". With the cooperation of various New Zealand government agencies, including Tourism New Zealand, Trade New Zealand and Film New Zealand, the country means to fully utilize the value generated by the film. In a reply from Don Badman, Senior Adviser in the Office of Hon Pete Hodgson, to my email enquiry, in the last two financial years (April 2001-March 2003) the Government has invested approximately NZ$2 million each year in activities that brand New Zealand alongside *LotR* movies.[15] In this financial year (April 2003-March 2004), about

---

[14] Erica Challis is a co-founder of "TheOneRing.net". She is also the Director of Red Carpet Tours.

[15] I contacted Tourism New Zealand by email on 21 October 2003 and asked how much the government had spent on *LotR* related projects. Stephen Griffith replied to my email and advised that Jane Dent, the person who works with other agencies on *LotR* issues, was unavailable. He suggested I contact the Office of the Hon. Pete Hodgson, "who is the Minister for the LOTR". Followed Griffith's kind suggestion, I emailed Hon. Pete Hodgson; this time I was more interested in the title "Minister for the LOTR". Don Badman answered my enquiry with updated figures on 22 October 2003. But as for the title, his answer was not as dramatic as I had hoped: "You asked about the title 'Minister of LOTR'. Mr Hodgson has been dubbed as such by the media (and some government officials), but it is not an official title. His work with LOTR is part of his responsibilities

NZ$4 million additional funding will be invested in similar projects associated with *RotK*. Of that about NZ$2 million are for activities directly associated with the world premiere of *RotK* in December 2003. (Hodgson, 2003) As mentioned above, we cannot treat any factor as a single entity any more. Nor can we figure out exactly how much government spending is contributing to tourism.[16] A report by the NZ Institute of Economic Research (Inc.) for the New Zealand Film Commission dated April 2002, which dedicates a section to investigating the "spin-off" of *LotR* to New Zealand tourism, however, shows another way of looking at the figure. It worked out that the estimated cost of the same kind of exposure of New Zealand as a tourist destination would have otherwise cost in excess of US$41 million (up to 12 March 2002). (New Zealand Institute of Economic Research (inc.), 2003) Given this evidence, the amount the New Zealand government has spent on *LotR* related projects is *not much* if we consider the value *LotR* has generated *so far*.

While the investment in *LotR* related projects is not solely for the purpose of promoting the New Zealand tourist industry, the industry does benefit considerably from it. An interesting report from the U.K. *The Observer* newspaper provides evidence of the success in New Zealand promotions connected to *LotR*:

> ...thanks to a bunch of elves, orcs, and hobbits, New Zealand has shrugged off its dull image to become one of the year's most fashionable tourist destinations... *The Lord of the Rings*, in which the scenery of North and South Island was used to evoke Tolkien's mystical Middle Earth, has sparked an unprecedented rise in holiday bookings. (Tourism New Zealand, 2002b)

Local evidence supporting the effect of *LotR* on New Zealand tourism is given by Henry Horne, Sales and Marketing Manager of Rings Scenic Tours Ltd. He opened the family farm in Matamata for "Rings Tours of Hobbiton" in December 2002. By September 2003, 9800 FIT (Free Independent Traveller) had visited the movie set. A

---

as Associate Minister of Foreign Affairs and Trade." So, New Zealand has not "officially" Disneyfied, yet!

[16] Knowing that I am examining at the cultural impact of *LotR* on New Zealand tourism, Don Badman kindly reminds me in his email: "[N]ot all of these funds have been or will be invested in tourism specific initiatives. The aim of these projects is to promote New Zealand's technology, creativity, filmmaking skills, exports and scenery. Promoting tourism is, of course, an important part of this, but tourism is not the whole story."

further 2500 tourists visited on organized tours. Of these visitors, 80% were international tourists and 20%, domestic tourists. Horne's company webpage (Anon, 2003a) has received over 700,000 hits and the figure is growing. (Tourism New Zealand, 2003e)

Down south, Queenstown tour company, Outback New Zealand has been offering "Safari of the Rings" tours (Anon, 2003d) since May 2002. According to the report in *Tourism News* dated 28 February 2003, from September 2002 to February 2003 the "Safari of the Rings" tours took 600-700 people per month on the tours, double the number of similar tours in 2001. (Tourism New Zealand, 2003e) Amanda Gatward-Ferguson of Outback New Zealand, told me in an email dated 21 October 2003 that the figure has been steady since then.[17]

If "Disneyworld Company" refers to the conflation of Disneyland Theme Parks, Disney films and associated merchandise, "*The Lord of the Rings* Empire" is aiming to achieve the same through the cooperation of different parties. The "Middle-earth" staged in Wellington could not succeed without the "backstage" efforts of different parties. The activities relating to *FotR* included proactively targeting major production houses and integrated studios such as Fox, Warner Bros and Disney; supporting film trade fairs; advertising in trade magazines; supporting missions to

---

[17] The above mentioned evidence contrasts dramatically with marketing research results published by NFO New Zealand for Tourism New Zealand on 4 April, 2003. NFO did two separate surveys during February and March 2003. One was conducted by face to face survey of 775 current international visitors who were users of Visitor Information Centres. One was an online survey on the purenz.com website with 916 potential international visitors. Ninety-three per cent of current international visitors (86% of potential international visitors) are aware of at least one of the two released *LotR* films; 72% of current international visitors and 75% of potential international visitors have seen at least one of the two films; 95% of current international visitors who were aware of the films knew that the films were filmed in New Zealand; 76% of international residents who had seen or heard publicity relating to the films indicated they had been made aware of the country in which the filming had occurred. Of the current international visitors who were aware of *LotR* films being filmed in New Zealand, 9% indicated *LotR* was "one reason but not the main reason" for coming to New Zealand. Only 0.3% indicated *LotR* was "the main reason" for visiting New Zealand. The report suggests that in order to fully capitalize on the increased interest in New Zealand as a destination, further promotion of the activities, attractions and events the "Home of Middle Earth" has to offer is needed. One should note this was a small scale survey. Nonetheless, it showed the eagerness of Tourism New Zealand to estimate *LotR* effects. (see NFO New Zealand, 2003)

promote New Zealand as a film location;[18] a revamp of the Film New Zealand Internet portal to profile *LotR*, to name just a few. (Tourism New Zealand, 2002b)

In striking a bargain with New Line Cinema and working with Tourism New Zealand, Air New Zealand also played its part in "*The Lord of the Rings* Empire". The airline has four of its fleet covered with images of the *LotR* film trilogy and New Zealand. The images are part of Air New Zealand's promotion as the "Airline to Middle-earth". Besides bearing images of *LotR* on its flying billboards, the airline also delivered *LotR* messages to thousands of potential consumers in the United States, Europe and the United Kingdom through events such as mailings, in-store events and cinema promotions. (Tourism New Zealand, 2003c)

Malcolm Roughead, head of marketing at VisitScotland, was impressed by the achievement of the "*Lord of the Rings* Empire". He recognized that

> ... an impressive degree of forward thinking was involved in the model: the national tourism organisation in New Zealand was in at the very beginning, Air New Zealand was a strategic partner and was able to take ownership of this from the very beginning. New Zealand's government also gave grants for filming. (Anon, 2003h)

Roughead added that all parties "joined up, got together and that makes life much easier". (Anon, 2003h) In terms of utilizing scenic and magical locations, we can draw many similarities between *Harry Potter* and *LotR*. But VisitScotland has not been as fortunate as Tourism New Zealand. VisitScotland is still working hard to tap into the *Harry Potter* effect. Warner Bros poses a very protective attitude towards the "brand" which may be "the most valuable commodity it has ever owned". (Anon, 2003h) If they are considered in relation to the "potential" theme tour,[19] with the more "Disney" elements of *Harry Potter*, the potential "*Harry Potter* Empire" will be closer to the Disneyworld Company than "*The Lord of the Rings* Empire" at surface level, yet fundamentally, all the three "Empires" are the same. So

---

[18] Tourism New Zealand opened a permanent "desk" at the Louis Vuitton Media Centre in Auckland to provide the international media with information about Auckland and New Zealand, as well as provide assistance with filming locations and itineraries. (Tourism New Zealand, 2003a)

[19] I used the word "potential" here because at present using images from *Harry Potter* movies is barred. Therefore, there is not yet a theme tour to Scotland.

far, *Harry Potter* remains a virtual space, whereas *LotR* has been *realized* by turning the *real* New Zealand into a hyperreal Middle-earth. To convert to a Disneyland Empire, the hyperreal needs the *real* to be ready and willing to allow its integration.

Whether joined together or not, they are all about consumption. Last year Mr Ordesky, executive vice-president and chief operating officer of New Line Cinema, said Wellington would lose the premiere if the Embassy Theatre was not brought up to standard. His comments followed Wellington City Council's decision, later revoked, to withdraw its $7 million backing for renovations. (*The Dominion Post*, 2003b) Wellington City Council is providing $4.5 million to underwrite the refurbishment and earthquake strengthening of the Embassy Theatre. Not only is the theatre renovation linked with *LotR*, but also with the consumption of the fans worldwide. Fans of *LotR* from all over the world will receive a chance to make their imprint on the theatre by sponsoring seats. According to *The Dominion Post* dated 6 October 2003, the seat appeal has so far raised $341,000. One devotee made a donation and said "(It's) going to a great cause". (*The Dominion Post*, 2003f) What cause is it? Will people generously sponsor a seat at the Embassy Theatre if the premiere does not take place there?[20] There can be a world of difference between the same theatre and the same seats, with or without *LotR*.

It is all about consumption and I will elaborate this in more detail: the *LotR* trilogy is a commodity for the audience to consume in the cinema (or through buying the video, CD or DVD). At the same time as a commodity of sign, it provides space for further consumption. Like all Disney products, *LotR* has its own wide range of merchandise. Like Disneyland, "Home of Middle-earth" provides a fantasy world for tourists to visit. The effects of Disneyland and Middle-earth are further enhanced by different events. The parade of well-known Disney characters and all sorts of performances around the theme of Disney films remind the tourists to shop and to buy souvenirs to remember the precious time spent at Disneyland. Ritzer and Liska argue that Disney World is in a sense a shopping mall. The ceaseless hawking

---

[20] The seats are not cheap. There are seventy-nine deluxe platinum seats which cost NZ$1850 each, 380 deluxe gold seats which cost NZ$650 each, 219 deluxe classic seats which cost NZ$150 each and seventy seats made from the floorboards of the original auditorium of NZ$200 each.

of Disney products, both in and out of the parks, is oriented to getting people to spend far more than they do on their daily pass. (Ritzer and Liska, 1997: 97) The film premiere creates a spectacle for the tourists, too. Merely attending the event is not enough; the audience/tourists feel the urge to buy something to commemorate the event. If there's nothing they can buy in the theatre, at least they can buy their own names for a "great cause". What kind of connection is left between the seats in the Embassy Theatre and the names of the Rings' fans after the premiere? Should the theatre change its name to *Rings Something* to commemorate it? What the Wellington City Council paid for is not the renovation of the Embassy Theatre, but the investment in the World Premiere. What the tourists buy is not the object itself, but the sign of the object. Baudrillard explains it well in his "The System of Objects":

> *In order to become object of consumption, the object must become sign*; that is, in some way it must become external to a relation that it now only signifies, a-signed *arbitrarily* and non-coherently to this concrete relation, yet obtaining its coherence, and consequently its meaning, from an abstract and systematic relation to all other object-signs. (Baudrillard, 1988: 22)

Another noteworthy aspect of *"The Lord of the Rings* Empire" is its mobility. Like the films themselves, the Empire mobilizes throughout the world in the incarnation of the *LotR* exhibition. Te Papa began developing the show in 1999, even before the first movie was completed. After a huge success in New Zealand, the exhibition has now been taken to London.[21] The show opened in 16 September at London's Science Museum with 19,000 tickets pre-booked. About 260,000 people are expected to see the show before it closes on 11 January 2004. After the London round, the exhibition will move to science museums in Singapore, Boston and Sydney. (*The Dominion Post*, 2003a) Again, it is about consumption. Attending the show is a kind of consumption, and the souvenirs sold there turn the museum into a shopping mall.[22]

---

[21] One in six visitors to Te Papa museum in the 2002-2003 financial year paid to see the Rings exhibition. The exhibition broke attendance records at Te Papa in 2003, being seen by about 220,000 people. (*The Dominion Post*, 2003d)

[22] In suggesting that museums and shops are getting less and less distinctive, Urry quoted Stephen Bayley, from the London Museum of Design, remarks: "... the old nineteenth century museum was somewhat like a shop... a place where you go and look at values and ideas, and I think shopping really is becoming one of the great cultural experiences of the

In addition to receiving a photo image of oneself as a Hobbit-sized creature in a re-created scene from *FotR* as an "inevitable" souvenir, the visitor is also tempted by *RotK* branded merchandise such as school bags, pencil cases and folders. (Anon, 2003f) Although you may withstand the temptation to go to Middle-earth to experience the events and gaze at the sites/sights of *LotR*, the mobile Empire is approaching you like the prevailing media to force you to consume it.

Preview

If you are sick of *LotR* after reading this chapter, you might prefer to view the preview of the next attraction: *Last Samurai*, starring Tom Cruise, set in 1870s Japan and location filmed at Mount Taranaki. The Internet location address is

    http://lastsamurai.warnerbros.com/home.php

I have good reasons to assume that the Nippon Travel Agency or other Japanese travel agencies will launch a special theme tour for their Japanese clients to come to New Zealand to tour "Mt Fuji" following the release of *Last Samurai* later this year. From then on, there will be two Mt Fujis and no one will be able to tell which one is real, and which one is a simulacrum. Or there will be Mt Fuji in Japan and Mt Fuji in New Zealand, when the country is dubbed as Japan. As Baudrillard says, "The real does not disappear into illusion; it is illusion that disappears into integral reality." (Baudrillard, 1996: preface page)

26 October, 2003

Bibliography

Anon (2003a), "Hobbiton Movie Set and Farm Tour":
    http://www.hobbitontours.com/matamata.htm

Anon (2003b), "Japanese Tour Agencies Design Theme Holidays" *Straits Times Interactive* July:
    http://straitstimes.asia1.com.sg/women/story/0,4395,200768,00.html

---

    late twentieth century... The two things are merging. So you have museums becoming more commercial, shops becoming more intelligent and more cultural. (Urry, 2002: 120)

Anon (2003c), "Late Rush Expected from Ring Seekers": http://www.stuff.co.nz/stuff/0,2106,2692922a2202,00.html

Anon (2003d), "Outback New Zealand" (company website): http://www.nomadsafaris.co.nz/rings.html

Anon (2003e), "Red Carpet Tour" (company website): http://www.redcarpet-tours.com/

Anon (2003f), "Te Papa's Rings Exhibition Opens in London" *NZPA* 16 September: http://www.stuff.co.nz/stuff/0,2106,2660838a2202,00.html

Anon (2003g), "View Looking up Pink and White Terraces" (photo): http://library.christchurch.org.nz/Heritage/Photos/Disc3/IMG0031.asp

Anon (2003h), "VisitScotland Seek Ways to Use Harry Potter's Magic" *Sunday Herald* 17 August: http://www.sundayherald.com/36076

Anon (2003i), "Wellington Production Base and Outdoor Sets": http://www.purenz.com/index.cfm/purenz_page/961F1242-9F5F-4858-81C2-28787EBAFAF0.html

Anon (2007a), "New Zealand Home of Middle-earth" (website): http://www.newzealand.com/travel/homeofmiddleearth/

Anon (2007b), "Tour 2 Korea" (website): http://english.tour2korea.com/02Culture/TVMiniseries/drama_wintersonata.asp?konum=subm1_1&kosm=m2_6

Anon (2007c), "Virtual New Zealand: Pink and White Terraces": http://www.virtualoceania.net/newzealand/photos/volcanic/terraces/

Baudrillard, Jean (1988), *Selected Writings*, trans. Mark Poster, Polity Press, Oxford (UK)

Baudrillard, Jean (1996), *The Perfect Crime*, trans. Chris Turner, Verso, London

Baudrillard, Jean (2003), "Disneyworld Company": http://www.uta.edu/english/apt/collab/texts/disneyworld.html

Boorstin, Daniel J. (1961), *The Image: A Guide to Pseudo-Events in America*, Harper Colophon Books, New York

Brodie, Ian (2002), *The Lord of the Rings Location Guidebook*, Harper Collins Publishers, Auckland

Burton, Mark (2003), "Celebrating New Zealand Place in the World Tourism Market" (transcript of speech) 10 September: http://www.beehive.govt.nz/ViewDocument.cfm?DocumentID=17806

Clark, Helen (2003), "Speech at Film Reception in Seoul" (transcript of speech) 26 July: http://www.beehive.govt.nz/ViewDocument.cfm?DocumentID=17433

Craik, Jennifer (1997), "The Culture of Tourism" in Chris Rojek and John Urry (eds), *Touring Cultures: Transformations of Travel and Theory*, Routledge, London, pp. 113-136.

Hodgson, Pete (2003), "Govt Ready for 'The Return of the King'" (transcript of speech) 24 October:
http://www.beehive.govt.nz/ViewDocument.cfm?DocumentID=18185

New Zealand Institute of Economic Research (Inc.) (2003), *Scoping the Lasting Effects of* The Lord of the Rings: *Report to the New Zealand Film Commission*:
http://www.nzier.org.nz/files/181.pdf

NFO New Zealand (2003), "Marketing Research for Tourism New Zealand":
http://www.tourisminfo.co.nz/documents/LoTR%20Research%20Report.pdf

Ritzer, George and Allan Liska (1997), "'McDisneyization' and 'Post-Tourism', Complementary Perspectives on Contemporary Tourism" in Chris Rojek and John Urry (eds), *Touring Cultures: Transformations of Travel and Theory*, Routledge, London, pp. 96-109.

Rojek, Chris and John Urry (1997), "Transformations of Travel and Theory" in Chris Rojek and John Urry (eds), *Touring Cultures: Transformations of Travel and Theory*, Routledge, London, pp. 1-19.

The Dominion Post (2003a), "Critics Attack Rings Exhibition" 18 September:
http://www.stuff.co.nz/stuff/0,2106,2662544a2202,00.html

The Dominion Post (2003b), "Last Minute Rings Filming" 14 October:
http://www.stuff.co.nz/stuff/0,2106,2690743a2202,00.html

The Dominion Post (2003c), "Late Rush Expected from Ring Seekers" 16 October:
http://www.stuff.co.nz/stuff/0,2106,2692922a2202,00.html

The Dominion Post (2003d), "Rings Exhibition Boosts Te Papa's Finance" 16 October:
http://www.stuff.co.nz/stuff/0,2106,2692961a13,00.html

The Dominion Post (2003e), "Rings Party Booked Out" 7 October:
http://www.stuff.co.nz/stuff/0,2106,2683116a2202,00.html

The Dominion Post (2003f), "Sponsors Fork out for Rings-side Seat" 6 October:
http://www.stuff.co.nz/stuff/0,2106,2681794a2202,00.html

Tourism New Zealand (2002a), "Best Supporting Country" *Tourist News* May:
http://www.tourisminfo.co.nz/cir_news/index.cfm?fuseaction=newscentre&subaction=news&article_id=355

Tourism New Zealand (2002b), "New Zealand on Film" *Tourist News* 11 September:
http://www.tourisminfo.co.nz/cir_news/index.cfm?fuseaction=newscentre&subaction=news&article_id=412

Tourism New Zealand (2002c), "New Zealander to Host New Zealand Night on US TV Network" (media release) 12 December: http://www.tourisminfo.co.nz/cir_news/index.cfm?fuseaction=newscentre&subaction=news&article_id=449

Tourism New Zealand (2003a), "Corporate Overview": http://www.tourisminfo.co.nz/cir_aboutus/index.cfm?fuseaction=12

Tourism New Zealand (2003b), "Extra Funding to Help Target US Visitors" (media release) 13 May: http://www.tourisminfo.co.nz/cir_news/index.cfm?fuseaction=newscentre&subaction=news&article_id=523

Tourism New Zealand (2003c), "Flying Rings Around the World" *Tourism News* 11 March: http://www.tourisminfo.co.nz/cir_news/index.cfm?fuseaction=newscentre&subaction=news&article_id=491

Tourism New Zealand (2003d), "Kiwis on Discovery" *Tourist News* 27 January: http://www.tourisminfo.co.nz/cir_news/index.cfm?fuseaction=newscentre&subaction=news&article_id=454

Tourism New Zealand (2003e), "Locations Bestseller for Brodie" *Tourism News* 28 February: http://www.tourisminfo.co.nz/cir_news/index.cfm?fuseaction=newscentre&subaction=news&article_id=471

Tourism New Zealand (2003f), "New Zealand Bucks Visitor Trend" (media release) 4 February: http://www.tourisminfo.co.nz/cir_news/index.cfm?fuseaction=newscentre&subaction=news&article_id=465

Urry, John (2002), *The Tourist Gaze*, Sage, London

The featured aeroplane belongs to Origin Pacific, a small budget airline in New Zealand which went into receivership in 2006. Does its disappearance have anything to do with its wearing the Ring secretly?
(photo by Bill J. Jerome)

6

SEEING THE PROMISED LAND FROM AFAR
The Perception of New Zealand by Overseas *The Lord of the Rings* Audiences

Martin Barker and Ernest Mathijs

EVER SINCE it was announced that Peter Jackson would be shooting *The Lord of the Rings* trilogy in New Zealand, it has become a "special place" for filmgoers.

Years before the trilogy was released Barry Keith Grant predicted that Jackson would seek "to make Middle earth look like it was shot on location", (Grant, 1999: 27) and New Zealand was increasingly hailed as a new cult location. (Wu, 2003: 84-108) In prefigurative coverage on the film, New Zealand became a prominent and persistent feature. A symptomatic narrative in that discourse tells how Jackson, as a young lad, was reading the books while on a train in New Zealand, and how, passing through the different landscapes, he could not help noticing the striking similarities between the book's descriptions and the views outside, imagining himself *really inside* Middle-earth. (Mathijs and Pomerance, 2006: 5)

There can be no doubt that the filming of *LotR* in New Zealand contributed significantly to the film's pictorial palette, and it certainly raised the world profile of New Zealand. But in what ways did audiences outside New Zealand take note of this, and how did "New Zealand" play a part in their appreciation of the films? This chapter uses materials from the 2003-2004 international *LotR* audience project to investigate how understanding of the film was shaped by its antipodean locations, and what this in turn added to people's ideas of "New Zealand".

The Locus of "Locations"

The role of film locations in generating meaning-potential has received little attention from film studies.[1] The long love affair with the concept of mise-en-scène, with its theatrical origins and emphasis on the pro-filmic's integration into narrative has surely helped in this marginalization. But the recent increase in attention to ancillary or satellite materials has begun to change this.[2] In discussion surrounding films, the actual filming locations often play a very large part. The relations between *LotR* and its New Zealand locations are a perfect type-case.

Fiction cinema often refrains from the costly and logistically complex organization of location shooting, and settings are instead recreated in studios or through special effects. Francis Coppola's *Bram Stoker's Dracula* (1992) famously does not contain one single actual outdoor shot, managing to imitate all of the Carpathians, Transylvania, London, Carfax Abbey and other locations either in the Columbia studios or through special effects. (see Pouroy, 1993)[3] But when fiction cinema does rely upon real life landscapes, with their own historical and ideological weights, two processes are set in train: the transfer of meaning from landscape to film, and from film to landscape.

The Transfer of Meaning from Location to Film

There are plenty of studies of how locations have impacted on understandings of film, the most obvious ones analysing how film can use real-life locations and their connotations to produce a certain frame of reference. It is for instance a much-heard claim that part of the appeal of Friedrich Murnau's *Nosferatu* (1922) are the qualities it deploys through its location shooting. The hyena, the running wild horses, the mountain ranges, the wild river, and the harbour town in which Nosferatu arrives have all added something extra to the feel of the story—making it, according to

---

[1] Note the small but significant number of studies on the 'cinematic city'; see for instance Clarke (1997).

[2] For an examination of this rise, see Barker (2004).

[3] Another famous example is *Titanic* (dir. James Cameron, 1997).

critics, more horrific because it looks so "real".⁴ Examples from this strain involving New Zealand include Ian Conrich's study of the Kiwi Gothic, and Estella Tincknell's analysis of landscapes in Jane Campion's *The Piano* (1994), which, tellingly, appeared in a collection entitled *New Zealand—A Pastoral Paradise?*. (Conrich, 2005; Tincknell, 2000)

Beyond the textual imprint which a location can leave, also of essential importance in framing a film culturally is when locations become a topic in tales *about* the film. When Steven Spielberg insisted for *Schindler's List* (1993) on filming the arrival of a train in Auschwitz outside the gates of the actual place, even though he could not obtain permission to shoot in that location, it was because he felt it would add gravitas to an already compelling historical narrative. The weight of the place could add a particular feel to the film, enriching it with additional meaning, regardless of whether audiences actually knew what the real Auschwitz looked like. It would be the *ancillary story that* Spielberg shot this scene just outside Auschwitz that would give many viewers the means to construct this meaning.⁵ Needless to say, the ancillary discourses of *LotR* abound with such stories and references.

Locations and Fantasy

But representations of places become particularly complex when the fiction concerned is fantasy. There is the sheer fact that fantasy makes no claims to a "real" against which it can be measured; its world never did and never will exist. Yet this does not mean no references are circulating, either through existing visualizations (previous adaptations of the story, book-jackets and illustrations, record-sleeves, landscapes said to have inspired the writer, artists inspired by the work, and so on) or through critical inference and interpretation (associations made when the work is discussed, topical connections with particular events and places in history). In the case of *LotR* there is a wealth of such references, each potentially impacting on

---

4   See for instance Göttler et al. (1990: 105-112).
5   Other such examples would include Werner Herzog's *Aguirre* (1972) and *Fitzcarraldo* (1981) filmed in the Amazon jungle, or David Cronenberg's *Crash* (1996), filmed in and around Toronto.

the film's reception, and on the audiences' viewing experiences. Here is, for instance, how Lin Carter, in 1969, describes the landscape and setting of Middle-earth:

> Tolkien's picture of Middle-earth during the Third Age is not very different from Europe during the Middle Ages. It is mostly made up of great and ancient forests, where dark things lurk, with here and there a patch of homely life—small farms and furrowed fields and little towns—forming islands of quiet, rural society amid the blackness of the wilderness. It is a world rising into the full noon of civilization, gradually exploring its limits and taming its wild places, half-remembering the high and noble civilizations of distant ages from whence it sprang. (Carter, 1969: 22)

Carter is not alone in visualizing Middle-earth. Since Tolkien's story became an entrenched part of popular culture, there have been numerous attempts to visualize the landscapes and locations of *LotR*, ranging from paintings, drawings, maps, book covers and illustrations, to Ralph Bakshi's 1978 animated version.[6] Each has added to the frames of reference available for producers and viewers of the movie trilogy, together creating a vast repository of imagery against which images of Peter Jackson's visualization could be seen, compared and tested.[7]

The depth and range of these make it unlikely that Jackson's version would be universally accepted—many would be disappointed at his choice of some images over others. Strangely, this disappointment seldom occurred. Instead, and to many observers' surprise, there was an overwhelming consensus that Jackson's visualization was not only very good, but by far the nearest to what Middle-earth "would", and "*should*", look like. Indeed, what is particularly striking is that the New Zealand setting of the film was seen as a major element in this achievement—it was often argued that New Zealand's landscapes and views were key to why Jackson's version was received as the ultimate Middle-earth. We will pass on the textual implications of this; on Jackson's claim that he wanted a realistic Middle-earth, to look as if it was shot on location, (Grant, 1999: 27) and on how his (and indeed the

---

[6] For an overview of popular culture artefacts using *LotR* in visualizations, see Mathijs (2006: 1-21, 43-60, 103-120, 287-303, and 321-335).

[7] We would like to emphasize at this point that by the name "Jackson" we actually refer to all personnel on the production involved in creating imagery, from the location scouts, to carpenters, to assistant cinematographers. We use the name "Jackson" not as an authorial label here but as a sign of collective corporate creativity.

audiences') conception of this realism relates to prior visualizations of Middle-earth, and ask instead under what conditions this consensus about the look of Middle-earth, and its connection to New Zealand, exist.

The Transfer of Meaning from Film to Location

Less attention has been given to the process by which films can, in their use of certain locations and landscapes, transfer meanings to them. But if film studies have said relatively little about locations, tourism researchers have made more valuable statements about the reverse processes. This attention arises from the "cultural turn" in tourism studies in recent decades, which has led to closer examination of the role of "images" and "myths" about peoples, sites and landscapes. The exemplar of such work is John Urry's *The Tourist Gaze* which drew on Michel Foucault's concept of the "medical gaze" to argue that contemporary tourists are involved in a global knowledge-making enterprise. In visiting "other cultures", which are increasingly displayed for visitors' consumption, the tourists are seeking in the form of myths the "authentic" that they have lost from their own lives. This is a power relationship, the "empire of the gaze", as Urry calls it. (Urry, 2002: 151) Urry does refer albeit briefly to the role within tourism of "mediated locations". But, be it the *Coronation Street* set or the stately home locations of a Jane Austen adaptation, these sites invite forms of participation which are hard to contain within notions of "authenticity".

In the case of New Zealand and *LotR* there are some examples of such an approach, most of them focusing on the impact of the production process rather than any change of perception. (Thornley, 2006: 103-120) Focusing particularly on landscapes, Stan Jones analyses how several tourist initiatives such as *The Location Guidebook*, the Te Papa exhibition, and the Hobbiton set produced a link between the production and local and indigenous cultural life. While stressing how difficult it is to ascertain how this impacts on perceptions of the country, Jones nevertheless notes that it equips New Zealand with a "wider out of frame reality than the actual". (Jones, 2006: 287-303) Similarly, Thierry Jutel has observed how *LotR* has created the possibility for a "geography of the virtual" in which the films' use of the landscape of New Zealand has transformed perceptions and attitudes towards it:

> First the discourse around New Zealand is firmly grounded in the imperialist projection upon the colonized land. Second, as a postcolonial society, Aotearoa produces multiple and often contradictory discourses about the landscape. Third, the landscape of New Zealand has come to represent a transposable "otherness"; and finally, New Zealand, especially as it is recognized as Middle earth, offers its land as a commodity, which inscribes it in the forces of the global economy. (Jutel, 2004: 55)

We want to test Jutel's claim by drawing upon evidence of the ways non-New Zealand audiences negotiated the presence of New Zealand. How did *LotR* audiences from elsewhere in the world perceive New Zealand? What did they think its landscapes added to the film? And, on the other hand, what kind of land, and place, did New Zealand become in their imaginations as a result of the filming? These questions need to be set within the context of "cultural tourism".

The Rise of "Cultural Tourism"

The recent growth in interest and research into cultural tourism has taken two main forms. There has been the inevitable rise of a substantial body of governmental and market research, often on a country-by-country basis, attempting to identify possible "brand" features of particular countries. This is in response to the realization that a considerable segment—and a wealthy one—of people travelling for leisure do so with the wish to access "local colour and culture". Such research has had to consider not only how to attract such visitors, but also, in many cases, how to manage the consequences of attracting them: the problems of security in countries liable to attacks on tourists visiting "ancient worlds" (Egypt, for example); the problems of unintended spin-offs of brand images (Thailand as a land of "innocence", and the growth of sex tourism); the problems of success, and the threats to the very culture that has attracted large numbers (Macchu Picchu is an evident example); and the problems of reconstituting local cultural features as tourist spectacles.[8] New Zealand, famously, has sought to build on the tourist

---

[8] See for instance Genocchio (1995: 35-46), and Bell and Lyall (2002: 35).

potential of the film locations for *LotR*, and subsequently *The Chronicles of Narnia: the Lion, the Witch and the Wardrobe* (dir. Andrew Adamson, 2005). But this was no pure invention; rather, it built on pre-existing structures (patterns of tourist organization and facilities) and constructions (touristic representations of New Zealand).

As we have seen, in the same period as the rise of policy-driven tourist research, there was a growth in critical studies, questioning not only their economic bases, but the ways in which tourists—predominantly from metropolitan countries—participate in ways of "knowing" the non-metropolitan world (and especially the "Third World"). But New Zealand, albeit not a metropolitan country, is hardly Third World. And the application of notions of the "tourist gaze" is not readily appropriate, as some studies have demonstrated. In an essay on the place of "adventure tourism" in New Zealand, Cloke and Perkins paint a historical portrait of the emergence of styles of tourism which eschewed conventional "beach holidays" and native tourism. (Cloke and Perkins, 1998) Instead, an image and a set of practices was constructed of New Zealand as an adventure playground against the backdrop of Vast Nature. One of the outcomes of their argument is a challenge to Urry's notion of the "gaze", from a case where the emphasis is on encounter, activity, and risky use. Wendy Larner meanwhile has addressed other aspects of this pre-Jackson tourist era. (Larner, 1998) She discusses tourist strategies in New Zealand in the context of radical shifts in government policy in the 1990s, away from a social democratic conception of the State towards a more market-driven, and Pacific Rim-oriented economy. Two features of this which she emphasizes are the drive for skill-led, new technology investment, and a sense of the country as a hub through which money, goods and utilities could flow. This marks a dramatic shift for an economy that had, until recently, been heavily based on agriculture. The *image* of the land could thence shift from one of farms with contented cows and sheep producing food for export, to an *empty but fertile* set of imaginary spaces.[9]

---

[9] As a younger person, Martin Barker recalls the intense marketing of New Zealand lamb, butter and cheese in the U.K., and the advertisements stressing the bucolic farm environments from which the products came. For an interesting consideration of the ways in which New Zealand's own film industry has incorporated many elements of this into its own representations of landscape, see Le Héron (2004).

According to Cloke and Perkins, the crucial step towards this was taken in 1993, via a Saatchi & Saatchi report, "The New Zealand Way", which proposed the conscious development of a "Brand New Zealand". This Brand did not attach to individual parts or aspects of the islands, but to the land as a whole, emphasizing that "it's a new place, youthful, fresh and still experimenting to find its feet in the world" (quoted in Cloke and Perkins, 1998: 191): a place of changes rather than traditions, leaving little space for Maori history. This was the brand conceived at the end of the twentieth century. But while the opportunities afforded by *LotR* could not be ignored, they were quite easily assimilated into this "personality": raw Nature mediated by high tech (digital) industry. Hobbit-like folklore offers miraculous experiences to the rest of the world. Expanding these themes, in 2001 and 2003 major reports commissioned by Tourism New Zealand, in the formulation of its "National Tourism Strategy 2010", identified cultural tourism as one of the foremost opportunities. The Reports focus on what is called the "interactive traveller", an Internet-savvy person who seeks, among other things, to feel "vital and alive", "social and carefree", "balanced and bonded", and "mentally stimulated". (Anon, 2001; Colmar Brunton report, 2003) "Natural wonders" are top of the wish-list, for this group. Interestingly, these reports make no mention of *LotR* or related experiences. Instead, they identify the problem of the so-called "cultural cringe"— New Zealanders' unwillingness to promote their *own* cultural productions and heritage. In a significant way, we might say that their unspoken concern is that the heritage of Jackson's films is *too temporary* to constitute a long-term substitute for local cultural traditions.

Alternatively we might see Peter Jackson's film as an event waiting to happen. Here is a film which celebrates the combination of a high-tech production regime and wild Nature, finding and putting "magic" into extraordinary locations. The general tale of the marketing of New Zealand via *LotR* is well captured in an essay by Rodanthi Tzanelli, who unpicks the curious ways in which the various production sites across the islands became "enhanced locales". (Tzanelli, 2004: 23) Tzanelli notes, among other things, that the official website for *LotR* was copyrighted by both New Line Cinema and Tourism New Zealand. She mounts an argument, through her essay, that in the relationship between New Zealand and

LotR we can see a new phenomenon: the merging of an old cultural industry and a contemporary tourist industry into a new "sign industry" leading to "an appropriation of the LOTR sign industry for purposes of economic growth". (Tzanelli, 2004: 23) She is particularly interested in the role of the State in these processes:

> The New Zealand state decided to take some initiative to protect commercial interests in the country. The stakes are high: the new Zealand Institute for Economic Research, an independent economic forecast group, predicted that "tourism will be the 'star' of the country's export sector in the next two years", attributing this change to the LOTR success.... Opinions converged behind one observation: New Zealand, a country that historically was seen as "the dullest place on earth with more sheep than people" (*Guardian*, 06/01/02) attained a new identity as the exciting Middle earth of Tolkien and Jackson. (Tzanelli, 2004: 37)

Thus, for Tzanelli, investment in the country/film crossover constitutes a "long-term investment in New Zealand's self-perception and global image". It is new in the sense that this is pure simulacrum. Not even the film sets remain (preservation rules requiring their complete removal)—all that remains is the *idea* of the film being made in different places.[10]

Whether one film and its associations can be sustained remains to be seen, but we do not doubt the force of a sustained series of fantastical crossovers. The question remains: what precisely *did* audiences, and in particular those who most promptly accepted the film's invitation, make of the New Zealand/*LotR* combination? To answer this, we turn to the body of materials gathered in the international *LotR* audience project 2003-2004.

---

[10] Taking a materialist approach, in their chapter entitled "On the Brink of a New Threshold of Opportunity: *The Lord of the Rings* and New Zealand Cultural Policy", Jenny Lawn and Bronwyn Beatty also consider the impact of Jackson's achievement on the New Zealand economy, on the government's export-driven creative industries policy, and on the longer-term shape and sustainability of local film production in New Zealand, in their discussion of the economic and cultural implications of the government's policy to make feature films a "value-added" export industry. (Lawn and Beatty, 2006: 43-60)

New Zealand in Overseas' Audience Perceptions

a. Methodology and Scope

This project was a fifteen-month study, originating from twenty countries but gathering responses across the world, of the launch and reception of the final part of the film trilogy.[11] It generated a unique data-resource. Its complex questionnaire, available in fourteen languages on the web and combining quantitative and qualitative questions, generated almost 25,000 responses across the world. No question asked specifically about New Zealand. But one open-text question—Question 5: "Where, and when, is Middle-earth for you? Is there a place or a time that it particularly makes you think of?"—produced a substantial number of spontaneous mentions of "New Zealand". There were more than 700 responses from across the world (excluding New Zealand). Of these, just under 600 were in English. For this chapter we explored these responses both quantitatively (to discover the kind of people who made these responses according to our demographic measures; and to further seek recurrent discursive patterns) and qualitatively (to build a model of the semantic meanings associating with "New Zealand" via *LotR*).

b. Who mentioned "New Zealand" in their Question 5 responses?

We limited ourselves to the English language responses for reasons of language competence. Also, we were unsure how to assemble all possible mentions of New Zealand in non-Latin scripts. Searching our database under various spellings

---

[11] This research was developed as part of the International Lord of the Rings Research Project, supported by a grant from the U.K. Economic and Social Research Council (ESRC Grant No. 000-22-0323) to whom we record our gratitude. The project had three stages: a study of the prefigurative materials in each country (marketing and publicity, press, magazine, radio and television coverage); a databased questionnaire combining multiple-choice with free-text responses, available on-line but also completed on paper in some countries; and follow-up interviews with individuals chosen to typify response-positions from the questionnaire responses. The volume and density of materials produced by the project was enormous: 24,739 questionnaires from around the world. Because of this, over time it should permit systematic investigation of many questions which have, until now, been the subject of speculative claims. A book of core findings from around the world is currently under development. (Barker and Mathijs, 2007)

(Zealand, Zeeland, Sealand, NZ, etc.) we could be sure of locating just about every English-language response. It was central to our investigation that people who mentioned "New Zealand" (henceforth "NZ-namers") in answering this question did so spontaneously, without any prompting from us. It was, for these people, one of the first things that occurred to them in thinking about the *kind of reality* that the film had achieved for them. Indeed, we were surprised at the frequency of this "naming". It was therefore important to determine how typical of a wider population the NZ-namers were.

Our research generated sufficient responses to permit internal differentiation, and groupings, in order to locate recurrent patterns and associations. In looking at our collection of 592 responses, we compared the nature of the group with all 11,429 English-language responses, to see how far they were representative of that wider set. The results were striking. On most measures, NZ-namers matched very closely the wider population. This held for age, for occupation (broadly), for country, and for familiarity with the books, and indications of the kind of story. In certain respects, one substantially, the others marginally, the group varied. While in the larger set, the gender breakdown was M=43.2% to F=56.8%, among the NZ-namers the proportion of females rose sharply: M=29.0%, F=71.0%. The other changes were more marginal, and apparently paradoxical. First, the relative ages of NZ-namers were higher than those of the full population. This increase was particularly noticeable in the age-ranges 26-45. Secondly, however, there was one shift within occupation, to a lower percentage of professionals, and a higher percentage of students—who might have been expected in the lower age groups. Finally, our group accentuated what was already a substantial tendency in our wider population, towards finding the film both "extremely enjoyable" (up from 75% to 80%) and "extremely important" (up from 69% to 79%). We will reflect on these variations later. But as a broad indication, the fact that in so many of our measures this NZ-namers group was representative of its base population suggests that this reference to New Zealand may be a direct response to the *film itself*, rather than arising from special features in the audience environments.

These responses some quite lengthy, turned out to be representative of our response population, except that nearly three quarters were from women, and showed slightly raised levels of reported filmic enjoyment and importance. In other respects (country, age, occupation, familiarity with the books, etc.) they reflected the overall spread of respondents. Our structured study of these answers explores the ways in which "New Zealand" operates as a figure within an imaginary world, focused around ideas of "nature" and "the mediaeval".

We took a random 200 set of the 592 English-language responses.[12] We did this expecting to develop, and then follow, a coding system which could capture differences among the responses, which might then be sorted for patterns, and then studied both quantitatively and qualitatively.[13] In fact this approach singularly did not work on this occasion, because there were no discernible differences, other than those arising from greater or lesser explicitness.

It is necessary to note the twenty-three respondents whose answers consisted of, for instance, "New Zealand" (henceforth we ignore variant spellings as irrelevant to our investigation), or "New Zealand most definitely!", or who perhaps took their account one stage further by extending this to "New Zealand in the Middle Ages". For these writers, the reasons for saying these things must have seemed so obvious as to be beyond elaboration. But as a result, while we may (reasonably) guess that their reasons are "mainstream", and thence of the kind that we find displayed among those who *do* elaborate, it is impossible to be certain of this. Simply, they have chosen complete implicitness.

Passing beyond these, we find different degrees of elaboration. Some people's responses only hinted at the nature of the associations linking Middle-earth with New Zealand. Other people (and we can say something about who they are) flesh out their pictures of these associations. What struck us forcefully was that these appeared to accumulate into a *single semantic model*.

Before we disclose this it may be helpful to first say what is revealed by asking: to whom do people appear to feel they are speaking, as they answer this question? We can see some signs of an agenda from which people wished to distance

---

[12] As previously, this was done using a facility within Microsoft Access, which allows all responses to be sorted alphabetically. By using the responses to another question, it is possible to ensure that nothing within the answers to this question is being privileged.

[13] See Martin Barker's article on patterns of character-choice for an example of how this works, and the kinds of understanding it permits. (Barker, 2005)

themselves. The main form this takes is a caution about appearing *over-involved* in the story-world, as in:

"Well I think of New Zealand, but of course I know that it's just an escape."

"But" here functions to circumscribe the implications of this thinking, and the adoption of "escape" reassures the writer that s/he is doing nothing inappropriate or nerdish. We see the same impulse, but managed differently, behind this answer:

"New Zealand! Just kidding..."

The implication here is that the writer is playing a game of over-involvement, to "have us on".

In between these extremes, we can depict a long chain of responses addressing the same semantic dimension, from those for whom New Zealand is never much more than a convenient place, a set of sites for filming (a true location), to those for whom it stands for something "fantastic". When we put these answers in a series of transitions we see increasing transference of meanings between the real and the fictional, on a semantic sliding scale, as follows:

Location...

    stand in...

        embodiment...

            a wished for place...

                where fantasy lives

It seems to make little difference to people's answers whether they have or have not visited New Zealand; or whether they dream, hope or plan to visit. Many people seem capable of making a strong separation between New Zealand as a physical reality—with its own history, peoples, problems, strengths and weaknesses—and "New Zealand" as a landscape invested forever with the supervenient meanings of Tolkien's world. This may in itself say much about the power of cultural tourism.

What is fascinating about these answers is that they are found among those who wish to distance themselves slightly from the experience of the film. From our wider researches into the questionnaire responses we have been able to identify which groups have the strongest and most committed relationship with the film. Most strikingly, our quantitative data shows that the highest levels of pleasure and importance are associated with those selecting *Spiritual Journey* as one way of characterising the *kind of story* Tolkien's world is for them.[14] Experimentally selecting one hundred Spiritual Journey respondents from the rest, and comparing them with one hundred others from within our NZ-namers, we discovered first, that the former gave markedly *longer* (and therefore more elaborate) answers than the latter. Second, there was a concentration among the latter of both entirely implicit answers, and of cautionary answers just described. Those experiencing *LotR* as in some sense a Spiritual Journey are sufficiently committed to it not to worry about how they might appear to us, and to want to express more fully what, for them, is the association between Middle-earth and New Zealand.

c. Elaborations of Time and Place

We also find this dimension of proximity and distance (of real and abstract) when we take into account references to time and place. We found that we could sort responses along three axes: 1) *implicitness*—those responses where references were fast, indexical, and unelaborated; 2) *distancing*—those responses where the time and space of New Zealand might have been acknowledged, but simultaneously denied too much "reality"; and 3) *explicit and connected*—those responses which combined the opposites of these, making simultaneously real and elaborated links with New Zealand, and tending to suggest links within and between the two strands of qualities. Table 1 captures the results of classifying responses in this way. The right hand column captures the responses of those with the highest levels of pleasure in and commitment to the film. We offer the following as an emergent portrait of the ways in which "New Zealand" as a site of representation plays on the meanings of LotR.

- **Time:** the temporal location of Middle-earth, and the qualities that New Zealand needs embody that location, are wonderfully imprecise. The point seems to be that this is precisely a *mythical* past, which can even—in one or

---

[14] The choice was between thirteen types of stories: allegory, epic, fairytale, fantasy, game-world, good vs. evil, myth/legend, quest, SFX film, spiritual journey, threatened homeland, war story, and "other".

two responses—be a "future" time. This is an *idea of pastness*, reaching into stories and fragments of moral narratives for the sufficient associations to place itself.

- **Place:** the qualities associated with New Zealand/Middle-earth range from the aesthetic to the moral. The cinematic qualities of the landscapes immediately become more than that for many. These are *clean* and *unsullied* places, before humans began despoiling them.

In combining these, respondents themselves sometimes puzzle over the complexity of the mental operations that they are performing. For instance:

"I actually believe it's somewhere on earth but not on earth. Confusing but I see it in my mind."

TABLE 1. References to Time and Place

	Implicit	Distanced	Explicit/Connected
Temporal location and qualities	-The past -1500s -The Middle Ages -The Dark Ages -Ages ago -A few thousand years ago	-This is nowhere and nowhen—Middle-earth isn't real -There is no equitable time period -Not a particular time -The book says it's 1300s	-Not here though maybe it was once here -Earlier than our knowledge -Predating written records. Before Christ -Before we went there -A timeless place that is just about anywhere -A more innocent time
Spatial location and qualities	-Wonderful -Awesome -Truly beautiful -Pristine -Primitive -Lush -Nature	-Good locations -Without the beautiful landscapes of NZ the films would have been difficult to make	-Pure and isolated -Such a beautiful and diverse world -Landscape with mountains, rivers and forest is perfect -The country has that primitive feeling with nature at its base -Fitting that it is NZ due to the immense variety of lands and characters

This would seem to derive from an awareness that they are creating a composite from different sources:

"I do borrow from the English middle ages to fill some of the gaps."

In other words, audiences know that they are constructing composites from a range of sources, and this very compositeness allows them to "manage" the kind of reality that they wish to apply to Middle-earth. Not a literal reality, but one which nonetheless *resonates* with their live world. This can be seen in the following two tendencies discovered in our materials.

d. A World Without Evil

First, this "land" is *enormous*. New Zealand—two mid-sized islands in the South Pacific—in the minds of those approaching it through *LotR* is able to contain an entire continent, a whole world which overspills maps, contains many peoples, and is almost unknowable to its own denizens. Viewers here encompass what the inhabitants of Middle-earth cannot. "New Zealand" can contain everything and everyone, through its expressive landscapes. They are simultaneously visual, cultural and moral, what one person describes as "the scenery and natural feelings". The landscapes force journeys and test characters.

Nevertheless, these landscapes are *without evil*. It may be a world of different cultures, but neither the Orcs, nor Saruman, nor the Balrog, nor Sauron even *belong* there. They live there, and threaten it, but it is not their world. Among the answers mentioning "New Zealand", many name different inhabitants. But only two mention the place of evil in this world, and both of these specifically place it as coming from "outside": one says that "a different kind of evil has permeated our world", the other identifies it as "the evil from the east". Evil does not truly inhabit New Zealand/Middle-earth, which thus retains its paradisal quality.

e. The Shire: Home

This portrait is uncannily common and shared, but carries within it one remarkable exception. In references to the Shire, a different dimension enters: "home". A number of people add a reference to another place to embody their feelings about

Hobbiton. And in each case where this is done, it is something very close to 'home'. In some cases, this is explicitly England. In one case it is Red River Valley in Minnesota (where the respondent grew up). In another one, it is Norway.

In each case, the writing reveals that this is the author's own "sense of home". What is interesting is that Tzanelli, working with quite different materials (a large sample of discussions about the film gathered from the Internet Movie Database), found precisely the same distinction at work:

> The idea of representing the "Old English" way of life was thought to be implicit in Tolkien's story. The little Hobbit houses with their gardens and the small Shire community occupied some space in English reviews of the LOTR trilogy (see for example IMDB, London, England, 20/11/04). Here, although the controversy was over the "appropriate" simulation of a fantastic community, the idea of an authentic "way of living" (which is British, not New Zealandish!) persists. (Tzanelli, 2004: 29)

Tzanelli suggests that this persistent Englishness might constitute a form of "cultural resistance" to the New Line/Tourism New Zealand proposition. We doubt this. To argue thus involves dividing people's responses to the landscapes into two parts: "dominated" responses to New Zealand, and "resistant" responses via their homelands, which makes little sense. We propose instead that it should be seen as a curious mental geography, with its own internal rationale.

New Zealand and "New Zealand"

There is nothing surprising about the idea that New Zealand has become a fantasy landscape for many fans of the *LotR* films. What is pertinent is the remarkable uniformity across English-speaking respondents in this regard, suggesting that this is a strong feature of the film itself and its marketing and established status, rather than a feature of the differentiated social lives of the audiences.

But it is also a landscape with a moral use, a *moral landscape*. Almost without exception audiences seem to approach the meanings Middle-earth embodies, through its placing in New Zealand, very seriously: as something that matters greatly to them. This is evident in the care with which they disconnect it from any "evil", and with which they try not to see the Shire (the true home ground) on the same level as other location-related meanings. It is as if they are determined to safeguard their feeling of "home" from any appropriation, not as Tzanelli suggests as cultural resistance but, rather, as a safe-haven.

We think that our sample's answers strongly indicate that degrees of time-distance and place-distance are used to situate value systems held by audiences, and which they want to ascribe to *LotR*. In film studies it is often suggested that such situating happens through identification with characters, but it is clear that for those people mentioning New Zealand, this country and its representation in the films carry value as well. It embodies good; it allows for elaborations of what matter ("nature", "purity", "innocence", "knowledge") in varying degrees of explicitness, and in varying degrees of closeness to the actual landscapes of New Zealand. Sometimes our respondents seem to ascribe these values to the actual locations, but more often they link the values to more abstract, distanced, *ideal* locations—the "New Zealand"—for which the New Zealand landscape (and its use in the films) functions as a trigger, an inference, or a stimulus.

Pilgrimage: "New Zealand" as a Touchstone for "Home"

We would go further. Beyond the use of the fixed place New Zealand we believe many overseas audiences use the idea of "New Zealand" as a touchstone for a journey of discovery, an abstract destination for a pilgrimage the films' stories invite them to take. This accords with Stan Jones in his chapter "Fixing a Heritage": "Seeking Middle earth does not mean wandering, but a form of 'grounded pilgrimage'. That is: there and back again between home and very distant goals already visualized." (Jones, 2006: 292) The idea of "New Zealand" as a destination for pilgrimage is a useful one. We suggest that the various meanings associated with "New Zealand" provide a possibility to find "home"—a home ground with its values, comfort and certainties—elsewhere. In this sense, it matters not so much where "New Zealand" is and what it looks like, but how it facilitates the journey from "home" (the Shire, and the real home this stands for) to a place one goes to in order to find home. There is no incongruity in this reasoning, it is in fact at the core of what a pilgrimage embodies.

For overseas audiences enticed by their appreciation of *LotR* to embark on a journey to (re)discover the values that underpin their own lives (or at least the place of *LotR* in their lives), "New Zealand" is a fleeting home away from home—a checkpoint for re-evaluating home values, much like Lourdes, or Salamanca, or Macchu Picchu or Tibet. It is in that sense no coincidence that we found the strong connection between explicit and connected mentions of New Zealand, and the choice of "Spiritual Journey" as a way of framing the story—it is indeed a journey for them. What distinguishes "New Zealand" from real pilgrimage locations, is that its representation filtered through *LotR* offers the possibility of completing this journey by proxy. In that sense, the glorious representation of the real New Zealand's landscapes in the films may possibly counter the tourist board promotions, since the real could hardly be as good as the "real".

Conclusion: The Utopian Impulse of "New Zealand" in *LotR*

In a famous essay, Zygmunt Bauman uses the metaphor of pilgrimage to explore modern quests for identity. He explains how pilgrimages involve distancing oneself from the locus of identity (home) to achieve a clearer view of one's personal identity and belonging: "'here' is the waiting, 'there' is the gratification," Bauman writes. (Bauman, 1996: 22) But he also adds that in modern times such a trajectory is no longer achievable: people find themselves embroiled in a senseless wandering, vector-less, in a world inhospitable to sense-seeking. As a stroller (purposeless), a vagabond (homeless), a player (inhibition-less), or as a tourist (value-less, or at least substituting moral with aesthetic values), the modern pilgrim finds it impossible to find meaning.

Bauman seems to point a damning finger at modern media for this loss, and especially at how its global village appeal has, in his eyes, erased all possibilities for a "there". That is where we differ. As our findings indicate, audiences of *LotR* do seem able to "travel" to a mediated location, "New Zealand", to form meanings about not just the film and the landscape (the aesthetic component, which the tourist board would like us to see), but also about themselves and their values, thence changing forever their perception of the location (the "grounded pilgrimage" Jones suggests). As Sean Cubitt writes: "...the country has not become Middle-earth, as some of the tourist board campaigns suggest, but it has achieved a certain imaginary power, as a utopian landscape for fantasies of a different humanity in tune with its world." (Cubitt, 2005: 7) It may surprise many that this "different humanity" also exists outside New Zealand in the form of numerous people seeing *LotR* as a journey.

We believe that using "New Zealand" in such a journey is not a senseless operation but rather one which we would like to call, with Ernst Bloch, a "utopian impulse". (Bloch, 1986, vol. 1: 12-18) It provides a powerful antidote for postmodern cynicism about meaning—it is not that our audiences find one single meaning, but that they believe that continuing to seek one counts.

Bibliography

Anon (2001), "New Zealand Tourism Strategy 2010": http://www.tourism.govt.nz/strategy/str-reports-2010/str-rep-2010sum.pdf

Barker, Martin (2004), "News, Reviews, Clues, Interviews and Other Ancillary Materials—a Critique and Research Proposal" *Scope: on-line Film Studies Journal* February: http://www.nottingham.ac.uk/film/scopearchive/articles/news-reviews.htm

Barker, Martin (2005), "*The Lord of the Rings* and Identification: A Critical Encounter" *European Journal of Communication* 20 (3), pp. 353-378

Barker, Martin and Ernest Mathijs (eds) (2007), *Watching the Lord of the Rings*, Peter Lang, New York

Bauman, Zygmunt (1996), "From Pilgrim to Tourist—or a Short History of Identity" in Stuart Hall and Paul Du Gay (eds), *Questions of Cultural Identity*, Sage, London, pp. 18-36

Bell, Claudia and John Lyall (2002), *The Accelerated Sublime: Landscape, Tourism and Identity*, Praeger, Westport and London

Bloch, Ernst (1986) [1960], *The Principle of Hope* 3 vols, MIT Press, Cambridge, Mass.

Carter, Lin (1969), *A Look Behind* The Lord of the Rings, Ballantine, New York

Clarke, David (ed.) (1997), *The Cinematic City*, Routledge, London

Cloke, Paul and Harvey C Perkins (1998), "'Cracking the Canyon with the Awesome Foursome': Representations of Adventure Tourism in New Zealand" *Environment and Planning D. Society and Space* 16, pp. 185-218

Colmar Brunton Social Research Agency (2003), *Demand for Cultural Tourism* (Report for Tourism New Zealand):

http://www.creativenz.govt.nz/files/resources/demand-for-cultural-tourism.pdf

Conrich, Ian (2005), "Kiwi Gothic: New Zealand's Cinema of a Perilous Paradise" in Steven Jay Schneider and Tony Williams (eds), *Horror International*, Wayne State University Press, Detroit, pp. 114-127

Cubitt, Sean (2005), *Ecomedia*, Rodopi, Amsterdam and New York

Genocchio, Bruno (1995), "Discourse, Continuity, Difference: the Question of 'Other Spaces'" in S. Watson and K. Gibson (eds), *Postmodern Cities and Spaces*, Blackwell, Cambridge, pp. 35-46

Göttler, Fritz, Frieda Grafe, Wolfgang Jacobse and Enno Patalas (1990), *Friedrich Wilhelm Murnau*, Carl Hanser Verlag, München

Grant, Barry Keith (1999), *A Cultural Assault: The New Zealand Films of Peter Jackson*, Kakapo Books, Nottingham

Jones, Stan (2006), "Fixing a Heritage: Inscribing Middle-Earth onto New Zealand" in Ernest Mathijs (ed.), *The Lord of the Rings: Popular Culture in Global Context*, Wallflower Press, London, pp. 287-303

Jutel, Thierry (2004), "*Lord of the Rings*: Landscape, Transformation and the Geography of the Virtual" in C. Bell and S. Matthewman (eds), *Cultural Studies in Aotearoa New Zealand*, Oxford University Press, Oxford, pp. 54-65

Larner, Wendy (1998), "Hitching a Ride on the Tiger's Back: Globalisation and Spatial Imaginaries in New Zealand" *Environment and Planning D. Society and Space* 16, pp. 599-614

Lawn, Jennifer and Bronwyn Beatty (2006), "On the Brink of a New Threshold of Opportunity: *The Lord of the Rings* and New Zealand Cultural Policy" in Ernest Mathijs (ed.), *The Lord of the Rings: Popular Culture in Global Context*, Wallflower Press, London, pp. 43-60

Le Héron, Erena (2004), "Placing Geographical Imagination in Film" *New Zealand Geographer* 60:1, pp. 60-66

Mathijs, Ernest (ed.) (2006), *The Lord of the Rings: Popular Culture in Global Context*, Wallflower Press, London

Mathijs, Ernest and Murray Pomerance (eds) (2006), *From Hobbits to Hollywood: Essays on Peter Jackson's The Lord of the Rings*, Rodopi, New York and Amsterdam

Pouroy, Janine (1993), "Heart of Darkness" *Cinefex* 53, February, pp. 22-53

Thornley, Davinia (2006), "Wellywood and Peter Jackson: the Local Reception of The Lord of the Rings in Welington, New Zealand" in Ernest Mathijs (ed.) *The*

Lord of the Rings: Popular Culture in Global Context, Wallflower Press, London, pp. 103-120

Tincknell, Estella (2000), "New Zealand Gothic? Jane Campion's *The Piano*" in Ian Conrich and David Woods (eds), *New Zealand—a Pastoral Paradise*, Kakapo Books, Nottingham, pp. 107-119

Tzanelli, Rodanthi (2004), "Constructing the 'Cinematic Tourist': The 'Sign Industry' of *The Lord of the Rings*" *Tourist Studies* 4:1, pp. 21-42

Urry, John (2002), *The Tourist Gaze* 2nd ed., Sage, London

Wu, Harmony (2003), "Trading in Horror, Cult, and Matricide: Peter Jackson's Phenomenal Bad Taste and New Zealand Fantasies Inter/national Cinematic Success" in Mark Jancovich, Antonio Lazaro Reboll, Julian Stringer and Andy Willis (eds), *Defining Cult Movies; the Cultural Politics of Oppositional Taste*, Manchester University Press, Manchester, pp. 84-108

7

WHOSE MIDDLE-EARTH IS IT?
Reading *The Lord of the Rings* and New Zealand's New Identity from a Globalized, Post-Colonial Perspective

Daniel Smith-Rowsey

> ...when all hope had faded, that Isildur, son of the king, took up his father's sword. Sauron, the enemy of the free peoples of Middle-earth, was defeated. The ring passed to Isildur, who had this one chance to destroy evil forever. But the hearts of Men are easily corrupted, and the ring of power has a will of its own.
> (Off-screen narration by Galadriel in the Prologue of The Fellowship of the Ring)

I REMEMBER as a child reading J.R.R. Tolkien's *The Hobbit*, and pausing to think about the evocative words "Middle-earth." Where was this place? Alice's Wonderland was down a rabbit hole. The Wizard's Oz was understood to be on the planet, hidden by surrounding deserts. Other "fantasy" novels seemed situated in the same mythical England that I associated with King Arthur. But Middle-earth seemed different. I pictured an underground world, much like our own, but where the skies, while looking blue to the world's inhabitants, were actually "ceilings" of an unusual sort. If the people there ever learnt to fly, perhaps they could drill up through their own skies and come into our world.

But I was wrong. Middle-earth has come to us through the cinema, and it turns out to resemble nothing so much as rural New Zealand. The New Zealand tourist bureau, through ubiquitous advertisements, is proud to assign to their nation much of the meaning of Peter Jackson's recent films. In other words, our planet has a "middle" world, a barely-touched rural paradise, steeped in medieval folklore, and it is in New Zealand. I am no longer a child, and this brought to mind a new question: How do the real-life "middle" nations of the world feel about these movies, and about New Zealand's new identity?

"Perception itself is embedded in history," according to Ella Shohat and Robert Stam. "The same filmic images or sounds provoke distinct reverberations for different communities.... Imported mass culture can also be indigenized, put to local use, given a local accent." (in Wilson and Dissanayake, 1996: 163) Ulf Hedetoft agrees, and expands: "(T)wo national contexts meet within the public communicative space of the movie theatre, producing a new national text framed by a more universalized 'transnational imaginary' of American origin." This "hybrid third" text is not necessarily alienated or unconscious or pro- or anti-American. Instead,

> ... at the level where a cognitive and emotional engagement with a film's unfolding plot, represented characters, and cognitive themes takes place, national audiences will apply the optic of their history, identity and values in a process involving a decoding and reframing of the film's content and "message". (in Hjort and MacKenzie, 2000: 282)

It is the intention of this chapter to attempt to understand how the people of underdeveloped nations might apply their "history, identity and values" to Peter Jackson's recent blockbuster film trilogy, *The Lord of the Rings*, with the awareness that no audience reacts monolithically the same way.[1] I conclude by suggesting some implications for New Zealand identity as it positions itself as Jackson's "Middle-earth".

LotR vs. Third Cinema

The *LotR* films have acquired as much (in Pierre Bourdieu's term) "cultural capital" as any film event might be expected to have. Taken together, they have earned about $3 billion in worldwide box office receipts alone, a figure that excludes video/DVD

---

[1] For this essay, I spent a great deal of time researching English- and Spanish-language newspapers from underdeveloped countries. I found almost no reviews of *LotR* at all—and the few I found, like in *The Manila Times*, were brief and complimentary. I now believe that most Third World newspapers do not routinely run film reviews. I was not able to get what I hoped for from "the horse's mouth", and instead must rely on scholarly inference.

rentals and sales. All three received the highest accolades from most of the world's film critics. All three films won Oscars, with the last of the trilogy earning the distinction of the largest sweep in Academy Awards history, winning all of the eleven categories nominated. It is extremely rare for any film, or group of films, to be so well received by the public, the critics, and the award-granters. If any films are influential, these are they. If any films deserve as many "readings" as possible, it is the *LotR* films.

What does it mean to "read" films in terms of post-colonialism and globalization? It means asking: is this film helpful or harmful for the actual oppressed and marginalized people of the world? Does the given film present images, situations, heroes, that globalization's victims can rally behind, relate to, or experience as further domination? Does the film present a normative white European subject (or subjects) as the centre of morality, and does the film present its antagonists as "otherized" or "Oriental"? In the case of the *LotR* films, the answers are unclear.

The *LotR* films are not Third World cinema in the sense of an Ousmane Sembene film, or even a Bollywood film. New Zealand filmmaking, even at its most localized, cannot be said to articulate the trauma of mother-language invalidation and economic underdevelopment that characterizes the indigenous cinema of Latin America and Africa. Even internationally embraced statements of native dissonance, like Lee Tamahori's *Once Were Warriors* (1994) and Niki Caro's *Whale Rider* (2002), are not typically categorized with Third World cinema. The *LotR* films are not closely aligned with any historically marginalized groups.

Plainly, the *LotR* films were unthinkable without Hollywood's (in this case, the New Line studio's) money and participation. They are no more "Third World" than Richard Attenborough's *Gandhi* (1982) or David Lean's *Lawrence of Arabia* (1962). On an extra-textual level, despite their New Zealand constitutions, the *LotR* films cannot avoid being seen as the Next Big Western Thing, comparable to Levi's, MTV, Starbucks, and a hundred previously released Hollywood blockbusters. As texts like *Global Hollywood* have explained, such ostentatious symbols of "cultural imperialism" tend to be divisive even before their quality has been examined. (Miller, Govil, McMurria and Maxwell, 2001: 28-29) If the citizens of the Third World actually watch *LotR*, one would expect them to do so with (at least in principle) arms folded. Only some will see more in the films than spectacle. Only some will judge the film on its artistic merits, bearing in mind that no film can feed a family, build a house, or incite a revolution. It is to this select group that the rest of this essay refers.

Can the Hobbits Be Seen as a "Subaltern" Race?

Each of the three *LotR* films has two versions, the version released into theatres and the "special extended" version saved for the later video/DVD releases. I believe my analysis will hold up for the shorter and longer versions, but the distinction is worth a mention.

The *LotR* films are based on the trilogy of novels of the same name, by J.R.R. Tolkien. Tolkien began work on the books before World War II but did not finish them until a few years afterward. The meaning and moral of the books is not agreed upon by everyone, but it seems to have something to do with honouring principles of courage, duty, community, and the necessity of actively opposing evil.[2] Some find Christian allegories, but I do not consider these obvious to a reader that is not looking for them.[3]

What to make of Tolkien's mélange of identity groups, lifted to the screen basically intact (though with far less attention to the Dwarves) by Jackson? Critics have posited all manner of far-fetched readings. Among others, Peter Gilet and J.S. Ryan read the Shire as some part of England, where Strider and his forces seem to represent the Maquis (the French resistance), while the forces of Mordor take on distinct German qualities. (Ryan, 1969: 79)[4]

Clearly Tolkien and Jackson don't wish any allegory to be the definitive interpretation. "Middle-earth", by its very nature, is both of this world and beyond

---

[2] Hal Colebatch gathers many of the extant readings of meanings. (Colebatch, 2003) Tom Shippey, claims that Tolkien has a Manichean view of good and evil, (Shippey, 2003: 215) but Scott Davidson specifically counters that claim (in Bassham and Bronson, 2003: 99-108).

[3] Janet Menzies claims that Gandalf is a very clear Christ figure. (Giddings, 1983: 56-72) J.S. Ryan carefully weighs a great deal of criticism and decides against direct Christian metaphor. (Ryan, 1969: 202)

[4] A sizable collection of half-baked theories can be found at www.theonering.net (Anon, 2006b: http://www.theonering.net/rumour_mill/readingroom/)

it. Tolkien and Jackson present a map of this unfamiliar world, and it is overreaching for any critic to try to parse out geographical features to find out which area is "really", say, Europe.

Yet Tolkien and Jackson are not quite free of the burden of representation. Saying that the *LotR* trilogy presents an ambiguously defined sectionalism is not the same as saying that all audiences will react to the story in more or less the same way, or that any reading is as sensible as any other. It is entirely justifiable to try to understand the metaphors in the *LotR* because the texts try to evoke our sympathy. To begin with, Mordor, the locus of evil, is often referred to as "the East," which could mean Germany, or Russia, but could just as well, in the more epistemological reading of "East," signify an Oriental land populated by people with darker skins.

The problem with a nation-state reading is that neither Tolkien nor Jackson uses the word "nation" or "national".[5] The equally anachronistic word that they do use repeatedly is "race". This is more of a break with "fantasy" tradition than it may appear at first—few if any novelists had previously grouped Elves and Dwarves (and trolls and goblins and fairies, for that matter) as "races". The potentially contradictory (yet evocative) phrase "the race of Men" may be a Tolkien original.

This leads to the first of two key questions when "reading" the *LotR* films in terms of post-colonial audiences: Can the Hobbits be seen as (using Antonio Gramsci's deathless term) a "subaltern" race? (Gramsci, 1971: 202) In the film narration quoted above, Galadriel says that the ultimate ring of power has come to "the most unlikely creature imaginable—a Hobbit". The films go to considerable effort, through effects and forced-perspective shots, to emphasize the Hobbits' smaller physical stature. At one point, Galadriel says to Frodo, "Even the smallest person can change the course of the future." This seems like a step toward what Ranajit Guha called subaltern consciousness. (in Ashcroft, Griffiths and Triffin, 1995: 408)

After the prologue, the film takes us to the verdant Shire, which the Hobbits call home. We learn that Hobbits drink and eat too much, and are known for

---

[5] It's a shame too, because if a nation-state reading were more plausible, there would be twice the amount of literature to support it, from Benedict Anderson's *Imagined Communities* to Roy Armes' *Third World Film Making and the West*.

wanting little more out of life than merriment. Though the Hobbits are bare of feet and crude of appetite, the story embraces them as repositories of virtue, warts and all. Abdul JanMohamed distinguishes between "imaginary" and "symbolic" stories, including in the former group a certain European tendency to make the (or a) character of the village "shamanic," a repository of mystical wisdom by which the more privileged characters can reify their own claim on moral authority. The Hobbits are not gurus, nor are they an "other" that will corrode and destroy the privileged man if he gets too close (as in, say, Werner Herzog's films). The Hobbits are JanMohamed's type of "symbolic"—they are more nuanced, and frankly more human. (in Ashcroft, Griffiths and Triffin, 1995: 18)

Their home, the Shire, is a virtual Miltonian paradise, celebrated without irony. Though the Shire scenes form only the first hour and last fifteen minutes of what can be seen as a twelve-hour film, they are not only the film's bookends but its emotional core. As Frodo says, they set out to save the Shire. (And in Jackson's films, as opposed to Tolkien's books, they succeed.) When all hope seems lost, they cling to their love of the Shire. It is with the Shire that the *LotR* films make their best claim for the sympathies of the rural, of the "backward," of the villages that know more than the cities. The portrayal of Hobbits as bucolic and multi-faceted is, certainly by the standards of the mostly upper-middle-class characters of Hollywood, a positive articulation of subaltern consciousness.

The main problem with seeing the Hobbits as heroes of the subaltern class is their white skin and their other trappings of European medieval culture. No matter how much the condition of Hobbits may allude to the state of a "noble savage" (as fraught with complications as that would be), they are still Caucasian, English-speaking, male-normative, and marked as Europeans in a hundred ways.

The *LotR* films do not go out of their way to explain their European markings, and it is just this presumption of familiarity that a non-European-descended audience may well find objectionable. Aime Cesaire famously declared, "Europe is indefensible." Yet Cesaire is also careful to assign the rottenness of Europe to a time no earlier than widespread mercantilism; he notes that there was nothing hypocritical about the conquests of Cortez and Pisarro. (Cesaire, 1972: 32-33) The Shire is a Paradise, but in a material sense it is a microcosm of Middle-earth itself, a land that exists (and maintains itself for thousands of years) before European colonialism and globalization. This gives the Hobbits, and the story, more "licence" with audiences from underdeveloped nations.

At the council meeting in Rivendell, the elf leader Elrond announces that the Ring must be destroyed in the only way possible—casting it into the fires from which it was forged, into Mount Doom. He says, "One of you must do this." Our subaltern Hobbits are enlisted into service, forced to bear the ultimate burden of the destruction of the one Ring. Such positioning may remind some of Gayatri Spivak's "native informant", a subservient member of the oppressed race who does the dominant race's "dirty work" while telling them what they want to hear.

At this point, motivation becomes the question. Throughout the films, Jackson emphasizes that the characters are fighting because of love for each other. Indeed, I know of no war film where brotherly love is mentioned half as often (and this aspect has done nothing to allay near-homophobic readings in some less reputable quarters). Aragorn and Legolas and Gimli are motivated entirely out of love and brotherhood for Merry and Pippin for the first half of *The Two Towers*; they do not seek them for strategic gain. Give Peter Jackson some credit: the presumptive leader of the "race of Men" consistently loves subalterns.

Keith Akers writes, "What Tolkien does is to evoke the *social* context of a great crisis, and that is what makes LOTR 'feel' like the Second World War." (Akers, 2006) I would counter that Jackson makes the story feel like any war in which the subject is personally invested, where he and his friends will come to the front lines. The sense of proximate conflict and crisis is one that the dispossessed know all too well. Some Westerners fail to consider the possibility that the Third World's ongoing beatification of Che Guevara has as much to do with ideology as it does with Che's willingness to fight on the front lines for his beliefs. Globalization's worst sufferers can relate, better than most complacent Westerners, to perhaps the cornerstone scene of *FotR*:

> Frodo: I wish the ring had never come to me. I wish none of this had happened.
> Gandalf: So do all who live to see such times. But that is not for them to decide.
>   All we have to decide is what to do with the time that is given to us.

The great achievement of the *LotR*, the recovery of a legendary past through radical de-historicization and reconstruction of myths, is likely to seem negligible to those that have not shared this past. On the other hand, many of the world's less fortunate, particularly in the Middle East and North Africa, recognize swords, chain mail and other flourishes from their own past.

Can the *LotR* Films Be Seen as an Allegory of Globalization?

Globalization is a complex process, and any attempt to summarize it will inevitably be coarse and over-simplified. Some aspects of globalization, like increased political agency and improved flow of information, seem felicitous to all concerned. Other aspects, like universal commodification and capitalism at the expense of human dignity, strike some as imperialism by more subtle means. How are the characters in Peter Jackson's film trilogy positioned in terms of globalization? The second key question this essay posits is: Can the *LotR* films be seen as an allegory of globalization?

In the text of the films, the spread of evil is clearly something to which our heroes react. They are "playing defence" until the final hour of the third film. If we consider that globalization is an active process, one sort of liberal-sympathizing interpretation might position Saruman and his minions as environment-wrecking, gene-splicing, despotic forces of globalization, and the Fellowship as a sort of organic resisting force, with some parallels to the 1955 Bandung conferees, or the Organization of African Unity, or even the protestors of the World Trade Organization and G8 summits.

However, a counter-reading does not seem difficult to imagine, if we consider the racial and "other" coding of Men and Elves. Saruman and the Uruk-hai who destroy all they see are warriors. The process of globalization is more insidious and may be closer to what the dawning "age of Men" promises. Perhaps Sauron and Saruman are the forces opposing what seems to the world of Men to be their quite "natural", even invisible, dominion over all that lives.

It is tricky to "map" a globalization allegory onto *LotR*, because globalization is inevitably understood in terms of capitalist exploitation. No one in the *LotR* story is ever turned away for lack of money; material possessions very seldom figure in the story. (This is not to suggest that such absence does not form its own disguised ideology—just that it is harder to detect.)

It comes down to how one sees the Ring that forms the engine of the plot. The Ring is classically golden and connotes jewellery. The Ring might be seen as the first hint of a material resource, akin to a newly discovered diamond, that forms the crucial first step in a cycle of exploitation and dispossession that Third Worlders understand all too well. Thus they may applaud Frodo's attempt to destroy it—even if Frodo is merely staving off the inevitable. But this line of reasoning may be too taxing. The Ring might also represent marriage, or achievement, not an intuitively grasped parable for anything.[6]

The Ring has at least two antecedents in Western high culture: Plato's Ring of Gyges, which renders its wearer invisible and corrupts his heart (as pointed out by Eric Katz in Bassham and Bronson, 2003: 5), and Wagner's epic cycle about a Ring that grants the power to rule the world (Anon 2006a). Tolkien always disavowed any direct allegories, especially any regarding the Ring and the atomic bomb, because the books were mostly completed before August 1945. He said: "The book is not about anything but itself. It has no allegorical intentions, topical, moral, religious or political. It is not about modern wars or H-bombs, and my villain is not Hitler." (Plimmer and Plimmer, 1968: 32)

Still, it is clear that the Ring is a foreign element that invites selfishness and the worst excesses of temptation. Our heroes must resist its charms even as they work toward its obliteration. (Conveniently, Frodo and Sam are conscripted as pacifists.) It is power, but it "cannot be wielded", as Aragorn puts it. It is power that knows no benevolent control and that can only be made to serve utter evil. This is a power that most victims of globalization understand. They may see Frodo's quest as quixotic, but his heart is right, and his voice is as honourable as it is representative of the subaltern.

---

[6] Alison Milbank reviews Marxist and Freudian readings of the ring in her essay "'My Precious': Tolkien's Fetishized Ring". (in Bassham and Bronson, 2003: 33-45) Patrick Curry also tackles much of the same ground in *Defending Middle-earth.* (Curry, 1997: 106-108) One is left with the impression that the ring's greatest function, on an extra-textual level, is to provide an irrefutable evil for liberal audiences that would ordinarily equivocate about the possibility of true evil.

It would not have been difficult for Jackson to have omitted Tolkien's subplot about the Ents, much as he removed the character of Tom Bombadil. In *TT*, the Ents— mobile tree-like beings that speak for the trees—refuse to be prodded (by Merry and Pippin) into war, but then reverse course when they see that Saruman has decimated a forest (to power his Uruk-hai-making device). The Ents rise up and use nature (by unblocking a dam) to destroy Saruman's base in Isengard. This sequence can be expected to resonate with the anti-pacifists and environmentalists among the subaltern class—a not insignificant percentage.

LotR is on much shakier ground in its characterizations of evil. In Tolkien's novels, evil and dread seem to lurk around every corner. In Jackson's films, evil is quite localized, personified by Sauron, Saruman, the Uruk-hai and the Ring-wraiths. Unlike some movie villains, their motivation is never comprehensively explained.

The Uruk-hai and the Ring-wraiths (a.k.a. Nazgûl) are notably dark. The Uruk-Hai and the villainous Harad are also the only dark-skinned characters in the films. Casting non-white actors in any of the leads would no doubt have created its own problems, distracting the flow of the images while opening up Jackson's re-articulation of medieval fables to charges of over-political correctness (while being arguably more accurately historicized; no doubt there were non-whites in Europe's ancient armies). Yet Jackson hardly counter-measures this difficulty by "darkening" all of the antagonists, save the malevolent Wizard Saruman. Frantz Fanon wrote at length about the role of colour symbols in maintaining blacks' belief that they are inferior, coining the term "anti-Negritude." (Fanon, 1967) The Nazgûl are a particularly blatant case of anti-Negritude, because we see them in the quoted prologue as white men. Their blackness signifies their centuries of corruption, just as Gandalf the Grey's transformation into Gandalf the White symbolizes his new purity. Were he alive today, Frantz Fanon would have a field day with *LotR*; why cannot black represent integrity and white represent debasement?

The Uruk-hai could have been white, but with a few pasty exceptions, they are not. Many Maoris, being of stronger build than the average white New Zealander, were cast as Uruk-hai—never as members of the race of Men. At one point during *The Return of the King*, a leading soldier appears on an oliphaunt, looking very much like a traditional Indian riding an elephant, presumably one of Tolkien's Haradrims. He is summarily dispatched without the chance to utter a line. Just as troubling are the film origins of the Uruk-hai. Jackson chose to present Tolkien's cross-breeding of Orcs and Men as a sort of genetic experiment by Saruman. This diminishes any reading of Saruman as a Nazi leader—the Nazis were nothing if not opposed to racial hybrids. As a white man dispatching a dark army (without getting his own hands bloody), Saruman represents the worst sort of colonial oppressor.

The nonwhites appear mostly as pure evil—one Ring-wraith intones sinisterly, "the world of Men will fall" (on the extended version of *RotK*)—or as bloodthirsty barbarians, as when the Uruk-hai become excited about Saruman's promise of "man flesh." They are assigned tragically little agency, but instead play the role of the dehumanized "other" whose deaths we are expected to cheer. The intentional coding of good as white and bad as black is hardly something that most post-colonial audiences, or in fact most audiences, should condone. It is here that the films fail severely on humanistic terms.

Further, it is probably safe to say that if we seek "imagined communities" (Anderson, 1983) without binaries, as Partha Chatterjee suggests, we are looking in the wrong place. (Ashcroft, Griffiths and Triffin, 1995: 164) Peter Jackson's shades of good and evil are, to put it mildly, rather over-drawn. Nor are the films formally disruptive—they're not "post-modern" in the sense of, say, the films of Alejandro Iñárritu or Fernando Meirelles.

Despite hiring two women (including his wife) as his co-screenwriters, Peter Jackson should not expect women in any country to applaud his film trilogy's attempts at female representation. It is not enough to say, as defenders sometimes suggest, that Tolkien ignored, not hated, women, or to say that Jackson is at least an improvement on Tolkien.[7] In a film trilogy that seems to be constantly bursting with new and peripheral characters, only three females have lines—Galadriel, Arwen, and Éowyn—and two of them spend most of their screen time mooning after Aragorn. There *is* a subplot where Éowyn asks why she cannot fight for the

---

[7] In *J.R.R. Tolkien: This Far Land*, at least two contributors explain the problem of Tolkien's casual sexism: Nick Otty in "The Structuralist's Guide to Middle-earth" (in Giddings, 1983: 154-178), and Brenda Partridge's "No Sex Please—We're Hobbits: The Construction of Female Sexuality in *The Lord of the Rings*" (in Giddings, 1983: 179-198).

ones she loves, secretly dons warrior garb, and faces off against the lead Nazgûl. It is a terrific moment when he says "No man can kill me," and she removes her helmet, says "I am no man," and kills him. But if Molly Haskell can declare that Katharine Hepburn and Bette Davis endure as feminist icons, despite their characters' compromises, because of how their characters *mostly* were, then by the same token, we mostly remember Jackson's Middle-earth as a place where women are clearly subordinate. (Haskell, 1987)

In many ways, *LotR* is a meditation on time and power, each presented as a boon and a burden. Arwen and Aragorn wrestle over her forsaking immortal life for his sake. In a story in which so many people are wounded, we rarely see any true healers. Extending life is mostly uncelebrated. Through the Nazgûl, and in particular through extended familiarity with the character Gollum, we are given to understand that some forms of immortality may well be worse than death. As Théoden dies, he tells Éowyn that he is happy to be honourably joining his fathers.

I would expect a mixed reaction from a subaltern audience about the theme of time. On the one hand, longer life is one of the rare virtues that European culture has to recommend it and to call it into question is a happy subversion. (I would also expect anti-colonialists to particularly savour the scene, during Elrond's vivid prognostication in the middle of *TT*, where the Europe-like towers of Rivendell fall into decay.) For a well-publicized sort of Fanonian radical, it is better to die in a blaze of glory and violence than to live in relative humiliation—"better to die on our feet than live on our knees."[8] On the other hand, when the West shows that it can treat extra time the way that it treats extra food, as wretched excess, the West should not expect the rest of the world's applause.

In the prologue we learn that Men are the ones that desire power above all things, but our subalterns, the Hobbits and Gollum, experience their share of temptation. The Ring-wraiths' souls are forever tortured because of their lust for power. We are meant to recognize Aragorn as a good Man because he resists the undue trappings of power. Gandalf and Saruman are the only Wizards we see, yet their power does not really come to much; these two cannot single-handedly turn the tides of great battles. In other words, the less endowed characters cannot hope

---

[8] Often attributed to Emiliano Zapata, Mexican revolutionary of the 1910s.

for a *deus ex machina*; they must face up to the limited range of their own powers. The Ring is the ultimate power, and stands metonymically for the ultimate evil.

Globalization's casualties can find much here on power that is resonant. The colonized subalterns have seen, more than most Westerners, how power can corrupt Men's souls. They know what it is for a leader like Pol Pot or Mobutu Sese Seko or Augusto Pinochet to empower them, ask for power, then turn around and use that power to treat them the same way as (or worse than) the colonial powers. To the extent that *LotR* promotes a loving community over such injustices, the world's oppressed can be expected to cheer the heroes. On the other hand, they may feel more betrayed in the end by the coronation of Aragorn, despite his gracious platitudes. While Westerners have known several (and may feel they remember many more) benevolent monarchies, the model is almost entirely unfamiliar in underdeveloped nations. The return of the king, as a Lacanian like Bhabha might note, is all too easily equated with the return of the repressed.

From what we know of Aragorn, he is unlikely to rule with an iron fist. (In the extended version of *FotR*, when Elrond tells Aragorn his fate, he replies in apparent sincerity, "I do not want that power. I have never wanted it.") Our subaltern Hobbits return to the unmolested Shire, presumably with no new governmental burdens. It is perhaps too convenient that Frodo has lost any desire for power that the Ring may have imputed. It is not the Hobbits' place to oppose the return of the king (to borrow Gandalf's line to the steward king Denethor in *RotK*). The kingdom has bowed before them—after Aragorn's elegant line "You bow to no one"—and returned them to their place, in much the same way that Nelson Mandela is received by world leaders nowadays. Thank you for your service, now get back to your mudhole.

But perhaps that is too harsh. Jackson's Hobbits at least have an undisturbed Shire, the chance to marry and bear children in peace, and even the chance to go on mystic voyages (as the Bagginses do in the final scene). This is commensurate with the goals of many of the world's oppressed. Additionally, Legolas and Gimli have buried the hatchet of their cultural Elf-Dwarf feud, while Arwen has foretold the child she will bear with Aragorn, half Elf and half Man, the presumptive future leader and role model of Middle-earth. (Some) races are coming together. The message could be worse.

How Middle Is New Zealand?

By way of conclusion, I consider the positioning of New Zealand in the films, and the positioning of the films *by* New Zealand.

Unlike Peter Weir, who went to Hollywood after his success Down Under and never returned, and unlike Philip Noyce and Gillian Armstrong, whose successes also took them to Hollywood only to return to Australia to work outside the American system once again, Peter Jackson basically brought Hollywood to New Zealand. The *LotR* films, especially considering their reliance on digital models, might have been filmed anywhere. He positioned New Zealand as Middle-earth.

In Jackson's films, the presumption of familiarity with medieval Europe is counter-balanced, to a significant extent, by a presumption of unfamiliarity with New Zealand itself. The country is positioned as a place that few filmgoers will know. The few that do know can be expected to react with pride, not resentment, at the "Hollywood treatment."

I can support this with a personal anecdote. Petra, located in what is now Jordan, is one of the great wonders of the world, the remnants of a lost civilization that built their temples into picturesque rocks. The local hoteliers never seem to tire of a nightly video viewing of Steven Spielberg's *Indiana Jones and the Last Crusade* (1989). Though the portions filmed in Petra are only in the movie's last third, and though there are doubtless many other non-Hollywood, more authoritative, films of Petra, this is the one that is repeatedly screened. It is as if to say, Look, Westerner, your most celebrated artist, Steven Spielberg, came here to end the adventures of his most famous character—to find his Grail. No Jordanian I met seems to regard this as defilement; it is instead confirmation of local richness.

If this experience in Jordan is any guide, then the post-colonial audience can be expected to relate to and enjoy the *LotR* films' presumption of unfamiliarity with New Zealand in background. (Naturally this elides the question of Maori claims to the land.) Had *LotR* been filmed in England, or America, or with mostly digital backgrounds, the films would not possess this quality. (Had they been made in a more oppressively colonized state, say, Mozambique, one could expect an entirely different flavour to their reception.)

New Zealand signed onto the Bandung conference of 1955, and declared itself part of the then-proud "Third World" alliance. However, New Zealand has a liminal status in post-colonial studies. It is that of a "settler" country, where the loyalty toward the mother country was stronger, the path to independence was less bloody, and a foreign language was less imposed than in most other former European colonies. Having said that, it can also be argued that because New Zealand remains at the margins, with only occasional gestures toward the centre, its experience is at least partly instructive for the post-colonial project.

In some ways, the Anglo-North American reception of the *LotR* films might be compared to the Anglo-North American reception of the rock band U2 twenty years earlier. Here is a voice from a relatively unfamiliar land, saying humanistic things in words we understand. If the subaltern must speak, surely this would be America's and the UK's favourite way—in clear tones that confirm the sentiments of the young and artistic. It may be that U2 and *LotR* fulfil a function not unlike a Bob Marley album or Salman Rushdie book on an otherwise Eurocentric shelf—a token gesture that assuages some small guilt, and complements (and compliments) taste. Perhaps it only harms the projects of other, more radical post-colonial authors, by setting a standard for them of whiteness and Englishness and Western sentimentalism that they can never echo.

Or perhaps this is, again, too harsh. Some post-colonial audiences may well understand New Zealand's relatively privileged status, but nonetheless see, in its unironic embrace by Hollywood, potential for similar representation and glorification for their own lands and peoples. Homi Bhabha rejects binarism in readings, preferring work that provides "articulation of antagonistic or contradictory elements." (Bhabha, 2004: 35) The film's promotion of hybridization and cultural heterogeneity, and the nuances of the rural Hobbits, combined with the New Zealand setting, go a considerable way toward his ideals.

The films are now part of cinema history, and New Zealand has moved to incorporate their reflection. Advertisements in magazines and on billboards name New Zealand as Middle-earth. And why not? "Middle" suggests liminal, a third way, something between two extremes. I believe most Kiwis are proud to be apart from the world's "superpowers" or even a distinct continent. "Middle" works for them, and so does "Middle-earth."

In the end, should they expect the world's less fortunate to agree, or even relate? On the one hand, Tolkien and Jackson's "Middle-earth" is not from a dispossessed culture, so why not let New Zealand claim it? On the other hand, New Zealand should not expect any particular valence with the Third World based on bearing the mantle of the *LotR* films. The films provide some comforting images, characters, and situations for the subaltern class, but also contain many objectionable elements. The fact that New Zealand can afford all these new advertisements, based on the fact that people want to see the locations of Jackson's films, means that this modern "Middle-earth" must be a site of capitalist advantage. That has to be a long way from the Shire.

Bibliography

Akers, Keith (2006), "Is *The Lord of the Rings* Christian?": http://www.compassionatespirit.com/LOTR-Christian.htm

Anderson, Benedict (1983), *Imagined Communities: Reflections on the Origin and Spread of Nationalism*, Verso, London

Anon (2006a), "The Ring Cycle" *Wikipedia*: http://en.wikipedia.org/wiki/Der_Ring_des_Nibelungen

Anon (2006b), TheOneRing.net website: http://www.theonering.net

Armes, Roy (1987), *Third World Film Making and the West*, The University of California Press, Berkeley

Ashcroft, Bill, Gareth Griffiths and Helen Triffin (eds) (1995), *The Post-Colonial Studies Reader*, Routledge, London

Bassham, Gregory and Eric Bronson (eds) (2003), *The Lord of the Rings and Philosophy: One Book to Rule Them All*, Open Court Publishing, Chicago

Benjamin, Walter (2006) [1936], "The Work of Art in the Age of Mechanical Reproduction", formatted by University of California: http://www.marxists.org/reference/subject/philosophy/works/ge/benjamin.htm

Bhabha, Homi (2004), *The Location of Culture*, Routledge, London

Cesaire, Aime (1972), *Discourse on Colonialism*, Monthly Review Press, New York

Colebatch, Hal (2003), *Return of the Heroes: The Lord of the Rings, Star Wars, Harry Potter, and Social Conflict*, Cybereditions Corporation: http://site.ebrary.com/lib/uon/Top?id=10041218&layout=document

Curry, Patrick (1997), *Defending Middle-earth: Tolkien: Myth and Modernity*, Harper Collins Publishers, London

Fanon, Frantz (1967), *Black Skin, White Masks*, Grove Press, New York

Giddings, Robert (ed.) (1983), *J.R.R. Tolkien: This Far Land*, Vision Press, London

Gramsci, Antonio (1971), "The Intellectuals" in Q. Hoare and G.N. Smith (eds and trans), *Selections from the Prison Notebooks*, International Publishers, New York, pp. 202-207

Haskell, Molly (1987), *From Reverence to Rape*, University of Chicago Press, Chicago

Hjort, Mette and Scott MacKenzie (eds) (2000), *Cinema and Nation*, Routledge, London

Ladaw, Dennis (2006), "Filmwatch: 'Return of the King'" *Manila Times* online: http://www.manilatimes.net/national/2003/dec/17/yehey/life/20031217lif8.html

Miller, Toby, Nitin Govil, John McMurria and Richard Maxwell (2001), *Global Hollywood*, BFI Publishing, London

Plimmer, Charlotte and Denis Plimmer (1968), "The Man Who Understands Hobbits" *The Daily Telegraph Magazine* No. 181, 22 March, p. 32

Ryan, J.S. (1969), *Tolkien*, University of New England Press, Armidale, Australia

Said, Edward (1991), *Orientalism*, Penguin Books, London

Shippey, Tom (2003), *The Road to Middle-earth: How J.R.R. Tolkien Created a New Mythology*, Houghton Mifflin Company, London

Spivak, Gayatri (1999), *A Critique of Post-Colonial Reason*, Harvard University Press, Cambridge, USA

Wilson, Rob and Wimal Dissanayake (eds) (1996), *Global/Local: Cultural Production and the Transnational Imaginary*, Duke University Press, Durham, NC

Yes, Gollum has been seen just about everywhere in New Zealand!
(photo by Bill J. Jerome)

SECTION II

Modernity, Ecology, Space and Environmentalism

8

ONE WALL AND NO ROOF MAKE A HOUSE
The Illusion of Space and Place in Peter Jackson's *The Lord of the Rings*

David Butler

IN 1982 IT became possible to wander in Middle-earth, talk to Gandalf and, if you'd had enough, ask Thorin to "kill Elrond with sword". The software publishers, Melbourne House, released *The Hobbit* into the fledgling home computer market: a pioneering text adventure game (with occasional graphics of selected locations!), which followed closely the action in Tolkien's book. One of the pleasures of the game, however, was to digress from the quest to retrieve the dwarves' treasure from the dragon Smaug and just go off wandering instead. The game's packaging and publicity emphasized the opportunity for the gamer to explore Middle-earth, to *be* in Tolkien's sub-creation and communicate with his characters ("... you will be able to roam freely throughout Middle Earth [sic], explore and discover this wonderful enchanted land," promised the game's inlay notes). For its time, the game was remarkably sophisticated in its ability to create the illusion of a wide and functioning world: it *seemed* that you could talk to whoever you wanted and go where you pleased, regardless of whether Bilbo had gone there in the book.[1] But if you wandered too far from Bilbo's footsteps you made a disturbing discovery. For example, travelling northeast from the Great River would elicit the following description:

---

[1] Characters were independent and it was not unheard of for the vicious Warg to stroll into Rivendell or the Dragon to follow one all the way back into Mirkwood—all of this independent roaming created a sense of a functioning world in which characters went about their business and had lives of their own.

> You go northeast. You are on the mountains.
> Visible exits are: southwest east southeast
> You see: nothing

Choosing southeast would take you to Mirkwood and the Forest River (southwest, of course, back the way you had come), but choose to go east—and you couldn't. Try as you might there was no way in. Instead, you received the message "the place is too full for you to enter." This was a shattering moment for the young gamer.[2] You could not "roam freely" in this Middle-earth. You could only roam as far as the programmers had chosen to go. This boundless alternate space was an illusion.

For many, the great achievement of Tolkien's mythopoeia is the vast, detailed and coherent world he constructed for his characters and readers to inhabit and explore. As Brian Rosebury has identified, the "quality of meticulously depicted expansiveness" in *The Lord of the Rings* encourages a sense of realism and acceptance of Middle-earth's marvellous properties. (Rosebury, 2003: 13) The diegetic depth of *LotR*—what Rosebury terms its "historico-geographical extension and density" (Rosebury, 2003: 15) (landscapes, histories, languages, cultures and folklore all covered in rich detail)—creates an effective illusion of space and a "believable" world that the reader can be immersed in. I would have to disagree here with Carl Freedman's assertion, in his excellent discussion of Darko Suvin's definition of science fiction as being centred on the dialectic between cognition and estrangement (with the cognition effect to the fore), that *LotR* does not produce a cognition effect. (Freedman, 2000: 17-18) As Freedman notes, hobbits and orcs may well estrange the reader through their "sharp break with known empirical reality" (Freedman, 2000: 17) but Tolkien's detailed accounts of the landscape (a landscape that is not "impossible" in its description of hills, marshes, woodlands and peaks) *can* be related back to our known world. Finding a correlative between, to use the most obvious example, the Shire and rural England is only one way to understand and make sense of Middle-earth.

---

[2] To be fair to the programmers, this mysterious impassable mountain range is in keeping with Tolkien's description in *The Hobbit*. The mountains in question are the Grey Mountains north of Mirkwood and Gandalf notes that the slopes are "simply stiff with goblins, hobgoblins and orcs of the worst description". (Tolkien, 1984: 127) So calling it "too full" is not inaccurate!

One Wall and No Roof Make a House 151

For Brian Rosebury, the level of diegetic detail in Tolkien's *LotR* takes it beyond a symbolic or allegorical relationship to our known world and bestows it instead a mimetic and spatial rigour more in keeping with the work of Tolstoy. As Rosebury outlines in his analysis of the Hobbits' arrival at the Prancing Pony in Bree:

> The Prancing Pony is no conceptual stopping-place on a Bunyanesque spiritual journey: there is far more detail here than could possibly be required for allegory. The reader's attention is drawn to spatial relationships (the lines of Road, dike and hedge, the topography of the inn and the sloping land, the turn to the left under the arch) [...] countless details of the episode at the Prancing Pony implicitly direct our attention to the rest of the huge world on which it is a tiny speck. If we are continually aware (as we are when visiting a real inn) of its geographical location, this is not simply a question of its appearing on a map in the end-papers. (Rosebury, 2003: 17)

In other words, the consistent and coherent detail of Tolkien's Middle-earth, its geography, history and cultures, operates as the means through which readers can overcome their estrangement and accept Tolkien's sub-creation. But this very strength of Tolkien's work has been, I suggest, the greatest challenge for filmmakers hoping to recreate the book's geographical and cultural intricacies on film. The resources and tools required to portray the expansive space of Middle-earth, without compromising or veering so far from Tolkien's detailed accounts that it might well be any generic fantasy world (stand up Boromir of the horned helmet and fur battle shorts in the animated film of *The Lord of the Rings*, 1978), have been beyond filmmakers until advances in computer generated imagery (and generous tax breaks offered by the New Zealand government) made Peter Jackson's sequence of films (2001-2003) a possibility.

The Jackson films are an extraordinary achievement—not least in terms of logistics and the marshalling of the thousands of individuals involved with the production. Sequences from Tolkien's novel are presented in stunning detail. The charge of the Rohirrim, for example, through the massed ranks of legions of Orcs and oncoming oliphaunts, but I want to consider instead how successful the films have been in generating the sense of coherent expansive space that is such an important feature of the book. To be sure, the scale of the Jackson films is astonishing. For example, John Boorman, one of the filmmakers who attempted to bring *LotR* to the screen in the 1970s (and invested considerable time and energy in the project), has acknowledged that Jackson's *The Fellowship of the Ring* (2001) is of "such scope and magnitude that it can only be compared to the building of the great Gothic cathedrals. My concept shrivels by comparison." (Boorman, 2003: 180) In this chapter, however, I want to suggest that the Jackson films have only been a *partial* success in maintaining the spatial illusion of a consistent and coherent geography for the spectator. While computer generated imagery (CGI) is often used sensitively in tandem with the New Zealand landscape to construct Middle-earth, numerous instances of Jackson's visual style risk disrupting the spectators' immersion in the on-screen world. The use of unmotivated camera shots, within the world of the film, serves to celebrate and fetishize the New Zealand landscape and the impressive technological achievements of Jackson's effects technicians at the expense of the films' illusion of space.

The Road to Jackson's Middle-earth: Tolkien and the Gaming Industry

I began the essay with a description of the early 1980s computer game *The Hobbit* not just for the sake of easy nostalgia but to introduce an important concept in the realization of alternative worlds on-screen: the sense that the world exists beyond the space of the immediate frame. The illusion that the artificial world presented to the spectator or gamer is not just confined to where the film/game directs them and what they can see immediately in front of them (in other words, if the spectator could somehow wrest control of the camera and pan left they would see a continuation of the diegetic landscape rather than green screens, car parks, film crew and the food van) is a time-consuming one to create but the rewards for the spectator are considerable. The writer Will Self has articulated the desire of the gamer to simply explore rather than be a slave to the prescribed task of slaying trolls and wolves or whatever. Discussing the PlayStation 2 game based on the film of *The Lion, the Witch and the Wardrobe* (2005), Self found his real interest in the game was in its detailed landscape and not the quest:

> Instead of focusing on the nature of good, they [the Pevensie children] all seem intent on kicking the shit out [of] anything they encounter. I find this particularly gnawing, because one thing does work for me, and that is the 3-D

world on-screen [...] How nice it would be—I muse as I frantically twiddle—to step aside and wander away down that avenue of pines, or across those snowy wastes. Who knows what might be around that rocky outcrop? (Self, 2006: 9)

This desire for exploration and the joy of discovery are recurring themes in Tolkien's work and there is a strong echo in Self's musing (about what lies beyond the parameters of the on-screen world) of Bilbo's wish (on the basis of the dwarves' song of distant lands) to "go and see the great mountains, and hear the pine-trees and waterfalls" (Tolkien, 1984: 15) or Frodo and his companions singing

> Still round the corner we may meet,
> A sudden tree or standing stone,
> That none have seen but we alone. (Tolkien, 1991: 90)

What Frodo, Bilbo and Will Self all express is not just the wanderlust to explore but also the act of imagining how the world continues beyond the known and available details presented to them.

It should be no surprise to discover the considerable influence of Tolkien's Middle-earth on the gaming industry (in its various manifestations). As a model of alternate world-building, Middle-earth was ripe for exploration and emulation by the computer and role-playing/battle games, which flourished throughout the 1980s. Numerous games were set either in Middle-earth itself[3] or took direct inspiration for their worlds from Tolkien. Among the most detailed of these alternate worlds was Games Workshop's Warhammer system, devised by Rick Priestley in 1983 and it was Priestley who would work on Games Workshop's *Lord of the Rings* battle game, officially licensed from the Jackson films in 2001. The official press release for the game, issued on 30 January 2001, noted the debt owed to Tolkien: "The opportunity to work on this game was one we couldn't ignore, especially as it was Tolkien's work, which, in part, inspired the fantasy wargaming hobby." (Anon, 2006b) Or, as the computer game producer and programmer, Ron Gilbert, has contemplated, "What would the games industry be like if Tolkien had been hit by a bus before writing those books? [...] If I was some wacko-conservative-anti-video-

---

[3] For example, Melbourne House's *The Hobbit* (1982), *The Lord of the Rings* (1986), *Shadows of Mordor* (1987) and *War in Middle Earth* (1989), or Iron Crown Enterprises' *MERP* (a Middle-earth role-playing game system first published in 1982 and discontinued in 1999).

game organization, I'd be building a machine to go back in time and take out Tolkien." (Gilbert, 2006)

Like role-playing and battle systems, computer games have also sought to create the sense of a world in which the gamer can be involved in an experience that is as detailed as possible. The promise of "immersion" has become an almost essential requirement of gaming PR—consider Electronic Arts' action-adventure game, *From Russia with Love* (2005) based on the original 1963 James Bond film, which entices the purchaser to "immerse yourself into an authentic recreation of the classic Bond world" and stresses elsewhere that the game is "a deeply immersive living world". (Anon, 2006a) The most significant of these "living" computer worlds has been, arguably, Cyan Worlds' *Myst* saga (1993-2005) (at the time of writing, sales of *Myst* have exceeded the twelve million mark). Again, like Warhammer, a rich backstory was developed (with novels based on the gameworld) but *Myst* (and its sequels *Riven*, 1997, etc.) heightens its immersive potential through rich sound design[4] and a narrative that is founded on real-time wandering (something that *Myst* shares with *LotR* and its emphasis, as Rosebury has argued, on the journey as much as the quest). (Rosebury, 2003: 31) Yet again, the influence of Tolkien's world-building is clear—as Rand Miller, co-creator of *Myst* with his brother Robyn, has confirmed when asked if Tolkien had been an inspiration:

> Absolutely. He [Tolkien] built massive worlds, and then created small windows to view them. The worlds were much larger than the books, and that was the key to their success. We're, as people, [...] used to complexity that goes beneath the surface. The reality of our world allows us to keep digging deeper and deeper. So when we build a story that allows for deeper digging, it feels real. (Miller, 2006)

In a 1951 letter, Tolkien wrote of how he had purposely left aspects of his "body of more or less connected legend" in sketch form so that they could be passed on to other tale-tellers: "The cycles should be linked to a majestic whole, and yet leave scope for other minds and hands, wielding paint and music and drama." (Tolkien, 1995: 144-145) If he had known what was to come, he could, perhaps, have added "pixels" as well. It seems fitting that developments in computer programming and

---

[4] As Geoffrey Rockwell notes, "no critique of *Riven* or *Myst* should ignore the use of audio to build the mysterious and lonely quality of their world." (Rockwell, 2002: 356)

imagery, spurred on by a gaming industry which owes so much to the inspiration of Tolkien's world-building, have been essential to the ability of the Jackson films to even consider approaching that "feels real" quality of Middle-earth. But as with the One Ring, the power to create through CGI can just as easily result in an excess that undermines and corrupts the reality effect being sought elsewhere in the films, and it is this tension that I want to consider next.

Creating the Illusion of Space

How successful have the Jackson films been in establishing this feeling of a "real" world and alternate space? And is the sense of a coherent geography essential to the films? I would suggest that it is—and not just out of a purist's desire to see Tolkien's world replicated faithfully on-screen. Viewed as big-budget action-adventure films, as opposed to an intricate exercise in alternate myth-making and world-building, the benefits of taking time to construct and portray the space of Middle-earth are considerable in terms of the films' dramatic effectiveness. The final sequences of Frodo and Sam's excruciating crawl across the plains of Gorgoroth and up Mount Doom, for example, *need* to have a convincing sense of space if the enormity of the task and Sam's heroism in carrying a ruined Frodo up the mountain are to have any chance of realizing their full dramatic and emotional potential for the audience. It's a concern not lost on the actors as Sean Astin (Sam) and Elijah Wood (Frodo) discuss in the cast commentary for the extended DVD edition of *The Return of the King*:

> EW: This is what I feel like we missed from the movie. It's just this *little* part of the journey—just to get you to where you need to be [...]
> SA: (commenting on a shot tilting up to reveal Mount Doom and Barad-dûr in the near distance from Frodo and Sam) Like that—look there—look at how far they must have had to go if they had to cross all that plain, wearing the heavy orc armour.
> EW: You see that's the thing and you don't really get that sense in the theatrical.
> SA: (later as Frodo stumbles to avoid the gaze of the eye of Sauron) It's still awkward to me—the topography—the "where are" y'know. I think in the earlier movies, when we leave the Shire—
> EW: You have more of a sense of where we actually are.

This understanding of the distances travelled in the film and the space between the various locations is crucial to much of the dramatic tension available to *LotR*. Will the Rohirrim arrive in time to save the besieged city of Minas Tirith? Can the Fellowship travel through the mountains and down the river Anduin without being seen by the spies of Mordor and Isengard? Can they reach the safety of Lothlórien before nightfall when the Orcs will pour out from Moria to pursue them? *LotR* is full of searching and hunting (e.g. the Fellowship are hunted by the Uruk-hai who are in turn pursued by Aragorn, Legolas and Gimli) and these sequences are in danger of losing much of their drama if an adequate sense of Middle-earth's spatio-temporal order is not established and sustained.

In this respect, the extended DVD versions of the three films have a far greater dramatic density than the theatrical releases. The characters and their relationships are enhanced (e.g. Gimli progresses from being a comic foil in the theatrical releases to a much more rounded character via the inclusion of his love for the Elven queen Galadriel, against the conditioning of generations of racial hatred), Middle-earth is fleshed out more thoroughly (Caras Galadhon "pops up" out of nowhere in the theatrical release but is given a proper establishing shot in the extended cut, thus generating a better understanding of where the Elves live and how the Fellowship arrived there, enabling the sequence to feel less like an isolated set-piece) and the overall result is, I consider, that the extended editions flow more effectively as films than their theatrical counterparts even though their running time is considerably longer (thirty, forty-five and fifty minutes respectively).

With more time given to portraying the characters, and the vastness of the space through which they travel, the more we are encouraged to care about their fates—and so the film moves further beyond being a glorified series of hack and slay vignettes. These added scenes *heighten* the impact of the action that occurs rather than dilute it. Throughout his DVD commentary on the extended cut of *FotR*, Peter Jackson constantly refers to the need to trim a scene to improve the pace of the movie, to wanting to "punch the film forward to its next act" but, without characters to care about, a series of punches is not necessarily the kindest way to treat your audience (an audio-visual pummelling does not need to take 178 minutes and, without the internal integrity of several of Tolkien's characters, the film flirts dangerously at times with generic sword and sorcery). As Denis Dutton observed in a damning review of the *LotR* films' dramatic merits:

> Take away the frenetic effects from this unremarkable action-adventure fantasy, and there is not enough on screen to keep even a subnormal human mind alive [...] Ignore Aristotle's advice, push spectacle to the top of the list, and you end up with such over-computerized, incoherent drivel as the recent versions of *The Hulk* or *Charlie's Angels*. (Dutton, 2006)

I would not go as far as Dutton in my critique of the theatrical releases but it is worth noting that all of the reinstated or extended scenes are given logical dramatic justifications by Jackson and his co-writers, Philippa Boyens and Fran Walsh, for their inclusion in terms of *enhancing* the film's storytelling (as Jackson notes on his *FotR* commentary, "you just trim these scenes out simply because you want to increase the pace not because they're not helpful to the movie"). In doing this, the extended cut draws a lesson from Akira Kurosawa and his 1954 epic adventure masterpiece *Seven Samurai*. For all its chaotic action and deafening battles, *Seven Samurai* still finds time for moments of quiet reflection and beauty (think of Katsushiro, lying back on a bank of flowers, gazing at the sun dappling the forest roof) that offset the violence and make the death of the samurai and villagers in the final battle all the more affecting.

If the extended editions offer a richer dramatic experience than their theatrical siblings, both versions of the Jackson films provide a portrayal of alternative expansive space far superior to anything on film before. Earlier attempts to portray epic fictional worlds on screen, such as *Excalibur* (dir. John Boorman, 1981) and *Dune* (dir. David Lynch, 1984), despite displaying great visual imagination, are severely limited in terms of the spaces they create and displaying the "connective tissue" of landscape between key locations.

Shot on location in and around the Wicklow hills in Ireland, *Excalibur* presents a Camelot that is never fully established as being the heart of a thriving kingdom—largely because the budget would not allow the film's director John Boorman to construct such a landscape (the film blossoms, ironically, in its sense of space during the excellent wasteland sequence of the Grail Quest where the camera is able to roam across barren moors without the need to include flourishing settlements). Camelot itself is usually seen in a fixed long-shot: a small model projected onto the camera lens via a mirror so that it appears to be nestling in the distant woods. It is an effective trick but it limits Boorman as to what he can do with Camelot—the camera has to remain locked in order to keep the image of the castle fixed in place, Boorman cannot track in closer to Camelot and establish the majesty of Arthur's castle (e.g. in a tracking shot following Lancelot as he returns to the kingdom on horseback) without ruining the illusion (as soon as the camera moves it leaves the reflected image of the castle behind). Camelot must remain a distant and barely discernible shape. There are similar problems with David Lynch's 1984 version of another epic imaginative work, Frank Herbert's *Dune*. As Elisabeth and Michael Liddell have demonstrated, for all the film's sumptuous design, Lynch's film does not create the necessary sense of diegetic space for the central desert planet of Dune (Arrakis), partly because it was filmed in a rubbish dump and Lynch was thus limited to tight angles and close shots: "There are no slow long shots in Lynch's film, and only the dust exists in his desert, and the odd mountainous dunes that have no other reference-point, no sweep of horizon behind and beyond them." (Liddell, 1992: 133)

By contrast, the *LotR* films are packed with reference-points which aid the spatial orientation of the spectator. There is no better comparison with Lancelot's approach to Camelot in *Excalibur* than Gandalf and Pippin's approach to the gloriously realized city of Minas Tirith in *RotK*. A combination of actual set, miniatures and digital imagery, Minas Tirith is a stunning illusion but what really convinces is its coherent occupation of space. The city is seen from a variety of angles and distances, always maintaining a consistent relationship with the surrounding geography. One of the finest shots of the city comes during Gandalf's interception of the Nazgûl as the remnants of Faramir's forces flee to Minas Tirith from the lost city of Osgiliath. The camera follows closely at speed behind Gandalf and Pippin, riding on Shadowfax, in a flowing arcing movement. As the camera arcs and tracks, the distant landscape continuously and smoothly comes into shot before settling on Minas Tirith, composited securely in the frame (even though the movement of the camera in its truck is somewhat erratic). As well as a thrilling rescue sequence, the spectator is given a clear understanding of the landscape, how far the retreat has to progress and how exposed the city is to the forces of Mordor.

The key to the Jackson films' superiority over these earlier films is the advancement in computer generated imagery. Throughout *RotK* there is an outstanding attention to geographical detail and spatial consistency, particularly during the scenes set in Gondor. The digitally composed malevolent skies over neighbouring Mordor are always present in the appropriate direction when the skyline is in shot, maintaining the presence of Mordor in the spectator's consciousness and thus the vulnerability of Minas Tirith as well (one of the best moments being when Frodo, Sam and Gollum approach the haunted city of Minas Morgul and a supernatural beacon erupts out of the Morgul tower into the sky—it is seen by the three travellers in close proximity but also in the distance as Gandalf and Pippin watch from the walls of Minas Tirith). It is an effective use of CGI—not just a moment of spectacle but a detailed piece of world-building that also serves a dramatic function.

The *spatial* fidelity to Tolkien's Middle-earth is exceptional and, across the three films, Jackson and his collaborators demonstrate a sensitive awareness of the need to emphasise this accuracy over *narrative* fidelity. As Mitsuhiro Yoshimoto has noted, the traditional focus in adaptation theory has been on fidelity criticism and the valorising of the original over the adaptation. (Yoshimoto, 2000: 258-261) It would be ridiculous to expect a film of *LotR* to be 100% faithful to the book and Jackson, Walsh and Boyens employ a range of adaptation strategies. It is useful to refer here to the work of the historian Robert Rosenstone and the set of approaches he identifies for the portrayal of historical events in film, as Tolkien's "alternate history" is so fulsomely documented (taking in the multi-volume history of Middle-earth edited by Christopher Tolkien, see Tolkien, 2003a-c). Rosenstone highlights omission, condensation, alteration, invention and anachronism as tools for the adapter of historical incident and all of these are employed by Jackson, Walsh and Boyens[5]. (Rosenstone, 1995: 134) But the careful construction in the films of a world

---

[5] To give one example from the films of each of these strategies: omission—the character of Tom Bombadil (superfluous to the plot); condensation—the Council of Elrond (again, too much backstory unnecessary to the progression of the essential plot); alteration—Frodo, not Gandalf, solves the riddle to open the Moria gates (foregrounding Frodo

faithful to Tolkien's (e.g. the presence on-screen of a geographical feature such as the island of Tol Brandir, even though it is not named in the film and simply travelled past in a landscape consistent with that described by Tolkien) acts as a buffer against any changes to the text, plot or action (e.g. Arwen, rather than Glorfindel, rescuing Frodo at the Ford of Bruinen): the films, with few exceptions, look like Middle-earth as described by Tolkien (and realized by two of his most prominent visual interpreters: the artists Alan Lee and John Howe who also worked on the art design of the films).

I want to focus on the boat journey down the great river Anduin past the Argonath in *FotR* as one of the best examples of sustained spatial coherency and diegetic fidelity in the films but which also demonstrates the stylistic excesses which act against a lasting "immersion effect". The huge statues of the Argonath are seen from the perspective of the Fellowship as they approach and then a remarkable shot swoops past the statues' heads in close-up (disturbing some birds nesting in one of the statue's eyes), then two reverse-shots after the Fellowship have sailed past into the lake beyond: one with the statues in the distance and a second with the statues in the extreme distance. In all shots, the statues and the surrounding landscape, including Tol Brandir and the falls of Rauros, are kept in consistent and correct proportion creating a strong sense of a coherent geography that has not just been manufactured for a single frame (as would be the case with older methods such as glass shots, requiring one camera to be fixed and the "expanded" world to be limited to a single shot).

But there are serious problems with the river sequence as well, not least the disruption of the otherwise impressive illusion of space through the use of unmotivated camera shots. Jackson's fondness for vertiginous camera movements creates many thrilling moments (Gandalf and the Balrog's plunge down the abyss in Moria, the charge of the Rohirrim through the legs of the stampeding oliphaunts, the Nazgûl soaring through the air on their fell beasts—all of which provide clear

---

whose character has been weakened through the omission of his defiance of the Nazgûl at the Ford of Bruinen); invention—the chief Uruk Lurtz (created to give the audience an identifiable corporeal villain—as Sauron isn't—who, in keeping with the classical narrative, can be killed at the end—cue audience cheer!—as he is an expendable invention) and anachronism—"Let's hunt some Orc!"

motivation for the camera movement) but the films contain many shots where the camera swoops and swirls impressively but without reason. There is a self-indulgent excess to these shots that damages the films' otherwise thoughtful visual world-building. Having gone to extraordinary lengths to construct Middle-earth, the films are less assured in the manner that the camera travels through and across it. There are too many examples to list here but a typical moment would be an early scene in the extended cut of *RotK* where the victors of the battle at Helm's Deep confront Saruman who is speaking to them from the top of the tower of Orthanc. The majority of this sequence is built, in classical fashion, through a variety of shots and reverse-shots of Gandalf, Théoden et al talking/looking up to Saruman and Saruman talking/looking down at his foes. Space is established well—we can see from Saruman's point-of-view shots how the tower stands in relation to the southernmost peaks of the Misty Mountains and the neighbouring forest of Fangorn. But in the midst of this "conversation" there is an odd shot that begins from high in the sky, looking straight down on the top of Orthanc, then floats down and around the tower in an impressive swirl before holding off, in mid-air, on a level with Saruman, now a tiny figure with the top of the tower and the mountains behind it dominating the frame. What does this shot achieve? It would seem to undercut Saruman—as the camera swirls past him he is trying to emphasize his authority over, and contempt for, Théoden while the end of the shot portrays him as a figure dwarfed by his surroundings—but a question remains: who is in control of the camera here? Whose eyes are we looking through? Are we somebody *in* Middle-earth—in other words, is the camera *immersed* in Middle-earth with the characters—or are we floating outside of it, an impossible outsider looking in? The nagging conclusion is that the shot's true function is to impress us with its virtuosity of movement, digital composition and the landscape beyond—it draws attention to itself rather than furthering the scene's drama.

These unmotivated shots create what Slavoj Žižek, discussing Hitchcock, calls an "impossible subjectivity" as the spectator realizes that "there is no possible subject within the space of diegetic reality who can occupy the point of view of this shot". (Žižek, 2001: 36) The principle of suture, in which the spectator is immersed in the world of the film, is broken and the camera draws attention to its presence through its virtuoso movements. The New Zealand landscape is covered lovingly in these instances but without any justification within the world of the film (i.e. no owner of the gaze is identified; the shot exists outside of and beyond the denizens of Middle-earth). There are moments where these shots work brilliantly *and* logically (the Nazgûl "bombing raids" on their fell beasts or the flock of crebain, winging their way back through the pits of Isengard to report to Saruman) but too many bring the presence of 21st century computer-assisted technology into the spectator's consciousness. As we watch and marvel, we are in danger of "seeing" Peter Jackson and his cameramen in a helicopter whizzing over the Misty Mountains instead of Gwaihir the Eagle Lord. There is a curious moment in the commentary of the extended version of *FotR* when Peter Jackson discusses the soaring shot past and beyond the Argonath, which disturbs some nesting birds. What causes the birds to abandon their nest? A passing eagle? Jackson's commentary provides a revealing answer: "(the birds were) frightened by the helicopter that's filming the shot". What is strange here is that the presence of a non-existent helicopter (the statues are miniatures and so a helicopter wasn't actually flying past them) is inscribed into the shot, through the activity of some computer generated birds which were not there in the first place—there is an attempt to *create* the existence of helicopters in this Middle-earth. Žižek suggests that the effect of Hitchcock's impossible subjectivity is to generate a "flavour of unspeakable, monstrous evil" (Žižek, 2001: 36) and it is apt, given Tolkien's concern about the perils of machines and industry used indiscriminately, that the nature of this evil in the Jackson films is the awareness of an impossible technology. Tolkien *does* provide occasional opportunities for a technologically-assisted gaze (the palantíri or the Seat of Seeing on Amon Hen, which allows Frodo to gaze across vast and impossible distances) and the films make the most of them but there is a lack of restraint elsewhere which is damaging to a sustained sense of immersion.

There is a marked contrast between Peter Jackson's approach to portraying epic landscapes and that of Akira Kurosawa in films such as *Dersu Uzala* (1975) set in the Siberian taiga, which is free from what Mitsuhiro Yoshimoto describes as

> moving aerial images of the Siberian forest shot from a helicopter. Instead of these commodified Kodacolour images, the film shows the forest and other

natural landscapes as they are actually experienced by Dersu, Arseniev, and other characters. (Yoshimoto, 2000: 346)

There is a wonderful moment in the film where Captain Arseniev stands on top of a mountain, gazing into the forest below. Tiny figures are barely visible walking along a path through a clearing. The camera zooms in on the figures as Arseniev spots and identifies them as his men, calling out to them—but, despite the partial zoom, they *still* remain small and indistinct! The landscape cannot be fully known by Arseniev/the camera. By contrast, the exposure of the landscape in the *LotR* films takes on at times a kind of National Geographic porn quality. Unlike Dersu and Arseniev, or Frodo and his friends, we as spectators do not discover this landscape *with* them—instead, these objective shots treat us as spectators to a privileged (and, yes, stunning) guided tour over Middle-earth the safari park rather than being *inside* the world of the film.

The potential illogicalities of these moments, in terms of the internal coherency of Middle-earth, have not been lost on the cast and crew of the films. Laura Crossley discusses the problems within the lighting of the beacons sequence elsewhere in this collection but it is interesting to note that the actual absurdity of this sequence, for all its ravishing beauty and undeniable emotional impact (yes, it is one of my favourite sequences too!), is discussed by three of the four commentaries (the cast, the design team and the writers/director) on the extended DVD. Each of these commentaries discuss the sheer impracticality of the beacons being positioned on top of the highest, most precarious and inhospitable peaks and undercut the moment of awe and majesty that the landscape, in tandem with Howard Shore's score, achieves so memorably.[6] There is a similar sacrifice of sense for sensation in the boat journey on the Anduin, just prior to the encounter with the Argonath, where a series of jarring overhead shots, swooping past the Fellowship's boats in conflicting directions and varying speeds, over vast expanses of forest and river valley, are only given a sense of continuity via the music score, which unites these otherwise disparate visual elements.

---

[6] It is worth noting that Barbara Strachey's maps in *Journeys of Frodo* place the beacons on the *flanks* of the White Mountains at heights of 2000-5000 feet rather than the peaks, which she estimates at 7000-11,000 feet. (Strachey, 1984: maps 42-43)

Are we aware of these moments? Umberto Eco, in a 1982 article on mise-en-scène in Italian film and television, suggests that

> the viewer of average intelligence [...] knows very well that [...] the meadow, even when real (usually located in the countryside around Rome or in Yugoslavia), is a meadow picked out, prepared, selected and hence *falsified* to some degree for the benefit of the shot. (Eco, 1995: 141)

Sequences such as those I have discussed may be less scrutinised when we are swept away by them in the cinema but on close scrutiny of the DVDs, which Peter Jackson clearly wants us to do, their incongruities become increasingly evident (why do Pippin and Gimli both speak with a Scottish accent if they come from completely different cultures and countries?). In his *FotR* DVD commentary (which was released before the theatrical releases of the subsequent films in the series), Jackson states that "the hope is that most people will get to look at this DVD ahead of the next film" in order to make sense of elements that are carried over into the theatrical release of *The Two Towers* but were not seen in the theatrical version of *FotR* (namely, the gifts given by Galadriel to the Fellowship). But who are "most people"? Who are the other people that the theatrical release of *TT* is being made for? Is there an underlying sense that the viewers who care will buy the extended DVDs anyway but nobody else will notice so it doesn't matter if elements in the theatrical release are inconsistent as long as the action flows thick and fast? In other words, there is an uneasy question about the integrity of the theatrical releases and their expected audience.

While writing this chapter I feel as if I have emphasized what I perceive as flaws in the Jackson films at the expense of their many and undeniable virtues. I do not take the view of Denis Dutton that "special effects are these films' raison d'être". The films, particularly in their extended forms, contain great moments of tenderness, quiet reflection and wisdom (Bilbo and Gandalf blowing smoke rings on the hill at Bag End comes to mind as one of the most charming) amid the spectacle and raging armies. But they are far from perfect in their realization of an alternative space. That might seem churlish of me but my main concern with the films is their stylistic *excess* not any *lack* of achievement. If we are convinced that Middle-earth is a location that the film crew actually visited, that a camera actually flew past giant statues overlooking a mighty river, then we are also reminded throughout these films that they are a construction and that there are helicopters just out of our view. This is not to allege that the films are inferior to the books. The self-indulgent flourishes of Jackson's camera can be thought of in the same way as the self-indulgent excesses of Tolkien's novel where, for example, swathes of the book are filled with poetry that does not progress the narrative, or characters speak in language that is not consistent with their background. As Tom Shippey has acknowledged, there are

> occasions where Tolkien himself seems to forget, or ignore, some of the very basic axioms of narrative [...]. Tolkien's narrative is on occasion unusually talkative, ready to bypass major dramatic scenes, and quite ready to leave the reader, or viewer, "up in the air". (Shippey, 2005: 413)

These traits of Tolkien's writing are not in keeping with the needs of a mainstream big budget action-adventure film (however careful and rich its attention to the cultures of Middle-earth, as conveyed through its detailed mise-en-scène) and the Jackson films are driven by a commercial imperative that Tolkien did not have to consider. It is not surprising, therefore, to find such differences of tone and approach when the aims and objectives of the films are inevitably different to those of the book. The films, like the book, have many other triumphant qualities. But as immersive experiences the Jackson films fall short of their full potential. In his study of the computer game as fictional form, Barry Atkins discusses the use of the gaming equivalent of Jackson's helicopter shots in the Second World War strategy wargame series, *Close Combat* (1996-2000). This point-of-view camera glides over the battlefield in such a fashion that calls into question the "realism" of the text:

> There is no equivalent of a [Gordon] Freeman or a Lara Croft, no "body" in which this point of view is housed. The all-seeing eye of the player floats at a fixed point above events, able to distinguish enough details so that he or she can discriminate between types of units and types of terrain, and so play the game effectively, but the player is always kept at a distance [...] this point of view reminds us of the artificiality of the vision we have access to, and acts to distance us from any possibility of mimesis. (Atkins, 2003: 95)

I would argue that the same awareness of artificiality is generated in the Jackson films through the type of shots I have discussed here. Jackson's marvellous array of *trompe l'oeil* acts against the mimetic rigour that Rosebury attributes to Tolkien's worldbuilding. In Tolkien, the discovery of the landscape is usually limited to what one of the Fellowship can actually see ("here and there through openings Frodo could catch sudden glimpses of rolling meads, and far beyond them hills in the sunset, and away on the edge of sight a dark line, where marched the southernmost ranks of the Misty Mountains", Tolkien, 1991: 400-401) and the reader discovers the landscape alongside them, as the spectator does the Siberian forest with Dersu and Arseniev. When Tolkien does offer the literary equivalent of a helicopter shot it is either, as I have noted, through the technologically-assisted vision of a sequence such as Frodo's gaze from Amon Hen or a character *within* Middle-earth describing the landscape that lies ahead[7] or the maps contained in the books: through each of these devices we remain *in* Middle-earth. The luxury of a character describing what the landscape does or will look like is not, of course, available as a regular strategy to Jackson and his colleagues in the films where there is a need to maintain narrative flow. The helicopter shot, then, is perhaps something of a necessary solution but, as I hope to have demonstrated, too often it is used injudiciously, to demonstrate technical virtuosity and the beauty of New Zealand rather than the experience of the Fellowship making their way through this extraordinary world. This solution, or (to be more accurate) the manner in which it is (over) used, is thus at odds with the "feeling of reality" that Jackson wanted and encouraged his design team to create.[8] The raised profile for New Zealand's landscape and outstanding creative talent is often achieved at the expense of a sustained illusion of alternative space.

---

[7] For example, Gandalf's account of the Fellowship's impending journey over the Misty Mountains: "... if we climb the pass that is called the Redhorn Gate, under the far side of Caradhras, we shall come down by the Dimrill Stair into the deep vale of the Dwarves. There lies Mirromere, and there the River Silverlode [...]. We must go down the Silverlode into the secret woods, and so to the Great River, and then—" (Tolkien, 1991: 300-301)

[8] See Peter Jackson's delightful account of the speech he gave to his design team at the outset of the project on the DVD feature "Designing Middle-earth" on Disc Three of the Special Extended Edition of *FotR*.

Bibliography

Anon (2006a), "From Russia with Love: Features": http://www.ea.com/official/bond/fromrussiawithlove/us/features.jsp

Anon (2006b), "Games Workshop Secures *Lord of the Rings* Licensing Deal" (media release) 30 January 2001: http://www.guildcompanion.com/scrolls/2001/feb/pressgwandlotrlicense.html

Atkins, Barry (2003), *More Than a Game: The Computer Game as Fictional Form*, Manchester University Press, Manchester

Boorman, John (2003), *Adventures of a Suburban Boy*, Faber and Faber, London

Eco, Umberto (1995), *Apocalypse Postponed*, Flamingo, London

Dutton, Denis (2006), "Dazzling, Sure—But to What Effect?": http://denisdutton.com/rings.htm

Freedman, Carl (2000), *Critical Theory and Science Fiction*, University Press of New England, London, Hanover

Gilbert, Ron (2006), "Tolkien" *Grumpy Gamer* 21 January 2005: http://grumpygamer.com/5274953

Liddell, Elisabeth and Michael (1992), "*Dune*: A Tale of Two Texts" in John Orr and Colin Nicholson (eds), *Cinema and Fiction: New Modes of Adapting, 1950-1990*, Edinburgh University Press, Edinburgh, pp. 122-139

Miller, Jennifer (2006), "Interview with Rand Miller" *Just Adventure*: http://www.justadventure.com/Interviews/UruRandMiller/UruRandMiller.shtm

Rockwell, Geoffrey (2002), "Gore Galore: Literary Theory and Computer Games" *Computers and the Humanities* 36 (3), pp. 345-358

Rosebury, Brian (2003), *Tolkien: A Cultural Phenomenon*, Palgrave Macmillan, Basingstoke

Rosenstone, Robert (1995), *Visions of the Past: The Challenge of Film to Our Idea of History*, Harvard University Press, Cambridge, Massachusetts

Self, Will (2006), "PsychoGeography №118: Space Invaders" *The Independent Magazine* 21 January, p. 9

Shippey, Tom (2005), *The Road to Middle-earth*, rev. ed., HarperCollins, London

Strachey, Barbara (1984), *Journeys of Frodo: An Atlas of J.R.R. Tolkien's* The Lord of the Rings, Unwin Paperbacks, London

Tolkien, Christopher (ed.) (2003a), *The Complete History of Middle-earth: Part I*, HarperCollins, London

Tolkien, Christopher (ed.) (2003b), *The Complete History of Middle-earth: Part II*, HarperCollins, London

Tolkien, Christopher (ed.) (2003c), *The Complete History of Middle-earth: Part III*, HarperCollins, London

Tolkien, J.R.R. (1984), *The Hobbit*, illustrated by Michael Hague, George Allen & Unwin, London

Tolkien, J.R.R. (1991), *The Lord of the Rings*, illustrated by Alan Lee, HarperCollins, London

Tolkien, J.R.R. (1995), *The Letters of J.R.R. Tolkien*, HarperCollins, London

Yoshimoto, Mitsuhiro (2000), *Kurosawa: Film Studies and Japanese Cinema*, Duke University Press, Durham

Žižek, Slavoj (2001), *The Fright of Real Tears: Krzysztof Kieślowski Between Theory and Post-Theory*, British Film Institute, London

9

DIGITAL PERFECTION OR, WILL MIDDLE-EARTH BE THE DEATH OF NEW ZEALAND?

Laura Crossley

I want us to imagine that we have been lucky enough to be able to go on location and shoot our movie where the real events happened. Those characters did exist and they wore costumes and I want the costumes to be totally accurate to what the real people wore. Hobbiton still exists, it's overgrown with weeds and it's been run down and neglected for the last three or four hundred years, but we're gonna go back in there and clean it up. We're the luckiest film crew in the world: we're able to shoot in the real locations that these real events actually took place in.

Peter Jackson[1]

WHEN DESCRIBING the speech delivered to the crew at the start of the design process of *The Lord of the Rings* trilogy, Peter Jackson stresses that the approach to the films should be that Middle-earth and the story that they, the filmmakers, are about to tell is real: that J.R.R Tolkien had, in fact, discovered a lost history and the crew are not so much building a set but excavating and restoring an actual historical site.[2] This approach has proved to be remarkably successful, both in terms of the meticulously detailed designs and constructions for *LotR*, and the audience reaction to the films' aesthetics. Middle-earth and New Zealand have become so synonymous that at a screening of *The Lion, the Witch and the Wardrobe* (dir. Andrew Adamson, 2005), the first instalment of *The Chronicles of Narnia*, which was also filmed on location in New Zealand, I half expected to see

---

[1] My own transcript from the documentary extra *The Appendices Part One: Designing Middle Earth*, in *The Lord of the Rings: Fellowship of the Ring* extended DVD edition (2002).

[2] *Designing Middle Earth.*

Aslan and company run into the occasional Elf or Hobbit. This intersecting of the diegetic and non-diegetic[3] worlds raises a number of related questions: how New Zealand itself is constituted as a character within *LotR*; and how landscape can be utilized as a site of cultural identity. The construction and presentation of New Zealand and the natural beauty of its landscapes as the "real" Middle-earth triggers questions about how the films' aesthetics illustrate the inherent concerns over industrialization and environmentalism in Tolkien's novels, and also engages with issues around the exploitation of this natural beauty as a marketing tool. Finally, the growing demand from filmmakers to use New Zealand for location filming and the increase in visitors to the country as a result of film induced tourism pose potential threats to the country's ecology.

The Authentic Middle-earth

> I didn't want movie design. I didn't want fantasy movie, Hollywood sort of style of design. I wanted something that felt authentic.
>
> Peter Jackson[4]

As a location for filming, New Zealand has a great deal to offer: apart from a wealth of natural scenery and the extensive conservation areas, it is also conveniently distant from Hollywood to allow the filmmaker a greater degree of independence and artistic control. The visual life of Middle-earth is rooted, not in generic, *faux*-Medieval Hollywood fantasy of the type apparent in *King Arthur* (dir. Antoine Fuqua, 2004), and *The Lion, the Witch and the Wardrobe*, but in a meticulous and intelligent design approach that, in its complete form, allows the spectator to differentiate between Elven, Dwarven or Human costumes, architecture and artefacts on the strength of their individual, fully realized design concepts. This authentication extends into every aspect of the mise-en-scène, including the use of landscape.

---

[3] Diegetic refers to the fictional world that is ocurring on-screen, i.e. the fictional reality as experienced by the characters. Hence diegetic sound, which is sound that occurs naturally on-screen, such as a character speaking or listening to the radio. Non-diegetic is something that is not produced from the on-screen world, a voice-over or added music, for example.

[4] *Designing Middle Earth*.

While all films require a suspension of disbelief on the part of the audience, the opening quotation in this chapter stresses that *LotR* requires not merely suspension, but an acceptance that we are seeing actual historical fact from actual historical sites. The construction of the landscape of Middle-earth as a real place is largely dependent on the visuals of New Zealand to authenticate it. The use of landscape to validate the realism of a story is not unfamiliar to film, as Rockett's study of Irish cinema explains:

> The inclusion of scenery was so important in establishing the realist credentials of these early Irish films that in some cases shots of well known beauty spots were inserted for their own sake, to authenticate, as it were, the setting for the main storyline. (Rockett and Hill, 1998: 223)

However, while the depiction of the Irish landscape in films such as *The Lad from Old Ireland* (dir. Sidney Olcott, 1910) or the more recent *Into the West* (dir. Mike Newell, 1992) serves to locate the narratives within the physical reality of Ireland itself, the *LotR* audiences are faced with a more complex set of dialectical relationships, simultaneously negotiating the acceptance of Middle-earth as a real spatial location with the knowledge that what we are seeing is the real New Zealand. In 2001 three government agencies, Tourism New Zealand, Trade New Zealand and Film New Zealand, converged in order to maximise the economic benefits generated by the films. This resolved in international marketing campaign, aided by production staff at New Line Cinema and the films' starring actors. The campaign emphasized the fact that *LotR* had been filmed in New Zealand by a New Zealand director. Tourism New Zealand estimated it had reached 200 million people world wide by 2003. Research undertaken by Tourism New Zealand in 2003 revealed that 86% of international visitors interviewed were aware, before they arrived, that New Zealand was the place where *LotR* was filmed. (Anon, 2006b)

The visual has played a significant role in culture throughout history. However, on the past decade, our globalized multimedia culture has become increasingly image-dominant. Cinema, television, and more recently the Internet and mobile phones, have displaced books and radio as the principal means of mass communication. It follows that film is the prime medium by which we represent ourselves. Since the earliest days of film the showcasing of indigenous landscapes to both local and international audiences has been a key component. Within the modernist vision of identity and subjectivity, enormous value is placed on judgment and cognition—on the visual and discursive over the tactile and figural. (Everett, 2000: 5) Our identity, therefore, is partly shaped by how we are represented quite literally through the vision or image we are shown. In *The Seeing Century*, Wendy Everett says,

> [T]he unprecedented degree to which the modern world has chosen to privilege sight, not only in conceiving of it as our primary access to ourselves and the world around us, but also in conflating sight with cognition, so that seeing and understanding have become synonymous in Western culture. (Everett, 2000: 5)

Images of the American West, as constructed in films such as *The Searchers* (dir. John Ford, 1956) and *The Big Country* (dir. William Wyler, 1958), assumed mythic, iconoclastic qualities, as the epically filmed landscapes became synonymous with myths of national identity. The spatial concerns in Middle-earth are far more complex: J.R.R. Tolkien's carefully crafted maps of Middle-earth, the genealogy of the Middle-earth languages, Tolkien's alleged translation of Bilbo and Frodo's *Red Book of Westmarch* all reinforce the illusion that *LotR*, *The Silmarillion* (1977) and all the attendant literature constitute a lost history of Europe, and of Britain specifically. Peter Jackson's films add another layer of complexity to the visual space of the film in that the trilogy was shot on location in New Zealand, so that discussions around colonialism, postcolonialism and cultural inheritance will inevitably develop.[5] The very act of creating Middle-earth in an existing landscape repeats the process of colonization: in the same way that colonial powers emptied a landscape of its original occupants and replaced their culture with their own settler history, so too does site-specific filming replace people and their histories with fictional inhabitants and stories. Yet New Zealand itself is still visible as a pentimento through the disfiguring layers of Middle-earth, in the same way that the Maori body—a constant reminder of New Zealand's colonial past—is present in the person of Lawrence Makoare upon whose physique the barbarism and animal savagery of the autochthonous Uruk-hai is constructed and encoded. In Tolkien's

---

[5] There is more to be discussed in relation to these issues, but as they fall outside the parameters of this essay I have merely alluded to them here.

novel the landscapes of the West Midlands, which inspired the Shire, are romanticized and mythologized. (Pearce 1999: 154) The manner in which the landscape is employed in Peter Jackson's films essentially mythologizes New Zealand before our eyes. The history of Middle-earth is told through the various volumes Tolkien devoted to his sub-creation: chronologically it begins with *The Silmarillion*, the creation myth, and ends with *LotR*, a myth of creating a national identity and building a unified Middle-earth. As with any postcolonial nation, the negotiation of cultural and national identity in New Zealand is strong. New Zealanders of both Maori and European descent have claims on the land, yet there is always the reminder that the Maori claim is a much older one and they are, in essence, a usurped people. While the all white heroes of *LotR* are presented as the rightful inhabitants and rulers of Middle-earth with the Uruk-hai as genetically mutated beings, deliberately bred for the sole purpose of destruction, this division of characters based on seeming ethnic differences unwittingly generates some disturbing allusions to New Zeraland's colonial history. Maori are neither autochthonous nor savage, but their displacement by white colonization and ongoing integration into contemporary New Zealand society is still a core issue of New Zealand identity. While the economic success of New Zealand's film and tourist industries has drawn international attention to the country, the successful negotiation of its colonial past and its embracing of its diverse cultural inheritance is a crucial aspect of how New Zealand will be perceived in a future more globalized society.

Mythic New Zealand

One of the most memorable and striking sequences in the final instalment, *The Return of the King*, is for me the lighting of the beacons between Gondor and Rohan. The camera tracks the progress of the mountaintop fires as they are lit, emphasising both the geographic distance between Gondor and Rohan and the temporal—the first beacon is lit during the day while the final one is only visible in Gondor the following morning. On an initial reading, the sequence is in keeping with the internal logic of the film, which is carefully constructed to reflect the scale of Middle-earth and the spatial relations of the different lands to each other. However, for the critical spectator the way in which this sequence is presented is problematic. Lasting one minute forty seconds—from when the camera begins to pan away from the first beacon to the moment Aragorn sees the flare—it is a prolonged sequence that affords the audience panoramic views of snow-capped mountains against an exquisite sunset merging into a starry night. From Gondor, we see the mountains and the fires kindling at regular intervals from an over the shoulder view of Gandalf. As the sequence unfolds, the camera pans across various mountaintops to give the audience an aerial view of proceedings. There is no character to whom this all-seeing gaze belongs, except that of the camera itself. The fires become dwarfed by the mountain range and the spectator could be forgiven for forgetting the purpose of this sequence and simply admiring the landscape. Ostensibly, we are being shown the splendour of Middle-earth: in reality Deer Park Heights, where the sequence was filmed, is showcased. For a New Zealand audience there is probably an undoubted pride at seeing these references of their own country. The cinematography and emotion-heightening musical score are designed to create spectator identification with Middle-earth and its inhabitants, but such grandeur is only possible through the authentic visual space of the landscape. We are obliged to admire not only Peter Jackson's mastery of film technique, but also the natural beauty of his homeland.

The multiplicity of spatial loci and the masquerade of New Zealand as Middle-earth may seem to reflect the *LotR* film experience as part of the self-reflexive, fragmentary postmodern condition. Negotiating the realities of New Zealand—for example, the necessity to respect Maori sacred lands such as Mount Ruapehu while simultaneously converting it into another fictional world—reflects New Zealand's ongoing project to present itself as a powerful modern figure on the world stage, while still engaging with its colonial history and Maori heritage. However, this negotiation of the real and the imaginary, of constructed myth, actual historicity and cultural identity falls within Marshall Berman's view of the great modernist project. His 1982 work, *All That Is Solid Melts into Air*, is a recognition that society will inevitably change, develop and move forward. The certainties of modern life, including the environments in which we live, whether urban or rural, are not necessarily certain; they will, eventually "melt", as space will inevitably be eroded by time. However, this negotiation of space and time is not approached from the Jamesonian view that formally links postmodernism with the spatial and modernism with the temporal—a view that reinforces these two fluid constructs as oppositional (Jameson, 1991; 1992)—but, rather, the low modernism espoused by Berman in relation to Heidegger's more complex view of space and time as intertwined and interchangeable concepts (Berman, 1982; Heidegger, 1992). New Zealand is its physical reality, the carefully packaged concept of itself as sold to locals and visitors, and the imaginary ideal of mythic history as conceived and presented in *LotR*. Yet, while the authentic, unspoilt New Zealand is an attractive proposition for those seeking the real Middle-earth *and* as a marketing strategy for the local tourist board, the image of both these reciprocal entities is mediated through the cinematic apparatus.

Digital Landscapes

Throughout the narrative trajectory of *LotR*, one of the dominant themes is that of unspoilt nature under threat from destructive, mechanized forces—a theme that is more apparent thanks to the dazzling visuals of Peter Jackson's films. Edoras, the Shire and even the Dwarven Mines of Moria are presented as places that are at one with, and sometimes even enhance, their idyllic surroundings. This is in sharp contrast with the bleak, dead lands around Mordor, and both these images merge through the sequences that map the destruction of Isengard and its eventual reclamation by the Ents.

Once the prologue in *The Fellowship of the Ring* is complete and the main body of the film proceeds, the audience is treated to a series of diverse landscapes: the greenery of Matamata in the North Island that represents Hobbiton to the russet glow of Kaitoke Regional Park, otherwise known as Rivendell. Our first view of Isengard is similarly idyllic: the establishing shot, as Gandalf rides towards it, shows a valley with the tower of Orthanc rising from an enclosure of trees. An aerial shot within, after Gandalf has passed through the entrance archway, reveals a tree-lined avenue and extensive greenery. Isengard may be the tamed edge of Fangorn Forest, but it is still, at this point, eco-friendly. As Saruman and Gandalf walk through the grounds at the base of the tower, the background of trees and the faint birdsong bring Isengard, visually and aurally, in line with the rural harmony already depicted in Hobbiton. The destruction of Isengard begins with the noctural felling of a tree similar to that which dominates the skyline above Bag End, thereby serving as a reminder of what Isengard used to be, and acting as a portent of the fate of Hobbiton and Middle-earth, should Sauron's power prevail. Once this first tree is felled, the camera provides another aerial shot of Isengard: the trees surrounding Orthanc are now punctuated by flames. The camera then cuts between the Orcs on the ground uprooting the trees, and another aerial shot from the top of the tower, gives the spectator a panoramic view of the unfolding destruction.

Another view of Isengard occurs in the following scene: once again at night, in the foreground the Orcs are standing guard on the outer wall with the tower visible behind it. The camera pans up and zooms in, giving us a high-angled shot of Isengard. We see a wasteland: the ground is scorched, bare and littered with the debris of rudimentary machinery. A tracking shot circles a fissure in the earth's surface where scaffolding and fire reveal evidence of mining and industrial development. This is confirmed in the next shot as the camera takes a vertiginous plunge off the top of Orthanc—where Gandalf is whispering to a moth, the only representative of the natural world to be found at Isengard—into a cavern below, the zoom ending on the red-hot blade of an Orc weapon. The trees that once stood around Orthanc are now being used as fuel for the mining and blacksmithing in the caverns. Once again the diegetic and non-diegetic worlds intersect on several levels.

Tolkien based the landscape of Hobbiton on the area around Sarehole, the hamlet on the outskirts of Birmingham where he first developed his love of trees and "loathing for those who destroyed them for no good reason". (Pearce, 1999: 4) The despoliation of the Shire (seen in Jackson's film only during Frodo's vision in Galadriel's Mirror) and Isengard was inspired by his deep reservations about the increase of heavy industry and its effect on the countryside during the late nineteenth and early twentieth centuries. (Pearce, 1999: 4) Tolkien's wariness about industrialization has been a point of contention for his critics, who believe he makes a "naïve equation of industry with evil, referring with disgust to the 'materialism of a Robot Age' and looking backwards to a medieval paradise". (Jackson, 1981: 155)

However, in the wake of two devastating world wars, it would be impossible *not* to dwell upon the threat posed by the *misuse* of industrialization. A preoccupation with the role of industrialization in the "war machine" was a dominant theme in the arts between the wars and after WWII. The Computer Generated Image (CGI) effects that depict the horrors of Saruman's mine and munitions factory recall the destruction and pollution wrought by industrial plants across the globe. The fantasy world, once again, highlights and engages with issues in the real world. These computer generated images also stand in sharp contrast to the natural landscapes of New Zealand. However, even though there are a significant number of protected national parks in both the North and South Islands, and the landscape is undeniably beautiful, these visuals of unspoilt nature are also digitally enhanced. At least 70% of *FotR* (and, one can assume, each subsequent film), not just the special effects, was processed by computer. Drama and landscape shots were also digitally graded to achieve the requisite look. As Peter Jackson explains:

> Even though the movie was shot on some amazing locations, I wanted to somehow just shift it, nudge it sideways from reality. New Zealand has got all of this amazing landscape, which we obviously used to maximum effect; but nonetheless it's still New Zealand, a real country, a real landscape.[6]

Hobbiton is one of the numerous settings that benefits from this process of digital grading; it is the expression of a rural idyll and therefore, as Peter Jackson explains, it needs to look like the "perfect picture postcard".[7] While Matamata is a beautiful and extremely green area of the North Island, the filmmakers desired a warmer look for the final print. By removing some green from the original negative and adding a magenta hue to eliminate the grey tones, and boosting the gold in the grass, the warm, verdant look of Hobbiton is more clearly defined in the finished graded print than it is in the non-graded image. Once again, a problematic is created between intent and presentation. Despite the fact that the original intent behind the digital grading was to convert the reality of New Zealand into the fairytale of Middle-earth, the fact that a real landscape is used to authenticate the fiction has the effect of encouraging the audience to believe that the visual fairytale is reality. The natural

---

[6] My own transcript from the documentary extra *The Appendices Part Two: Digital Grading*, in *The Lord of the Rings: Fellowship of the Ring* extended DVD edition (2002).

[7] *Digital Grading*.

beauty and the enhancements generated by cinematography and post-production combine so that the spectator may believe that the digital perfection presented on film is the reality. With tour guides offering holidays in the "real" Middle-earth, and Tourism New Zealand emphasizing the purity of the land and the links between it and the film, the perception of New Zealand as an unspoilt wilderness is rapidly becoming a profitable marketing tool. There is a possibility that the commercialization of the "Middle-earth Experience" in New Zealand and the exploitation of the tourist trade may, eventually, cause untold damage to the New Zealand ecology—the possibilities of which I address in the next section. The CGI enhancements that contribute to the image (within the films) of New Zealand as unspoilt may become increasingly necessary to "perfect" future projects if the land is damaged by developing industries.

Destination, Middle-earth

With fourteen National Parks and one third of the total land mass protected as parks and reserves, New Zealand's culture is strongly inclined towards conservation. The presentation of a clean, green image is important to New Zealand in the international arena. While Tourism New Zealand is keen to highlight the country's conservation programmes, the report of a survey of the New Zealand population in 2002 notes that 42% of respondents believe that the clean, green image of their country is a myth. (Hughey et al, 2002: 18) Of the studies that investigate the state of the New Zealand environment, the comprehensive 1997 publication on behalf of the Parliamentary Commissioner for the Environment, *Management of the Environmental Effects Associated with the Tourism Sector*, focuses on the impact that an influx of tourism could have on the urban and rural New Zealand habitat and ecology. The paper, which refers to international studies of the environmental impact of tourism, especially the North American model, links the intensity of tourism numbers and the level of damage. (Kearsley and Higham, 1997)

In 2002, the year following the release of *FotR*, international visitors to New Zealand totalled 2.04 million, an increase of 14.3% compared to 2000. The release of each subsequent film saw a rise in tourism figures and the DVD releases extended the synonymous marketing of New Zealand and Middle-earth across a four year period. The enormous economic impact of *LotR*'s success has comprised a vital part of New Zealand's ongoing tourism strategy outlined in *New Zealand Tourism Strategy 2010* and launched in 2001, which is committed to capitalizing on the 85% tourism growth during this decade, while also balancing the needs of the Maori population and environmental sustainability. Yet, as the *New Zealand Tourism Strategy 2010* itself notes, tourism growth is producing a demand for an upgraded and increased capacity infrastructure. (New Zealand Tourism Strategy Group, 2001) This is a problem—the economic imperatives to maintain a viable industry while still safeguarding the environment—faces many tourist destinations. However, as the 1997 study by Kearsley and Higham emphasises, increasing tourist numbers create a demand for facilities and amenities, the constructions of which inevitably impact upon the environment,

> Tourism cannot take place without the provision of services and facilities. This is confirmed by the fact that tourists must be transported and accommodated regardless of the environment in which their visitor experiences take place. However, the provision of facilities consumes space and may act to compromise the naturalness of the setting in question [...] Development of facilities for tourism takes place in any setting that tourists visit. These forms of impact, therefore, exist wherever tourism takes place. (Kearsley and Higham, 1997: 10-11)

While the conservation areas enjoy protection from development, rural areas are under pressure from numerous demands. Agricultural demand may require a change of conventional rural landscape, but demands by tourism can be both insistent and conflicting. Tourists expect amenities to be available wherever they go, yet visitors also expect, and are encouraged to do so, pristine rural areas. In some cases the demand for "authentic", unchanged landscapes may outweigh or at least defer the building of commercial projects.[8]

A press release on the media branch of Tourism New Zealand's extensive web site highlights the environmentally friendly filming that occurred during the production phases of *LotR*. New Line Cinema worked with environmental agencies

---

[8] The 1997 Kearsley and Higham study refers to the conflict over the hydro development of the Kawarau River in the 1980s, but postulates that landscape changes due to logging or new agricultural practices may be resisted in favour of retaining the more tourist-friendly pristine landscape. (Kearsley and Higham, 1997: 33)

to minimise the damage done by filming: of the more than 150 locations used during filming, thirty were Department of Conservation sites. Plants which were uprooted during filming, were temporarily housed in custom made nurseries and replanted when filming ended; in Queenstown, the location of one of the big set-piece battles in *The Return of the King*, red carpet was laid in order to protect plant life from the estimated 1100 people who were on set daily. (Anon, 2006a) However, despite the most assiduous and wholehearted preservation efforts, the volume of traffic through conservation areas will have an effect. Examples from across the globe are already in evidence, as Dr Martin Price's studies into the double-edged effects of tourism on mountain communities and environments notes: "Tourism can help to stem depopulation and increase incomes by bringing new sources of revenue, but it also tends to destabilize societies and environments." (Price 2006) Similarly, Kearsley and Higham's 1997 report details the disruption of wildlife and their habitat due to tourism, be it "track erosion and physical wear and tear" due to visitors walking rural tracks to visit areas of beauty, or the accumulation of litter and pollutants that encourage rats, ferrets and other predators, to the detriment of the local wildlife. (Kearsley and Higham, 1997: 21)

With tax breaks that make it more profitable to work in New Zealand than the United States and with a highly skilled domestic workforce, more filmmakers are opting to film there. With *The Chronicles of Narnia* franchise, there is an assurance of major feature films in production during the next decade. As film-induced tourism becomes increasingly popular, and based on the evidence since 2001, it can be assumed that the rise in New Zealand based productions will have a commensurate effect on the influx of international visitors. Of the 775 international visitors interviewed through Tourism New Zealand, two thirds stated that their visit was a direct result of having seen *LotR* and discovering that the trilogy was filmed on location in New Zealand. (Anon, 2006c)

Reclaiming the Land

When Isengard is attacked by the Ents (Tolkien's eco-warriors) it is a turning point in terms of both narrative and visual impact. It marks the first significant victory of the remaining Fellowship and their companions over the forces of evil, coming, as it does, immediately before the vanquishing of the Orcs at Helm's Deep. Even though the Ents, as depicted in Jackson's film, are computer generated and their triumph is over computer generated destruction, they and their narrative appear to embody some of the contradictions of modern life, that is the perceived oppositions of space and time and of nature and industry. At the dawn of the Age of Man, we witness their last march; their timeline draws to a close and their spatial locus is encroached upon. As the most ancient of Middle-earth's inhabitants, their last stand could be read as the reassertion of the temporal over the spatial. With their physical appearance as walking, breathing trees, the images in which they tear down the walls around Isengard and flood the compound in order to quench the fires in the mine are a visceral reminder that nature is, ultimately, more powerful than man-initiated industry (illustrated by the Asian Tsunami on Boxing Day 2004). As an audience we applaud this triumph of the natural world over the evils of Saruman's industrial manipulations. Yet we live in a world where the mastery of nature has formed the core of our modern development.

These are the paradoxes of life in the modern era and it is the struggle to engage with these dialectic concerns that form the modernist condition:

> To be modern is to live a life of paradox and contradiction. It is to be overpowered by the immense bureaucratic organizations that have the power to control and often to destroy all communities, values, loves; and yet be undeterred in our determination to face these forces, to fight to change their world and make it our own. It is to be both revolutionary and conservative: alive to new possibilities for experience and adventure, frightened by the nihilistic depths to which so many modern adventures lead, longing to create and hold onto something real even as it melts. (Berman, 1982: 14)

The negotiations of past and present, and of preservation while simultaneously embracing the future are, as Marshall Berman explains, the fabric of our modern existence. At present, New Zealand is conducting a balancing act between expanding its global presence and maintaining its natural assets. Even though government agencies and conservation groups are at pains to ensure that the ecology is sufficiently protected, past experience shows that increases in infrastructures and human presence pose a potential risk to natural environments. It would be a tragedy if the branding and packaging of the New Zealand experience, and exploitation of it as a commodity, should result in damaging the very things that make New Zealand unique in the first place. Berman says, "The deepest modern seriousness must express itself through irony." (Berman 1982: 14) It would be irony indeed if Tolkien's *LotR* resulted in the sort of commercialization and environmental damage that he warned against in the first place.

BIBLIOGRAPHY

Anon (2006a), "New Zealand Tourism Online: Environmentally Friendly Filming": http://www.newzealand.com/travel/media/story-angles/film_ecofilming_storyangle.cfm

Anon (2006b), "New Zealand Tourism Online: The Lord of the Rings Increases Profile for New Zealand": http://www.newzealand.com/travel/media/story-angles/film_increaseprofile_storyangle.cfm

Anon (2006c), "New Zealand Tourism Online: Visitors Drawn to Middle Earth": http://www.newzealand.com/travel/media/story-angles/film_visitorsdrawn_stroyangle.cfm

Berman, Marshall (1982), *All That Is Solid Melts into Air*, Verso, London

Everett, Wendy (2000), *The Seeing Century*, Rodopi, Amsterdam

Heidegger, M. (1992) [1924], *The Concept of Time*, trans. William McNeill, Blackwell, Oxford

Hughey, Kenneth F.D. et al (2002), "Public Perceptions of New Zealand's State of the Environment: How 'Clean' and How 'Green'?" paper presented at New Zealand Association of Economists Conference 26-28 June, Wellington

Jackson, Rosemary (1981), *Fantasy: The Literature of Subversion*, Routledge, London

Jameson, Frederic (1991), *Postmodernism, or, The Cultural Logic of Late Capitalism*, Verso, London

Jameson, Frederic (1992), *The Geopolitical Aesthetic*, B.F.I, London

Lash, Scott, and Jonathan Friedman (eds) (1991), *Modernity and Identity*, Blackwell, Oxford

Kearsley, Geoff and James Higham (1997), *Management of the Environmental Effects Associated with the Tourism Sector: Review of Literature on Environmental Effects*, Parliamentary Commissioner for the Environment, Wellington

New Zealand Tourism Strategy Group (2001), *New Zealand Tourism Strategy 2010*: http://www.tourism.govt.nz/strategy/str-reports-2010/str-rep-2010full.pdf

Pearce, Joseph (1999), *Tolkien: Man and Myth*, HarperCollins, London

Price, Martin (2006) [2001], "Taming the Tourists": http://www.peopleandplanet.net/doc.php?id=967&section=11

Rockett, K., L. Gibbons, and J. Hill (1998), *Cinema and Ireland*, Routledge, London

Tolkien, J.R.R. (1954a), *The Lord of the Rings: The Fellowship of the Ring*, Allen and Unwin, London

Tolkien, J.R.R. (1954b), *The Lord of the Rings: The Two Towers*, Allen and Unwin, London

Tolkien, J.R.R. (1955), *The Lord of the Rings: The Return of the King*, Allen and Unwin, London

Tolkien, J.R.R. (1977), *The Silmarillion*, Allen and Unwin, London

Is it before or after? Power lines installed (or not yet been digitally eliminated) over Anduin River, Middle-earth.
(photo by Nataliya Oryshchuk)

10

BLOCKBUSTER PASTORAL
An Ecocritical Reading of Peter Jackson's *The Lord of the Rings* Films

Thomas Murray Wilson

PETER JACKSON'S *The Lord of the Rings* film trilogy had made US$2.9 billion for New Line Cinema by August 2004. (figure from Anon, 2005) In this chapter I want to answer the question: Why have these films been so popular? This discussion of the films, however, is a pretext to examine a much wider question, the place the trope of pastoral has assumed in the popular culture of the contemporary West. Before I examine Jackson's films I will look at the origin of the arts. An evolutionary account of the arts demonstrating the relevance of the way nature is represented on film for contemporary environmentalism culminates in a green critique of the audience reception of *LotR*.

The Art of Environmentalism

The human prefrontal cortex has undergone rapid expansion over the past two million years. However according to anthropologist Robin Fox, the myths that we live with today as highly intelligent modern humans draw on "phyletically old material in the limbic system—dreams, memory, and emotion". (Fox, 1994: 309) As creatures who possess self-consciousness and language, myths give us an evolutionary advantage in making sense of the world inside our heads, the result of both "dreams, memory, and emotion", and a highly sophisticated neocortex. Thus it should not surprise us that "myths are a more powerful and satisfying way of apprehending the world than is logic", and that they persist in the lives of all of us, acknowledged or unacknowledged. (Fox, 1994: 309) I believe that the same applies to enduringly popular patterns of narrative. Such sequences of narrative literature echo cognitive models that resonate well with our evolved limbic and cerebral systems.

This is the view of Edward O. Wilson. Prehuman populations were once, like other animals, simply guided by environmental cues which triggered behaviour patterns. Like other animals they fitted their particular niche in the environment and eco-system very well and did not concern themselves with anything beyond their adaptation to this niche. However with the escalation in intelligence that coincided with the advent of *Homo sapiens*, we formed a more flexible set of responses to our environment and an ability to imagine future states, such as our own deaths. With our high level of generalized intelligence, language and culture we humans were given an edge over other species in the struggle for existence. This was to our benefit; however, as Wilson rightly points out, these acquisitions: "also exacted a price we continue to pay, composed of the shocking recognition of the self, of the finiteness of personal existence, and of the chaos of the environment." (Wilson, 1999: 245) For Wilson the product of this escalation of general intelligence, over and beyond the immediate gains it conferred in terms of survival and reproductive success, is art, the imposing of order on the confusion caused by our extremely high level of intelligence.

The work of arts ethologist Ellen Dissanayake, has added further credence and detail to Wilson's view. Dissanayake views elaborating (her term for participating in the arts) as a fundamental element of human behaviour. She argues that elaborations, such as paintings, songs, chants, poems or plays, provide humans with pleasurable feelings of mastery and control in the face of chaos and uncertainty, and serve to highlight and draw attention to significant themes in human society, as well as facilitate social cohesion. She argues that the formalization inherent in most arts has its precursors in the emotion-suffused, rhythmic-modal interactions between mother and infant. Her work plausibly advances the view that the arts are as essential to human well-being as are warmth, food and shelter. (Dissanayake, 2000: 203)

In 2003, Klaus Toepfer, Executive Director of the United Nations Environment Program called on marketers and advertisers to promote sustainable products "cool" and trendy. (Toepfer, 2003) He was wise to do so. According to Dissanayake, the ceremonies on which modern Western societies lavish extraordinary communal effort are advertisements and the products they enhance. However, while in traditional societies ceremonies were the means by which perennial human concerns were articulated (such as caring for the body, finding love and sharing a worldview), today our secular market-driven society uses the arts (vivid, attention-grabbing images and narratives) to promote and promise youth, sexiness and power. (Dissanayake, 2000: 202) In the words of Dissanayake, "the goods and services elaborated by the modern media are more important to the health, fecundity, and survival of the international market-place than that to that of human individuals and populations." (Dissanayake, 2000: 203) Considering the way in which narratives, images and poetic language use all influence human attention more effectively than rational argument and pure intellectual analysis, we would be wise to champion art works in any genre or context which celebrate the natural world, in promoting a culture of sustainability.

In a widely discussed conference paper on climate change politics, Michael Shellenberger and Ted Nordhaus called on environmentalists and left-politicians in general to focus more on articulating inspiring visions and connecting with basic values: "Environmentalists need to tap into the creative worlds of myth-making, even religion, not to better sell narrow and technical policy proposals but rather to figure out who we are and who we need to be." (Shellenberger & Nordhaus, 2004) Neil Evernden has extended a concordant view. Environmentalism must involve values, and in Evernden's words, "values are the coin of the arts. Environmentalism without aesthetics is merely regional planning." (quoted in Love, 2003: 28)

Ecocriticism is an emerging field in academia which examines the relationship between culture and the environment. I write ecocriticism because I believe that the planetary ecocrisis largely precipitated by the over-consumption of members of market-driven and technocratic Western nation-states will not be remedied purely by resource management and political decision-making. In a biodiversity crisis, such as the one we are now experiencing, drawing attention to hitherto under-appreciated and highly sensitive attitudes, images and narratives concerning nature as they are expressed in language or on film is, well worth doing.

Ecocritism on Pastoral Narratives as a Popular Genre

Returning to my original question: Why were the *LotR* films so popular in the twenty-first century market?

A recent international audience study conducted by Martin Barker, Ernest Mathijs and Janet Jones, collected nearly 25,000 responses to a questionnaire which asked, among other things, "What kind of story is *The Lord of the Rings* for you?" The most frequent response (19.2%) was "Epic", followed by "Good vs evil" (15.8%), and "Fantasy" (14.5%) a close third. (Barker and Mathijs, 2008 forthcoming) "Pastoral" was not listed as a potential response. However, it is unlikely that many viewers would be familiar with this term due to its contemporary association with literary-critical discourse. It is my contention that the representation of the natural world in film, rarely absent throughout the narrative, figured largely in the trilogy's ability to draw audiences. That most respondents to the said questionnaire interpreted the films as "epic" in no way precludes such a judgment.

More people are becoming city-dwellers. The United Nations predicts that by 2050 there will be more people living in cities than presently live on the entire earth. (Tudge, 2003: 46-47) With ever fewer people living in close proximity to the land, the time is ripe for the writing and filming of pastoral. In defining pastoral I use Peter Marinelli's definition: pastoral as narrative "which deals with the complexities of human life against a background of simplicity" that simplicity usually being a country landscape. (Marinelli, 1971: 3) Thus my definition refers to a general area of content rather than a specific literary form.

Shepherds do not usually write pastorals. As Marinelli notes, pastoral is "a genre which arises only when an original beauty has been lost". (Marinelli, 1971: 17) One might argue that this is what occurred in nineteenth-century England. During the 1800s the Industrial Revolution saw the nation's demography changed dramatically, from the beginning of the century when most people lived off the land, to the century's end where the majority of the population were denizens of the city. And yet, as W. J. Keith writes, "the nineteenth century, which saw the decline of the English countryside, is also the great age of nature writing." (Keith, 1975: 10) The suburban Victorian reading public voraciously consumed the works of writers such as Richard Jefferies, and even contributed to the emergent popularity of earlier rural writers such as Izaak Walton and Gilbert White. (Keith, 1975: 10)

According to Ellen Dissanayake "only the most 'civilized' or artificial groups and societies glorify nature, as did the members of the French nobility in the eighteenth century, who dressed rustically as shepherds and milkmaids." (Dissanayake, 1992: 136) In most traditional cultures, Dissanayake continues, "shiny, new-looking, bright and conspicuously artificial things" are valued more than natural things. In Sri Lanka, for example, new sarongs are often stitched by village women so that manufacturing marks will show. We in the affluent West, on the other hand, prefer worn and faded when it adds to an item looking natural and authentic. (Dissanayake, 1992: 137)

With regard to recent literary works, the English ecocritic Terry Gifford updates this notion by speculating that the novel *Cold Mountain* sold so well in London, New York and Sydney because it was a pastoral, and pastorals speak to us as we endure increasingly urban patterns of habitation at this time in history. (Gifford, 2001: 89) Modern Westerners live in a virtual disinhabitory coma, busily efficient among the angled surfaces and concrete walls of our built-environments, yet the urge to regain the natural frequently appears in our cultural creations.

But I am assuming that humans love nature. Edward O. Wilson coined the term "biophilia", a term he used to characterise our "innate tendency to focus on life and lifelike forms, and in some instances to affiliate with them emotionally". (Wilson, 2002: 134) To give just two of the examples Wilson cites as evidence for his hypothesis that part of the physically based component of human nature includes a "biophilic instinct", a large portion of society gardens, fishes, backpacks, and bird-watches for leisure; in the United States and Canada alone more people visit zoos and aquariums than attend all professional sporting events combined. (Wilson, 1992: 350) The "biophilia hypothesis" posits a theory of prepared learning for human habitat selection. It suggests that humans have an innate tendency to enjoy being in environments which mimic their ancestral home (large park-like grasslands dotted by groves and scattered trees, the terrain of the African savannah). Wilson also argues that people prefer entities that are growing, and sufficiently unpredictable to be interesting. (Wilson, 1984: 115) This led him to the following conclusion:

> People can grow up with the outward appearance of normality in an environment largely stripped of plants and animals, in the same way that passable looking monkeys can be raised in laboratory cages and cattle fattened in feeding bins. Asked if they were happy, these people would probably say yes. Yet something vitally important would be missing, not merely the knowledge and pleasure that can be imagined and might have been, but a wide array of experiences that the human brain is peculiarly equipped to receive. (Wilson, 1984: 118)

According to Wilson, in a predominantly urban or suburban world that has become blind to the value of wild, green life, the human mind will not be activated to its full, evolved capacity. With potted plants and household pets, or trees in the suburbs, substituting for our ancestral home—an often mysterious and more-than-human, wild biota—we will inevitably receive a diminished experience of daily life.

Peter Jackson's *LotR* as Blockbuster Pastoral

From this evolutionary and species-centric perspective it is to be expected that pastoral should increasingly become a popular genre. Glen Love, the ecocritic who has done the most to bring science into dialogue with the pastoral tradition, has remarked that the continuing appeal of pastoral over recent millennia of human history is attributable to the biophilic instinct. (Love, 2003: 72-83) In saying this, however, Love fails to register that pastorals are not traditionally written by country folk. An alert attentiveness and emotional responsiveness to the natural world has always been an epigenetic rule of human nature, but an increase in the production and reception of pastoral narratives in imaginative literature or film at the present juncture in human history would, from an ecocritical perspective, signal a unique discontent with the life-world provided by modern Western societies. I am here adducing the popularity of Peter Jackson's trilogy and stress that this popularity is, to some extent, a sign that the entombed in concrete human animal is trying to right itself.

We can do more than evince the image of the Ents shepherding their trees to give relevance to Lawrence Buell's ideal of giving the biota more than a bit part in each of the films. (Buell, 1995: 22) Many of the scenes from Jackson's film trilogy are traditional pastoral, principally the grassy, rural idyll of the Shire. The films' narratives are, unlike most blockbuster films, about being in, or moving through, natural places. The audience hears, not siren and engine, but hoof-fall and bird-call. In beautifully photographed detail we become acquainted with bowers, crags, villages, rivers, streams, hills and valleys. Tolkien's descriptions of the natural world are both poetic and grittily realistic. Jackson retains this aspect of the novels by using few computer generated graphics, and letting the wilds of New Zealand speak for themselves. Whether the Fellowship is galloping across the foothills of the Southern Alps under a cold sky to the sound of Howard Shore's equally rarified score, or trudging through Fangorn Forest, where glimpses of rustling woodland environments present beguiling suggestions of greater and more complex wholes, a sense of the mystery and sanctity of natural creation is imparted to the attentive viewer.

In the words of film theorist Noel Carroll,

> Insofar as movies are constituted of a mode of representation connected to biological features of the human organism [visual recognition of objects and events], they will generally be more accessible than genres in other media, such as the novel, that presupposes a mastery of learned conventions, such as specific natural languages. (Carroll, 1988: 143)

Film is even more compelling as narrative (if less reflective than verbal story) because it employs immediate and spectacular visuals, and music that can rapidly mobilize the emotions.

To summarize, I argue that the natural world is deeply appealing to modern humans, especially at a time where the world population is becoming predominantly urban. I also argue that narrative literature appeals to humans because of their evolved neuro-physiology, and film narratives even more appealing on some levels because of their ability to readily elicit emotion using music and visuals. The recent *LotR* films depict a group of companions inhabiting and encountering a series of strange, mysterious and beautiful natural places. One of the main reasons these films have made so much money and are so popular is that they deploy pastoral, narrative patterns which celebrate the natural and wilderness space. I am sure that there are other reasons for the trilogy's popularity, such as the appeal of plausible and compelling representations, community, kinship, love and dignity in an age of urban alienation, social fragmentation and a confusion of identity. However I maintain that the representation of a sometimes majestic, sometimes comforting, wild biota is central to the films' attraction.

Certainly Jackson's films offer plenty of human drama, including war, valour, love, jealousy, but all is situated amongst the rough-hewn textures of nature. The audience is absorbed by the quest to destroy the ring and triumph over Mordor, and yet this anthropocentric narrative drive is contextualized by trunks, shadows, rough-knit garments, unrefined victuals, sweaty saddles, shining waters and cloud-tossed skies. Contra to the illusory human/nature divide foisted upon us by an urban twenty-first century, the dirt-smudged faces of Sam and Frodo are envisaged as a link on a continuum of biology and terrain. Aragorn's brown locks fall along side the brown mane of his horse, and close-up shots of the future king's face are enframed by a granite boulder. Sam carries some salt from home, to connect him with his homeland. The film trilogy does not only use symbols from the natural world as substitutes for human attributes or ideals (although it often does this), but also venerates the natural world in and of itself. The scene where Shadowfax runs to Gandalf the White glories in the brilliant physicality of the horse in a way which exceeds the horse's significance in the overall plot.

In *The Two Towers*, when Merry and Pippin abandon hope of the Ents' arrival to tip the balance in the battle against Saruman and Sauron, Merry sinks into despondency. He sees a dark future and says: "All that was once green and good in this world will be gone." The normative ethical benchmark of Middle-earth thus links green intrinsically with the good. When Gollum goes deep into the mountainside he forgets the sounds of wind and the softness of trees and he leaves behind the health-giving goodness of a natural ecosystem. As the characters travel further into Mordor there is less green and more rock and fire. At a late stage in *The Return of the King* the struggle against Sauron and his forces appears desperate. When Frodo and Sam see a huge stone statue of the King of Gondor on their journey towards Mordor, the statue is headless. Then, the camera pans to the right and we see the statue's head on the ground crowned by a wreath of white flowers, which are momentarily spot-lit by a ray of sunlight. In this moment, growing plants provide a redemptive epiphany amidst the atmosphere of darkness and fear. In

Jackson's trilogy the characters are not only encompassed by nature, but also enobled by its presence.

To Problematize Blockbuster Pastoral such as *LotR*

I seem to be saying that the filming of the recent *LotR* trilogy in New Zealand and its subsequent popularity at the box office was good in that it catered to deeply held, evolved capacities and needs in the mind and emotional repertoire of *Homo sapiens* at a time when that species is removing itself ever further from its ancestral cradle.

Is this the end of the story? No.

In his essay "The Trouble with Wilderness" William Cronon asserted that "wilderness represents a flight from history". (Cronon, 1996: 79) However, if we think of history as the history of our species, wilderness is our home, and paying homage to it can indeed take the form of a "flight *to* history". If the 2.2 million-year history of the genus *Homo* was compressed into seventy years, a human life span, humanity occupied its ancestral environment and practiced a hunter-gatherer lifestyle for sixty-nine years and eight months, whereupon some of us took to farming and moved into villages for the last 120 days. (Wilson, 2002: 136) When charged with the accusation that he wanted to go backwards, the American poet of ecology Gary Snyder was right to remark that "[i]t's only a temporary disturbance I'm setting myself against. I'm in line with the big flow." (Snyder, 1999: 106)

Where Cronon's essay is useful, however, is in its highlighting of the fact that odes to the glories of wilderness can in some instances risk becoming abnegations of our responsibility to confront environmental problems outside the wilderness space. As Cronon writes: "By imagining that our true home is in the wilderness, we forgive ourselves the homes we actually inhabit," homes that usually contain such weapons of mass consumption as cars. (Cronon, 1996: 81) In answer to Cronon I think we should be encouraging more of the post-pastoral genre championed by Terry Gifford: visions of accommodated man that celebrate nature while retaining an admirably sober realism about how we treat it. Traditionally, pastorals, such as Shakespeare's *As You Like It*, celebrated nature as a benign realm of sunny indolence, while the counter-force of the anti-pastoral, a well known example being Stella Gibson's novel *Cold Comfort Farm*, debunked this picture with satirical cynicism.

Gifford's post-pastoral is a poetry or pattern of narrative which escapes this closed circuit of pastoral and reactive anti-pastoral, and "take[s] responsibility for our problematic responsibility with our natural homeground, from slugs to our solar system, from genes to galaxies, or as Marvell puts it, all that can be encompassed by 'a green Thought in a green Shade'."(Gifford, 2002: 57) While the divine beauty of the living creation will lie under the protectorate of this green Shade, so too will representations of the effects of global warming and an associated consciousness of the environmental impacts of over-consumption in the contemporary West.

Are we moviegoers receiving blockbuster post-pastorals? At this point one might argue that the trilogy's narrative opposition to Saruman's industrialism and clear-felling of Fangorn forest moves the films towards a post-pastoral aesthetic. I leave this line of thought for others to pursue. I maintain that the veil of fantasy places is, to a significant extent, a domesticating muzzle on the narrative's anti-industrial critique. It is far from obvious that the splendidly wicked Saruman, enacted by Christopher Lee, with a "mind of metal", could in some respects be the suburban everyman next-door who owns shares in ExxonMobil and loves his 4WD. We movie goers are, I more pessimistically suggest, not getting blockbuster post-pastorals; we are getting films such as *LotR*, or *The Last Samurai* (dir. Edward Zwick, 2003), another big-screen pastoral recently filmed in New Zealand. So one must understand that Cronon's critique is in this context immensely salient. There is a split-personality at large in Western society at the start of the twenty-first century. Tens of millions of Westerners act and vote in an environmentally irresponsible manner and then live with the cognitive dissonance required to vicariously partake in the celebration of the wilderness space depicted in Jackson's films. I dare not do more than mention the way the advertising industry has scandalously hijacked the staging of pastoral (consider blithe magazine images of Ford Explorers vanquishing tropical rivers and alpine tundra).

The causes of the currently slow progress towards a culture of environmental sustainability are many and over-lapping. Jared Diamond, in his recent book *Collapse*, effectively explained why in the West we are, as a society, choosing to fail, and may be heading towards self-induced collapse. However there is room for hope—even Diamond dubs himself a "cautious optimist". (Diamond, 2005: 521) The corollary of my preceding argument is that we ecocritics should encourage any cultural creations which constitute revelations of dwelling with the earth from an environmental *praxis* perspective.[1] If we desire a new, greener Jerusalem we should be championing the narrative genre of the post-pastoral. Jackson's film trilogy is a major expression of biophlia by a human species increasingly divorced from the wild biotas it evolved in concert with. Regardless of whether we conclude that the representation of the mountains, plains, forests and skies of Middle-earth in the recently filmed *LotR* trilogy constitute a post-pastoral aesthetic, the irony bites deep when we realize that this biophilic creation is abetted by a culture of market-driven and largely unreflective consumerism. Hopefully others will prove me wrong, but my observations lead me to believe that viewers consume Middle-earth. And mostly they do so between courses. The main dish is our earth.

Bibliography

Anon (2005), http://film.guardian.co.uk/new/story/0,12489,1286421,00.html

Barker, Martin and Ernest Mathijs (eds) (2008 forthcoming), *Watching The Lord of the Rings: Tolkien's World Audiences*, Peter Lang, New York

Bate, Jonathan (2002), *The Song of the Earth*, Harvard University Press, Cambridge

Buell, Lawrence (1995), *The Environmental Imagination: Thoreau, Nature Writing, and the Formation of American Culture*, Harvard University Press, Cambridge, Mass.

Carroll, Noel (1988), *Mystifying Movies: Fads and Fallacies in Contemporary Film Theory*, Columbia University Press, New York

Cronon, William (1996), "The Trouble with Wilderness; or, Getting Back to the Wrong Nature" in William Cronon (ed.), *Uncommon Ground. Rethinking the Human Place in Nature*, W.W. Norton, New York, pp. 69-90

Diamond, Jared (2005), *Collapse: How Societies Choose to Fail or Survive*, Penguin, London

Dissanayake, Ellen (1992), *Homo Aestheticus: Where Art Comes From and Why*, Macmillan, New York

---

[1] The English ecocritic Jonathan Bate has been doing just this in *The Song of the Earth* (see Bate, 2002).

Dissanayake, Ellen (2000), *Art and Intimacy: How the Arts Began*, University of Washington Press, Seattle

Fox, Robin (1994), *The Challenge of Anthropology*, Transaction, New Brunswick

Gifford, Terry (2001), "Terrain, Character and Text: Is *Cold Mountain* by Charles Frazier a Post-Pastoral Novel?" *The Mississippi Quarterly* 55:1 Winter 2001-2002, pp. 87-96

Gifford, Terry (2002), "Towards a Post-Pastoral View of British Poetry" in John Parham (ed.), *The Environmental Tradition in English Literature*, Ashgate, Aldershot, Hampshire, pp. 51-63

Keith, W.J. (1975), *The Rural Tradition*, Harvester Press, Hassocks

Love, Glen (2003), *Practical Ecocriticism: Literature, Biology, and the Environment*, University of Virginia Press, Charlottesville

Marinelli, Peter (1971), *Pastoral*, Methuen & Co., London

Shellenberger, Michael and Ted Nordhaus (2004), "The Death of Environmentalism; Global warming politics in a post-environmental world" essay released at the October meeting of the Environmental Grantmakers Association

Snyder, Gary (1999), "The 'East West' Interview" in *The Gary Snyder Reader: Prose, Poetry, and Ttranslations, 1952-1998*, Counterpoint, Washington D.C., pp. 91-128

Toepfer, Klaus (2003), Interview with Alexandra de Blas, Earthbeat, Radio National, Australian Broadcasting Association, broadcast on Saturday 19 July

Tudge, Colin (2003), *So Shall We Reap*, Penguin, London

Wilson, Edward O. (1984), *Biophilia*, Harvard University Press, Cambridge

Wilson, Edward O. (1992), *The Diversity of Life*, Harvard University Press, Cambridge

Wilson, Edward O. (1999), *Consilience: The Unity of Knowledge*, Vintage, New York

Wilson, Edward O. (2002), *The Future of Life*, Little Brown, London

11

MILLENNIALISM IN MIDDLE-EARTH
An Examination of the Relevance of *The Lord of the Rings*

Michael J. Brisbois

AT EVERY OSCAR CEREMONY, nominations for best picture are presented to the audience. As Sir Ian McKellen, one of the finest Shakespearean actors of his generation, introduced the film that has made him a household name, he struggled to define *The Lord of the Rings: The Return of the King*'s value, asking:

> ...what is it that made it so momentous? What made it so popular, worldwide, *The Lord of the Rings*? Is it the unique scale of the almost impossible task [of making the films]? Traditional storytelling mixed with new technology? Is it the beauty of New Zealand...? Or is it simply the story itself, good people travelling together, young and old, in a fellowship of friends?[1]

People share this fantasy for essential reasons, and through examining the process by which they develop their social groups we can further understand their needs. A general theory of communication put forth by Ernest G. Bormann, "symbolic convergence theory", is best suited to discuss the formation of fan culture. In basic form, this theory proposes that the basis for communication and group consciousness is "shared fantasies [which] provide group members with comprehensible forms for explaining their past and thinking about their future." (Bormann, 1985: 128) The details of *LotR* are important to fans because they

---

[1] My transcription from "76th Annual Academy Awards", television broadcast, American Broadcast Company, aired on 29 February 2004.

represent a shared language used to identify both those within the group and those without. (Bormann, 1985: 129)

The development of shared identity is first apparent in the reading groups who asked questions of Tolkien. Nearly half of the correspondence published in *The Letters of J.R.R. Tolkien* is written to his fans. More examples of the emergence of the Tolkien subculture as an expression of ideology and community can be found in the formation of clubs and societies in the 1960s and 1970s and, more recently, the development of Internet groups like TheOneRing.net, which has been the impetus for the publication of two books: a primer on medieval literature, *The Tolkien Fan's Medieval Reader: Versions in Modern Prose* and *The People's Guide to J.R.R. Tolkien*. (Hebdige, 1979: 5-19)[2]

The existence of the fan culture of *LotR* is apparent in the costumes worn to theatres, as well as groups dedicated to recreating Middle-earth. Even non-Fantastic medieval re-creationists could be said to be participating in a comparable activity, either explicitly, in the case of Dagorhir Battle Games, whose slogan is "You've seen *Lord of the Rings*. We live it," (Anon, 2006a) or implicitly, in the case of the Society for Creative Anachronism (Anon, 2006b).

Why do people turn to Middle-earth? Why do they find so much meaning in a story about Hobbits, Elves, and Orcs? Shared group fantasies, like those of the fans of *LotR* or *Star Trek* (TV series and films since 1966), are a "creative and imaginative shared interpretation [...] that fulfils a group psychological or rhetorical need." (Bormann, 1985: 130) Just as communication experts can demonstrate the way in which certain topics of conversation elicit more exuberant discussion, literary critics can examine why certain texts elicit such an excited response in their readers. (Bormann, 1985: 130-131) People respond to fantasy literature because it provides them with something; it fulfils the readers' needs.

---

[2] While the fantasy fans of Tolkien are not as overtly subversive or as "spectacular" a subculture as the punks whom Hebdige discusses, throughout the body of my argument ideology, semiotics and subversion all play a role in our understanding of subculture. (Hebdige, 1979: 18)

An Opportunity for Collective Escape

Tolkien's success as a writer lies in his ability to respond to the reader's need for escape. Not desire, not want, but an actual need to achieve complete psychic escape from the crushing weight of modernity. We need only look at the title of Tolkien's masterpiece to see the reason people find it so fulfilling: the defeat of the Lord of the Rings. Sauron is an abstract element in the novel, never actually seen or interacted with. This is an intrinsic part of what Sauron represents: the modern condition. He represents technology and pollution as connected to the hegemony, tyranny, and the lust for power that seems to consume our ever-quickening society. While the latter evils are not entirely modern, Tolkien clearly considers them to be so. (Tolkien, 1997: 155) For Tolkien, and others like him who served in World War I and lost many friends, the world seemed to have derailed. The old Victorian notions of progress suddenly became questionable, and the fate of modern society seemed difficult to map out. He wrestled with the same crisis of European civilization as did his contemporaries.

The way that fantasy achieves this complex expression of modern anxiety without being allegorical is through the exchange of semiotic signs. Tolkien's insistent denial of any allegorical intention in *LotR* is widely known, but he did allow for "applicability:"

> I dislike Allegory—the conscious and intentional allegory—yet any attempt to explain the purport of myth or fairytale must use allegorical language. (And, of course, the more "life" a story has the more readily will it be susceptible to allegorical interpretations: while the better a deliberate allegory is made the more nearly will it be acceptable just as a story.) (Tolkien, 1981: 145)

The "life" of *LotR* is what allows the reader to perceive a meaning in it where there is not necessarily one. This meaning invariably responds to the needs and desires of the reader.

LotR asks questions of modernity, questioning its apparent lack of moral focus or spirituality. It asks questions of its intentions and its possible endpoints. The growing isolation of the individual and the growing power of hegemony are expressed through Sauron and the emptiness of Middle-earth. One of the reason the Shire is so appealing is the sense of community found in those sections of the novel.

Further questions of power and the nature of governance are raised through the One Ring and Aragorn.

Of course, some of the answers are Christian. Pity, mercy and Christian charity are dominant themes in the book, through both Gollum and Aragorn's stories. Many of the novel's events are very conservative and based on monarchism. But throughout the narrative, a response to modernity can be found. This response is millennialism—the renewal of the past and the arrival of a golden age.

LotR is a novel with two climaxes. The destruction of the One Ring is the obvious one, but the climax of Aragorn's story is subtler. The curing of Éowyn and Faramir's illnesses (Tolkien, 1991: 847-848) is the true climax of his story, for everything that follows, from his victory on the field of battle[3] and his crowning as king, hinges on this moment. Through this act, Aragorn fulfills the prophecy known among the commoners of Gondor: *"The hands of the king are the hands of the healer, and so shall the rightful king be known."* (Tolkien, 1991: 844) The moment of his healings and the prophecy are complex images that should be examined.

Firstly, the actual healing is done with *athelas*, or kingsfoil, an herb with the ability to restore a victim of the Black breath and the Shadow. It is the same herb that keeps Frodo alive after he is stabbed by the Witch King's Morgul knife on Weathertop. Something with the ability to refute the raw corrupting quality of evil is, by extension, raw good. It is the most manifest use of the divine good that permeates the nature of Middle-earth. In the healing of Faramir, Aragorn takes Ambient nature (the expression of God) and makes it manifest (Brisbois, 2005: 204). His act is to restore the divine order of the world, to put things right. This is why the description of the healing uses so much natural imagery. The "living freshness" is at once like the Holy Spirit and also the renewal of nature. It is part of the "monotheistic world of 'natural theology'" that Tolkien designed. (Tolkien, 1981:

---

[3] Some readers may initially disagree with this statement, as the destruction of the Ring destroys both Sauron's guiding will and the Nazgûl's. However, one should note that Aragorn is the decisive element in the Last Debate. The other lords all bow to his position as heir to the throne. If he did not possess the authority to command the lords of Gondor, the delaying action fought at the Black Gates might not have provided Frodo with the opportunity to reach the fires of Mount Doom. The two stories are entwined and there is a sense of providence to the order of events.

220) In the Houses of Healing, Aragorn fulfills the prophesy and changes from hero to king.

Secondly, the prophecy is entwined with Christian resonance. Christ was a king—not by battle, but by healing. Aragorn must take on the same characteristic to be successful. He cannot be king by violence. Of course, both Christ and Aragorn are kings by virtue of birth (a major factor in divine providential rule) but their actions define their kingships. The prophecy speaks volumes about Aragorn's role: he is a healer, and only through mercy and grace shall the king be recognized. It might seem odd to some readers how quickly Aragorn is accepted by almost everyone as the rightful heir. Denethor rejects him, but the Steward's mind was damaged and corrupted by his use of the palantír, which provided Sauron access to his thoughts via his crying. His monstrous attempt to burn himself and Faramir alive demonstrates what can happen when a person is cut off from the moral nature of Middle-earth.

Tolkien did not write for a specific audience, but in writing for himself, Tolkien hoped that there were others in his generation like him. While critics often deride *LotR* as "a work which many adults will not read more than once", "balderdash", and "juvenile trash", it has held an audience for fifty years. (Shippey, 2001: 306; Wilson, 1956: 312-314) This audience, as we have discussed, is complex and thoughtful; a tightly knit fan culture that is very fluent in fantasy. They have a need fulfilled in the genre, and for fans of Tolkien that need is a millenarian story.

In his study of millenarian activities, *New Heaven and New Earth*, anthropologist Kenelem Burridge provides a structure to these real-world social movements. He defines millennialism as a process by which a social group's lost power becomes transferred into religious expression through a prophet who is a magician powered by charisma in the Weberian sense. (Weber, 1991: 46) Historically, movements like cargo cults and the Ghost Dance movement of the Sioux are examples of this process. (Wallace, 1966: 30-31; Burridge, 1969: 65-72, 78-82) In Fantasy, the narratives often express the same process, especially in the most popular and successful stories. Burridge creates a socio-cultural model that is based upon a set of basic requirements which enable a social process to occur in the culture.

The most basic requirement is the presence of religious elements at work. (Burridge, 1969: 4) Tolkien's world is subtly Christian in morality. The Fantastic device of magic, with its mysterious and unexplained process, is essentially faith-based and can be considered as a religious motif. Even in more science fiction-styled works (such as George Lucas' *Star Wars: A New Hope*, 1977 and Leonard Nimoy's *Star Trek III: The Search for Spock*, 1984), psychic powers, the Force, or Vulcan telepathy provide the magical with a gateway into the rational world. With religion comes the notion of redemption, through which the fallen world can be returned to a state of grace. (Burridge, 1969: 5-8) In *LotR*, Middle-earth is a barren land of ruins and small pockets of civilizations which are isolated, besieged or fallen from their former glory.

The notion of redemption is also tied to the concept of renewal, and this is a key aspect of millennial movements: the idea of returning the past to the present and turning the future into a golden age. This is the promise of the second coming of Christ found in "Revelations 20:1-6",[4] and also the manifest intent of many real world movements. (Burridge, 1969) Fantastic narratives work in the same way. In Tolkien's story, the "Return of" signals the renewal of past traditions which symbolize the return of prosperity. The kingship of Aragorn indicates that core moral values can be made new and resonant for the future.

In order for a millennial movement to spring from this religious base there must be a level of oppression at work. (Burridge, 1969: 9-10) This is often a ruling power, the threat of conquest or, for our readers, the crisis of modernity. This oppression can only be resolved through the appearance of heroes and prophets. (Burridge, 1969: 10-12) These characters touch upon the religious elements in the work (Gandalf the Wizard, or more contestably, Tom Bombadil) and ignite the process of change that results in a millennial movement. In the real world, this can take the form of a religious movement or occasionally, armed conflict. The Ghost Dance of the Sioux tribes is an important example of this process. A prophet named

---

[4] Specifically "Revelations 20:4-6: [...] They came to life and reigned with Christ for a thousand years. (The rest of the dead did not come to life until the thousand years were ended.) This is the first resurrection. Blessed and holy are those who have part in the first resurrection. The second death has no power over them, but they will be priests of God and of Christ and will reign with him for a thousand years." (*Bible*)

Wovoka became a messianic figure for the tribe and taught the Ghost Dance as a way in which the ghosts of the past could be made real and the tribe could live out their days in a revitalized Sioux society. Ultimately, the Ghost Dance came to a violent end in 1890, as the U.S. army confronted the tribes involved. (Mooney, 1965) In the fantasy novel, the narrative always moves towards conflict and resolution.

The Process of Millennialism: Phase One

Burridge delineates a clear three-phase process for Millenarian activities. Each of these phases can be related first to the readers of *LotR* and second to the narrative structure of the novel. The first phase consists of three stages. First, the culture experiences a "disenfranchisement and severance" that marks its loss of power and authority. (Burridge, 1969: 115) For the audience of the Fantastic, the disenfranchisement has been ongoing since the post-World War I period. Modernity's disruptive effect on the mind of its participants forces them into a position of confusion and isolation. Many artistic expressions rely on this experience, but unfortunately we do not have the space to examine them all.

In the second stage, "lone individuals seek the basis of a common experience." (Burridge, ibid) Fan groups are brought together through common experience and knowledge. Therefore, this period is the one in which the fans are beginning to become interested in and exposed to the Fantastic; they intellectually and socially vacillate, seeking a common experience with which to construct peer groups, often using a novel, television series or film as a starting point.

The third stage is based on a "loss of integrity turning on: (a) Qualitative measure: Industriousness; capacities of intellect; courage or warfare [or] (b) Quantitative measure: Handling money." (Burridge, 1969: 115-116) In the real world of our readers, they often experience a loss of integrity over all these elements. From a Marxist position, money plays an important part of power dynamics in modern society, and therefore exerts a pressure on the reader. It can also be seen as the impetus for the proliferation of the genre, because publishers and producers would not engage in the production of the novel and films if it were not profitable. Burridge allows for a political concession at this stage, which mitigates the actual process of revolution. In modern Western societies, democracy functions on the illusion of constant political concession to the will of the electorate (i.e. hegemony). Therefore, modern citizens are rarely able to organize into groups and form effective social movements.

Although an argument could be made that feminism and racial equality are examples of successful social movements, I would suggest that they were responding to Althusser's Repressive State Apparatus (RSA) and the millenarian voice of the Fantastic is responding to the Ideological State Apparatus (ISA). (Althusser, 1971) Althusser describes a process by which all states maintain power and the status quo through processes of coercion. In absolute monarchies and totalitarian states, the state primarily relies upon processes of repression: military and police violence. In democratic states, the technique is subtler. Governments use ideological processes, such as voting, participating in capitalism, or discussions and legislation enforcing gender and racial equality to maintain the status quo. (Althusser, 1971: 127-186) One might further argue that part of the complex process of modernity and hegemony is the incorporation of feminism and racial equality into the ISA upon the failure of the RSA's efforts to contain the problem.[5] This idea of ideological coercion is related to ideas of hegemony, the process by which we are complicit in our own oppression. By adopting the values of the ideology, we continue to oppress others and ourselves. It is this mechanic of oppressive thought from which fantasy allows the reader to escape. It is the psychic strain that Tolkien thought Imagination allows us to recover from and to clear our perspective.

The Process of Millennialism: Phase Two

The second phase of the millenarian movement is the most active. This is the "externalization of thought or ideas" resulting in either a lack of a prophet and the collapse of the movement into "diffuse and inchoate activities" or the "emergence of [a] prophet" and organized actions with the potential of transcending the social problems. (Burridge, 1969: 116) We might view the multitude of conventions held worldwide for fans of the Fantastic to be indicative of social activities. But because

---

[5] Of course feminism and the equality movements have not entirely accomplished their goals. They have made significant social gains, but now have to deal with a much more complex and systemic form of oppression.

the group lacks a real-world prophet, the fans become a disparate group and do not create a serious threat to authority. A few figures have the potential to be prophets—J.R.R. Tolkien, Gene Rodenberry, or George Lucas—but the political concession of hegemony does not allow for the fans to express their millennial crisis in the real world. Instead, they must turn to their imaginary worlds for release.

The Process of Millennialism: Phase Three

The third phase is the "aftermath" of the socio-religious movement. (Burridge, 1969: 116) The millennial movement then ends in one of three possible conclusions: "Complete victory; or sect; or recurrence into Phase 1." (Burridge, ibid) In the real world, the fan subculture becomes a sect—a small quasi-religious group based upon exclusive knowledge and practices. In the narratives they enjoy, victory is experienced vicariously, allowing the reader to alleviate their modern condition and experience a simulated millennial experience. However, the reader's victory is not complete. As a vicarious experience, the reader's triumph passes with the reading. It is a momentary respite that passes too swiftly. Hegemony and the status quo it creates forces the individual back into modern existence and causes them to re-gather the strain released by the novel. This is why the Fantastic has flourished as a genre throughout the twentieth century, selling umpteen books and films, and it is also why so many of the its narratives are similar. Whether the reader experiences the same story over again or enters into a new world of fantasy does not matter, the excitement and psychic release of the work is what is important.

Millennialism in Middle-earth

Now that the millennial process has been mapped out and we understand why fans gravitate towards millennial stories, we are left to examine the process in the actual narrative. In *LotR*, Elendil's death and Isildur's failure to destroy the Ring is the moment of severance that marks the beginning of the third stage of Phase One. Isildur's failure to act seals the doom of the kingdom, and marks the beginning of the Third Age and the slow decline of Man (sic). (Tolkien, 1991: 51) The loss of the kingship and the appointment of a Steward to take charge of Gondor further illustrate this disenfranchisement.

The period of "lone individuals wandering" is found in Aragorn's travels to Rohan and Gondor, where he serves under kings and stewards, "exploring the hearts of Men". (Tolkien, 1991: 1035) Aragorn eventually becomes dissatisfied with what he finds and with the burden of his doom (the kingship and its connection with the One Ring), he loses faith in humanity. (Tolkien, 1991: 1035) A key element of Aragorn's character becomes fully formed at this point in his life: his role as a Ranger. Aragorn's knowledge of the wilderness and his easy, skilled way with animals are clues as to his special role in the story. Throughout *LotR*, good characters are connected with nature: the intrinsic natural theology of Middle-earth. This symbolism directly connects Aragorn with the prophecy and divine purpose (the renewal of Middle-earth) of his ascension to the throne.

Phase Two is the basis of the novel. Gandalf serves as the prophet figure. Like Aragorn, he is connected with natural imagery, and characters such as Treebeard think highly of his actions. We are provided with further evidence of "natural theology" in the other Wizards, or Istari, in the story. The Istari, of whom there were five, were sent to Middle-earth to oppose Sauron. (Tolkien, 1998: 502) In *LotR*, we only learn the names of three of the Istari: Gandalf, Saruman, and Radagast. All three are in some way related to nature. Gandalf describes Radagast as "a worthy Wizard, a master of shapes and changes of hue; and he has much lore of herbs and beasts, and birds are especially his friends." (Tolkien, 1991: 250-51) Gandalf is in turn described by Treebeard as "the only wizard that really cares about trees". (Tolkien, 1991: 455) Saruman is a fallen figure: Treebeard does indicate that the white Wizard once walked among the trees and cared for nature, but he grew steadily distant and finally turned against nature. (Tolkien, 1991: 462)

All the Istari are related to a colour: Saruman the White, Gandalf the Grey, Radagast the Brown. It can be safely assumed that this is something of a ranking system or a way of indicating the role of the Wizard within the Order, because Gandalf is returned to Middle-earth as Gandalf the White. Saruman's fall is likewise represented in his adoption of the title Saruman the Many-Coloured. This adoption of all colours indicates his hubris: to master the world and bend the moral nature of

Middle-earth to his will. As he is excommunicated, from the Order by Gandalf, he is told: "You have no colour now." (Tolkien, 1991: 569)

In his role of prophet, Gandalf creates two heroes, Frodo and Aragorn, and becoming a more pivotal character after his transformation into Gandalf the White. Through Gandalf's initial actions, Aragorn takes steps to become king, and following the Council of Elrond wields his re-forged hereditary sword and frequently declares his lineage, such as his declaration to Éomer. (Tolkien, 1991: 423)

The final phase culminates in the victory of the forces of good. Throughout the final books of the novel, Gondor is described as a city of "doubt and great dread". (Tolkien, 1991: 937) Once evil is shown to be selfish and self-defeating as in Gollum's tragic end, the world begins to change: "the days that followed were golden." (Tolkien, 1991: 925; 942)

It is important to understand the symbolism of Aragorn's crowning. The new Steward, Faramir, meets Aragorn at the Gate of Gondor. This happens amidst rumours of the healing prophecy being fulfilled. Aragorn does not seize the white rod of the Steward as his own, but generously allows Faramir to retain his familial role. Faramir then announces Aragorn's titles, intertwining current deeds, a renewal of the past, and prophetic fulfillment:

> Here is Aragorn son of Arathorn, chieftain of the Dúnedain of Arnor, Captain of the Host of the West, bearer of the Star of the North, wielder of the Sword Reforged, victorious in battle, whose hands bring healing, the Elfstone, Elessar of the line of Valandil, Isildur's son, Elendil's son of Númenor. (Tolkien, 1991: 946)

When the people are asked if they will accept him as king, they unanimously agree. The crown of Gondor is a magnificent piece of craftsmanship, tied, we are told, through symbols to the kings who came over the Sea. Those kings from across the Sea hailed from the divine land of Valinor, home of the Valar (or Angels). Through the crown, the religious is made manifest, and the crowning begins its millennial ascension. Aragorn proceeds towards the symbolic climax of the ceremony by connecting himself to the kings from the West and through them the divine:

> *Et Earello Endorenna utulien. Sinome maruvan ar Hildinyar tenn' Ambar-metta!* And those were the words that Elendil spoke when he came up out of the Sea on the wings of the wind: "Out of the Great Sea to Middle-earth I am come. In this place will I abide, and my heirs, unto the ending of the world." (Tolkien, 1991: 946)

Then Aragorn sets into motion a key semiotic event: the transmission of narrative authority. As mentioned, Gandalf has created two heroes. In order for the millennial process to complete itself, one of these heroes must become the focus. Because he must be king to provide stability and closure to the millenarian movement, Aragorn needs achieve a transmission of authority, not only from the prophet, but also from the other hero. Aragorn is therefore humble and acknowledges his debts "by the labour and valour of many have I come into my inheritance" asking that "the Ring-bearer bring the crown to me, and let Mithrandir set it upon my head, if he will; for he has been the mover of all that has been accomplished and this is his victory." (Tolkien, 1991: 946) This allows for a transition of power to occur: Frodo takes the crown from Faramir and transfers his role as hero as he passes the crown to Gandalf, who in turn transfers his authority to Aragorn by placing the White Crown upon Aragorn and declaring: "Now come the days of the king, and may they be blessed while the thrones of the Valar endure!" (Tolkien, 1991: 946)

Aragorn achieves kingship and reunites his people under one nation. His ceremony does not diminish Frodo's role in the story, but only deepens the readers' understanding of why the Ring-bearer must leave Middle-earth. Frodo has undertaken a terrible journey, in some respects journeying deep into the heart of evil, and, through the power of the ring, experienced the separation from life and the natural theology of Middle-earth.

As for Aragorn, he must fulfil his self-described role as *"Envinyatar*, the Renewer". (Tolkien, 1991: 845) His successful ascension to the throne is achieved not through military conquest, but through Christian morality. He fights no war of unification; neither does he lead a band of knights on a quest. Instead, he fulfills the prophesy of healing. (Tolkien, 1991: 844) Aragorn's ultimate act, the healing of Faramir and Éowyn, parallels Christ's acts of healing and advocates compassion and love over violence. Frodo's journey likewise embodies Christian notions of sacrifice, pity and compassion.

Aragorn's success marks the beginning of the Fourth Age for Middle-earth, a period of prosperity and peace. It thus marks the culmination of the millennial narrative. It is important to point out that fantasy authors do not necessarily deliberately map out these stages. It is through observation of the genre that we can apply the template Burridge designed to the literature. Perhaps fantasy fans are expressing religious phenomena, as Durkheim suggests. We can definitely observe the workings of religious expression in the majority of fantasy novels and films, and therefore we might consider them as such. (Durkheim, 1994: 93-98)

However, there are difficulties in adopting this position. Certainly there are semiotic commonalities between the religious and the Fantastic, but the former is an important social institution and the latter a literary genre. While it is far beyond the nature of this study to attempt to answer all the possible relationships between faith and fantasy, I can venture some summary comments.

First, magic lies at the heart of Middle-earth. In *The Sociology of Religion*, Max Weber defines magic as a kind of "charisma" through which a magician affords himself social power and economic influence. (Weber, 1991: 2) This social power applies to the notion of the prophet in our model of millennialism. Furthermore, in complex societies, symbolic acts and images become integral parts of religious activities. As concluded earlier, the fan culture of *LotR* and the verisimilitude of fantasy are based upon a consistent set of symbols and terms, through which social sub-groups form and propagate themselves.

Weber also discusses the role of prophets and rebirth in his study. He argues that there is no serious distinction between "a 'renewer of religion' who preaches an older revelation—actual or superstitious—and a 'founder of religion' who claims to bring completely new deliverances". (Weber, 1991: 46) Perhaps this is an important point of divergence between fantasy and religion. While Weber attempts to define large, cross-cultural trends, fantasy is often rooted in a specific culture's mythic imagination. The time and needs of that imagination differ with circumstance. In Tolkien's lifetime and afterwards, modernity is the key circumstance to respond to. Millennialism is the best possible response because it moves forward into a golden age while renewing the past. This dualism of past and future allows the reader to become comfortable in the present, just as Aragorn's journey along the paths of the dead put to rest the dark history of betrayal that plagued the Kings of Gondor. The confrontation with the dead is another key prophecy of the King, as spoken by "Malbeth the Seer, in the days of Arvendui, last king at Fornost",

> The heir of him to whom the oath they swore.
> From the North shall he come, need shall drive him:
> he shall pass the Door to the Paths of the Dead. (Tolkien, 1991: 764)

Aragorn's kingship allows Middle-earth to embrace the new and the hopeful out of a dark period. With a complex mixture of religious metaphor, natural images and symbolic passage, the millennial message of *LotR* can reach the reader.

The explosion of fantasy genres in the twentieth century owes its success to the audience it generates. Many authors are indebted to Tolkien, especially those whose works of fantasy from the 1960s and 1970s, are if not pale copies of Tolkien, often explicitly similar in terminology and plot. This duplication of *LotR* in other narratives is demonstrative of the development of the fan culture and shows a growing consistency in the language. The stock scenario or character allows readers or viewers of fantasy to develop consistent themes in their subculture, which are understood in much greater detail by those "in the party" than those not. (Bromann, 1985: 132)

In popular culture studies, audience is critical. A scholar must seek to understand how and why society responds strongly to a text. Often the media will describe these phenomena as fads, but in the case of nearly every fantasy group, they are long lasting and increasing in relevance. Peter Jackson and his cast and crew were shrewd on Oscar night. They may have somewhat undermined their position on stage, but their choice of after-ceremony parties spoke volumes about the power of fan groups. After attending the Governor's Ball (a required post-Oscar party), Jackson and his fellow victors, including the actors, did not rush to New Line Cinema's lavish event. Instead they met several hundred fans at a much humbler party organized by TheOneRing.net and celebrated foremost with the reason for their success: the popular subculture borne of *LotR*.

Bibliography

Althusser, Louis (1971), *Lenin and Philosophy and Other Essays*, trans. Ben Brewster, Monthly Review Press, New York

Anon (2004a), Dagorhir Battle Games website: http://www.dagorhir.com/dagorhir/dagorhir.htm

Anon (2004b), Society for Creative Anachronism website: http://www.sca.org

Anon (2004c), TheOneRing.Net website: http://www.theonering.net

Bormann, Ernest G. (1985), "Symbolic Convergence Theory: A Communication Formulation" *Journal of Communication* 35, pp. 128-37

Brisbois, Michael J. (2005), "Tolkien's Imaginary Nature: An Analysis of the Structure of Middle-earth" *Tolkien Studies* 2, pp. 197-216

Burridge, Kenelm (1969), *New Heaven, New Earth: A Study of Millenarian Activities*, Copp Clark Publishing, Toronto

Challis, Erica (ed.) (2003), *The People's Guide to J.R.R. Tolkien*, TheOneRing.net, Simon and Schuster, Toronto

Durkheim, Émile (1994), *Durkheim on Religion*, ed. W.S.F. Pickering, Scholar's Press, Georgia

Hebdige, Dick (1979), *Subculture: The Meaning of Style*, Routledge, New York

Keegan, John (1994), *A History of Warfare*, Vintage Canada, Toronto

Mooney, James (1965), *The Ghost-Dance Religion and the Sioux Outbreak of 1890*, University of Chicago Press, Chicago

Shippey, Tom (2001), *J.R.R. Tolkien: Author of the Century*, HarperCollins Publishers, London

Tolkien, J.R.R. (1981), *The Letters of J.R.R. Tolkien*, ed. Humphrey Carpenter, HarperCollins Publishers, London

Tolkien, J.R.R. (1991), *The Lord of the Rings*, Houghton Mifflin, Boston

Tolkien, J.R.R. (1997), "On Faerie Stories" *The Monsters and the Critics and Other Essays*, ed. by Christopher Tolkien, HarperCollins Publishers, London, pp. 109-161

Tolkien, J.R.R. (1998), *Unfinished Tales*, ed. Christopher Tolkien, HarperCollins Publishers, London

Turgon (David E. Smith) (2004), *The Tolkien Fan's Medieval Reader: Versions in Modern Prose*, Cold Spring Press Fantasy, Cold Spring Harbor, New York

Turner, Jonathan H. (2004), *The Structure of Sociological Theory* 7th ed., Wadsworth/Thomson, Toronto

Wallace, Anthony F.C. (1966), *Religion: An Anthropological View*, Random House, New York

Weber, Max (1991), *The Sociology of Religion*, trans. Ephraim Fischoff, Beacon Press, Boston

Wilson, Edmund (1956), "Oo, those Awful Orcs" *Nation* 14 April, pp. 312-14

River Kawarau or Anduin? Perhaps New Zealand is Middle-earth.
(photo by Bill J. Jerome)

SECTION III

The Pilgrims in and beyond the Tale

12

ALL I REALLY NEED TO KNOW ABOUT NEW ZEALAND I LEARNED FROM PETER JACKSON[1]

Bill J. Jerome

It is 1 February 2004. I am watching Super Bowl XXXVIII at a pub inside LAX airport with my father. We're on our third order with the waitress. We keep the drinks coming to retain our seats, even though the view of the game is so poor on the small distant television that I don't learn of "the wardrobe malfunction" for nearly four weeks. I've left this continent only once before to go to Europe, and this country otherwise only to slip into Canada and back. So how is it that this scene is both real and the direct fault of one Peter Jackson?

In December 2001 my father and I first saw *The Fellowship of the Ring*. I had read the books and liked them; my father had read the books a number of times, and liked them more. I knew little about the movie when I decided to see it. Our expectations were low due to the mutual feeling that a movie couldn't be done and couldn't evoke the feeling of the books. However, it was the holiday season, I was back home in New York for a visit, and it seemed a reasonable way to kill an evening in Albany. The theatre, a large and relatively nice one, was attached to a mall.

After leaving the screening we barely spoke. We wandered through the mall oblivious to the holiday shoppers caught up in buying presents and cards. At some point we began to talk... about wanting to "return" to whatever magical place the

---

[1] The following writing is based on a trip taken by the author and his father to New Zealand in 2004. A travelogue written by the author during the trip is available online at http://www.billjerome.com/nz, and his father's journal of the trip has been since digitized and is available at http://www.billjerome.com/nz/journal. All photographs were taken by the author.

movie had taken us. As stunned as I was by the initial experience, and recognizing that it was somehow transforming, I still would never have guessed that years later I would be many miles from home in an airport pub watching the Super Bowl, while waiting for an Air New Zealand plane bound for adventure (or, as the ticket read, Auckland).

~

In part, this could be attributed to the fact that, at that moment, I had no idea whatsoever where the film had been shot, and that many of the places I had seen in the first movie were *real* locations, or that the subsequent movies would contain progressively more stunning locations.

In the years following my first viewing of *FotR*, the journey was a continuous one. I reread the books. I talked often with family and friends about the movies and books. I recall one evening when a group of us went out to dinner, many weeks after the release of *FotR*. Apart from about five minutes, all of our conversation revolved around the movie; what we loved, what we missed, what we loved again, and how much we looked forward to seeing our favourite moments. We also indulged in a bit of speculation, "Why would they do paths of the dead? I bet they cut it; it's too hard to explain without the book," "I can't wait to see Shelob!" On other occasions, we'd simply marvel over the movies, or wonder aloud, "What would *I* have done differently?"

The level of interest in all things related to the film reached such heights that once the Argonath "bookends" were announced, we began to speculate about what future "accompaniments" might include. Two Towers candle holders? An Oliphaunt piggy bank? (I myself still believe that a Tomb of Balin to hold all the discs would be fantastic.) Was this the evolution of a fanatic? Not necessarily. Then came the sword.

~

For Christmas 2002, a year after first seeing *FotR*, a large box arrived at my house—a gift from my father: a sword, a replica of Sting from the Noble Collection, to be specific. He already had Glamdring hanging in his house. (He had to "test one out to be certain of the quality," of course, before getting one for me.) It is proudly displayed on my fireplace.

How did this come to pass? Two words: Peter Jackson.

As the DVDs were released, I became aware of a man who had an undeniable passion for Middle-earth. Yet he was also level headed and knew exactly whom to surround himself with to give life to his vision. Although I have never met him in the flesh, I cannot help but feel that I have after watching the DVD documentaries and listening to the film commentaries.

In addition to providing a window into the people involved with the project, the available DVD materials also introduced the viewer to New Zealand as a beautiful place on Earth, as well as home to a dedicated citizenry who helped breathe so much life and energy into the production.

Perhaps it is the obsession, passion and determination displayed that helped fuel my own interest. Doubtless, I am not alone in my fascination with the films and books. Even aside from my own friends and family, anyone mildly aware of the public consciousness (in the United States, anyway) could tell I'm not alone. There is even a small documentary release about the fan frenzy called *Ringers*.[2]

Still, I surprise myself when with a chunk of vacation approaching, I phoned my father in December 2003 and said, "Let's go to New Zealand in February."

~

At first it was in fun despite my real desire to go there. Over a week or two we discussed it. I bought travel guides at a local bookstore. We both called travel agents. Then less than two months later, we were jumping headlong into our own Middle-earth adventure (albeit less perilous than some other famous tales from that land!).

We had our plane tickets to Wellington, a flight back from Auckland booked for three weeks later, a rental car, our first two nights reserved in a hotel, and absolutely no idea where we would go and what we would do when we got there.

---

[2] *Ringers: The Lord of the Fans* (dir. Carlene Cordova, 2005)

Only on our third day did we try to determine where we would go after we left Wellington.

~

While exploring New Zealand, we avoided guided tours of *The Lord of the Rings* sites, favouring the spirit of adventure in finding locations on our own. The only paid tour we took was of Hobbiton, because that was the only way to see the sets. Otherwise, we relied only on one paperback book to aid us on our *LotR* journey: Ian Brodie's well-known guidebook to Middle-earth.[3]

We decided that we both loved and hated that book, much like Gollum and the one ring. It was fantastic to have many of the locations identified, but for us, the directions would usually get us 90% of the way there and then leave us stranded without a GPS device handy. Perhaps some day someone will show me where on Mt. Ruapehu I might find the stone on which Isildur lay. That said, by and large the book served us well as we journeyed the countryside. We first put it to the test at Mt. Victoria. We have no idea if we found the "get off the road" locations as the book didn't seem to indicate just *which* entrance to the park we were to start at. But we enjoyed exploring, we enjoyed the park, and the feel of the films was obvious even if the locations were not exact.

~

We spent many evenings wandering around Wellington. It was a delightful city and I am glad we spent as many days there as we did. At a recent concert here in Pittsburgh, Pennsylvania, Billy Boyd sang during a performance of *The Lord of the Rings Symphony*.[4] I had the pleasure of greeting him briefly for a photo, and used the

---

[3] Ian Brodie (2003), *The Lord of the Rings: A Location Guidebook*, Harper Collins, Auckland.

[4] *The Lord of the Rings Symphony: Six Movements for Orchestra and Chorus* was adapted from Howard Shore's film scores by Shore and John Mauceri with each movement corresponding to a book of *LotR*. Interestingly, I have seen the symphony conducted by both Shore and Mauceri here in Pittsburgh. Mauceri is the music director of the Pittsburgh Opera.

The Witchking of Angmar

opportunity to ask him for a recommendation on his favourite place to eat in Wellington. I look forward to trying it on my next trip to New Zealand.

While we were in Wellington we saw *The Return of the King* at the Embassy Theatre. It was guarded by the lord of the Nazgûl, which amazingly could be seen from the top of the trolley run in Wellington. Afterward, we crossed the strait to Picton, before driving south. This was our first introduction to rural New Zealand, and to sheep.

~

Not that I had never seen a sheep. I hadn't, however, seen *Sheep*. If you don't know what I mean by that difference, there is no point in saying more. I can, however, say more about the roads.

We drove all around the South Island, and were often led to (quickly) wonder, "Is this the last road I'll ever live to see?" My father did the driving due to insurance issues with the rental. I'll have to find out what those issues were so I can ensure they happen again next time. To be clear, the "wrong side" of the road was not the issue.

Here in the United States we have these things called guard rails. I suppose we've become reliant on their comforting presence, but like any good thing you take for granted, you sure miss them when they're not there.

From page eight of my father's journal, regarding Highway 1: "The twistiness of the road is amazing." From page ten: "The roads are narrow and twisty." Page eleven reads: "The drive out to the peninsula is 45 minutes of the worst road I've ever seen." Page eighteen: "Our NEW WINNER in the world's worst road contest!"

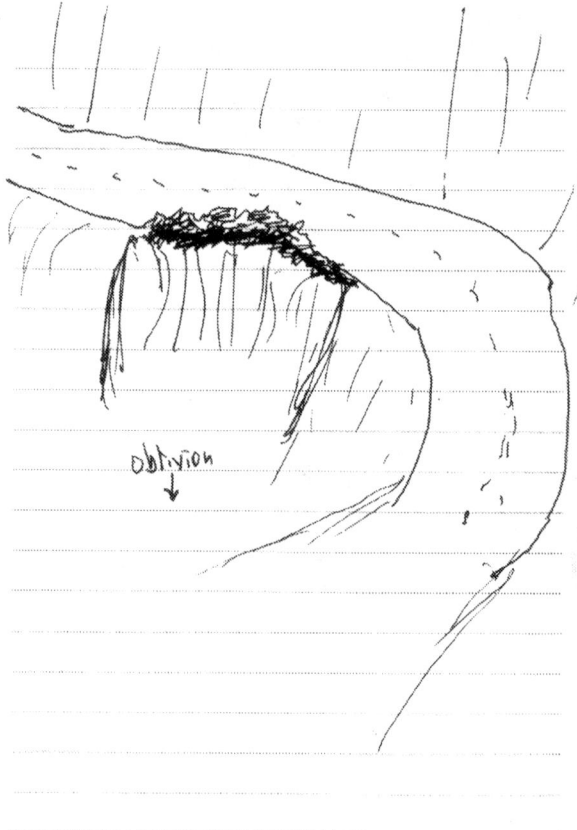

My father's sketch of Akatarawa Road, in less than prime condition, from his travel journal

That road, it turned out, had been worsened by storms the previous night and although it had been closed on one end, the end we started on had yet to be closed. The rain had caused slips not only on to the road but, in this case, from underneath part of it. Elsewhere there was a cliff where I spotted a car that had gone through the fence—a jeep—that was wedged nose-down a *loooong* way below. At least all of these aforementioned roads were paved, as opposed to the teeth-chattering gravel road that leads to Erewhon.

All I Really Need to Know about New Zealand

Probably the most fantastic location we visited was Mt. Sunday, site of Edoras. We got as close as the road allowed, which was actually closer than I'd hoped. It's surprisingly... small! But perfect. As we rounded the first bend we could see it from where we pulled off the road. A gentleman was standing beside his car as well, and before I could wonder aloud if that was really Mt. Sunday, he turned around, looked at me and said, "Yep, that's it!" We drove on, and took photos from what was really the first place I stood and thought: "There is no mistaking this for any other place in the world, and no mistaking it as the landmark in the films." It took hours to reach and hours to leave, but it was a highlight of the trip.

Less than a highlight was our only attempt at cooking. We weren't sure how we ruined the frozen shepherd's pie, but we took it as a sign that we weren't meant to cook while on vacation, and accepted our destiny.

~

Mt. Sunday

Other than the cooking experiment, the food throughout the trip was surprisingly good. Many small town eateries seemed to have gourmet chefs in the back. The only time we were led astray was when we became curious about what "American" cuisine was like in New Zealand. Although some places made strenuous attempts to reproduce a 1950s American diner atmosphere, the food was rarely right, and usually quite off. A note to one particular restaurant: we call it "Tex-mex", not "Mex-tex". Subway is nearly identical, McDonald's has some extra offerings (including egg and beets on their burgers) but is otherwise the same or better, and Pizza Hut carries different assortments of toppings worth trying.

Sampling such culinary experiences was part of our strategy of not planning our destinations too far ahead, so that we could adapt our plans while we were there. This meant we often stayed over night at places off the beaten path. Waitangi Day was one such example.

~

I was only vaguely aware of Waitangi Day beforehand. The standard celebrations we observed most reminded us of our own Independence Day celebrations. We should have realized that finding a place to stay without a reservation on Waitangi Day would be like finding a place to stay on 4 July here in the States, which is to say, almost impossible. This was a great example, however, of how friendly and helpful New Zealanders are. We had to go to the next town, but we were directed to an off-road location which had room for us only twenty minutes away.

As hard as it was finding a room on Waitangi Day, we were nearly thwarted the following night by a much greater force: Rugby. Specifically, a major tournament taking place in Dunedin the night we arrived. Again, the citizenry did not let us down.

Each place we visited seeking a vacancy would refer us to another, showing a genuine concern for where we might stay. Eventually we found a Bed & Breakfast which, although it did not have a room, placed a call to a friend, and found us a place to stay.

These impressions of friendly, good-natured people we met all along the way were a wonderful, integral part of the experience, and we left the South Island wishing we'd had more time to stay... Next time.

Upon returning to Wellington and spending a few more days there, we plotted the film-inspired part of our trip. We visited smaller locations, such as Isengard's gardens and the river bank where Aragorn is rescued by Brego around some rather inspiring destinations like the Putangirua Pinnacles, which doubled for the Dimholt Road in *RotK*. Our budget did not run to helicopters as used by the film crew, so as with Mt. Sunday, we used car and foot to reach our film destination!

Does Friday the 13th mean anything in New Zealand? If you are aware of the superstition of the date, you'd have thought we'd pick a different day to visit the Pinnacles. We opted for the "low road" though sometimes I would have preferred the path that ascended with a view into the valley. The three hours we spent there that day were enthralling, and a bit... surreal, like the Moeraki boulders in the South

Pinnacles featured in Brodie's guide

Island. Only I hadn't seen the Moeraki boulders on screen with ghosts inside them. The boulders were fascinating, especially as I'd never seen such formations, and the explanation for their existence appears to be only a theory, but they failed to generate the spine-tingling awe that the pinnacles produced. As creepy as the environment feels on film, it really *is* just as disturbing and awe-inspiring to walk through them yourself.

~

After resting in Napier to take in some quality beach time, we visited the National Aquarium. Unbeknownst to us this housed yet another surreal New Zealand treasure, which, despite being in the aquarium, was not at all aquatic: the kiwi. From my travelogue :

> They're a lot larger than I'd thought, and very odd. I didn't have my camera, but that didn't matter a lot given the low light, glass, and the fact that to really appreciate how odd and extra-dimensional they are, you need to see them move. No wings. I don't think. [...] but nothing for balance. As my father put it, they're like little furry people without arms.

Watch for kiwis!

This was the only time we saw live kiwi, though we did see a couple of illustrated road signs warning of their presence as we drove from Napier to our next film-geek location. Mt. Ruapehu was the name of the mountain that we could see about ten feet of through the fog when we arrived.

Our first assault on the mountain was treacherous, and although it definitely resembled Mordor shrouded in fog, we could not find any definable locations. This was because the road continued from where we stopped, but we didn't realize this because we couldn't see it. The visitor centre suggested the best walk on the mountain that day: "From the couch to the fridge and back."

On the evening of our second day there, we were blessed with a few hours of cloud break and stormed the mountain again to see some breathtaking scenery. Some film locations may or may not have been specifically found, but the whole area was astonishing regardless. One place that we think we looked was the rock Gollum creeps down at the start of *The Two Towers*. Some locations had to be guessed

Gollum's rock on Mt. Ruapehu

Mt. Taranaki from the road at the foot of Mt. Ruapehu

at because the book uses car park numbers which were no longer posted due to construction.

On our descent, I took a photo of Mt. Taranaki, which is currently serving as the desktop image on my laptop computer.

Not yet finished with visiting *LotR* destinations, the next day we headed for Hobbiton.

Matamata (aka Hobbiton) was a required stop on the trip, and worth the time. Not surprisingly, we were not the only Americans on the tour (the only kiwis on board were the driver and the tour guide). Although we generally preferred to explore on our own during the trip, seeing the party tree was no less thrilling for having been led there, and a good time was had, (even if it was a good time covered in sheep).

Our geek-inspired destinations came to a close with this guided tour of Hobbiton, and we decided on a little more beach time before Auckland.

In between rests on the beach, we walked up "The Mount" (on the Coromandel Peninsula). As we descended (passing the sheep), a man stopped and politely informed us about signs we would see as predicted by Nostradamus. Again, in true New Zealand fashion, he gave us a few warnings, told us where to read more, wished us a pleasant journey, and went on.

All I Really Need to Know about New Zealand

What's left of Bag End

For those who may be concerned, at the time of writing we have yet to observe any of the signs.

Auckland was a nice city to spend a couple of days. It felt, however, much more like home than Wellington. The citizens seemed busier, the streets more crowded. It was enjoyable, but served as a small reminder that we were on our return journey.

The trip home was solemn, and best expressed with words written at the end of my travelogue, en route from LA to Pittsburgh:

> ... the truth of having left New Zealand behind is sinking in. The people aren't (anywhere near as) friendly, the mood is different, the pace of life, the feeling of it all... as we walked from terminal 2 to terminal 1, I took an unfortunate deep breath, which drove home that the air sure is different over here.

And the last lines of my father's written journal:

In LA. It's Monday 7:30 am when we land. Security, getting bags, customs, re-checking takes like an hour. LA smells like the U.S. No more magic.

That is where the answers lie.

~

The draw is the New Zealand countryside, its citizenry, and what it all represents. Not only did New Zealand and its people meet our high expectations from the movies and opinions formed through the DVDs, but all those expectations were surpassed. Those mountains *are there*. Those rivers *are there*. You *can* reach out and touch them. You *can* go see Mount Sunday. But although those destinations draw fans, they are just the teasers to bring you there. There is far more than that.

There *are* people like those so dedicated to the vision of the books. There *are* people who care so much about their land that no trace remained at Mount Sunday. Many are the same people who cared that a pair of travellers from across the world had a place to stay on Waitangi Day.

But even if you've never set foot there, you already know. You know for the same reason I've been able to write this chapter. The same reason this book has been created, and the reason you have a copy in your hands right now. You may have already learned all you need to know about New Zealand from Peter Jackson, just as I did.

13

TO SEX UP *THE LORD OF THE RINGS*
Jackson's Feminine Approach in His "Sub-creation"

Elise McKenna

FILM, as a visual medium, branches out and forms a lush canopy between the written word of literature and the static art of painting, as it progresses beyond the "plastic representations" of life to become an "exaltation of the mental vision". (Waston, 1998: 210) *The Lord of the Rings* trilogy, directed by Peter Jackson, is exactly that. Not only does Jackson's film epic adhere to the basic story by J.R.R. Tolkien, but the LotR tale is also modernized to express a stronger feminine element. Jackson's vision bridges the gap between written word and visual image, and consciously or unconsciously, he relies upon the archetypes of Mother, Nature, Hope, and the Wiseman. (Campbell, 1949: 17-20) Jackson stepped into the marginal space between literature and art, internalized Tolkien's words, and returned with a new fantasy. Interestingly, Tolkien addressed this idea in his essay, "Tree and Leaf", stating, "Art, [is] the operative link between Imagination and the final result, Sub-creation." (Tolkien, 1966: 68)

The impact that Jackson's sub-creation has had on society can be directly related to the archetypes that are peppered throughout. If one were to examine his sub-creation through Joseph Campbell's understanding of Carl Jung's "Phenomenology of the Self", it becomes clear why Jackson's films resonate deep in the recesses of the mind; "the mythical sense of the world and its eternal figures" play a strong role within us. Jung's theory of the *anima* and *animus* is an idea of balance. The masculine is "compensated by a feminine element" known as the *anima*.

(Campbell, 1978: 152) Likewise, Jung argues that the feminine is compensated by a masculine element or *animus*. (Campbell, 1978: 151) Issues arise when these two are not in symbiosis or balance and this is where Jackson shines.

Jackson brought Tolkien's story out of a completely male-dominated world by altering the roles of particular female characters, adhering to what Joseph Campbell called the monomyth (Campbell, 1949: 30). Specifically, Jackson blurred the defined masculine roles of warrior and provider through the characters of Treebeard and Gandalf, making them more transitory and less defined. At the same time, he bolstered the feminine through the characters of Galadriel and Arwen, giving those females more scenes than in Tolkien's original. However, Jackson does not change the character of Éowyn; her role remains essentially the same. Theoretically, there is no need to strengthen Éowyn's character, since her *animus* assures her a place in the Battle of the Pelennor Fields and her *anima* is integral to the downfall of the evil avatar, the Witch-king of Angmar, who cannot be killed by any son of Man. Following this trend, if a balance of masculinity and femininity is achieved, then Nature, reflected through Treebeard, should not yearn for the feminine; and therefore Jackson omits Treebeard's "Song of the Entwives", a call to the restorative powers of the feminine in the theatrical release. However, Jackson does reincorporate this yearning in the extended version.

Of Ents and Elves—Mother Nature Restored

Jackson's *The Fellowship of the Ring* opens with a woman's voice speaking Elvish, "[t]he world has changed. I see it in the water. I feel it in the Earth. I smell it in the air." This dynamic opening introduces the pastoral and dark world of Middle-earth. It is Galadriel—the Lady of Lothlórien—who introduces the world that Tolkien created. At once the audience is plunged into a foreign, yet familiar place; we are lulled into acceptance by the soft feminine voice. However, Tolkien originally assigned these words to Treebeard, Shepherd of Fangorn Forest, and, most importantly a male. To hear them spoken by a woman, instead of Tolkien's male nature spirit, prepares us for the influence that the restoration of the feminine in this film will achieve. Jackson's movement towards Jung's anima, by re-introducing the archetype of Mother as the Gaia myth defines her, attempts to restore the atrophied feminine.

Jackson's Galadriel speaks demurely when the Fellowship arrives at Lothlórien, and the only sense we have of her power is the lower-tone register of her whispered warnings inside Frodo's head. Yet, Aragorn and Legolas lower their eyes and bow their heads in reverence, while Boromir shrinks from her gaze, and all others stare speechlessly enthralled by her. By showing the deference given her by the naturally more powerful male characters, Jackson demonstrates Galadriel's power.

She is the ringbearer of "Nenya—ring of adamant—ring of water", and her pool is like the primordial waters of creation. Through this pool, she perceives past, present, and future. Her strength is within the female bailiwick, which for Campbell is shrouded in the mysteries of the night and the creation of life. (Campbell, 1999: 224) When Galadriel is offered the One Ring, she affects the image of a dark queen, simultaneously beautiful and terrifying. Galadriel's hair flows wildly about her like tentacles—no longer the neatly tressed blonde, and her outfit changes from pristine white and sparkling to a shade of green complete with metal breastplate and torn material that enhance an image of her as a sea-witch—her face no longer placid and serene, but wild and terrifying and her layered voice seems to rise from the "foundations of the earth". (Campbell, 1999: 224) The special effects team of Weta Workshop created for Galadriel an eerie backdrop of shaded greens, possibly reminiscent of creation or water. This is very different to the backdrop they created for the dark Lord Sauron, where there is very little colour and the world moves in shades of grey. Possibly this is meant to allude to the regenerative and restorative aspect of the Mother and the anima of Nature, where the animus of masculine power is unsupportive, destructive and stagnant.

Jackson's vision of Galadriel's transformation further encompasses the elemental forces of earth, air, fire, but especially water, so it is quite proper that she voices the knowledge of a changing Middle-earth. When Galadriel reaches for the Ring, we are suddenly plunged into a nightmare. The shaking ground belies volcanoes and earthquakes. Explosions of sound rush forth, while her hair and clothing whips about, clearly representing the elemental force of air. Her face is lit with a strange golden light as if a fire is burning within. The vision of her as a dark and alluring witch, her appearance both "beautiful and terrible", gives us a connection to the element of water.

Ultimately, Galadriel's transformation is accompanied by the same sound heard when the Dark Lord was defeated—that inhalation of noise and centrifugally outward explosion of change. For the audience, this sound heralds that a change is coming—for good or for ill—and it supports the duality of the Nature archetype which can be as kind as it can be cruel. This is where we see Jackson's vivid imagination most clearly. He was inspired by Tolkien's words, but his portrayal of Galadriel is more than a mimetic representation. Tolkien did not direct Galadriel's depiction by Jackson; the text provided only an inspiration. The archetype of the feminine and of Nature, as well as the knowledge that Galadriel bears the Elven symbol of water through her ring, Nenya, are mixed into the dynamic image of a terrible dark and beautiful Queen of Middle-earth that will never be. She wanted "to rule [...] a realm at her own will", (Tolkien, 1977: 89) but she did not ultimately take the Ring. She manifests the Jungian *shadow* by briefly experiencing "the dark aspects of [her] personality as present and real", (Campbell, 1978: 145) and "pass[es] the test". (Tolkien, 1973: 474) After that, Galadriel's voice is low and clear and her eyes sparkle.

There are many words synonymous with the feminine; the one Jackson relies on is enchantment. To heighten this cinematically, Jackson uses close-ups and places emphasis on the eyes. Galadriel's ability to enchant is seen through the flickering and twisting lights that are reflected in her eyes, making it difficult for us to look away. Galadriel not only enchants the members of the Fellowship, but the audience as well. It is said that Hope also enchants and Jackson's next augmentation to the *LotR* involves the character of Arwen Undómiel. She is the epitome of Hope for the Fellowship, for Middle-earth, and for those around her. Jackson cleverly reinforces this through the butterfly motifs that are reflected in her accoutrements. The Evenstar becomes the outward expression of Hope.

Of Elves and Men—A Forged Alliance

One cannot underestimate the power of Hope in Middle-earth and Jackson embodies that Hope in his portrayal of Arwen Undómiel, which means Evenstar, the most treasured star of the Elves. Aragorn was given the name Estel, Elvish for hope, because he was a hope for the future of Men. Our first glimpse of Arwen's presence is her sword, Hadahafang, lightly lifting Aragorn's chin as we hear her voice. This pivotal scene reverses the roles of Arwen and Aragorn. Aragorn is cropping the *athelas* plant in order to heal Frodo, which is based on prophesy, but Arwen enters as a warrior. The two most striking aspects of this scene are Arwen's off-screen voice—again, demonstrating Jackson's preference for his female Elves to speak in the lower register—and the visual as she catches Aragorn unaware in a subservient position, stooped like an old woman gathering herbs. Immediately we see Arwen's strength and realize that she has the upper hand. Our second vision of her is through the eyes of Frodo, as she emerges from a dazzlingly white light with the soft singing of upper register voices. Arwen fairly glows in her gown of white and silver that shines like Frodo's mithril shirt. This vision of her gives hope to the Hobbits that Frodo will be healed. It is the feminine that restores hope, not the healing powers of Aragorn as the returned king.

At the Ford, Arwen commands the waters, a feminine symbol that we see with Galadriel. Jackson has Arwen, not Glorfindel, nor Gandalf, call upon the waters of the Ford as a barrier between herself and the Nazgûl. She brandishes her Elven sword while issuing the challenge, "If you want him, come and claim him!" Out of her hope for Middle-earth, she protects and delivers Frodo to her father, but out of her hope for a life with Aragorn, she sacrifices her immortality and does not rescind it, even when Aragorn attempts to return her Evenstar charm. She simply states, "Keep it. It was a gift." Giving the audience Arwen is Jackson's gift—a twenty-first century woman who is empowered to make a difference in the reconstructed medieval culture of Middle-earth. Jackson's Arwen is crucial, because she is the one who brings hope to the male characters in the film; in fact, she is the personification of Hope. Arwen is a natural choice for Jackson since she played a very small role in Tolkien's story. This left her character open for Jackson's creative endeavours.

Jackson's visual representation of Arwen's presence and immortality is her necklace, the Evenstar, which is a delicate silver fairy/butterfly. Hope further supports faith that Frodo will be victorious in destroying the Ring. Even when Elrond states that there is no hope, Arwen says, "There is always hope." This is the half-Elf who has lost all hope in the line of Men when Isildur refused to throw the Ring into the fiery chasm of Mount Doom. Elrond's vision of his daughter is a bleak one. He sees her in a landscape with decaying fortresses, devoid of life and people, as she stands shrouded in a black mourning gown on a windswept platform beside the sarcophagus of Aragorn. But Arwen remains faithful to her belief in hope. As she accompanies the last group of Elves on their way to the Elven ships, Arwen catches a glimpse into a possible future where an older Aragorn scoops up a young boy, with her striking blue eyes. The child wears her Evenstar, and as a continuance of her, is also hope. Realizing that this future is still possible, she rides back to Rivendell and confronts her father. He tells her that he looked into her future and saw only death, to which, she counters, "But there was also life." And while there is life, Arwen herself still has hope. She reads a prophesy that speaks of the elemental forces and of the re-forging of the sword that was once broken:

> From the ashes a fire shall be woken,
> A light from the shadows shall spring;
> Renewed shall be blade that was broken:
> The crownless again shall be king.

Here, Jackson takes a crucial turn towards strengthening the voice of the feminine by giving Bilbo's lines (Tolkien, 1973: 325), spoken in indignation at the Council of Elrond, to Arwen after she convinces her father to secure the prophesy, speaking the words in voice-over as her brothers Elladan and Elrohir re-forge the sword of kings, Narsil.

Arwen has the power of Hope to awaken Aragorn after his fall from the cliff. She has the ability to keep Frodo clinging on to life and not succumb to the wound of the Morgul blade as she intones, "What Grace has given me, let it pass on to him." Arwen can sustain as only the archetype of Hope can. It is not her place to heal, but to sustain Frodo. With her marriage to Aragorn, which Jackson saves for the end, the secular male and the sacred female embodiment marry and then truly there is hope for Middle-earth and the continuance of the race of Men. And, thus, balance is restored to Nature.

Of Wizard and Warrior —Deconstructing the Masculine Power

Gandalf the Grey was written as a trickster figure in *The Hobbit*. In fifty years shire-time, he grows into the role of Wiseman, a term used by Campbell. (Campbell, 1949: 9-10) Jackson's Gandalf looks, talks, and for the most part, acts as Tolkien wrote him. However, Jackson's Gandalf is humorous, which reveals a part of the younger character. Traditionally, the Wiseman is the archetypal keeper of knowledge, and the one who has knowledge and wisdom at his command. When Gandalf gives advice or answers questions, he speaks as the archetypal Wiseman. As the Fellowship leaves Rivendell, Frodo queries silently, "Mordor, Gandalf. Is it left or right?" Gandalf replies, "Right." Frodo asks the Wiseman, not the ranger, who should know the way. Later, with a single look, we know that Gandalf is not happy to enter the Mines of Moria. Here, Jackson plays towards the archetype by removing action from Tolkien's Gandalf through the lines, "Let the Ringbearer decide." Returning from the masculine role of decision-maker, Gandalf does not choose to go into the Mines, as in Tolkien's book; instead he acquiesces to Frodo's decision.

At the Gates of Moria, Gandalf uses his wizardly knowledge of spells and incantations to no avail. Defeated, Gandalf subsides, waiting for inspiration. The riddle must be solved by someone who is not so wise as to "miss the forest for the trees". Once inside the Mines, Gandalf leads for a while before exclaiming in horror, "I have no memory of this place." This truly is frightening! All were depending on the knowledge and experience of this Wiseman. Jackson allows a brief scene of Gandalf in a library, consulting ancient parchments before making the strong recommendation that the Ring is not safe in Hobbiton. However, Gandalf is dumbfounded when his wisdom or memory and experience fail him. Once again, he sits down to ruminate, seemingly learning from his earlier experience at the Gates. As the Wiseman, Gandalf seeks wisdom from the written knowledge, in fact the first item he seeks in Balin's tomb is a book that has been half slashed through, preferring to read what has happened rather than to view the corpses strewn about the Chamber.

Gandalf, according to Tolkien, secretly wears the ring of fire, Narya. As with Galadriel, Jackson plays with archetypal elementals, this time fire. As Gandalf attempts to hinder a creature from the ancient realm, a Balrog, creature of fire and flame, Gandalf calls upon the Secret Flame of his ring and is lit with a golden glow. But fire cannot vanquish a creature whose life is fire, and Jackson has Gandalf resort to the sword, Glamdring, obtained from the troll's lair in *The Hobbit*. (Tolkien, 1973: 53) Now Gandalf has been moved from inactive player to a warrior's role. Thus playing with different archetypes, Jackson blurs the lines of the typical masculine role.

In *The Two Towers*, rumour has spread that a white Wizard roams the forest of Fangorn. No one knows who this is, but everyone assumes it is Saruman the White. When Aragorn, Legolas, and Gimli encounter the white Wizard, the light of his presence is blindingly bright. Each of the three fires one shot which is easily deflected by the Wizard. The voices of Saruman and Gandalf are blended into one mighty voice that is somewhat deceiving—a brilliant move on Jackson's part because Gandalf the Grey is now Gandalf the White. He has assumed the role that Saruman had occupied before a fall from grace. However, when looking at archetypes, Gandalf, reborn after his fight with a manxome foe, (Carroll, 2002: 939) is no longer the Wiseman; he is a quasi-warrior. Jackson films scenes with Gandalf charging the Orcs at Helm's Deep with Éomer and the Rohirrim. Gandalf saves Faramir, strikes Denethor, and slices through Mordor's army at the gates of the White City. Now Gandalf has been moved from a top hierarchal status—the patriarch of wisdom and knowledge—to a minor position—that of a mere warrior who resorts to physical strength and weapons. Through such devolution the patriarchal power—the ideological foundation of masculinity—is wittily challenged. This physical masculinization of Gandalf blurs and denounces his higher status as a patriarchal Wiseman, making his character barely equal to if not inferior to some female characters in the film. Ironically, the physical masculinization of Jackson's Gandalf can be viewed in terms of social politics as feminization of this character.

Jackson's films are far more feminine than Tolkien's story could have ever envisaged. The cinematographic version moves Tolkien's male-oriented story of war and brotherhood into the present by acknowledging the power of the feminine. Peter Jackson, as a "sub-creator", has brought to life his own vision of Middle-earth—a part of, not a mere reflection of the literature on which it was based.

Bibliography

Anon (2005), Joseph Campbell Foundation website: http://www.jcf.org/about_jc.php

Campbell, Joseph (1949), *The Hero with a Thousand Faces* The Bollingen series 17, Pantheon Books, New York

Campbell, Joseph (1978), *Portable Jung*, trans. R. F. C. Hull, Penguin Books, New York

Campbell, Joseph (1999), *The Hero's Journey: Joseph Campbell on His Life and Work*, ed. Robert Walter, Element, Shaftesbury

Carroll, Lewis (2002), "Jabberwocky" in Robert DiYanni (ed.), *Literature: Reading Fiction, Poetry, and Drama* 5th ed., McGraw-Hill, New York, pp. 939-940

Tolkien, J.R.R. (1966), "Tree and Leaf" in *The Tolkien Reader: Stories, Poems, and Commentaries but the Author of The Hobbit and The Lord of the Rings*, Ballantine Books, New York, pp. 29-124

Tolkien, J.R.R. (1977), *The Silmarillion* 1st ed., ed. Christopher Tolkien, Ballantine Books, New York

Tolkien, J.R.R. (1986a), *The Hobbit*, Ballantine Books, New York

Tolkien, J.R.R. (1986b), *The Lord of the Rings: The Fellowship of the Ring*, Ballantine Books, New York

Watson, G. (1988), "Discovering the Imagination: Platonists and Stoics on phantasia" in John M. Dillon and A.A. Long (eds), *The Question of "Eclecticism": Studies in Later Greek Philosophy*, University of California Press, Berkeley, pp. 208-233

Pinnacles: towers consume us or towers consumed by us?
(photo by Bill J. Jerome)

14

IN LIGHT OF ZEN BUDDHISM
Reading Frodo Baggins' Journey to Rivendell

Lalipa Nilubol

The Lord of the Rings as a modern Buddhist myth? Not very plausible, on the face of it... Although neither God nor a Redeemer is ever mentioned, the tale expresses some Christian influence, according to Tolkien's own admission (he was a devout Roman Catholic)... There is no hint, either in the story or in its sources, of any Buddhist influences....

And yet...Tolkien's masterpiece achieves what he intended, which was to create a modern myth; and myths, as he also knew, have a way of growing beyond their creator's intentions. The Lord of the Rings is much more than an endearing fantasy about little hobbits, gruff dwarves, and light-footed elves. It has been repeatedly voted the novel of the century—according to some, it is the novel of the millennium!—because so many readers find it deeply moving as well. What is it about the tale that makes it so compelling, so mythic? One answer, for us at least, is that despite its European origins it resonates with Buddhist concerns and perspectives.

(Loy and Goodhew, 2004: 20-21)

THE FACT THAT Buddhist themes can be read into *LotR* is one of the most compelling testimonies to the universal qualities of Buddhism. As suggested in the above passage, *LotR* is not overtly Buddhist in its mythical qualities, and henceforth, Buddhist themes in the story have not been widely studied. On the other hand, studies on Christian themes in Tolkien's literary works are so varied and expansive that it may be plausible to say that such Christian themes contribute significantly to defining *LotR* as a modern Anglo-Saxon, or Western, myth. A Zen Buddhist analysis of *LotR* does not necessarily become mixed with or even undermine the tale's Christian roots. Instead, a Zen interpretation is a valid alternative to a Christian interpretation, especially as Tolkien's writing materialized during an era when Zen Buddhism was becoming increasingly popular in the West. This chapter does not attempt to prove that such Zen influences in Tolkien's novels were overtly intentional enough to compete with the significance of the Christian influences. Instead, this chapter provides a Zen reading—independent of any contentious issues with Christian themes—of a significant episode in the film version of *LotR*. This episode begins in Troll's Clearing, and progressively incorporates an apparition scene, action sequences, and surreal visual assemblages that suggest Frodo's spiritual elevation. Together, these presentations portray the powers of immortal Elves fusing with the consciousness of a mortal Hobbit, accelerating the expansion of the Hobbit's consciousness so that the Hobbit comes to experience what can be argued as an equivalent of Zen enlightenment.

A Zen reading of these successive scenes holds to the premise that Zen is "the art of seeing into the nature of one's own being, and it points the way from bondage to freedom". (Suzuki, 1970: 13) As an access and a view into one's true nature, and a means towards liberation, Zen thus becomes a universal ideal. This universal quality significantly heightens the appropriateness of a Zen analysis of *LotR*, as the story itself contains the widest range of multi-cultural and multi-lingual themes.

Zen and Its Relevance to Reading *LotR*

Zen, according to Sohaku Ogata's, is described as "the essence of the Oriental mind". (Ogata, 1973: 11) Being founded on and closely connected with various Eastern cultures (such as Indian, Chinese and Japanese), Zen has a far more universal quality. Many Western writings of Zen Buddhism praise Zen as one of the greatest jewels gifted by the East to the West. And the likelihood of Professor Tolkien's receptiveness to Zen influences in his writing would have been especially high, as he wrote *LotR* during the 1930s—1950s, a period when the novelty and popularity of Zen among the Western educated class appeared to take on celebrity proportions.

In 1956, Alan Watts wrote in the Preface of his book *The Way of Zen*, that since the 1930s, and indeed since World War II, interest in Zen Buddhism among Western intellectual and artistic circles had increased extraordinarily. Watts argued that despite the spiritual deterioration of modern Western society, the middle of the twenties century was also the time when the West was undergoing its most creative period. New insights and discoveries in Western science, psychology, philosophy, and communications might have been the result of influences from Asian philosophy. Watts referred to this as a "parallelism" rather than a direct influence, evidently alluding to the notion that Asian philosophy, and indeed Zen Buddhism, have all-encompassing qualities that can be easily applied universally or cross-culturally. (Watts, 1995: vii)

The publication of the works of Dr. Daisetz Teitaro Suzuki, which first introduced Zen Buddhism to the Western audience, became a turning point in the history of reception of Eastern ideas in the West. Since then the popularity of Zen Buddhist philosophy among Western readers has been unflagging. It became typical to address Zen as a "universal point of view", (Blyth, 1942: vii) for "[l]abels vanish and there is no East/West dilemma in the realm of pure thought". (Benoit, 2004: 7)

In order to substantiate a Zen interpretation of a modern Western myth such as *LotR*, it is important to establish those elements of modern Western culture that converge with Buddhist teachings. According to Alan Watts, it is perhaps the idea of psychotherapy, the objective of which is to change one's state of consciousness. Fundamentally, Oriental disciplines are more concerned with the evolution of states of consciousness; for as the average human being is often deluded, "it is thus that the very word 'Buddha', in Buddhism, is from a root in Sanskrit, *buddh*, which means to awaken." (Watts, 1995: 8-9)

In *The Fellowship of the Ring*, the first instalment of Peter Jackson's film trilogy, Frodo Baggins' journey to the Elven haven of Rivendell deals entirely with a re-awakening to a higher state of consciousness. Expansion of consciousness also underlies Frodo's Ring Quest. The entire odyssey consists of a series of rites of symbolic death and rebirth that repeatedly strip Frodo of his conditioned status and persona. From an Eastern perspective at least, it is these rites of humility (status-stripping by nature) that determine the success of the Ring Quest. Significantly, *LotR* bestows the most credit to the powerless—little Hobbits of the Shire who, according to the film prologue of *FotR*, "would change the fortunes of all".

The official forging of Frodo Baggins' new identity as Ringbearer is not designed to glorify any kind of heroism. On the contrary, the great necessity for a Fellowship to accompany Frodo during the earlier part of the Ring Quest signifies that Frodo is an "anti-hero". Frodo's need for an accompanying Fellowship demonstrates that he is weak, timid, vulnerable, and infantile in the ways of the world, and naturally requires a Fellowship to protect him. As Frodo is protected by these mighty fellows of great status and power, and as they display their martial brilliance and heroic valour in the exertion of such protection, Frodo is, in a sense, belittled, despite his most important position in the Fellowship. Through this belittlement, Frodo Baggins comes to represent an "anti-ego", which is more in harmony with the Eastern devaluation of the ego.

According to Joseph Campbell, the doctrine of individualism so common in modern Western society has no real equivalent in the East. "There the ideal… is the quenching, not development, of ego." (Campbell, 1962: 22) Because of this discouragement from clinging to the restrictions of ego, the Eastern psyche, to a large extent, remains "wide open to the seizures of completely uncritical mythic identifications." (Campbell, 1962: 23) The devaluation of the ego is one of the principles that perfectly validates reading *LotR* from an Eastern perspective. At least from a Zen perspective, the devaluation and ritual cleansing of the ego, featured prominently in Frodo's journey to Rivendell, eventually lead to a state of greater realization equivalent to an experience of Zen enlightenment, referred to as satori.

It can be interpreted that the experience of satori is brought about by a transcendence of personality, status, conditioning from external circumstances, and even intellect. Only through such a transcendence does Frodo's being merge with a superior form of collective intelligence that has given rise to and nurtured the existence of the world of the Elves. This process of merging between Frodo and the superior collective intelligence, however abstract that may sound, occurs towards the end of the crossing to Rivendell. As will be argued in the latter part of this chapter, the mystical, dream-like quality of the cinematic presentation of this phenomenon provides substantial allusions to the Zen experience of satori:

> Zen writings commonly refer to satori as realization of the "original mind" as it is in itself, the universal ground of consciousness, concealed beneath the temporal conditioning that forces people to experience life through outlooks arbitrarily limited by their cultural, social, and personal histories. (Cleary, 2001, vol.1: 3)

One of the reasons for the classic appropriateness of using the cinematic portrayal of Frodo Baggins' journey to Rivendell as a case study in this chapter is that this episode in the film signifies Frodo's transcendence of his previous cultural conditioning and personal history. This transcendence not only directly parallels the aim of Zen and the nature of Zen enlightenment, as described above. More importantly, Frodo's transcendence of his previous Hobbit conditioning is an appropriate case study for this chapter, as it presents Zen as a universal ideal, transcending the limitations of cultural, social, and personal divergences.

Zen after all, seeks to transcend separateness and dualism, and to be liberated from such constructed patterns of thought and action. In the same spirit of transcendence and liberation, Frodo's entry into an Elven haven signifies an inter-dimensional fusion that transcends the rift that could be potentially generated by the aloofness of the Elves and the long-standing suspicion that Hobbits hold towards the world outside their native Shire. In establishing the concept of Zen liberation as the principal theme running through Frodo's journey to Rivendell, I will initially apply the Zen notion of emptiness in my discussion of the earlier episode of Frodo's crossing. I will then apply the Zen notion of enlightenment, referred to as satori, in my discussion of the completion of Frodo's crossing, as well as his re-awakening in the Elven haven of Rivendell.

"Emptiness" in Frodo Baggins' Journey to Rivendell

In order to enter Rivendell as a new being who will officially take on the task of Ringbearer, it is essential that Frodo is purified from the curse of the evil wound inflicted upon him by the Nazgûl Ringwraiths, his previous status as a more or less carefree Hobbit gentleman brought up in the confines of the remote Shire, and his ignorance, suspicion, and fear of the external world outside the safety of the Shire. If purification is defined as a surrendering of and release from a previous state, then the passage to Rivendell magnifies this concept to clear extremities, as it already appears at Troll's Clearing—the starting point of the passage—that Frodo's body is quite ready to relinquish even its own life due to his tortured state of physical and spiritual paralysis. This death-like state is predominantly characterized by a sense of emptiness, a Zen ideal whose aspect of surrender is described by Zen master Yuanwu as cited in Thomas Cleary's *Classics of Buddhism and Zen*. Yuanwu's teaching conveys a surrendering of former knowledge and conception, to the point of emptying one's mind of thought and potential speech. This emptying opens up the heart, bringing about the merging of one's mind with "the fundamental source, sinking into the infinite, spontaneously attaining inherent wisdom that has no attainment." (Cleary, 2001, vol.1: 167)

In the film, Frodo's passage to Rivendell begins with an experience of emptiness, free of the processing of speech and thought. The stab from a Morgul blade to his chest has reduced him to a crippled state, resulting in a delirium where he is being psychically tortured by the forces of the Dark Lord. However, it is this state of delirium that causes his mind to empty itself of any sense of logic, coherency and rational conception of the tangible world. And it is this emptiness in Frodo's mind that allows him to perceive an other-worldly phenomenon that is evanescent and dream-like, but whose sole purpose is to heal him.

Frodo has a vision of a white light radiating from among background trees where a tall, graceful woman emerges on a horse which is galloping in slow motion. As the mysterious woman dismounts, the white light conceals the details of her appearance. She slowly approaches Frodo and she emerges from the concealing light. Frodo's vision of her becomes clearer.

> Frodo, im Arwen. Telin le thaed.
> Lasto beth nîn, tolo dan na ngalad.
> *(Frodo, I am Arwen. I come to help you.*
> *Hear my voice, come back to the light.)*

Her introduction, which happens in slow motion, generates a sense of airiness, appearing to diminish the earthly influence of gravity. There is also an allusion that time on the earthly plane has slowed down especially to grace her entry. She is evidently not of this world. There is a translucent layering of the image of Arwen and the image of Frodo that produces a telepathic intimacy between the beholder and the object of his vision. Frodo is clearly not perceiving her through his intellectual faculties, as these faculties have been severely crippled. He is not even "trying" to perceive this other-worldly phenomenon, as this "trying" would be an act that the intellectual component of the mind would attempt. This is simply a spontaneous vision that happens to Frodo magically without any conscious preparation on his part. This supernatural vision, thus, signifies that Frodo has been emptied of his intellect in order to perceive such ethereality that, arguably, only his true nature or his "soul"[1] has the power to experience. The layering of the image of Arwen and the image of Frodo signifies a union between the knower (in this case, Frodo) and what he knows (in this case, his vision of Arwen).

This union is accomplished through the emptying of and purification from Frodo's intellect, an intellect that, according to Zen, is more given to perceiving duality and separation. According to Daisetz Suzuki, "[t]he intellect can yield an understanding of life, indeed, many possible understandings of life, but it cannot bring man into union with life and with himself." (Phillips, 1962: xxi) For intellect tends to separate the subject from the object, and the knower from the knowledge. The intellect tends to objectify, and refrains from involvement and unity. Even when one tries to understand oneself intellectually, one must stand outside oneself to look at oneself. According to Suzuki, it is not by intellectualizing about ourselves that we unite with ourselves, as Zen would say, "but only plunging into ourselves." (Phillips, 1962: xxi) Uniting with ourselves, thus demands a kind of perception that is the opposite of intellectualizing.

In perceiving the apparition of Arwen, Frodo has involuntarily, even unconsciously, perceived in a manner that is the opposite of intellectualizing. All he did was to look without meaning to look, to see without meaning to see. Even such subtle acts of perception occur with minimal effort but profound consciousness. I contend that the spontaneous operation of this profound consciousness transcends any conditioning by the external world. For if this profound consciousness were subject to the external world, such a vision of ethereal beauty would not have been visible to a mortal Hobbit who had grown up within the confines of the remote Shire. This extraordinary perception generated by minimal effort, directly converges with the Zen concept of purification from the unnecessary that, in this case, extends to unnecessary efforts to perceive the other-world. The emptying of and purification from what can be considered, in this context, the excesses of the mind is summed

---

[1] I am defining the "soul", for purposes of convenience, as a divine source that is eternal and the storehouse of extraordinary gifts. I am arguing that throughout the crossing to Rivendell, the soul is Frodo's only faculty that has not been fatally wounded. The soul is, thus Frodo's only chance to experiencing the equivalent of satori, an instance of Zen enlightenment which, as I will argue, occurs at the end of the crossing.

up by Stephen Addiss: "The power of... Zen... lies in its elimination of the nonessential." (Addis, 1989: 13)

The camera then shifts to Sam and Merry. "Who is she?" Merry asks in wonder. The camera returns to the mysterious woman. She is no longer in white. Within the space of the single image diverted from her, she has transformed, the transformation process itself remaining unknown and unseen by the audience. The mysterious woman has made a "second entry". She is now in a dark, much thicker riding outfit. This transformation process, unseen by the audience, bestows extreme ambiguity upon the enchantress's character: we do not know whether an actual transformation took place at all, or whether it was witnessed by Frodo's companions if indeed it actually happened, or whether the woman in white was merely, unknown to his companions, a figment of Frodo's hallucination.

The ambiguity of this transformation is a classic exemplification of the Zen notion of emptiness of form. This does not refer to physical emptiness. In this context, it is the fleetingly impermanent quality of form that we are concerned with. Arwen's transformation from her first disguise to her second disguise epitomises, in a magical context, the notion that form is in an incessant state of flux. This signifies that, at any given moment, the present state of form does not last, and is thus evanescent and empty. The fact that Arwen's transformation occurs away from the audience's vision, and the fact that the protagonists do not appear to notice this transformation, altogether convey the emptiness of the transformation itself. The emptiness of this transformation lies in the fact that the transformation becomes entirely immaterial after it has taken place. The scene then progresses in a way that immediately detaches from this transformation. The focus of the scene and the attention of the audience are brought back to Frodo's fatal condition.

Thus, Arwen's transformation is not fixated on the tangible presence of form as such, but comprises rather of the miraculously swift metamorphosis from one form to another, causing any appearance of form to become a mere memory. In Zen terms, the essence of form does not last, and is thus empty: "The emptiness of emptiness means that emptiness itself is empty. That does not mean empty as in physically empty, but its emptiness means emptiness is not itself a thing." (Cleary, 2001, vol.3: 592) Emptiness, as an elusion of form or of any concept of fixation, becomes a predominant theme that runs through the crossing sequence. This is because the crossing sequence is directed by an epic escape, the escape theme maximising the extremity of elusion.

Emptiness, as an ultimate elusion of form that characterizes Arwen's transformation, is seen again in the action sequence of River horses that occurs shortly before Frodo's arrival at Rivendell. Although contrasting stylistically with the emptiness portrayed in Arwen's transformation, the sequence of Water horses just as significantly portrays the Zen notion of emptiness as it presents the enormity and rage of a terrorising but protective force wielded by incorporeal creatures who elude any sense of physical substantiality. Leading up to this sequence, Arwen and Frodo reach the Ford of Bruinen, the outskirts of a territory protected by the power of the Elves. The Nazgûl horses halt at the far side of the river as they are forbidden to cross by powers that are as yet unseen. The presentation of this invisible resistance re-introduces an emptiness imbued with divine power, initially portrayed in Frodo's first encounter with Arwen at Troll's Clearing. Arwen then chants an invocation that resonates and echoes towards the expanses of the immense rock-scape in the background:

> Nîn o Chithaeglir lasto beth daer;
> Rimmo nîn Bruinen dan in Ulaer!
> *(Waters of the Misty Mountains listen to the great word;*
> *Flow waters of the Loudwater against the Ringwraiths!)*

A giant flood of water rushes forward with wrath-like force from the upper river. There is a brief "profile" image of the flood, this time with horses' heads emerging from the deluge. As the Water horses gallop forward, the immensity of their might becomes heightened by their resemblance to assemblages of rapidly expanding clouds storming mercilessly forward. The River horses rise majestically higher and higher, their bodies always attached to the cloud-like formations. They do not gallop "out" of the clouds, even though the enormity of their force makes them appear about to do so. In their feat of gallant ascension, the River horses overwhelm the Nazgûl. Then, in all their rage and magnificence, the Water horses return to the River from whence they came.

The River horse sequence exemplifies the paradoxical nature of the Zen notion of emptiness. It demonstrates the water element operating in an animalistic form. Simultaneously, the sequence bestows an entirely aquatic nature on animals that are normally earthlings. The conventional division between animal traits and aquatic traits disappears, hence the Zen notion that divisions or differences are essentially empty. Duality and separateness are thus empty—and are merely subject to the binding constructs created through intellectualizing—especially as the complete and utter fusion between the animalistic and the aquatic in this sequence shows clearly that horse and water are of the same flesh, however intangible that flesh may be. This intangibility in itself suggests that the substance that constitutes and identifies the being or object concerned is ultimately empty.

Thus, the River horse sequence conveys an underlying Zen concept of ultimate reality as a non-dual emptiness. According to Moti Lal Pandit's interpretation, beings and things are essentially of the Buddha-nature, and therefore, "[a]ll beings have the possibility of attaining to Buddhahood because reality is of the nature of emptiness." (Pandit, 1998: 171)

The manner in which the River horse sequence is presented is in itself empty. The horses emerge from the unfathomable water, a highly elusive element to physically grasp, let alone contain. Its fluidity determines that water will always elude, and thus be empty of, any sense of fixated form or substantiality, similar to the case for Arwen's transformation at Troll's Clearing. Therefore, water in the River horse sequence can be referred to as the "great emptiness". The Water horses which rise from this great emptiness release the fury and enormity of their powers, and disappear back into the great emptiness. The epic action wielded by the River horses is negated by the very brevity of this action and the immediate disappearance of the River horses back into the water. Even the action sequence, elegant and wrathfully savage as it may be, holds no substance, and is thus empty of it. And like Arwen's transformation at Troll's Clearing, the disappearance of an evanescent state, followed by a regression or return into another, conveys the ultimate emptiness of form that cannot be explained by logic but can be known or intuited through experience.

As the scene unwinds from the action sequences, it becomes evident that the invincible wildness of water has symbolically become a living character in the deluge sequence, accentuated by water's role as cleanser and destroyer of evil:

> ...both on the cosmological and the anthropological planes immersion in the waters is equivalent not to a final extinction but to a temporary reincorporation into the indistinct, followed by a new creation, a new life... In whatever religious complex we find them, the waters invariably retain their function; they disintegrate, abolish forms, "wash away sins"; they are at once purifying and regenerating... (Eliade, 1959: 130-131)

Thus, through the literal and symbolic "washing away" of his previous ordinary identity, Frodo's new identity—one that will achieve its birth in the ethereal dimension—is well and truly in the process of being forged. In forsaking his previous ordinary identity, Frodo relinquishes the previous habitual patterns of his ego, overcoming many of the fears and weaknesses conditioned throughout his life within the confines of the Shire.[2] This relinquishment of the previous ways of the ego can be considered equivalent to the Zen notion of the Great Death, according to Bernard Phillips: "No one is prepared to take that last step [the Great Death] until he has first exhausted all his other resources, and finally stands emptied of all contrivances for meeting life." (Phillips, 1962: xvi) Phillips continued to suggest that the Great Death is also the Great Awakening, and that "the existential awakening to one's true Self is called *enlightenment* (*satori*, in Japanese)." (Phillips, 1962: xvi)

The Equivalent of Satori

The scene finally returns to Arwen and Frodo. As Frodo's condition worsens, Arwen realizes that he is beginning to pass into darkness, and that he will eventually become a Ringwraith like those who wounded him. She softly utters a prayer:

> What grace is given me, let it pass to him, let him be spared, save him...

The scene fades into a dream sequence that provides the first glimpses into the architecture of Rivendell, one of the sacred realms governed by the Elves. The images are faded and dissolved into a foggy whiteness. The dream sequence is a series of multiple layers of faint images varying in degrees of translucency, with the more opaque images lapsing into one another amidst the other fainter images. Image

---

[2] As we see in the film trilogy, Frodo's lack of direction and purpose in life and his display of fear in the presence of Ringwraiths—significantly portrayed in the earlier part of *FotR*—hardly reappear after he is officially named Ringbearer at the Council of Elrond at Rivendell.

contents are "fragmented", as they depict only small segments of indistinguishable architectural components. The dream sequence clearly embodies the Zen ideal of eluding the binding principles of logic. The camera now acquires a sense of surpassing earthly grasp, its movements suggestive of hovering, floating, and trance-like gazing in the direction of the celestial. Nothing is grounded.

Can this experience be identified as an equivalent of satori? At this early stage of the dream sequence, Frodo's transcendental experience tends to encompass evident characteristics of it. The fluid, weightless, almost ghost-like slow motion of the camera arguably represents Frodo's consciousness. The translucent layering of faint and opaque images (which also occurred at the beginning of the crossing when Frodo first encounters Arwen) represents Frodo's "translucent vision", capable of penetrating a multitude of dimensions, both ordinary and ethereal.

Thus far, we cannot see Frodo. But it seems likely that the dream sequence represents Frodo's vision, which has already departed from worldly constructs of logic. As it occurs immediately after the defeat of the Ringwraiths, the dream sequence is an experience of liberation, an expanding pristine quality that has overcome and detached from all physical and mental exhaustion. According to Hubert Benoit, satori is described by a number of Zen masters as encompassing the following characteristics:

> ... the initial profound calm with a sensation of being in a state of suspension as though both awake and asleep at the same time, the cessation of all mental restlessness (the Zen monk says that he is then "like an idiot, like an imbecile"), the part played by a sense-perception in triggering a global shift in perspective, the suddenness with which this happens, the impression of clarity and unity brought by the new perspective. (Benoit, 2004: 54)

The above characteristics—the blurring of the boundaries between unconsciousness and waking, the profound sense of rest, and the sudden unfolding of a previously unknown vision—all describe Frodo's inner state during this dream sequence. Frodo's inner state has now cleared itself of previous hindrances and spontaneously opened itself to merge with a higher consciousness that can be described as satori. According to Suzuki, "[w]hen poetically or figuratively expressed, satori is 'the opening of the mind-flower', or 'the removing of the bar', or 'the brightening up of the mind-works'." (Suzuki, 1970: 231) All these tend to mean the clearing up of a passage, or of one's means of expression.

While the camera remains "floating", wandering in slow motion, an image of Frodo appears, still partly unconscious, amidst a peaceful hymn sung in an ethereal tongue and a white light radiating from the faded background. The white light glows around Frodo like an aura, the same white light that accompanied Arwen's entry into the film and illuminated Frodo's first vision of her. The white light moving across to become part of Frodo is an early indication that the immortal Arwen has succeeded in passing over "what grace is given me" to the mortal Frodo, partly sanctifying him in the process. Then, an image of Lord Elrond emerges as Frodo's image disappears. With the serenity that similarly characterizes his daughter Arwen, he softly utters an invocation:

> Lasto beth nîn, tolo dan na ngalad.
> *(Hear my voice, come back to the light.)*

After that, the sequence cuts to a blank white image. The origin of this whiteness remains ambiguous. If it is a momentous signification of ritual purification—thus symbolising a void where a new state of being is to be created—then this image of blank whiteness becomes a component of satori where destruction and rebirth are fused into one and the same experience. Although seemingly opposites by way of logic, the destruction of Frodo's former ordinary status and the rebirth of his new ethereally-forged identity are united into an organic whole when viewed in terms of spiritual evolution. Through Frodo's experience of a death-like satori, the opposition between destruction and rebirth dissolves. Rebirth is, in a sense, "birthed" by destruction, and destruction attains birthing qualities through its generation of rebirth, and therefore destruction becomes neutralized through rebirth. This transcendence of opposition is elaborated extensively in Zen writings, particularly those of Suzuki:

> Satori may be defined as an intuitive looking into the nature of things in contradistinction to the analytical or logical understanding of it. Practically, it means the unfolding of a new world hitherto unperceived in the confusion of a dualistically-trained mind. (Suzuki, 1996: 84)

After this new awakening, one's spiritual evolution accomplishes a rebirth of perception where everything feels new. (Suzuki, 1970: 262) This Zen ideal of a revolution in perception that clears the passage for full expression of intuitive powers is conveyed significantly in the dream sequence upon Frodo's entry into Rivendell. In the dream sequence, the images washed over in a foggy whiteness and the camera's hovering, trance-like movements—all representing Frodo's vision as the forces of light (i.e. the Elves) accomplish their triumph—suggest that time itself has slowed down.

Arguably, time loosening its own grasp easily suggests a sense of "eternity", the concept of eternity considered to be the transcendence of time. This dream sequence is, in other words, a cinematic portrayal of the slowing down of time, and hence, arguably, is an allusion to eternity. Thus, in an almost poetic sense, this sequence demonstrates Frodo "visiting" eternity, and eternity "visiting" Frodo, if the term "visiting" can be at all poetically synonymous to the concept of "'allusion" (referring to the expression "allusion to eternity", mentioned in the previous sentence). According to D.T. Suzuki, the visiting and visitation of eternity also define an aspect of satori: "Satori obtains when eternity cuts into time or impinges upon time, or, which is the same thing after all, when time emerges itself into eternity." (Suzuki, 1970: 262) It can be claimed that satori occurs when the physical and mental laws to which worldly existence is bound have been transcended. This is perhaps the new awakening mentioned earlier. Significantly, the blank white image concluding Frodo's passage to Rivendell is almost iconic of the fusion between purification and renewal.

Following this image of blank whiteness, we see Frodo awakening in Rivendell. The journey to Rivendell demonstrates that the destruction of Frodo's previous status, that he had acquired from his upbringing in the Shire, is necessary to bring about his identity-renewal. In this new identity, Frodo Baggins is officially pronounced Ringbearer, the chosen one who will fulfil the Ring Quest. The path to this new identity was fraught with near-death and death-like phenomena, after which an experience of illumination equivalent to satori symbolically provided the initiatory key to Frodo's new identity as the Ringbearer. After this experience of death-like satori, Frodo is "reborn" into a new identity as the "chosen one", an identity that is sanctified in every sense, as it is forged by ethereal forces and, henceforth, eternally at one with the ethereal.

The Universal Quality of Zen as Portrayed in Frodo Baggins' Journey to Rivendell

Frodo Baggins' journey to Rivendell demonstrates an elusion and elusiveness of all the technical prerequisites to being a conventional hero. Since Frodo is a hero who does not conform to conventional heroic qualities, he transcends any kind of dualism between what is traditionally considered heroic and non-heroic. This alludes to the Zen ideal of transcending opposites through the attainment of a sense of wholeness that is all-encompassing, (Phillips, 1962: xxxiv) and henceforth universal. And thus lies the universal quality of Frodo's journey to Rivendell, as Frodo's transcendence of the traditional opposites of heroism and anti-heroism also liberates this aspect of *LotR* from confinement by the restrictions of cultural constructs.

After Frodo experiences the equivalent of a death-like satori during his completion of the crossing to Rivendell, he generates an original and innovative brand of heroism that belongs entirely to the powerless and the humble. Frodo's rather unconscious creation of a new brand of heroism has an infinitely more far-reaching and universal appeal. Because it is not founded upon idealized traditions of heroism and valour, the universal appeal of Frodo's crossing to Rivendell lies in its underlying message that higher states of consciousness, empyrean visions, and peculiar guises of heroism can also be accomplished by the ordinary and the inexperienced.

In the journey to Rivendell, Frodo does not demonstrate his heroic qualities through physical brilliance. This is even further proven in his utterly helpless reliance on Aragorn and Arwen who epitomise the conventional heroic couple, exerting their protection through their cultivated warrior qualities and fluency in an ethereal tongue whose mere utterance has the power to cast away evil. Instead, Frodo's heroic qualities are brought forth by a state of physical and spiritual paralysis. Such qualities are derived, quite unconsciously, from his psychic strength, which transcends the confines of his small being, as Lord Elrond speaks of him to

Gandalf: "And yet, to have come so far still bearing the Ring, the Hobbit has shown extraordinary resilience to its evil."

As for as the journey to Rivendell, Frodo has shown only severe ineptitude in the martial arts, exemplified by his attempts to fight the Ringwraiths at Weathertop. So Frodo's strength definitely lies in his spirit, as opposed to the intellect or any development of technical skill in the physical and mental planes of operation—in other words, those constructs that merely shape worldly standards. The strength of Frodo's spirit being maintained consistently throughout the journey to Rivendell alludes to the Zen ideal of living in the true essence of being, which is to transcend the defining characteristics and actions that merely constitute types or aspects of personas (in this case, the personas of hero or anti-hero):

> The spirit of Zen is then the going beyond conceptualization, and this means to grasp the spirit of the most intimate manner... Zen holds in itself something which eludes all systematized technical skill but which is to be somehow grasped in order to come in the closest possible touch with Life, all-generating and all-pervading and all-invigorating. (Suzuki, 1980: 58)

Zen by its nature is a universal philosophy. It aims to experience the Formless Self, or the True Self, "which is prior to and free from any form", (Hisamatsu, 1982: 18) and it is the consideration of this concept of the true essence that underlies the universality of Zen. This universality appropriately converges with the common appeal of Frodo's journey to Rivendell. The journey portrays miracles, or spontaneous exposures to various manifestations of higher consciousness, that are unexpectedly experienced by an ordinary creature of Middle-earth, who had known nothing other than a blithe life in green meadows.

From a Zen perspective, Frodo's journey refutes the conventional divisions between heroism and anti-heroism, and reduces such divisions to nothing, hence the Zen notion of emptiness. For Frodo's heroic path is not paved with glory. As the Ringbearer, Frodo has to forsake the interests of his ego: no overt demonstrations of flair or genius, not even any attempts to impress, and no seeking of an exalted prize. In his quest to destroy the Ring, Frodo is destined to serve the world, and to serve other beings of every dimension of existence—divine, earthling, and underworld. Through this pledge of service, Frodo's own sense of self actually diminishes. As the Ring of Power, in every sense, embodies all the malice of ego, the Ring Quest almost succeeds in destroying Frodo. But it does not. At the end of the story, it is the humble one who prevails, whose hands bring the Fourth Age to Middle-earth, and who sails away with ethereal beings to the Undying Lands. Throughout the story, Frodo Baggins demonstrates that humility is the foundation of all planes of existence—divine, earthling, and underworld. Thus, humility can be referred to as the true essence, in much the same way that Zen seeks to experience the True Self.

Bibliography

Addiss, Stephen (1989), *The Art of Zen*, Harry M. Abrams, New York

Benoit, Hubert (2004), *The Light of Zen in the West: Incorporating The Supreme Doctrine and The Realization of the Self*, trans. Graham Rooth, Sussex Academic Press, Brighton and Portland

Blyth, R.H. (1942), *Zen in English Literature and Oriental Classics*, The Hokuseido Press, Tokyo

Campbell, Joseph (1962), *The Masks of God: Oriental Mythology*, The Viking Press, New York

Cleary, Thomas (2001), *Classics of Buddhism and Zen: The Collected Translations of Thomas Cleary* vols 1-4, Shambhala, Boston and London

Eliade, Mircea (1959) [1957], *The Sacred and the Profane: The Nature of Religion*, Harcourt Brace Jovanovich Publishers, New York and London

Hisamatsu, Shin'ichi (1982), *Zen the Fine Arts*, trans. Gishin Tokiwa, Kodansha International, New York

Loy, David R. and Goodhew, Linda (2004), *The Dharma of Dragons and Daemons: Buddhist Themes in Modern Fantasy*, Wisdom Publications, Boston

Ogata, Sohaku (1973), *Zen for the West*, Greenwood Press, Westport, Connecticut

Pandit, Moti Lal (1998), *Śūnyatā: The Essence of Mahāyāna Spirituality*, Munshiram Manoharlal Publishers Pvt. Ltd., New Delhi

Phillips, Bernard (ed.) (1962), *The Essentials of Zen Buddhism: Selected from the Writings of Daisetz T. Suzuki*, Greenwood Press, Westport, Connecticut

Suzuki, Daisetz Teitaro (1970) [1949], *Essays in Zen Buddhism* 1st Series, Rider and Company, London

Suzuki, Daisetz Teitaro (1972) [1950], *Living by Zen*, ed. Christmas Humphreys, Rider & Company, London

Suzuki, Daisetz Teitaro (1963) [1907], *Outlines of Mahayana Buddhism*, Shocken Books, New York

Suzuki, Daisetz Teitaro (1980), *The Awakening of Zen*, ed. Christmas Humphreys, Prajña Press in association with The Buddhist Society, Boulder and London

Suzuki, Daisetz Teitaro (1996) [1956], *Zen Buddhism: Selected Writings of D.T. Suzuki*, ed. William Barrett, Image Books, Doubleday, New York

Watts, Alan (1995), *The Philosophies of Asia: The Edited Transcripts*, Charles E. Tuttle, Boston

Watts, Alan (1989) [1957], *The Way of Zen*, Vintage Books, New York

15

THE WEIGHT OF EXISTENCE
A Camusian Analysis of Frodo's Journey

Gerald A. Powell

Be not afraid of life. Believe that life is worth living,
and your belief will help create the fact.

(James, 1956 [1987]: 62)

PETER JACKSON'S *The Fellowship of the Ring* is an epic film that chronicles the travels of nine heroes (Frodo, Sam, Merry, Pippin, Gandalf, Gimli, Legolas, Boromir, and Aragorn) who forge an alliance in Rivendell, the land of the Elves, to destroy the Dark Lord Sauron's Ring of Power and save Middle-earth. At Rivendell, Frodo is beckoned to take the Ring to the fiery pits of Mount Doom. With the Ring around his neck, Frodo embarks with the alliance on a daunting journey to Mount Doom to destroy the Ring. Along the way, Frodo discovers the value of camaraderie and trust, central principles that aid him in his perilous journey.

I primarily focus on Frodo's philosophical dilemma. In my mind, the appeal of *The Lord of the Rings* is its rich philosophical commentary. Bassham and Bronson assembled an anthology of essays that reflects the philosophical significance of the film. (Bassham and Bronson, 2003) Issues ranging from Nietzsche's will to power, to issues of Stoic morality are discussed. Little, if any, commentary, however, references Frodo's existential predicament. With this in mind, my thesis is that prior to bearing the Ring Frodo is best characterized by his *lack of being conscious*; however, the wielding of the Ring of Power is the impetus for Frodo's existential provocation—*becoming* conscious and recognition of his absurdity, parallel to what Camus articulates in *The Myth of Sisyphus*.

Thus the immediate significance of this chapter is best understood in Camus's awareness that "... the conditions of the modern life imposes on the majority of men the same quantity of experiences and consequently the same profound experiences." (Camus, 1983: 61) Though the specifics of Frodo's dilemma are fictitious, he suffers and experiences absurdity as any human being suffers and experiences the absurd; therefore, exploring Frodo's dilemma, his confrontation with the absurd can be self-reflexive for our own lives. As a result, a more comprehensive understanding of our own existential dilemma and the absurdity shadowing it becomes clearer. Like Frodo, we can learn how to transcend our dilemma and become absurd heroes.

Lack of Being Conscious

Staying faithful to Tolkien's depiction of Hobbits, Jackson in *LotR* presents them as sensual creatures of the earth, characterized by their affinity to an uncomplicated lifestyle of drinking, smoking, dancing, and farming and their lack of *being* conscious concerning the outside world. By lack of *being* conscious, I am referring to what Bassham and Bronson noted:

> Hobbits are merry, good-natured folk who delight in simple pleasures[....]They live uncomplicated, rustic lives in 'close friendship with the earth,' dislike complex machinery, have no real government, and enjoy simple comical songs about hot baths and shinbone-munching trolls. (Bassham and Bronson, 2003: 49–50)

Having renounced the desire for power, domination, and greed, Hobbits, unlike the species of Men and Dwarves, are quite content with their pleasures, are reflexive in routine, and live without a sense of inner turmoil. For example, in *FotR* in response to Gandalf's murmur concerning the predictability and timeliness of Hobbits, Frodo emphatically replies, "Before you came along, we Bagginses were very well thought of. Never had any adventures or did anything unexpected." (And I suppose this is characteristic of Hobbits.) To the point, it is this lack of *being* conscious, a "run of the mill" a priori existence that is characteristic of Hobbits, particularly Frodo.

Nowhere is this point clearer than in the following example in the film. Before exiting the Shire, Sam and Frodo have this conversation:

> *Sam*: This is it.
> *Frodo*: This is what?
> *Sam*: If I take one more step... it'll be the farthest away from home I've ever been.
> *Frodo*: Come on, Sam. Remember what Bilbo used to say, "It's a dangerous business, Frodo, going out your door. You step on the road, and if you don't keep your feet, there's no knowing where you might be swept off to."

Indicated in this dialogue and mentioned previously, the outside world, or the world beyond the Shire, is mysterious and taboo for Hobbits. Warned against by Bilbo Baggins, adventure and voyage are unsavoury activities for them. For good reason, this is the case. Adventure and voyage contaminate the simplicity of the Hobbitian worldview; they raise questions of culture, rationality, and morality. Upon the modern man *becoming* conscious, the quotidian of life diminishes and man awakens in his sleepwalk wondering whether or not he can live without appeal. (Camus, 1988) This feeling of lassitude—*becoming conscious*—is expressed in the dialogue between Frodo and Gandalf in *FotR*:

> *Frodo*: I wish the Ring had never come to me. I wish none of this had happened.
> *Gandalf*: So do all who live to see such times. But that is not for them to decide. All we have to decide is what to do with the time that is given to us. There are other forces at work in this world, Frodo, besides the will of Evil. Bilbo was meant to find the Ring. In which case, you also were meant to have it. And that is an encouraging thought.

Frodo's continued failure to understand the gravity of the Ring, his specific responsibility to carry the Ring, and the Ring's connection to Middle-earth and all races is amplified by his indifferent comment to disclaim the Ring and the journey. Camus reported, "I am linked with men by all my pity and my gratitude with the world by all my acts." (Thody, 1957: 10) The point is that the modern man (Frodo) argued by Camus cannot engage in perspective taking—that is, he cannot see beyond his own worldview. He does not recognize the common universal bond that intersects all kind. As such, he is chained to his indifference, his lack of *being* conscious. In other words, he is paralyzed and inebriated by his own solipsism/romantic vision.

Becoming Conscious

The wielding of the Ring is a turning point in both the film and the psyche of Frodo because it is his first encounter with the absurd that transforms him and gives him an inexhaustible passion. The levity once characteristic of Frodo prior to bearing the Ring is now defaced with bewilderment and uncertainty. According to Camus, the absurd is "the confrontation of this irrational and the wild longing for clarity whose call *echoes* the human heart. The absurd depends as much on the man as on the world. For the moment it is all that links them together." (Camus, 1983: 21) Hence, the Ring signifies an unfathomable existential burden. By unfathomable, I am referring to a *fatiguing of* consciousness in which, out of pure exhaustion, the mind searches and finds answers and cognitively reaches limitations of rational thought, only to find the soul shadowed in doubt. At this juncture, even the best reasoning, although reassuring, seems futile. Rivendell, the Shire, Bilbo's truisms, and Gandalf's sagacity no more console Frodo than antagonize him. Even more disconcerting for Frodo is what *becoming* conscious illuminates that the *lack of being* conscious does not elucidate—there is no transcendental truth or meaning; rather, the two are phenomenological-induced inward expressions of the mind and soul's present standpoint. Splintered, with little hope of reconciliation, Frodo's metaphysical burden brings focus to the blurred unbridgeable chasm between mind and soul. Camus noted, "But if I recognize the limits of reasoning, I do not therefore negate it, recognizing its relative powers." (Camus, 1983: 40) Hence, schism between the mind and soul is manifest in the following queries.

First, what is the impetus for one to know—to reason, and if reasoning is synonymous with rationality, where does it begin and end? The question mirrors Aristotle's metaphysical reply to human curiosity—all men desire to know. Nonetheless, for our purpose here, Aristotle's lamentation is better understood existentially; men desire to know in order to exist, for self-preservation. Unamuno lamented, "Knowledge is employed in the service of necessity of life and primarily in the service of the instinct of personal preservation." (Unamuno, 1954: 23) Differentiating between what is epistemologically rational and absurd (irrational) seems rather inane, existentially speaking, because what is paramount to understanding Frodo's predicament is a matter of the *will*, an inward absurdity that analytically is tantamount to drivel and a diseased mind.

Second, is reasoning solely limited to the mind or does it include the soul? What follows from our first query is that analytic reasoning does little to elucidate Frodo's disposition because it burgeons from an inward *will*. Reasoning for Frodo is holistic, involving both rational and irrational states of stupor; it is a matter of *both/and*, not *either/or*. Further proof comes from Camus who stated that the absurd man "recognizes the struggle, does not absolutely scorn reason, and admits the irrational. Thus he again embraces in a single glance all the data of experience and he is little inclined to leap before knowing." (Camus, 1983: 37) Like Frodo, we are torn between both worlds, are fragmented in our thinking, and have lost our path—neither the mind nor the soul is a compass of resolve; at this juncture, the *will* navigates, endures, and protests, but does not seek, resolution. In the same line of reasoning, the absurd hero, Frodo, does not seek clemency or cessation; rather, he wants to know "whether [he] can live with what [he] know[s] and with that alone." (Camus, 1983: 40)

Given the limitations of both the mind and soul, how does one make sense of the absurd? As suggested in our second query the absurd is something to be endured not conquered or demystified—it is a *willful* matter of negotiation, living in negation and affirmation; two worlds, two minds, forever splintered without resolve. Making sense of the absurd is absurdity in itself. Unamuno brought perspective to our query:

> [Absurdity] is not the mere adherence of the intellect to an abstract principle; it is not the recognition of a theoretical truth, a process in which the will merely sets in motion our faculty of comprehension; [absurdity] is an act of the will—it is a movement of the soul towards a practical truth, towards a person, towards something that makes us not merely comprehend life, but that makes us live. (Unamuno, 1954: 191)

Be it hope in something greater than, capitulation, or a profundity not yet comprehended, how can one know what prompts Frodo to stay the course and endure the absurd? Whether Frodo's life has some transcendent meaning or his current predicament is predestined, how can one know with certainty? What is clear to me is that absurdity withdraws humankind from their perfunctory living;

thus, one can not hide behind the prevaricated veil of living. One has to *live*, not just in action but also in feeling and thinking. This is living, a harrowing passion to exhaust the limits of the self through the absurd.

Lastly, forever branded by the absurd, how does one live without appeal? Frodo grapples with several of these questions; however, the last question is most significant and deserving of attention. Gandalf's remark to Elrond: "[Frodo] will carry [the wound] the rest of his life," alludes to the absurd state of consciousness that the Ring brings (*becoming* conscious derails the certainty, clarity, and orderliness) to Frodo that he must grapple with. Once conscious, Frodo cannot return to the state of naïveté in which smoking pipes, drinking ale, and singing songs secured a happy existence; these activities have been replaced with a parasitic spirit of seriousness that cannibalizes the soul. Frodo has become an altogether different person, expressing feelings of regret, doubt, and rancor. Now, all that is for Frodo to decide is how to live with such perversity, revealed to him in Galadriel's mirror.

> *Galadriel*: Will you look into the mirror?
> *Frodo*: What will I see?
> *Galadriel*: Even the wisest cannot tell. For the mirror shows many things. Things that were... things that are... and some things... that have not yet come to pass.

Bemused by Galadriel's comment, Frodo walks with caution toward the mirror and witnesses the Shire in all of its brilliance; then, to Frodo's surprise, he sees the Shire set ablaze by Orcs, his fellow Hobbits in bondage, and the eye of Mordor. After Frodo withdraws from the mirror, Galadriel telepathically discloses to Frodo, "I know what it is you saw. For it is also in my mind. It is what will come to pass if you should fail." Indicative of *becoming* conscious and evident in what is witnessed by Frodo is that all discoveries derivative of consciousness are violent and Frodo is in no way exempt. Since bearing the Ring, Frodo finds himself free-falling without end to the deepest and unfathomable depths of consciousness—death.

When one is conscious of something, it is only because one can locate and understand the object or idea of one's consciousness within the determined temporal continuum of life.

Frodo soon realizes that death nullifies and makes trite any thoughts of heroism, victory, or failure that may come to be, and yet, Frodo remains headstrong, first to the welfare of the fellowship, and second, to the Ring's destruction. This idea is worthy of deliberation because it calls into question how a sense of duty comes about and whether it can be justified when there seems to be no basis for justification. Frodo's duty goes beyond the predictable Western cinematic hero in that he upholds principles of humanity and compassion for a common good and does not falter in the face of evil. The reality of Frodo's duty is his interest in *existing*, his *passionate* concern, as he stands in the crisis of decision to move from possibility (thinking) to action (being) when there is no logical purpose to do so. In other words, Frodo's duty is *self-emanated*, propelled by a voluptuous tension: thinking—being that violently births a new way of seeing and awareness that erodes "logical sensibility". Camus noted, "To an absurd mind reason is useless and there is nothing beyond reason." (Camus, 1983, 35) It is precisely this type of *self-emanated* rationale that takes the place of reason and propels Frodo into the absurd and allows him to go on. When the naïveté that guided one's life no longer has currency in the face of the absurd, it is the embracing of the absurdity that provides lucidity and kindles consciousness. This idea is especially clear in the dialogue between Frodo and Galadriel:

> *Frodo*: I cannot do this alone.
> *Galadriel*: You are a Ring-bearer, Frodo. To bear the Ring of Power is to be alone. This task was appointed to you. And if you do not find a way... no one will.
> *Frodo*: Then I know what I must do. It's just... I'm afraid to do it.
> *Galadriel*: Even the smallest person can change the course of the future.

Similarly, in Bergman's *The Seventh Seal* (1957), the knight, clouded by anguish and existential emptiness, realizes that his existence and God's presence is a sordid joke. Upon this revelation, the knight at once stops trying to outwit and best Death in the game of chess, affording him the opportunity to distract Death and make provision for Mia, Joseph, and their son to escape Death for a time, ultimately postponing their death. Bergman presented the knight's intervention as an absurd but meaningful gesture of humanity, only possible through embracing absurdity. Nihilism becomes the logic of reason that allows the knight to extricate himself from himself and to aid Mia, Joseph, and their son. Fundamentally, then, Bergman, Camus, and Jackson all communicate the fundamental absurdity. Be it emptiness, God, or death, how can one know, or understand, these metaphysical issues with certainty? Given the time one has to live, however, one can perform meaningful acts of humanity. Analogously, considering Frodo's ominous task, although Frodo's chances of getting to the mountain are less than minimal, he continues to wield the Ring for any unforeseen good that may come from the journey—hence, performing a meaningful act of humanity. With every step toward the mountain possibly his last, Frodo knows his death is inevitable; still, hopeful, he continues to wield the Ring toward the mountain. What is this buoyancy that keeps Frodo afloat in trepid waters? Absurdity. For Frodo to die is a forgone conclusion and a great loss, but in his mind if the very idea he is persevering for dies, then his life is intolerable; in the waning space between life and death, acts of compassion and humanity give the absurd meaning. "From the moment absurdity is recognized, it becomes a passion, the most harrowing of all." (Camus, 1983: 22) This amorphous passion burns in the soul until it is refined, clear, and purposeful. Its purpose and one's decision to take action, Camus notes, is the revolt.

"[Revolting] is a constant confrontation between man's awareness and his own obscurity—the constant presence of man in his own eyes," (Camus, 1983: 54) which brings courage to trepidation and value to life. The revolt is the decisive moment at which one chooses action over contemplation. Camus reminded his audience of Sisyphus, who ceaselessly pushed an oversized stone up a hill only to have it roll back to the base. It is at the moment before the stone rolls back to the base that Sisyphus's revolt occurs and he is lucid. Percolating through Sisyphus's veins is an indomitable resolute not to acquiesce or plead for salvation but to accept his condition as his; the same is true for Frodo. Two important scenes come to mind, exemplary of Frodo's revolt in which Frodo decisively knows what he must do.

When leaving Lórien, Galadriel says to Frodo: "Farewell, Frodo Baggins, I give you the light of Eärendil, our most beloved star. May it be a light for you in dark places, when all other lights go out." Toward the end of the film, when Frodo, in tears, stands at the edge of the shoreline, ready to do away with the Ring and the journey, he remembers Gandalf's wise words: "So do all who live to see such times... but that is not for them to decide. All you have to decide is what to do with the time that is given to you." Both scenes illustrate Frodo's revolt, a steadfast disciplined resolute to carry onward, in spite of his uncertainty. It is in revolt that Frodo is drawn out of seclusion and finds within himself a beacon of encouragement and lucidity. Similar to Sisyphus's pause that brought lucidity, Frodo experiences a pause of lucidity when leaving Lórien and after hearing Gandalf's inspirational comment. Frodo, now more than ever, clearly understands what he must strive to accomplish and how he must tackle it—alone. Thody noted, "[The revolt] is both a call to action and an indication of how that action should be carried on." (Thody, 1957: 25) Hence, the revolt steps beyond contemplation and is a perpetual journey of action through negation in which, alone, one takes a courageous stand. Above all, revolts are personal passions of the heart that spawn an indomitable attitude of protest in the face of the abyss that stirs a greater intensity for life—an inspiration of transcendence. And it is with this resolve that Frodo sets forth on *his* journey.

Final Thoughts

In bringing closure to this chapter, I presume that most individuals have experienced Frodo's existential attitude—even if, for a brief moment, one asks the questions. Why me? Is this fair? Does anyone understand my suffering? At one point in time everyone has likened his or her condition to that of the biblical Job. Like Job or Frodo, perseverance can triumph, although there is no guarantee that will necessarily be the case. Gandalf reminds Frodo that there are other powers in this world besides evil, and I have to believe Gandalf was referring to the human spirit—Frodo's resilience and unbreakable spirit. Although it is true that living is never easy, at the bottom of utter loneliness, silence, and frustration, the human spirit refuses to succumb. The moral is to never count oneself down and out. What counts in life, at least in my mind, is not whether one is successful in completing the task at hand, but whether one compromises *principle* to complete the task. This implies that we must toil with optimism but without the guarantee of accomplishment. Each waking moment is a chance to make a difference—"Even the smallest person can change the course of the future." This is encouraging because the future always remains at a distance, so what truly counts for Frodo and all of us is the present.

And it is in the present where we all can find purpose and meaning amid a cold and vacuous world.

Bibliography

Bassham, Gregory and Eric Bronson (eds) (2003), The Lord of the Rings *and Philosophy: One Book to Rule Them All*, Open Court, Chicago

Camus, Albert (1983) [1942], *The Myth of Sisyphus*, Random House, New York

James, William (1956) [1897], *The Will to Believe and Other Essays in Popular Philosophy*, Dover Publications, New York

Unamuno, Miguel de (1954), *Tragic Sense of Life*, Dover Publications, New York

Shippey, Thomas (2003), *The Road to Middle-earth: How J.R.R. Tolkien Created a New Mythology*, Houghton Mifflin, New York

Thody, Philip (1957), *Albert Camus: A Study of His Work*, Grove Press, New York

PART THREE

WHERE DOES THE KING RETURN TO?

SECTION IV

Interpretations Forever

16

SURPRISED BY JOY
Eucatastrophe in Tolkien's and Jackson's *The Lord of the Rings*

Christopher Garbowski

AS A SCHOLAR Tolkien worked in a period of transition. His own research paradigm, that of philology, was being slowly overtaken by that of literary studies even in the stronghold of Oxford. Keenly aware of this, Tolkien defended his discipline fiercely. (Tolkien, 1997: 224-240) If we accept Tom Shippey's interpretation of *The Lord of the Rings*, the work is a sort of celebration of philology. (Shippey, 1992) Shippey, a philologist, even suggested that a reason literary critics were so slow in accepting the novel was a kind of spite on their part that someone on the wrong side of the barricades had produced a work of such stature. (Bailey, 1992)

I mention this because at a time when Tolkien's opus has finally attained a modicum of respectability among literary scholars, literary studies themselves are in trouble. In some English departments they are crowded out by cultural studies, in most they merely accommodate them. What is interesting is that *LotR* remains a focus of attention for the new field, as can be attested by some of the topics in this volume.

My particular view of *LotR* as narrative art, both in its literary and film form, will attempt to produce an examination of the works as well as provoke questions with ramifications for both literary and cultural studies. This will be connected with the turn to ethics in theory, which has had some impact on literary studies,[1] although to the best of my knowledge has not been reflected yet in the field of cultural studies. Within this "turn" I am particularly interested in the problem of human flourishing, which attracts me in part to virtue ethics, to whom belong such moral philosophers as Martha Nussbaum, Charles Taylor, and Alisdair McIntyre. In his magisterial *Sources of the Self*, Taylor claims that, "because we cannot but orient ourselves to the good, and thus determine our place relative to it and hence determine the direction of our lives, we must inescapably understand our lives in narrative form, as a 'quest'." (Taylor, 1989: 51-52)

Tolkien's Eucatastrophe

What are the ethics of *LotR*? In the foreword of the 1964 American paperback edition Tolkien claims that one of his intents in writing his "tale" was to "delight" his readers. (Tolkien, 1964: 9) This could be interpreted as simply meaning that he wished to entertain readers, and certainly in part the author had this in mind, since in a further clause of the same sentence he adds that his intent was to "amuse" them.

However, it should be noted that in his Andrew Lang lecture of 1939 "On Fairy-Stories", Tolkien suggests that the purpose of fantasy is to evoke "eucatastrophe": "the sudden, joyous 'turn'" which leads to the "imaginative satisfaction" of profound human desires. (Tolkien, 1997: 153) Since critics have discerned eucatastrophe at the structural base of *LotR*, it can be claimed the work is "essentially comedic (in contradistinction to tragic)." (Rosebury, 2003: 70)

Tolkien has intimated a religious quality to the concept of eucatastrophe. And, indeed, there seems to be a quality in his opus that harkens back to the comedy of the Middle Ages, where, as Francesca Murphy puts it: "The hero ascends toward a community of love. He uses prudence and discernment to reach it. He suffers as much as the tragic hero; he struggles against evil forces. But the swing of the comic plot hauls him up." (Murphy, 2000: 7) Suffering on the part of the hero and the possible experience of both "sorrow and failure", is accepted by Tolkien and termed

---

[1] One of the better known proponents of this vein of the "turn" is Australian David Parker. See Parker (1994).

"dyscatastrophe", but eucatastrophe gives the fullest resolution for fantasy. Part of the imaginative satisfaction of eucatastrophe likewise involves achieving what the author calls "recovery" and "restoration": a sense of defamiliarization of the known world in order to better appreciate its qualities: in other words, to recognize the miracle of the ordinary.

It was Dante that discerned three essential levels of comedy: the infernal, the purgatorial, and the paradisial. According to Murphy, in paradisial comedy the heroes achieve their dreams with minimal effort, while in the infernal comedies darkness and even the possibility of death are experienced. The heroes of purgatorial comedies face tremendous struggles when they leave their wholesome homes for less familiar territories. Along the way they meet Beatrice figures that act as guides in the new circumstances. (Murphy, 2000: 1-28)

Due to its complexity all three levels of comedy are present in *LotR*. However, its location in "Middle-earth" suggests the predominance of the purgatorial, especially once the dominant extended metaphor of life as a journey develops in earnest, (Rosebury, 2003: 29-31) and the Hobbit fellowship leaves the paradisial Shire behind. In a passage after Iluvatar blesses the created earth, which "shall be a mansion for [Elves and Men]," he goes on to claim that people have the power of self-determination, but this freedom bears the weight of finding no rest upon this earth. (Tolkien, 1977: 42) Thus there is the Augustinian sense of the inhabitants of Middle-earth being on a pilgrimage. During their ordeal the Hobbits meet foes: "some open, some disguised", (Tolkien, 1964: 330) and different Beatrice figures: some male, some female. Beyond the purgatorial struggle the journey through Mordor has an infernal dimension to it, with Gollum a Virgil who is more of a threat than a guide. For the "joyous turn" to be effective dramatically, there must be an extended struggle. This *LotR* delivers.

Upon closer examination of this tradition there is no contradiction between the inherently religious nature of *LotR* and the essentially earthly vision of paradise offered in the *annus mirabilis* in the final portion of the book. In a manner analogous to Jeffrey Burton Russell's observation on Dante's *Purgatorio*, "[t]he earthly paradise makes us wish even more keenly for the celestial paradise." (Russell: 1996: 163)

However, the "earthly" aspect of eucatastrophe bears further examination if we wish to explore the relationship between eucatastrophe and human flourishing. Brian Rosebury observes that in *LotR* the "eucatastrophe is compelling[...] because its optimism is emotionally consonant with the work's pervasive sense of a universe hospitable to the humane." (Rosebury, 2003: 71) Among others, Tolkien achieves this ethical sense by the variety of the good, as, for instance, in the multiculturalism of the benign societies of Middle-earth.[2] From this perspective evoking a powerful sense of the good life based on its diversity undergirds the attainment of the correct emotional tenor along with its resolution in the work.

The ethical system at the base of Middle-earth is connected with its eudaimonism: the conviction that happiness is a goal of the good life. Eudaimonism was accepted as the ethical goal of most philosophical and religious systems of the Occident from ancient times almost until the Enlightenment, even if the means of attaining happiness were variously understood. At that juncture Immanuel Kant forwarded his deontological ethical teleology, and eudaimonism has been largely marginal in philosophical discourse since then.[3]

Perhaps the above goes some way to explaining the initial difficulty critics had in accepting Tolkien.[4] To some extent concomitant with religious eudaimonism there was the aesthetics of beauty as delight, as Aquinas defined it. (Maritain, 1949: 19) After the Enlightenment, again on account of Kant, beauty was thought of in terms of the sublime, which was supposed to instil aesthetic distance. To a greater or lesser degree the object of art was an entity unto itself.

In contrast, Andrew Greeley makes the provocative claim that much of Western art from the Middle Ages was inspired by the Catholic liturgy, and that the liturgy affects the Catholic imagination to this very day. (Greeley, 2000: 34-35,

---

[2] Cf. Lynnette Porter's account of Gimli and Legolas' relationship. (Porter 2005: 151-155)

[3] A rare example of a contemporary moral philosopher who develops an ethical system based on his understanding of eudaimonism would be John Kekes. (Kekes, 1995) However, the work of the virtue ethicists is not too distant from the concept, especially that of the rather optimistic Charles Taylor. (Taylor, 1989)

[4] I can now explain the allusion from my title, which at one level connects Tolkien's "joyous turn" with C.S. Lewis' conversion story *Surprised by Joy: The Shape of My Early Life*. (Lewis, 1956) However, in my title it is also the critics who are currently surprised by an aesthetics of delight.

passim) From his description of the Catholic sensibility it can be inferred that it retains its foundation in eudaimonism.[5] It might be that Tolkien as a devout Catholic and a scholar steeped in the works of the Middle Ages would intuitively opt for an "aesthetics of delight".[6]

Peter Jackson's Participation in the LotR's Role-Playing Games

One might go further: the connection of delight to Tolkien's work means that, as with the liturgy, it invites participation. If this is the case, then much of what is called the Tolkien phenomenon, that is, the various Middle-earth products: encyclopaedias, illustrations, the influence of *LotR* on role-playing games, etc., is not so much ancillary to the trilogy as a work of art, but a valid response to a successful instance of a work steeped in an aesthetics of delight.

At one level Tolkien seemed aware of this. Among the reviews of his novel that he felt captured something of its essence was the opinion that *LotR* represented "an elaborate game of inventing a country." (Tolkien, 1990: 196) If the work is a game, however serious that game it might be, it provokes participation. Tolkien was known to be critical of the initial craze inspired by his Middle-earth opus, but this, together with the above mentioned phenomena, is at least in part a legitimate response to the aesthetics he followed.

One of the most elaborate forms of "participation" in LotR was Peter Jackson's impressive enterprise. A Polish fantasy magazine aptly wrote when the films were in production that the set was the world's largest role-playing game,[7] while even on the extended DVD commentaries designer Richard Taylor uses vocabulary from

---

[5] For the theist, the religious imagination has two contrasting, but ultimately complementary aspects. The theist's picture of God focuses in turn on His transcendence and on His immanence. That is, one focus relates to God's distance to His creation, the other to His nearness. The theologian David Tracy claims both these perceptions of God influence the religious imagination, although for different faith communities one or the other might have more significance. (cf. Greeley, 2000: 5) Catholics tend to focus on the closeness of God to creation, hence the belief in the presence of grace within the sacraments, and a generally optimistic world-view.

[6] I realize my usage of this term is rather imprecise. To some extent its meaning is developed during the course of my argument.

[7] I cite this information from memory.

that realm to describe some of his ideas for presenting Orcs.[8] No doubt part of the pleasure of viewing the films for Tolkien aficionados has been recognizing references to elements of the Tolkien phenomenon that have accrued over the years. For instance, in the line where Bilbo offers Gandalf good "weed" from South Farthing Jane Chance has noted an allusion to the Harvard Lampoon spoof *Bored with the Rings*. (Chance, 2002: 82) Indeed, it is likely that the quality of the fan base made its own impact on the calibre of the cinematic product. As Rosebury suggests:

> What *The Lord of the Rings* shows is that even a very challenging and immensely complex film adaptation of a work of fiction can survive the necessarily collective elements of production, if the original has created a posterity capable of understanding it. (Rosebury, 2003: 210)

Having arrived at Jackson's adaptation we might ask how the filmmaker's work fares as a work of art: a status which the literary original has only recently attained. One of the reviewers of Peter Jackson's *Two Towers* declared that the film presents Middle-earth with remarkable beauty. (Coombs, 2003) Regardless of the validity of that statement, it can be said of any film adaptation of *LotR* that, no matter how faithful otherwise, without beauty something essential would be missing. There is, however, an additional ethical dimension to Tolkien's understanding of beauty, since, as the author complained, in our times "goodness is itself bereft of its proper beauty." (Tolkien, 1997: 151) We may surmise that in his fiction he made an effort to restore the balance. Fantasy for Tolkien is a quest to bestow tangible shape upon invisible desires, and is a valid form in which to search for beauty.

Fortunately, the cinematic *LotR*, even though it is darker at times, is likewise underpinned by an aesthetics of delight and moves inexorably toward eucatastrophe: an essential part of the spirit of Middle-earth is thus present. The different levels of comedy are also present. Moreover, Jackson succeeds in evoking an almost unimaginable Tolkienian quality. As Rosebury observes, the filmmaker manages "the realization of Middle-earth as a diverse and expansive world of lands

---

[8] For that matter the realm of scholarship is likewise represented on the film, such as in the costume design of the Riders of Rohan in which elements of Sutton Hoo armour are evident.

and cultures under threat, a world we need to fall in love with in order to sufficiently care about the outcome of the plot." (Rosebury, 2003: 213)

However, in discussing eucatastrophe in Jackson's work we encounter a problem involving the general nature of film art. Whereas twentieth century major literary works based on an aesthetics of delight were rather unusual, this is not the case when we look at film: the very fact that happy endings, whether genuine or not, are the most frequent convention attests to this. Indeed, there is something of a parallel situation when we recall that motion pictures had similar difficulties to *LotR* in being treated as art, on account of their popularity, which counted against film receiving serious treatment.[9] Even today, critics who defend optimistic filmmakers like Capra stress an underlying "darkness" to their oeuvre.[10] In other words, their works are deemed valuable despite rather than because of the aesthetics of delight on which they are founded, and the importance of eucatastrophe for them is ignored or reduced.

There is another similarity between classical Hollywood film and Tolkien's opus. *LotR* is a continuation of *The Hobbit*. Albeit much darker in tone, it remains true to the spirit of the children's story, which is due in no small measure to its ending in eucatastrophe. This possibly contributes to its intergenerational popularity: no small achievement as at the time of its publication the generation gap in popular culture was notoriously widening.[11]

As is generally known, because Hollywood motion pictures were initially regarded as entertainment rather than art, they did not gain protection from the First Amendment when the self-censorious Production Code was set in place. Since it was felt that it would be difficult for children not to be exposed to inappropriate material—a prophetic concern!—films were supposed to be suitable for every age group.[12]

---

[9] Obviously there was more at issue. For instance, the collaborative nature of film art raised the problem of the "author" of the finished work.

[10] A number of the texts in Sklar and Zagarrio (1998) take that approach.

[11] For an account of this intergenerational reception, see Stanecka (2005).

[12] Long before the Production Code reformers such as Jane Addams or John Dewey were worried about the effect the new medium might have on children. (Blake 1991: 17)

Such a restriction meant that more provocative filmmakers resorted to various types of subterfuge to convey their message, as in some of the intelligent films by Billy Wilder. Nonetheless, as in the case of Tolkien's *LotR*, some filmmakers' work was genuinely intended for general viewing. Films by directors such as Leo McCarey, John Ford or Alfred Hitchcock, among others, helped achieve an era of art that critic Robin Wood claimed was a period unmatched since the Elizabethan theatre in reaching audiences at different levels. (Blake, 1991: 29)

It might be more than a coincidence that Capra and the three filmmakers mentioned above were Catholics and to varying degrees an aesthetics of delight can be attributed to their work.[13] For instance, Lesley Brill argues that Alfred Hitchcock's *North by Northwest* (1959) is best understood as embodying the romantic mode, which according to Northrop Frye expressed the struggle of "innocence to maintain integrity against the assault of experience." (Quoted in Brill, 1986: 6) Brill points out that scenes like the airplane attack against the film's protagonist utilize the same type of aesthetic hyperbole as that provided by monsters such as dragons in fairytales. (Brill, 1986: 7)

However, although their religious background cannot be excluded as a factor, I think that it would be insufficient to ascribe the eudaimonism inherent in such Hollywood films only to the Catholicism of their directors. A hint is provided by Capra, when he claimed that the popularity of his films provided him with the patronage he needed as an artist to have freedom from "subsidies or strictures from government, pressure groups, or ideologists." (Capra, 1997: 139) Another source of eudaimonism in the American tradition has obviously been the Declaration of Independence, which intellectually stands at the end of the long-standing tradition of eudaimonism, but contributed to encoding the "pursuit of happiness" in the national consciousness, despite various unfavourable intellectual trends. V.S. Naipaul claims that this ingrained "pursuit", which the American quest merely epitomizes, makes the West rather unusual and attractive outside its bounds.

---

[13] For a discussion of the influence of Catholicism on Capra, Ford and Hitchcock, see Blake (2000: 49-176).

(Naipaul, 2005)[14] Currently, some trends in humanistic psychology, notably those initiated by David Myers, stress the importance of happiness for personal and social development. (Myers, 1993) That such studies have been so rare in the past is itself telling. For the moment, the artists of popular culture are more perceptive than the critics. Thus filmmakers following Capra, Spielberg and Lucas, for instance, can count on this deep-rooted base to provide an audience for their feel-good films. (Brown, 1997: 219-232)

Peter Jackson's Cinematic Representation of Heroism

Nevertheless, since eucatastrophe is less rare in cinematic narrative art, there must be more to an adaptation of *LotR* than its inclusion to make it distinct. Here it must be stressed that an aesthetics of delight does not mean that weighty themes were not broached by Tolkien. However, in as much as these could be developed by the idiosyncratic means available to the author of a literary work the collaborative nature of filmmaking makes it difficult for certain nuances to be communicated. What were some of the themes from Tolkien that might pose particular difficulties for a filmmaker? One perhaps counterintuitive matter that would require going against the cinematic grain to retrieve at least part of Tolkien's spirit would be the heroism in *LotR*.

Since heroism plays such an important role, it requires a brief preliminary examination. In his review of Jackson's *Two Towers* in *The New Yorker* Anthony Lane emphasizes that "*The Lord of the Rings* is an epic, and one of the defining restrictions—not to say pleasures—of epic is that it both predate and outwit psychology." (Lane, 2003) This witty observation coincides with a more thought-provoking question posed by the Polish poet Czesław Miłosz who, reflecting on the issue of heroism in respect to world literature in the twentieth century, noted that the proclivity toward psychoanalysing the character was not conducive to or even antithetical to accepting the heroic will: "This happened in contrast to reality, which in the wars throughout the century was full of examples of tremendous heroism." (Miłosz,

---

[14] Yi-Fu Tuan and Steven D. Hoelscher similarly claim that while the American dream revolves around happiness, the Chinese dream centres on contentment. (Tuan and Hoelscher, 1997: 191)

2002: 9) As a witness to, among others, the Warsaw Uprising of 1944 during World War II Miłosz knew this first hand. "Reflecting on Tolkien," he continues, "forced me to postulate the question some time ago: 'Why is it that in twentieth century literature the only heroic character is not a person but a hobbit'." (Miłosz, 2002: 9)

Miłosz might be overly harsh in his evaluation of twentieth century literature, but certainly the depiction of Frodo and his heroism is a significant literary achievement. Tolkien seems in part to have been influenced by the *Beowulf* hero. Obviously Hobbit heroes are revisionist toward the epic hero, reflecting the author's own experience of trench warfare in World War I. However, part of the aesthetic treatment of Frodo harkens back to the insight the author gained from his study of *Beowulf*. Analysing the central figure of the Old English epic, Tolkien observes: "Beowulf is not, then, the hero of a heroic lay, precisely. He has no enmeshed loyalties, nor hapless love. *He is a man, and that for him and many is sufficient tragedy.*" (Tolkien, 1997: 18) In Tolkien's creation of Frodo there is a similar removal of all extraneous elements from the character. His "hapless love", if we can call it that, is primarily for the Shire and those he holds close within it, which renders his ultimate sacrifice on its account all the more poignant.

Moreover, in a sense related to the above, Tolkien avoids the problem Milosz observes by not giving Frodo an overly elaborate psychological portrait. Especially after the breaking up of the Fellowship we see Frodo's heroism from the outside through Sam's eyes. The latter's observations are astute, befitting his background as a gardener who must be observant, but they also leave room for the mystery of the heroic will.

Since a film adaptation is often more like its cinematic times than its literary sire, to present this aspect of Tolkien's opus with any depth Jackson had to go against a number of deep rooted prejudices in Hollywood cinema, not all of them successfully overcome. Among the most obvious concerns is the temptation to escalate the sensational elements in accordance with the predominant aesthetics of today's blockbusters. Unfortunately, Jackson did not pass this particular trial with flying colours: Aragorn's "no mercy" speech at Helm's Deep, for instance, goes against the grain of Tolkien's work and is dramatically redundant.[15]

Nevertheless, at an even deeper level Tolkien's heroes are antithetical to a strong vein in the Hollywood tradition, since the latter are quite closely connected to the dominant cultural code in America. Robert Bellah claims this code of expressive individualism evolved from the near sacralization of the conscience stemming from the influence of Roger Williams and the American Enlightenment on the Bill of Rights. (Bellah, 1999: 10-13) The "flaw" in the cultural code is a tendency toward "radical individualism" which after a certain point leads to the "porous institutions" of civil society that currently plague the country.

Bellah's analysis contributes to understanding Hollywood's penchant for the "outlaw hero": an individual whose own code of right and wrong at best converges with society's for the matter at hand, but often scorns its norms. (Ray, 1985: 59-66) Bellah protests Greeley's claim that the Protestant imagination tends to look upon society as a prison, yet Hollywood's expressive individualism often portrays society as just that: the metaphor is quite literal in films such as *One Flew Over the Cuckoo's Nest* (dir. Milos Forman, 1975) or *The Shawshank Redemption* (dir. Frank Darabont, 1994). Subsequently, deeply imbedded in American culture is a desire for "fables of liberation". (McClay, 2001: 397)

It should be noted in this context that after the fall of the Production Code in the 1960s and the trauma of the Vietnam experience, antiheroes became a powerful presence in Hollywood cinema. This has had its positive and negative sides. As educator Peter H. Gibbon succinctly puts it:

> By questioning convention and exposing hypocrisy, antiheroes can be appealing and even useful[....] Antiheroes permit us to explore our dark side safely. But antiheroes can be dangerous when, instead of seeing them as characters to be wary of, we are seduced into antisocial behaviour. (Gibbon, 2002)

Much like the hardly distinguishable outlaw hero, the antihero has an important role to play but requires a counterbalance.

---

[15] Greg Wright examines this aspect of Jackson's trilogy. (Wright, 2004: 107-108) Moreover, Kristin Thompson notes that Jackson's trilogy is directed at the teen audience to a greater extent than the literary original. (Thompson, 2003: 47-53)

Bearing this in mind, we see that although his rendition of Tolkien's heroes is not completely faithful, Jackson has nevertheless managed to break some Hollywood prejudices. Among others, the heroes of *LotR*' emphasis on cooperation set them apart. Consequently, there is little room for the macho hero. Tellingly, the closest to a macho hero is Gimli the Dwarf: not only the butt of most of the humour in the film, but a fantasy character whose diminutive stature is in itself a visual commentary on his tragicomic heroic ethos. Most importantly Jackson captures the Tolkienian emphasis on community and sense of place, and the heroes, particularly the Hobbits, are to a large extent determined by this ethos.

In the context of the above it is necessary to indicate that although the filmmaker's *LotR* is less inherently religious than Tolkien's,[16] there remains an important sacramental quality to the film that is crucial to the literary original. Why is this important? After discussing the question of "porous institutions" of civil society, Bellah claims that what his society needed was an injection of a sacramental sense of the world, since "sacraments pull us into an embodied world of relationships and connections[...] rather than a world in which individuals attempt to escape from society." (Bellah, 1999: 13) One aspect which Jackson has managed to preserve quite well in his adaptation is just such an understanding of the sacramental inherent in Tolkien's prose.[17]

Essential to achieving this was rooting the Hobbits in the Shire. Obviously the opening sequences of *FotR* instalment—after the stunning prologue—are a key here. And the Shire is continually referred to in the films, as in the touching early sequence in *TT* where while climbing down a rock face in Emyn Muil Sam drops a box of "the best salt in the Shire". Even during the vision Frodo has of Galadriel when he collapses in Shelob's tunnel the grass seems to evoke the greenness of the Shire as much as Lothlórien. A key frame for the Shire and its relationship to heroism is Sam's garden, which we see in the extended DVD edition of the *FotR* and

---

[16] I have suggested elsewhere it is better to speak of spiritual values in discussing Jackson's work. (Garbowski, 2005)

[17] Maintaining Tolkien's celebratory sense of meals in the film narrative could have strengthened this sacramental sense. Whereas the filmmaker could obviously relate to the author's sense of place, his depiction of meals communicates the feeling of today's fast food culture.

again at the conclusion of *The Return of the King*, where, after the great ordeal, the garden is enriched by the Hobbit's young family.

However, an aesthetics of delight does not mean everyone ends up "happy". Frodo's sacrifice ultimately removes him from the very Shire he helps save. Nonetheless, through sacrificing himself for the sake of his community he achieves what the psychiatrist Viktor Frankl terms self-transcendence: he has gained meaning for his actions.[18] This is analogous to the classical problem of happiness in eudaimonism, where for Plato and Aristotle, greater happiness was attained by directing one's actions toward the higher good than through mere pleasure-seeking.

Moreover, both in the book and the films, Frodo obviously also gains meaning through his work as a writer. When mentioning Frodo's self-transcendence as a writer the reflexive nature of *LotR* should be mentioned, which requires a brief discussion of reflexivity in the Middle-earth legendarium.[19] Tolkien intimated that his creation story pertains to what he called sub-creation, that is the artist's imitation of the Primary Creator, or God, during his or her creative activity. My own hypothesis is that the gender division of the Valar reflects the author's possible attraction to Renaissance theologian Nicholas of Cusa's claim that God is a "composition of opposites,"[20] comprising both a male and a female side. Thus any human sub-creators would also have to draw upon their male and female sides during the creative act.

The masculine and feminine qualities of Middle-earth are obviously not evoked through anything resembling affirmative action for female characters. Although the few women in Middle-earth are generally characterized in a fairly conventional manner, I tend to agree with critic Sandra Miesel that "[i]n Tolkien, feminine virtues make life worth living." (Miesel, 2004)[21] But more than this, in *LotR*

---

[18] The most succinct version of Frankl's psychology is presented in Frankl (1973).

[19] For a somewhat different discussion of reflexivity in Tolkien's legendarium, see Bolintineau (2004: 263-276).

[20] For a succinct explanation of Nicholas of Cusa's concept of composition of opposites, see Bro[die] (1995: 619).

[21] Porter makes a similar point regarding heroes. (Porter, 2005: 93-96; passim) One might add that the virtues of service that Sam embodies (see discussion below) are more typically gendered female in narrative art.

the author achieves a certain plenitude in his imaginary world that simultaneously absorbs and transcends both gender sensibilities.

Nevertheless, Frodo as a writer in Jackson's version joins Galadriel in the white-out near the conclusion of *RotK*. In a sense they are complementary "authors". The connection between Frodo and Galadriel is stressed earlier in the films' Mirror sequence, where Sam is absent, as well as in Frodo's vision in Shelob's lair: notably, after Frodo's has entered the lair alone.[22]

Galadriel represents "orality" in art. The screen is completely black at the beginning of the entire epic when she utters the first words in Quenya, that she further interprets into today's "common tongue": English, initiating the entire narrative. Even the fires of this early sequence that break the darkness evoke the sense of a tale spoken with listeners seated round a bond fire. Shortly before the film ends Frodo hands his book over to Sam, and we subsequently hear his voice citing a passage from his written work—as a "contemporary" author, with a more "natural" voice than the aristocratic Elf. However, since the filmic art comes from what seems to be Galadriel's Mirror, it is really she who lends Frodo his voice. Much like in the creation story with the Valar, a "composite of opposites" occurs: male and female are in dynamic dialogue to create an artistic whole.

Nonetheless, important as it may be, the theme of reflexivity in Tolkien does not end with creation. In the dialogue between Sam and Frodo on their place in future stories—which in Jackson's version takes place shortly before the *TT* instalment concludes—there is discussion on the question of reception, indicating an awareness that a "story" needs to be heard and meet the needs of those listening to it.

What are the needs of those on the receiving end of such tales? Noël Carroll talks about near universal moral themes that recur in "mass art", like the "recognition of positive duties of mutual support, loyalty, and reciprocity[....] it is also the case that romantic love can be recognized, appreciated and morally assessed cross-culturally." (Carrol, 1998: 357-358) This is hardly surprising then that Paul

---

[22] In *The Lord of the Rings: The Return of the King* extended edition DVD commentaries Phillipa Boyens even gives this as the main purpose for adding the major quarrel between Sam and Frodo.

McCartney continues to sing "silly love songs": this is what listeners genuinely need.²³ Jackson felt that his audience needed the romantic element of the Aragorn-Arwen tale forwarded from the literary work's appendices to the main body of his cinematic work.²⁴

Returning to the question of heroism in this context, Gibbon observes that "[h]eroes are a response to a deep and powerful impulse, the need to emulate and idealize." (Gibbon, 2002) Significantly, Tolkien's tale offers a number of heroes. Lynnette Porter makes the provocative point that "although the characters [of *LotR*, whether literary of filmic,] live in the mythic past, they are relevant as heroes and role models in a modern world." (Porter, 2005: viii)

More specifically, Aragorn, Sam Gamgee and Frodo have been discussed as protagonists by different critics and depict three different roads to meaning: purposeful action, service and suffering.²⁵ Albeit in their own manner, Jackson's Aragorn, Frodo and Sam largely follow Tolkien's in this respect. However, the hero most against the vein of expressive individualism is Sam and his model of heroic service. His significance stems from the fact that while few of us are called on to be leaders, or to make heroic sacrifices, most of our callings entail lesser or greater degrees of service, which includes the "heroes" who edit books such as this one. Frankl's existential analysis would see this service as a valid way to find meaning and achieve self-transcendence.

It might be too early to answer whether or not Jackson's adaptation is a significant work of art. At this juncture it is more important to confirm that it embodies the aesthetics of delight of the literary original to an extraordinary degree. From the perspective of his fidelity to this aesthetic the films' tremendous

---

[23] "Silly Love Songs" was a McCartney single from 1976 in which he defends his penchant for sentimental songs. For an analysis of the former Beatles' work from the perspective of his optimism, see Dempsey (2004: 27-40).

[24] Here the right tenor is also essential. I feel Jackson may have been influenced by the treatment of a similar theme in *Wings of Desire* of 1987 (dir. Wim Wenders). His treatment of Aragorn's death is appropriately influenced by art cinema.

[25] I discussed this further in *Recovery and Transcendence for the Contemporary Mythmaker: The Spiritual Dimension in the Works of J. R. R. Tolkien*. (Garbowski, 2000: 198-203)

popularity—not to mention the sense of participation it has inspired[26]—is not a mark against it in answering the question. The fact that despite its moments of gravity Jackson's *LotR* is "essentially comedic" may also be an explanation for a good measure of its acceptance. As Mary Nichols puts it,

> what popular culture senses when it[...] demands comedies [is] that moments of joy enfolded in ordinary life are more profound that those of suffering and despair and that the former redeem the latter, even if it is life's suffering that makes possible the full experience of its joys. (Nichols, 1999/2000: 76)

Unlike a sense of well-being, which can be more stable, joy is rather fleeting. It often comes upon us unexpectedly, hence its narrative expression in eucatastrophe. Moreover, eucatastrophe is closely connected with hope in both the religious and humanistic sense. Hope has been defined as the unique human capacity for generating positive expectations concerning the future regardless of present circumstances. (Reading, 2004) A work of art, whether prose fiction or film, that achieves a profound sense of eucatastrophe is most simply understood as a forceful expression of the aesthetic fulfilment of hope.

Bibliography

Bailey, Derek (dir.) (1992), *J.R.R.T.: A Film Portrait of J.R.R. Tolkien*, Landseer Films and Television Productions

Bellah, Robert (1999), "Religion and the Shape of National Culture" *America* 181 (3), pp. 10-13

Blake, Richard A. (1991), *Screening America: Reflections on 5 Classic Films*, Paulist Press, New York

Blake, Richard A. (2000), *Afterimage: The Indelible Catholic Imagination of Six American Filmmakers*, Loyola Press, Chicago

---

[26] This participation has taken on various forms: movie tie-ins have been taken to a higher level with replicas of the cinematic swords, with even their price indicating an adult market. These are hardly comprehensible without considering the re-enactment movement, where adults simultaneously "play" and deepen their historical consciousness. Not for the fist time, the staid National Geographic Society has likewise "participated" in the film, producing *The Lord of the Rings: The Fellowship of the Ring. Beyond the Movie* (2001). Internet fan sites such as TheOneRing.net are another phenomenon that may even have influenced the development of the films themselves.

Bolintineau, Alexandra (2004), "'On the Borders of Old Stories': Enacting the Past in *Beowulf* and *The Lord of the Rings*" in Jane Chance (ed), *Tolkien and the Invention of Myth: A Reader*, University Press of Kentucky, Lexington, pp. 263-276

Brill, Lesley (1986), *The Hitchcock Romance: Love and Irony in Hitchcock's Films*, Princeton University Press, Princeton

Bro[die], A[lexander] (1995) *Nicholas of Cusa in The Oxford Companion to Philosophy*, Ted Honderich (ed.), Oxford University Press, Oxford

Brown, Stephen (1997), "Optimism, Hope, and Feelgood Movies: The Capra Connection" in Clive Marsh and Gaye Oritz (eds), *Explorations in Film and Theology: Movies and Meaning*, Blackwell, Oxford, pp. 219-32

Capra, Frank (1997)[1971], *The Name Above the Title: An Autobiography*, Da Capo, New York

Carroll, Noël (1998), *A Philosophy of Mass Art*, Oxford University Press, Oxford

Chance, Jane (2002), "Is There a Text in this Hobbit: Peter Jackson's *The Fellowship of the Ring*" *Literature Film Quarterly* 30 (2), pp. 79-85

Coles, Robert (1989), *The Call of Stories: Teaching and the Moral Imagination*, Houghton Mifflin, Boston

Coombs, Marian Kester (2003), "A Joy Forever: *The Two Towers* As a Cultural Renaissance" *Online Human Events*: http://www.humanevents.org/articles/01-13-03/coombs.htm

Dempsey, J. M. (2004), "McCartney at 60: A Body of Work Celebrating Home and Hearth" *Popular Music and Society* 27 (1), pp. 27-40

Frankl, Viktor E. (1973), *Man's Search for Meaning: An Introduction to Logotherapy*, Pocket Books, New York

Frith, Simon (1996), *Performing Rites: On the Value of Popular Music*, Oxford University Press, Oxford

Garbowski, Christopher (2000), *Recovery and Transcendence for the Contemporary Mythmaker: The Spiritual Dimension in the Works of J.R.R. Tolkien*, Maria Curie-Sklodowska Press, Lublin

Garbowski, Christopher (2005), *Spiritual Values in Peter Jackson's* The Lord of the Rings, Maria Curie-Sklodowska University Press, Lublin

Gibbon, Peter H. (2002), "Making the Case for Heroes" *Harvard Education Newsletter* July/August: http://www.edletter.org/past/issues/2002-ja/heroes.shtml

Greeley, Andrew (2000), *The Catholic Imagination*, University of California Press, Berkeley

Kekes, John (1995), *Moral Wisdom and Good Lives*, Cornell University Press, Ithaca

Lane, Anthony (2003), "Fantasyland" *The New Yorker* 6 January: http://www.newyorker.com/critics/cinema/?030106crci_cinema

Lewis, C.S. (1956), *Surprised by Joy: The Shape of My Early Life*, Harcourt, Bruce, New York

Maritain, Jacques (1949), *Art and Scholasticism With Other Essays*, trans. J.F. Scanlan, Sheed & Ward, London

McClay, Wilfred (2001), "Individualism and its Discontents" *Virginia Quarterly Review* 77 (3), Summer, pp. 391-405

Miesel, Sandra (2004), "The Ladies of the Ring" *Independent Women's Forum* 1 February: http://www.iwf.org/articles/article_detail.asp?ArticleID=424

Miłosz, Czesław (2002), "Hobbit: bohater XX wieku" *Tygodnik Powszechny* 8, 24February, p. 9

Murphy, Fransesca Aran (2000), *The Comedy of Revelation: Paradise Lost and Regained in Biblical Narrative*, T and T Clark, Edinburgh

Myers, David (1993), *The Pursuit of Happiness: Discovering the Pathway to Fulfillment, Well-Being, and Enduring Personal Joy*, Avon Books, New York

Naipaul, V.S. (2005), "Our Universal Civilization" (Wriston Lecture, 30 October 1990 at the Manhattan Institute for Policy Research): http://www.manhattan-institute.org/html/wl1990.htm

Nichols, Mary (1999/2000), "A Defence of Popular Culture" *Academic Questions* 13 (1) Winter, pp. 73-79

Parker, David (1994), *Ethics, Theory, and the Novel*, Cambridge University Press, Cambridge

Porter, Lynnette (2005), *Unsung Heroes of* The Lord of the Rings: *From the Page to the Screen*, Praeger, Westport, Connecticut

Ray, Robert (1985), *A Certain Tendency in Hollywood Cinema*, Princeton University Press, Princeton

Reading, Anthony (2004), *Hope and Despair: How Perceptions of the Future Shape Human Behavior*, John Hopkins University Press, Baltimore

Rosebury, Brian (2003), *Tolkien: A Cultural Phenomenon*, Palgrave MacMillan, Hampshire

Russell, Jeffrey Burton (1996), *A History of Heaven: The Singing Silence*, Princeton University Press, Princeton

Shippey, T.A. (1992) [1982], *The Road to Middle-earth: How J.R.R. Tolkien Created a New Mythology*, HarperCollins, London

Sklar, Robert and Zagarrio, Vito (eds) (1998), *Frank Capra: Authorship and the Studio System*, Temple University Press, Philadelphia

Stanecka, Zofia (2005), "Tell Me a Story Mum... Or the Child in the Land of *The Lord of the Rings*" *Aiglos* Summer, pp. 130-139

Taylor, Charles (1989), *Sources of the Self: The Making of Modern Identity*, Harvard University Press, Cambridge

Thompson, Kristin (2003), "Fantasy, Franchises, and Frodo Baggins: *The Lord of the Rings* and Modern Hollywood" *The Velvet Light Trap* 52 Fall, pp. 45-63

Tolkien, J.R.R. (1964), *The Lord of the Rings* Part One: *The Fellowship of the Ring*, Ballantine Books, New York

Tolkien, J.R.R. (1977), *The Silmarillion*, Houghton Mifflin, Boston

Tolkien, J.R.R. (1990) [1981], *The Letters of J.R.R. Tolkien*, edited by Humphrey Carpenter, HarperCollins, London

Tolkien, J.R.R. (1997) [1983], *The Monsters and the Critics and Other Essays*, ed. Christopher Tolkien, Harper Collins, London

Tuan, Yi-Fu and Steven D. Hoelscher (1997), "Disneyland: Its Place in World Culture" in Karal Ann Marling (ed.) *Designing Disney's Theme Parks: The Architecture of Reassurance*, Flammarion, Paris, New York, pp. 191-199

Surprised by joy, or surprised by horror? Balrog's choice nowadays is a newspaper, not palantiri.
(photo by Nataliya Oryshchuk)

17

J.R.R. TOLKIEN AND THE CHILD READER
Images of Inheritance and Resistance
in *The Lord of the Rings* and J.K. Rowling's *Harry Potter*

Lori M. Campbell

Don't adventures ever have an end? I suppose not.
Someone else always has to carry on the story.

Bilbo Baggins (Tolkien, 1981:. 306)

IN HIS often-quoted 1938 Andrew Lang lecture "On Fairië-Stories" J.R.R. Tolkien defends Faerie and its tales from being "relegated to the 'nursery'". (Tolkien, 1966: 58) What Tolkien calls "sub-creation" equals a "human right" and the fairy-story, if "worth reading at all[...] is worthy to be written for and read by adults." (Tolkien, 1966: 67) He does not mean to suggest, of course, that children *should not* read and *cannot* enjoy the fairy-story, only that the form should not be solely identified as childhood reading. His impulse to defend Faerie refers to the long tendency of readers and especially of critics to associate the imaginative with the non-rational or childish. Although rising to become "the dominant literary mode of the twentieth century", (Shippey, 2001: vii) fantasy continues to some extent to be "a word commonly disparaged by literary and nonliterary voices alike." (Armitt, 2005: 1) Yet, the genre known for its "subversive treatment of established orders of society and thought" (Attebery, 1992: 1) easily rises above its detractors, especially in the last few decades. Also emerging as a genre in the nineteenth century, children's literature has faced a similar problem, enjoying popularity among the public while often being overlooked or undervalued by scholars.

J.K. Rowling's *Harry Potter* provides a case-in-point, with critics such as Jack Zipes and Harold Bloom acknowledging mostly to dismiss the books as unworthy of the hype. Those who persist in underestimating fantasy and/or children's literature must at least notice the 6.9 million record-breaking sales on its first day on the shelves for the sixth book in the series, *Harry Potter and the Half-Blood Prince* in 2005. In 2006, the film version of the fourth book, *Harry Potter and the Goblet of Fire* (dir. Mike Newell, 2005), made $54.9 million in its opening three-day weekend, earning more than $200 million in America alone in its first ten days of release. (Germain, 2005) As of publication, the latest film *Harry Potter and the Order of the Phoenix* (dir. David Yates, 2007) and the final book *Harry Potter and the Deathly Hallows* have easily surpassed these numbers to become the biggest money-makers of the series. Such popular success indicates that the demographic of fantasy is not limited to children, although the reading audience remains difficult to categorize as adults normally pay for "children's" books. Obviously impressive sales—at bookstore or box office—do not equate quality, but the success of fantasy films significantly contributes to growing the genre. Notwithstanding Peter Jackson's Oscar sweep for *The Return of the King* though, massive ticket sales can also create a backlash that undermines the value of fantasy, with franchises such as *Star Wars* film series (George Lucas et al, 1977-2005) attracting more commercial than critical affirmation. Besides Jackson's adaptation of Tolkien as a noteworthy exception, the *Harry Potter* films, while garnering much less acclaim and no significant awards, have also mostly avoided the condescension that fantasy films often receive.

Using a mode "deeply rooted in human experience", (Swinfen, 1984: 231) Tolkien and Rowling create invaluable spaces for readers of all ages to explore and enact personal experience of the "real" world. What has unfolded since Tolkien felt the need to defend fantasy compels a reassessment of *LotR* as a work with accessibility, or to use his term, "applicability" to the younger audience. To clarify, in regard to books, I refer to childhood as ages six or seven through adolescence, when "[r]eading is a prime tool at one's disposal for gathering and organizing information about the wider world and learning how that world works." (Appleyard, 1990: 59)

It remains important to recognize that Tolkien took pains to alert his publisher that the sequel to *The Hobbit* would not be a children's book in the terms he understood, and I certainly do not wish to argue he did not mean what he said. Even less do I mean to send the magical tale back "to the nursery", nor to undermine the popular and critical appreciation fantasy and children's literature have achieved in the past few decades. Much remains to be done, however, to solidify and elevate their place in literary, film, and cultural studies, as recent works by Lucy Armitt, Beverly Lyon Clark, and Ann Lundin aid and confirm. Using Rowling's texts, Jackson's films, and to a lesser extent, the *Harry Potter* books/films for comparison, in this chapter I look at two key image patterns of *LotR*, each of which plays an important role in maturation: inheritance and resistance. But first, it is necessary to understand what "children's literature" means in terms of Tolkien's vision for his masterwork.

Framing Children's Literature and *The Lord of the Rings*

Responding in 1959 to Walter Allen's invitation to participate in a symposium for publication in a Children's Book Supplement of *The New Statesman*, Tolkien declines for health reasons, and because, he says, "I am not specially interested in children, and certainly not in writing for them: i.e. in addressing directly and expressly those who cannot understand adult language." (Carpenter, 2000: 297) Here Tolkien the linguist provides insight into his definition not of children's literature but of a child's book: one that "expressly" speaks to a person of limited vocabulary. Those who write, read, and study children's literature make a similar distinction: texts of literary quality speak on multiple levels and those odd texts meant *only* to speak to children probably fail to speak at all. As a category children's literature is "imaginary", because "'children' and 'childhood' are social constructs that have been determined by socioeconomic conditions and have different meanings for different cultures." (Zipes, 2001: 44) Tolkien probes this idea in his letter to Allen:

> What are "Children"? [....]Life is rather above the measure of us all (save for a very few perhaps). We all need literature that is above our measure—though we may not have sufficient energy for it all the time. But the energy of youth is usually greater. (Carpenter, 2000: 297-298)

Thus in Tolkien's estimation, children have a *greater* capacity than adults to understand—or at least to try to understand—what seems to be beyond them.

While some books are probably not for children due to excessive violence or sexual content, even these aspects can be clouded by perspective and personal morality. Adult assumptions about what children should not read "imply that individual children are more like each other in being children than unlike each other in being individuals." (Nodelman, 1996: 74) Further, if a younger reader does not consciously understand the deeper meaning of a text, does this mean he or she does not still absorb its more intricate themes as with say, Carroll's *Alice's Adventures in Wonderland*, or to name a non-fantastic example, Charles Dickens' *Oliver Twist*? That the issue of the child reader continues to weigh on Tolkien shows in a letter to his aunt Jane Neave in 1961, several years after *LotR*'s initial publication. Here Tolkien reiterates that the work "was *not* written[...] for any kind of person in particular" but "for itself" and notes, "If any parts or elements in it appear 'childish', it is because I am childish, and like that kind of thing myself *now*." (Carpenter, 2000: 310) Rejecting that children are a "class or a kind" he sees instead "a heterogeneous collection of immature persons, varying, as persons do, in their reach, and in their ability to extend it when stimulated." (Carpenter, 2000: 310) Tolkien uses "childish" and "immature" neutrally, without their usual negative connotations. Indeed, for Tolkien being "childish" would be a compliment and "immature" refers to chronological development. He sees his work as accessible to any literate person with the interest and energy to enter the "perilous realm" of Faerie.

As mentioned above, one factor in judging a text "appropriate" is violence, yet adults often forget about the remarkable darkness of many tales normally classified "for children". In but one example from the *Grimms' Fairy Tales*, Cinderella's stepmother insists her daughters mutilate their feet in order to fit into the glass slipper and thus win the prince. Looking back on his own childhood reading Tolkien notes,

> I do not think I was harmed by the horror in the fairy-tale setting, out of whatever dark beliefs and practices of the past it may have come[...]They open a door on Other Time, and if we pass through, though only for a moment, we stand outside our own time, outside Time itself, maybe. (Tolkien, 1966: 56)

In other words, children recognize fiction as fiction. Similar to Bruno Bettelheim, psychoanalytic children's literature and/or fantasy scholars such as Perry Nodelman, Lucie Armitt, Nina Mikkelsen, and Karen Coats, go further, seeing stories as necessary for children to confront and work through complex internal processes. Mikkelsen believes fantasy provides children with "exciting, inventive ways of shaping and reshaping their worlds", arguing the importance of adults "tuning in" to their responses to a given text. (Mikkelsen, 2005: 3) Nodelman echoes Zipes, identifying innocence in children's literature as an adult construct inherent to the form rather than as a reflection of the way a boy or girl actually appears in or sees the world. (Nodelman, 1996: 166) Although from different angles, these critics all see fantasy as a site of exploration and learning where darkness is an expected and pivotal part of the process.

On the tail end of what critics call the genre's second "Golden Age" in the mid-twentieth century, in what has become known as postmodern children's literature, writers such as Roald Dahl, Dr. Seuss—and more recently, Lemony Snicket (*A Series of Unfortunate Events*, 1999) and Neil Gaiman (*Coraline*, 2003) increasingly moved beyond the Romantic ideal to recognize the child as capable of enacting "inappropriate" or rebellious emotion and thought. Eva-Maria Metcalf explains how the postmodern impetus toward "questioning and erasing borders between the real, the fictional, and the fantastic" enables authors to "broach epistemological questions in a format that is understandable but challenging for children." (Metcalf, 1997: 55) Such flattening of categories engenders this incarnation of children's literature, which more explicitly acknowledges "the full range of issues and topics addressed in adult fiction." (Metcalf, 1997: 55) Often these are irreverent, darkly twisted tales that easily rival the more gruesome moments of *LotR*, often without the eucatastrophe, or "fleeting glimpse of joy" Tolkien identifies as a stock trait of the fairy-story. (Tolkien, 1966: 86) Thus the consideration of darkness or violence as a reason for limiting Tolkien's readership to adults applies even less today.

Complexity is another factor often used to distinguish child from adult reading. A glance at the children's section in just about any book store will reveal authors such as Bram Stoker, Mary Shelley, Robert Louis Stevenson, and others who not only did not write solely for children but whose books contain material many adults today would see as too complicated for younger readers. Perhaps the best classic example is Dickens, whose novels such as *Oliver Twist* and *Great Expectations* were in his day considered to be "family" reading.[1] His stories abound with child and adolescent characters, but such figures do not necessarily make a "children's" book, and Dickens invariably places them in a decidedly dark, adult world defined by injustice, poverty, and cruelty. Known for courting mass appeal, Dickens stands as arguably the most popular of the Victorian "social problem" novelists. His works consistently aim to convey messages for adults as well as for the next generation, both of whom have the capacity to effect change. Still the contemporary child would probably find his style and subject matter a bit uninviting, especially in America where his novels are not usually taught until high school or college.

Concepts of children's literature and age-based categories for reading collapse with relative ease, particularly in recent years. Although by no means postmodern, Tolkien's work is a complex mythology that may be "understandable but challenging for children" (Metcalf, 1997: 55) to varying degrees depending on age, experience, and adult participation in their reading. As Shippey puts it, along with *The Hobbit*, *LotR* has "largely created the expectations and established the conventions of a new and flourishing genre[...] hav[ing] said something important, and meant something important, to a high proportion of millions of readers." (Shippey, 2001: xxiv) Adding filmgoers to this list, as such Tolkien's work exemplifies and confirms his belief that "[w]e all need literature that is above our measure." (Carpenter, 2000: 298) To fully comprehend the relation between *LotR* and a younger audience lies as it does with any work, in the content. Next I will discuss two predominant messages that would resonate for readers of varying ages, but particularly for children, by looking at Tolkien's imagery in tandem with Jackson's adaptations, together with key examples from Rowling's *Harry Potter* series and their film versions.

---

[1] In Dickens' day this meant the middle- to upper-classes who could afford to buy books, which most often (to keep down costs) appeared serially in periodicals, including his own *Household Words* (1850-1859), and *All the Year Round* (1859-1870). Dickens viewed these ventures as forums for voicing his social and political opinions, yet selling them meant including his fiction and humorous pieces, which also dealt with the plight of poor and/or unfortunate children.

Inheritance and Resistance in *The Lord of the Rings* and *Harry Potter*

The concept of inheritance literally refers to the passing on of property, but also connotes the carrying on of traditions, memories, and beliefs from one generation to the next. When Frodo reluctantly accepts the One Ring from Gandalf he symbolically does much more: he takes a step toward maturation and assumes his place in a long line of (British) heroes. Literally, Frodo becomes a carrier of tradition by receiving from Bilbo an object whose long history parallels and propels that of his culture. Bilbo says as much when at their joint birthday party he puts on the Ring for the last time, saying, "[Frodo] comes of age and into his inheritance today." (Tolkien, 1981: 29) Frodo also shoulders the burden of responsibility that goes with the Ring: to fight evil and save his world. Verlyn Flieger sees Frodo as part of Tolkien's synthesis of the medieval and the modern, saying Frodo "conforms to mythic patterns and yet evokes the identification and empathy which the modern reader has come to expect from fiction." (Flieger, 2004: 135)

Harry Potter easily fits this description, too, and a similar blending of past and present drives Rowling's series, with Hogwarts and the Wizarding world looking decidedly medieval alongside contemporary Muggle Britain. For Frodo, Harry, and countless others like them, inheritance means accepting one's place in history, assuming a role pre-cast by ancestry, and making a personal contribution to what has come before. Such a condition includes dangerous trials meant to test the heir's worthiness, revealing depths and capabilities, often to the surprise of the character and those around him, including his enemies. Outside the text each child enacts a similar process in transitioning from childhood into adolescence and adulthood.

J.A. Appleyard maps these as reading stages, from the pre-school "confident player in a fantasy world that images realities, fears, and desires in forms that the child slowly learns to sort out and control," to the school-age child who becomes the hero or heroine in the story, and the adolescent who "looks to stories to discover insights into the meaning of life[...] and authentic role models for imitation." (Appleyard, 1990: 14-15) For each stage the text provides a way for the reader to engage actual feelings and experiences. Peer relations undoubtedly play a role in development, but much of what the child knows is derived or inherited from older people, as he or she personally envisions an adult self. Reading fantasy becomes "a practice and example of[...] discovering interrelations of individual, community, and cosmos; discovering past, present, and future; feeling, thought, and action; the human, the natural, and the supernatural." (O'Keefe, 2004: 18) With Tolkien's work representing all of these experiences, through Frodo, Aragorn, and others whose inheritance makes them guardians of Middle-earth, the reader carries out his or her own quest.

Along with Aragorn, whom I discuss later, Frodo must make a choice of how to handle his inheritance. Brian Rosebury pinpoints Frodo's talk with Gandalf about the Ring as the "moment" of acceptance, but underestimates the subtlety of Tolkien's message by saying, "Frodo and his friends[...] have an unwelcome responsibility thrust upon them by ill-fate." (Rosebury, 2003: 28) Given the abundant lucky coincidences in the story, this remains valid, yet Rosebury downplays the notion of choice, and that the "philosophic core" of Tolkien's work is his "belief in the workings of Providence[...] But that Providence does not overrule free will, because it works through the actions and decisions of the characters." (Shippey, 2004: 252) In Tolkien's universe, inheritance may be accepted or postponed, but not wholly rejected, and avoidance carries dangerous risks. Frodo accepts the Ring from Gandalf in the Shire, but does not realize what this means until after he has been hunted by Nazgûl and stabbed at Weathertop. He makes a deliberate, more informed and therefore more courageous decision at the Council of Elrond when he volunteers to take the Ring to Mordor. Clearly fate presents Frodo with an "offer he can't refuse" but he does retain the *ability to choose*. No one at the Council names Frodo; he names himself by stepping forward.

After Gandalf politely declines Bilbo's offer to take his old Ring on its final journey, the members sit "with downcast eyes, as if in dark thought." Feeling "a great dread" Frodo struggles with "an overwhelming longing to rest and remain at peace by Bilbo's side," not unlike a child might feel in leaving home to go to school, effectively going into the world alone for the first time. Frodo overcomes this anxiety and speaks "as if some other will was using his small voice. 'I will take the Ring,' he said, 'though I do not know the way.'" (Tolkien, 1981: 354) These last famous words stress Frodo's inexperience, making his gesture that much more powerful. Jackson spotlights this moment in the film version by revising Tolkien's text, choosing sound instead of silence. Frodo's voice rises above the din of an argument over ownership of the Ring raging between the different representatives of the races of Middle-earth. As with Tolkien's text, in the film, "It is the small and physically insignificant characters, the hobbits, who dominate the plot." (Shippey, 2004: 240) Confirming this the film reveals Frodo's capacity to succeed by having his voice rise above the noise to command the attention of those who are at least physically bigger and stronger than he. Jackson intensifies Frodo's obstacles, compounding the Hobbit's fear of the journey with that of speaking out in such an atmosphere. As Shippey notes, Jackson maintains "the vital words" the Hobbit says, but "stresses them above and beyond the original." (Shippey, 2004: 240) In the book the narrator's description of Frodo speaking "as if some other will was using his small voice" confirms the workings of fate, yet Frodo's voice is his *own*, and more importantly, the Council accepts the offer of one whose size and experience make him an unlikely candidate for the task.

Although certainly not children, the Hobbits' size and innocence of the world outside the Shire allow a discussion of them in similar terms. For the child reader or filmgoer, Frodo's stepping forward at the Council becomes charged by his physical size and a sense of powerlessness that comes with not being in control of one's own comings and goings. Of course Jackson is bound by budget and time constraints that go along with filmmaking, but his desire to remain true to Tolkien's most important themes, which he discusses in the DVD appendices, drives his decision to emphasize Frodo's diminutive stature. (Jackson, 2002) Jackson also uses camera perspective in the Council scene to enhance Frodo's smallness, showing him as if from the viewpoint of Gandalf, the first to turn, gaze *down* at the Hobbit, and acknowledge his words. The film follows Tolkien's text by expressing for either the adult or child audience "the means by which we are all dwarfed throughout our lives—by challenges and circumstances we struggle to master." (Armitt, 2005: 63) In taking on the quest Frodo overcomes his sense of his own limitations, accepting control not only of his own destiny but also of the future of Middle-earth.

As with many fantasy and children's literature protagonists, Frodo develops over the course of his travels, from relative innocence to experience. In *volunteering* to take the Ring to Mordor, Frodo accepts a position as a deliverer of his culture and the choices he makes irretrievably alter him, particularly after he no longer has

Gandalf to rely upon, and when he and Sam part from the rest of the Company. Evidence of his alteration unfolds by degrees in the story, but a vivid example occurs when he and Sam first meet Gollum/Smèagol and Frodo gets him to "swear[...] on the Precious." Here Frodo *becomes* the Ring in the once-Hobbit's eyes:

> "No! not on it," said Frodo, looking down at him with stern pity. "All you wish is to see it and touch it, if you can, though you know it would drive you mad[...] Swear by it, if you will. For you know where it is. Yes you know, Smèagol. *It is before you.*" (my emph. Tolkien, 1984: 285)

Here Sam sees Frodo having "grown" while Gollum does the opposite, so that "the master" appears as "a mighty lord who hid his brightness in a gray cloud." (Tolkien, 1984: 285) Still the narrator says Frodo and Gollum are "in some way akin and not alien," that they can "reach one another's minds." (Tolkien, 1984: 285) Not only does Frodo access the Ring's power by lording over a subject who mirrors himself, he also appears physically larger to Sam, his already faithful servant and friend. Although his journey will ultimately drag Frodo nearly to the ground as Gollum appears in this scene, it will also make him wise beyond his years and Hobbit-kind. The way Sam perceives Frodo here illustrates the extent to which this has already happened.

Of course, Frodo's physical enlargement is a trick of the Ring meant to ensnare him. His ability to resist the lure that turns Smèagol into Gollum confirms an inherent goodness in Frodo, in the same way that Gandalf, Galadriel, Aragorn, and Faramir confirm theirs by refusing the Ring. The difference between Gollum and Frodo helps to define the latter's heroism according to Joseph Campbell's definition of "[s]omeone who has given his or her life to something bigger than oneself." (Campbell, 1988: 123) In terms of growth, by seeing the threat of the Ring, Frodo implicitly recognizes development and even death as positive conditions. He accepts his inheritance unconditionally, knowing a large part of this acceptance means throwing away the Ring along with its (illusory) power. For the child reader, such acceptance means recognizing, whether subconsciously or consciously, the loss of freedom from responsibility that maturation demands.

Chance makes the important point:

> Instead of going on a quest to obtain some significant knowledge or item of value, Frodo goes to divest himself (and the world) of this power. If in life, maturity means the loss of the child self to adulthood, then this quest reverses that idea: the adult Frodo must attempt to recuperate the child, as the Ring returns to its origin. (Chance, 2001: 32)

The key phrase here is "must attempt": the destruction of the Ring, albeit not ultimately accomplished by Frodo himself, does not actually allow him to "recuperate the child" at all. Frodo returns to the Shire as an experienced Hobbit-of-the-world and in the book the Shire is also greatly affected. In the film version, *The Return of the King*, Jackson opts to revise Tolkien's ending chapters; rather than a "scouring" the Hobbits return to find the Shire pretty much as they left it. While this scene evoked some ire from many Tolkien purists, besides the obvious practicality of saving the film from extraordinary length, Jackson's approach powerfully highlights how much the Hobbits have changed. The scene where the four sit at a pub table, looking meaningfully at each other and separating themselves from the merry chatter around them, makes clear that they are not the same "boys" who set out, according to Frodo's voice-over, thirteen months before. If this were not enough, Sam's wedding scene follows, reiterating the idea of generations moving forward, which is also suggested by Frodo telling Sam the red book still has "a few pages left".

By the time Frodo returns to the Shire, he has done and seen so much that although he technically fails in his quest to destroy the Ring, he succeeds in destroying his child self. Enlarged, his experience also refers to the Shire and to Middle-earth: both suffer losses and irretrievably change as a result of Frodo's journey. Rather than contradicting Tolkien's idea of eucatastrophe, such losses confirm his effort "to dramatize th[e] 'theory of courage'" in the story. (Shippey, 2004: 156) Further, we must not lose sight of the fact that the Ring *is* destroyed and that Frodo plays the most important part in this outcome. With the widely held view of fantasy as inherently realistic, Tolkien's emphasis on loss throughout *LotR* also coincides with the inevitability of evil, in one form or another, in a fallen world. *Resisting* evil equals the key idea. Even if the effort results in personal loss, the outcome allows for a "fleeting glimpse of joy" (Tolkien, 1966: 86) and the ability to see the journey as successful. To move forward often takes great courage for a child or adult. Tolkien embeds messages about finding such strength even when—or especially when—things appear to be the darkest.

The idea of overcoming fear or insecurity also occurs in *LotR* through Aragorn and Thèoden, both of whom feel haunted by their ancestors. While Thèoden fears he may not live up to the glory of his fathers, Aragorn worries he may come too close to re-enacting the weakness of Isildur, whose choice to keep the Ring after taking it from Sauron ultimately compels Frodo's journey. Anne C. Petty makes the point, "It's the internal expression of an inward weakness that Tolkien felt was such a dominating trait of being human," with Aragorn being a primary representative. (Petty, 2003: 167) Jackson intensifies the idea of Aragorn's conflict by revising one encounter with Boromir. In Tolkien's text, Elrond presents Isildur's Bane at the Council and Boromir looks at Aragorn, comprehending his identity as heir to the throne his own father now keeps as Steward. Aragorn tells Boromir, "Little do I resemble the figures of Elendil and Isildur as they stand carved in their majesty in the halls of Denethor. I am but the heir of Isildur, not Isildur himself." (Tolkien, 1981: 325) Here Aragorn acknowledges his past without showing sign of being overwhelmed by it as he goes on to describe his trials as a ranger. (Tolkien, 1981: 325-326)

In the film these lines go to Arwen, coming upon Aragorn after a charged encounter with Boromir in a room where the Sword of Elendil lies in shards on an altar. Jackson places this scene prior to rather than as part of the Council meeting in *The Fellowship of the Ring*, spotlighting the moment. Boromir recognizes the shards, picks up the sword, and is cut. Saying "it's still sharp" he turns with dawning recognition to the silent Aragorn, then runs from the room, dropping the sword. That the broken weapon cuts Boromir indicates his impure motives and foreshadows his downfall, along with Aragorn's rise. Aragorn replaces the hilt on the altar just as Arwen enters, saying, "*Why do you fear the past?* You are Isildur's heir, not Isildur himself. *You are not bound to his fate.*" (my emph.) Giving the lines to Arwen probably stems from Jackson's concern to create a more compelling story by embellishing the romantic angle. More important here, though, is what Arwen says. Adding to Tolkien's text with the lines italicized above, Jackson underscores the fear that keeps Aragorn from claiming his inheritance. The ranger confirms the point when, referring to Isildur, he says, "The same blood flows in my veins, the same weakness." Until now Aragorn has provided a necessary, protective, yet largely anonymous service to Middle-earth, but a greater place for him appears to be pre-determined. By making Aragorn's fear of failure explicit in the film, Jackson foregrounds a key theme in Tolkien's text, one that would play especially well to a younger audience.

As with Aragorn in his guise as a ranger, and Frodo whom most other Hobbits initially view with suspicion due to his daring, heroes in fantasy and in children's literature often appear as marginalized from their societies. Arguably Rowling personifies this idea even more fully since the reader first meets Harry Potter as an infant with a scar marking him as "the chosen one". He remains ignorant of being a wizard until the significant age of eleven, but by then he has already been famous in his community for most of his life. From the start, Harry's life is defined by a combination of inheritance and resistance. At its most basic level Harry's quest is deeply personal, deriving from his need to carve an identity: he is an orphan whose parents die when he is too young to know them. Harry does not belong to anyone, yet he belongs to *everyone*. From the moment of his parents' deaths he becomes a symbol of victory and resistance against evil for the Wizarding world, who toast him as the narrator tells of "people meeting in secret all over the country[...]holding up their glasses and saying in hushed voices: 'To Harry Potter—the boy who lived!'" (Rowling, 1997: 17)

While the celebration might seem inappropriate given the tragedy, the Potters die protecting Harry, and serving the greater good by seemingly eliminating a grave threat. Harry literally inherits a place in the Wizarding world through his parents, along with their money, magical powers, and genetic traits. More importantly, as "the chosen one" he personifies the larger resistance of the Order of the Phoenix against Voldemort, a mission he never seeks and could conceivably refuse, yet one he accepts and slowly embraces. His legal inheritance of the Order's "headquarters" in Book Six further reinforces the point. As the series unfolds Harry recognizes his relationship to his culture, suggesting a transition from the self-centredness of childhood to a more external, adult view.

Still, in typical adolescent fashion, Harry also bucks authority and resists every effort designed to protect him. Closely associated with resistance is rebellion, a stance especially relevant to the young reader who may feel the pressure of adult rule and one that also defines the mission of Tolkien's Fellowship. One clever way both Tolkien and Rowling express this theme is through the idea of invisibility, a ubiquitous fantasy convention. Enlarged, invisibility connotes avoiding notice or acknowledgement, an idea bound up with a child's sense of being in the world. Either he or she might already feel invisible to busy parents, or might wish to be invisible to prying adults and teachers whose notice implies censure. With similar implications, avoidance of notice applies in opposite ways for Frodo and Harry. In *LotR* putting on the Ring means slipping by less perceptive enemies (Orcs, Uruki); while standing directly in the most dangerous foe's line of sight (Nazgûl, Sauron). In other words, the Ring bestows power along with unparalleled vulnerability.

Also, wearing the Ring literally wears on a person, resulting in a physical wasting as we see in Gollum. Frodo's journey becomes defined by his capacity to resist the Ring's hold, that is, Sauron's dominion, over him. In this way inheritance becomes ironically complicated by resistance: vowing to undertake the quest passed to him from Bilbo means Frodo must continually resist the pull of the tangible emblem of that quest, the Ring. Further, while the power it bestows is obviously negative, a positive effect does emerge from it. Throughout the journey Frodo finds within himself dormant qualities that will make him an admirable "adult". In this way, the Ring can be viewed as a conduit between childhood and adulthood, innocence and experience. Petty identifies the "most unique and potentially dangerous feature" of the rings of power as their use "as a gateway between worlds[...] The wearer of such a ring becomes invisible to those in the third-dimensional physical world but can at the same time see beings who were non-physical, such as wraiths." (Petty, 2003: 155-156) Viewing wraiths the way a child or adolescent might see unimaginative, over-authoritative adulthood, one can interpret Frodo's possession of the Ring as his metaphorical position on the brink of maturation, a time that includes much that is painful and seemingly insurmountable, as well as inevitable and instructional. The confusion coinciding with such a time symbolically occurs in the way the Ring alters a person's vision while wearing it; an idea Jackson vividly captures in the films.

Although without the dark side effects of the Ring, Harry's invisibility cloak similarly marries inheritance and resistance. The cloak last belonged to his father, and was passed to Harry through Dumbledore, his most powerful paternal surrogate. As part of a long-standing effort against evil, the cloak connects Harry to the past in terms of both his biological and Hogwarts families. Interestingly, in the sixth book Dumbledore tells Harry to carry the cloak with him everywhere as an instrument of protection or defence and Harry uses the cloak more in this one book than he has in the previous five combined. Harry's choosing of moments to be invisible usually comes from a desire or need to break at least one of Hogwarts' rules. Invariably students in my children's literature courses want to know why Harry "gets away with" going against the behaviour code of Hogwarts, and we usually come to the conclusion that he avoids expulsion for serving a higher purpose. While he does so pretty readily, one does not get the sense that Harry breaks rules arbitrarily or for the thrill, but rather because he knows his survival is bound to the perpetuation of good. Likewise, Frodo must destroy the Ring or he will be responsible for the downfall of Middle-earth, so despite great personal harm, he is sometimes forced to use the Ring in service of the greater good.

Harry's supreme rebellion is, of course, aimed at Voldemort. According to one interpretation of the prophecy as revealed by Dumbledore in *Harry Potter and the Order of the Phoenix*, either Harry or Voldemort is destined to kill the other. (Rowling, 2003: 741) From his appearance in the first book Harry grows increasingly stalwart. One of his greatest shows of strength against evil occurs in *Harry Potter and the Goblet of Fire*. Near the end the Dark Lord finally takes his own physical shape after luring Harry and using his blood to create the potion that enables the transformation. (Rowling, 2000: 689-697) Rather than quickly killing Harry, Voldemort turns the moment into a competition. Harry experiences great physical and emotional suffering in these scenes, being forced to watch a schoolmate die, then to fend off Voldemort's attacks in the ultimate "wizard's duel". (Rowling, 2000: 691, 721-724) Still Harry determines not to falter. The narrator describes Harry's response to his enemy's insistence that he perform a perfunctory gesture before battle: "Harry did not bow. He was not going to let Voldemort play with him before killing him[...] he was not going to give him that satisfaction." (Rowling, 2000: 715) Coming to Harry's aid out of the wand are those who died in a similar effort, most of whom are adults, and among them, his parents, which suggests a strength of character or grace within him that goes beyond even that shown by them when alive, as far as we know.

While all the films so far have stayed true to the major themes of Rowling's books, the most recent three films seem to most accurately capture the complexity of Harry's situation and the heroic role he must play, not only to survive, but also to enable his culture to survive. In the film version of *Harry Potter and the Goblet of Fire*, director Mike Newell unfortunately compresses the champions' final task of the labyrinth, omitting the specific tests Harry overcomes in the book. The scene where Voldmort kills Cedric and faces Harry in the first direct confrontation since Harry's birth remains mostly intact, however, bringing to life descriptions that might be troubling for younger viewers. With each book (and film), Harry's world grows more "adult" and forbidding, but his readership grows along with him, both in age and quantity. Upon its release much was made of the fact that *Harry Potter and the Goblet of Fire* marked the first of the *Harry Potter* films to receive a rating of PG-13 (for sequences of fantasy violence and frightening images). While the media quickly tried to make this into a story, Warner Brothers, the film's American distribution company, dismissed its importance by saying, "We've learned the audience has grown older with the movies, so the[...] rating just played into the core of the audience." (Germain, 2005: online)

Fantasy Literature for Broader Audiences

Being notoriously possessive about her characters, Rowling shares creative control over the films, but ultimately these decisions lie in the hands of the producers and directors. Interestingly, while Chris Columbus remains as producer, he stopped directing after the first two films, which were decidedly child-friendly in style and almost cloyingly true to the books. *Harry Potter and the Prisoner of Azkaban* (dir. Alfonso Cuarón, 2004) and *Harry Potter and the Goblet of Fire* (dir. Mike Newell, 2005), as well as *Harry Potter and the Order of the Phoenix*, have different directors, and progressively stray from such close adherence to the books. Clearly the changes are due to the fact that the later instalments are longer, requiring extensive trimming, but while the *Harry Potter* films (and books) attract increasingly older audiences,

J.R.R. Tolkien and the Child Reader   307

Jackson's adaptations of *LotR*, all filmed simultaneously, seem to attempt the opposite: using effects and action to attract the younger audiences who may only be interested in an entertaining film, as well as the adults who know Tolkien's original.

While Tolkien rejected possible film adaptations in his lifetime, he did so because the technology simply did not exist to convince him that his Middle-earth could effectively translate on to film. Conversely, Rowling may have dreamt of seeing her vision on film, but this did not seem to significantly drive her writing process, at least initially. Rowling has often said she had the entire series planned and the last chapter of the last *Harry Potter* book conceived before having an inkling of being published, let alone selling the film rights. (Chaundy, 2003: online) Since the films have become reality, though, like *LotR*, the *Harry Potter* series has become a franchise, making efforts to maintain artistic integrity increasingly complicated.

Apart from the obvious marketing machinery surrounding both Tolkien and Rowling, technology marks perhaps the most important component in terms of seeking and attracting particular audience demographics. Specifically in regard to a younger audience the Internet and gaming create new frontiers that have extended the works of both Tolkien and Rowling in interesting yet potentially troubling ways. Indeed for *LotR*, "two-and-a-half years in advance of the movie release and nine months before the first frame of film was shot," Senior Vice President of Worldwide Interactive Marketing and Business Development for New Line Cinema Gordon Paddison built "www.lordoftherings.net". He started by making contact with "more than 400 fan sites", then

> ... created an online event to show the first look at never-released footage almost a year before the theatrical teaser trailer. The result was 1.7 million fans downloaded it in twenty-four hours; almost double the number for the previous *Star Wars/Phantom Menace* trailer. (Braswell, 2003)

This *LotR* site is, of course, one of many, and the interest in the films does not seem to have diminished despite the passage of time. In fact due to Jackson's concern for making Tolkien's themes the star of his films, the adaptations have given long-time fans of the original a new way to appreciate and relive it, while continually drawing new readers/viewers until, perhaps, further advances in technology demand a remake. The controversy over Jackson's possible directing of *The Hobbit* as a prequel to *LotR* certainly confirms the continued enthusiasm for fans and movie industry executives.

Tolkien famously despised "machines", but enjoyed seeing people appreciate the world he created, so one can only speculate about his response to websites and video games representing Middle-earth and its battle against evil. Still whether the battle occurs at Helm's Deep or in cyberspace, the overarching messages in both *LotR* and *Harry Potter* are that evil must be resisted, that each generation will fight this fight in its own way, and that just as a new evil will arise, a new hero will pick up the sword. In this sense Harry is a successor to Frodo and a long line of heroes, the latest in a literary tradition that transcends labels of "adult" or "child" reader to speak to the human experience. *LotR* is no more specifically *for* adults than the *Harry Potter* series is *for* children. Certainly *Harry Potter and the Half-Blood Prince* and *Harry Potter and the Deathly Hallows* both include darkness and violence that might make an adult think twice before giving the book to a child under twelve. Yet, upon its release, many critics saw *Harry Potter and the Half-Blood Prince*, for example, as an invaluable text for helping children to confront loss.

The most important and powerful feat of Tolkien, Rowling, and Jackson is to open a "good book" to a wider audience, helping to ensure and further elevate the status of fantasy and children's literature for generations to come. While this carries some capitalistic side effects, those who care about these texts will continue to fight to uphold their value and relevance. Just as Rowling's stories of the boy wizard's fight against evil have countless men and women lugging copies through subways and airports, once introduced, Tolkien's portrayal of Frodo's "errand" can inspire the child reader to carry the book through the phases of growth, gaining something new with each encounter.

Bibliography

Appleyard, J.A. (1990), *Becoming a Reader: The Experience of Fiction from Childhood to Adulthood*, Cambridge University Press, New York

Armitt, Lucy (2005), *Fantasy Fiction: An Introduction*, Continuum, New York

Attebery, Brian (1992), *Strategies of Fantasy*, Indiana University Press, Bloomington

Braswell, Ty (2003), "In Search of QEIB: Gordon Paddison Interview" *iMediaConnection* 8 March: http://www.imediaconnection.com/content/1179.asp

Campbell, Joseph (1988), *The Power of Myth*, Doubleday, New York

Carpenter, Humphrey (ed.) (2000), *The Letters of J.R.R. Tolkien*, Houghton Mifflin, New York

Chance, Jane (2001), The Lord of the Rings: *The Mythology of Power* rev. ed., University Press of Kentucky, Lexington

Chaundy, Bob (2003), "Harry Potter's Magician" *BBC News* 18 February

Clark, Beverly Lyon (2003), *Kiddie Lit: The Cultural Construction of Children's Literature in America*, Johns Hopkins University Press, Baltimore

Flieger, Verlyn (2004), "Frodo and Aragorn: The Concept of the Hero" in Rosa A. Zimbardo and Neil D. Isaacs (eds), *Understanding The Lord of the Rings: The Best of Tolkien Criticism*, Houghton Mifflin, New York, pp. 122-145

Germain, David (2005), "Harry's 'Goblet' Nets $54.9M at Box Office" *ABC News* 28 November

Metcalf, Eva-Maria (1997), "The Changing Status of Children and Children's Literature" in Sandra L. Beckett (ed.), *Reflections of Change: Children's Literature Since 1945*, Greenwood Press, Westport, pp. 49-63

Mikkelsen, Nina (2005), *Powerful Magic: Learning from Children's Responses to Fantasy Literature*, Teacher's College Press, New York

Nodelman, Perry (1996), *The Pleasures of Children's Literature* 2nd ed., White Plains, Longman, New York

O'Keefe, Deborah (2004), *Readers in Wonderland: The Liberating Worlds of Fantasy Fiction*, Continuum, New York

Petty, Anne C. (2003), *Tolkien in the Land of Heroes: Discovering the Human Spirit*, Cold Spring Press, Harbor, New York

Rosebury, Brian (2003), *Tolkien: A Cultural Phenomenon*, Palgrave Macmillan, New York

Rowling, J.K. (1997), *Harry Potter and the Philosopher's Stone*, Bloomsbury, London

Rowling, J.K. (1999), *Harry Potter and the Prisoner of Azkaban*, Bloomsbury, London

Rowling, J.K. (2000), *Harry Potter and the Goblet of Fire*, Bloomsbury, London

Rowling, J.K. (2003), *Harry Potter and the Order of the Phoenix*, Bloomsbury, London

Rowling, J.K. (2005), *Harry Potter and the Half-Blood Prince*, Bloomsbury, London

Shippey, T.A. (2001), *J.R.R. Tolkien: Author of the Century*, Houghton Mifflin, New York

Shippey, T.A. (2004), "Another Road to Middle-earth: Jackson's Movie Trilogy" in Rose A. Zimbardo and Neil D. Isaacs (eds), *Understanding* The Lord of the Rings: *The Best of Tolkien Criticism*, Houghton Mifflin, New York, pp. 233-254

Swinfen, Ann (1984), *In Defence of Fantasy: A Study of the Genre in English and American Literature Since 1945*, Routledge, Boston

Tolkien, J.R.R. (1966), "On Fairië Stories" in *The Tolkien Reader*, Ballantine, New York, pp. 33-99

Tolkien, J.R.R. (1981), *The Fellowship of the Ring*, Ballantine/Houghton Mifflin, New York

Tolkien, J.R.R. (1984), *The Two Towers*, Ballantine/Houghton Mifflin, New York

Tolkien, J.R.R. (1985), *The Return of the King*, Ballantine/Houghton Mifflin, New York

Zipes, Jack (2001), *Sticks and Stones: The Troublesome Success of Children's Literature from Slovenly Peter to Harry Potter*, Routledge, New York

18

ONE RING TO RULE THEM ALL
Power and Surveillance in the Film Adaptations of *The Lord of the Rings*

Cherylynn Silvia

FILM ATTEMPTS to be all-seeing. But while it captures every movement and expression within the frame, it is unable to capture the characters' thoughts or feelings. Emotions, such as fear, are usually conveyed through acting and reaction shots. Much of our fear while watching Peter Jackson's *The Lord of the Rings* revolves around the possibility of the characters (particularly Frodo) being observed. For example, in Jackson's *The Fellowship of the Ring*, when the Hobbits hide in a ditch beneath the roots of a tree to avoid being seen by the Ringwraith, we are afraid for the Hobbits because we see that the Ringwraith is right above them. Our fear is accentuated because we assume that, since we as the audience can see the Hobbits, the Ringwraith can see them as well. Jackson further underscores the vulnerability of the characters by filming the Ring as an observing character in its own right. Throughout the film, Jackson uses close-ups, lingering middle and long shots, and even reaction shots of the Ring to suggest its sentience and malevolence. These shots increase our fear for the characters and legitimize the Ring and Sauron as objects of fear.

The Ring as a Character

By cinematically emphasizing the Ring as a character, Jackson's adaptation of *LotR* intensifies and extends the novel's emphasis on the Ring's and Sauron's power. Through the transformation of narrative elements in the source text and cinematic techniques such as the framing or absence of the Ring within various shots, the film trilogy reinforces the extent of Sauron's control and the fear associated with it. By vividly depicting the Ring's and Sauron's power and the mechanisms of surveillance they engender, these films effectually constitute a Foucauldian reading of Tolkien's text.

If power is always related "to the historical production of truth", as Michel Foucault maintains, then any examination of power in *LotR* must take into account the role of history. (McHoul, 1993: 57) In the prologue to *FotR*, Galadriel's voiceover reveals that the history of the Ring's creation, the Great War that ensued, and the severing of the Ring from Sauron's hand. Galadriel relates this history because, with the exception of Sauron and Treebeard, she is the oldest character portrayed in the *LotR* films. Galadriel is aware of the One Ring around the time of its creation and helps to hide the three Elven rings from the domination of the One. Because of her direct involvement, as well as the fact that she eventually bears one of the Elven rings, Galadriel is an ideal voice for the history of the Ring.

In addition to setting up the Ring's history, Jackson uses the prologue to foreground the fear of Sauron and the Ring. At the battle of the Last Alliance in *FotR*, the initial shot of Sauron is a full-screen close-up of his hand wearing the Ring and wielding a mace. Combined with Galadriel's words "But the power of the Ring could not be undone,"[1] this frame epitomizes fear of the Ring by focusing on the hand that wears it holding a legitimate object of fear, a large mace. In succeeding frames, even when Sauron is barely visible, his imposing physical presence is emphasized by recurring extreme-angle shots. The first shot pans back to look down at the army from over Sauron's head. The second looks up at Sauron from the point of view of the men in the army. This makes the army, as well as the audience (who identify with them), appear insignificant. This same framing is used when Sauron approaches Isildur. We first see Isildur from over Sauron's shoulder—we are never shown Sauron's exact point of view—and from this angle we see not only Sauron's height but also Isildur's fear. The film cuts to an extreme low angel shot of

---

[1] Dialogues from *LotR* cited in this chapter, unless otherwise specified, are all from the extended DVD editions of Jackson's films.

Sauron, and in the next few frames, a giant foot seems to crush us as an audience. The foot, however, is stepping on Narsil, and as Isildur grabs for the sword, Sauron's foot lands in front of Isildur, breaking the sword. We then share Isildur's point of view as Sauron's ringed hand comes towards us. As the Ring is sliced from Sauron's hand, the emphasis is no longer on Sauron and the Ring but on the Ring alone. Sauron falls back out of the frame as the camera follows the Ring to the ground in front of Isildur. Once Isildur has the Ring, Jackson deliberately keeps it out of the prologue when it is not important to the scene. The Ring is shown in close-up as the voiceover declares, "but the hearts of Men are easily corrupted and the Ring of power has a will of its own," and then it is kept out of sight until Isildur uses it to escape from the Orcs. Jackson keeps the image of the Ring out of the shot by focusing on Isildur in close-up and later by having Isildur cover the Ring with his hand until he is ready to use it. When he uses the Ring to become invisible, the Ring again becomes the focus of the shot. By removing the image of the Ring from all shots in which it is not influencing Isildur, Jackson ensures that we recognize the Ring as an active, manipulative force.

In choosing to open the film with this visual emphasis on Sauron and the Ring's history, Jackson effectively makes the fear of Sauron and of the Ring the basis of his film. Tolkien, on the other hand, begins *LotR* with a depiction of the innocence of the Shire and slowly builds up to the fear of Sauron and the Ring. When Jackson moves this history to the opening of the film, this fear, and the fact that it has been passed down through history, is brought to the fore.

Jackson also alters Gandalf's relationship to the Ring, representing it as a more intense object of fear. In *FotR*, Gandalf tells us that Sauron endured his apparent defeat because "his life force is bound to the Ring and the Ring survived," thus characterizing the Ring as a legitimate metonymy of Sauron's power. He further explains that he "would use this Ring from the desire to do good. But through [him], it would wield a power too great and terrible to imagine." While the films vividly reinforce this fear by physically separating Gandalf from the Ring, the novel leaves a sense of ambiguity regarding Gandalf's tactile relationship to the Ring. For example, in an early passage of Tolkien's *FotR*, Gandalf asks Frodo for the Ring:

> "Give me the ring for a moment."
> Frodo took it from his breeches-pocket, where it was clasped to a chain that hung from his belt. He unfastened it and handed it slowly to the wizard[....] Gandalf held it up. It looked to be made of pure and solid gold[....] To Frodo's astonishment and distress the wizard threw it suddenly into the middle of a glowing corner of the fire. (Tolkien, 1994: 48)

It seems uncertain whether the repetitive "its" all refer to the (soon to be capitalized) Ring or whether Gandalf is holding the chain and not the Ring itself. But if Gandalf is holding the chain, the referent pronoun "it" inexplicably switches meaning mid-passage. Since the "it" in "where it was clasped to a chain that hung from his belt" clearly refers to the Ring, it follows that "unfastened it" also refers to the Ring. It may be odd for a ring to be "unfastened," but as the previous sentence states, it was "clasped" to the chain, and so the Ring would need to be unfastened. There is further evidence that Gandalf comes into contact with the Ring when he removes it from the fire:

> For a moment the wizard stood looking at the fire; then he stooped and removed the ring to the hearth with the tongs, and at once picked it up. Frodo gasped.
> "It is quite cool," said Gandalf. (Tolkien, 1994: 49)

Gandalf's action of "at once pick[ing] it up" could refer to lifting the Ring with either tongs or his fingers. Yet Frodo would have no reason to gasp at the supposed heat of the Ring if Gandalf did not touch it. Gandalf would also know it was "quite cool" only if he held the Ring with his fingers before handing it to Frodo; if he held the Ring with the chain still connected, the chain would have burned him even if the Ring did not. This scene in the novel suggests, therefore, that Gandalf does actually touch the Ring. Yet Jackson's filmic version significantly alters this scene by keeping Gandalf physically separated from the Ring. In the film, Gandalf transports the Ring only in an envelope or with the use of tongs, emphasizing the separation of Gandalf and the Ring and foregrounding his fear of the Ring's active power.

This fear is further illustrated for the audience in *FotR* during the Council of Elrond scene. Here Jackson employs extreme close-ups of the Ring when the characters are arguing over who will take it to Mordor. By including this argument, Jackson differentiates this scene from the calmer discussion that takes place in the novel. (Tolkien, 1994: 233) As the characters argue, they are not only reflected in but also contained by the Ring, in a shot that emphasizes its control over them. The fire around the edges, which consumes the Ring and the council members in subsequent frames, points to Sauron's presence. His influence is further emphasized through sound effects: the voice coming from the Ring chants "ash nazg durbatulûk, ash nazg gimbatul, ash nazg gimbatul" ("one Ring to rule them all, one Ring to find them, one Ring to find them")—as if Sauron is claiming to be the cause of discontent among the council members and is exulting in the fact that the darkness of the Ring has found them. Although Frodo does appear to hear Sauron's voice, the image of the Ring wreathed in flame is visible only to the audience. This extreme close-up vividly demonstrates the Ring's active connection to Sauron in a way that language alone, i.e. history and hearsay, cannot. This vision of Sauron in the Ring reinforces our belief in Sauron's power; this belief is important to the plot, because if we do not fear Sauron's ever-present evil, then we have no sympathy for the trials of the quest. And although the argument could have started without Sauron's influence, this scene reminds us of his presence and reinforces our belief that the Ring must be destroyed.

While Sauron and the Ring can control and debase others, such as the men who become Ringwraiths, Sauron's power stems primarily from the belief—held by the Free Peoples of Middle-earth—that he is omnipotent. If, as Michel Foucault states, "there is no[...] knowledge that does not presuppose and constitute[...] power relations," (Foucault, 1995: 27) then the characters' knowledge of the Ring's history and the fear associated with it create its actual power over them. The characters' knowledge of Sauron enhances and extends his power so much that even when Sauron is disembodied and no longer wields the Ring, the fear of him remains. Thus Sauron's ultimate power relies on the fear that has been propagated about him, particularly Galadriel's assertions that "the power of the Ring could not be undone" and "the Ring of Power has a will of its own." (*FotR*)

That this unquestioning belief in Sauron's omnipotence is created through knowledge is clearly demonstrated when Saruman, the greatest of the Wizards, succumbs to despair. Saruman, who is never in the physical presence of the Ring, allies himself with Sauron because of the information he receives through the palantír. This information leads him to believe that "[a]gainst the power of Mordor there can be no victory." (*FotR*) The capitulation of Saruman reinforces the Foucauldian notion that power produces truth through knowledge. The truth as Saruman sees it is that Sauron is insurmountable. Yet if Saruman did not believe that Sauron was omnipotent, then that truth would have no power over him, and he would not renounce his position as one of the wise to mimic the Dark Lord.

Denethor also succumbs to despair as a result of trusting a palantír. While Denethor's use of the palantír is not directly recounted in Jackson's *The Return of the King*, he does proclaim "Do you think the eyes of the white tower are blind? I have seen more than you know," implicitly admitting that he has looked into the palantír. In the novel he speaks these words while directly referring to the palantír in his hand. (Tolkien, 1994: 835) Denethor's further assertion that "[a]gainst the power that has risen in the east, there is no victory" is related to the knowledge, gained through the palantír, that the Black Ships are approaching Gondor. What he does not know is that those ships hold Aragorn and his army, not the enemy. The information Denethor gains through the palantír produces his despair and thus consummates Sauron's power over him.

Although the other characters believe in Sauron's supremacy, they do not yield to the despair he promotes. As Kocher notes,

> The whole venture of the Ring always looks desperate[....] Yet against all persuasions to despair, Gandalf, Aragorn[...] and all those who fight beside them hope on and keep on acting upon their hope. Without that, Sauron would have won a dozen times over. (Kocher, 1972: 55-56)

Their persistence indicates that although they acknowledge the produced truth, they do not fully submit to it. These characters possess a gleam of hope, symbolized by the journey of the Hobbits. Although Frodo and Sam's mission is often deemed a "fool's hope", the remaining characters protect Middle-earth from the encroaching armies of Mordor and Isengard to give Frodo and Sam time to destroy the Ring. In this way, they resist the "discourse of truth". (Brown, 2000: 31) As Brown explains, "discourses are loci of knowledge [that are] neither stable nor monolithic," and "no discourse [can] cover the diversity of truths." (Brown, 2000: 31) Each character resists the produced discourse of truth that Sauron is invincible by believing that there can be an outcome other than their destruction. By doing this, they oppose the dominant idea and create their own truth. It is the possibility of truths other than the one produced by the dominant power that makes Sauron's downfall ultimately achievable.

Control without Contact; Contact without Control

Even though he carries the Ring, Frodo has no control over it because it is the physical representation of Sauron himself. As the Ringbearer, Frodo becomes "a reality fabricated by this specific technology of power that [Foucault calls] a 'discipline'." (Foucault, 1995: 194) Even though he bears the Ring, Frodo is, as Foucault would say, disciplined by it. While this discipline may not be as rigorous as the prison timetable in Foucault's *Discipline and Punish*, wherein every moment of the day has a specific and regimented purpose, Frodo has an explicit purpose: to go to Mordor and destroy the Ring. He must do this before he is found or Sauron's armies overwhelm Middle-earth. And while "[t]raditionally, power was what was seen[...], disciplinary power[...] is exercised through its invisibility." (Foucault, 1995: 187) The completion of the quest depends on Frodo's ability to escape the observation inherent in bearing the Ring. In order to avoid capture, Frodo changes his name, hides his purpose, and prohibits any obvious firelight. But capture is an ever-present possibility, as Sauron has many creatures searching for Frodo, including the ubiquitous Ringwraiths.

Frodo can escape observation by corporeal entities if he wears the Ring, which makes him invisible. But in doing so, he subjects himself to the "all-seeing eye" of Sauron. The more he wears the Ring, the more he subjects himself to this "inspecting gaze[...] which each individual under its weight [begins] interiorising to the point that he is his own overseer." (Foucault, 1980: 155) Thus he constantly fears being seen, whether he is physically visible or not, and "it is the fact of being constantly seen, of being able always to be seen, that maintains the disciplined individual in his subjection." (Foucault, 1995: 187) When wearing the Ring, Frodo's situation parallels that of the prisoners under the surveillance of the Panopticon; the prisoners are kept under endless surveillance, and yet they are invisible to each other. Similarly, when Frodo is wearing the Ring, he cannot clearly see the world around him, but he can see—and be seen by—Sauron's great "lidless" panoptic eye.

While Sauron may be the "all-seeing eye", he is far from the omnipotent force that Saruman believes him to be. As Foucault observes, "the perfect disciplinary gaze would make it possible for a single gaze to see everything constantly." (Foucault, 1995: 173) But Sauron cannot do this: his inability to see beyond his realm without the assistance of palantiri and Ringwraiths illustrates his lack of omnipotence. To effectively use his palantír, Sauron must rely on the weakness of other individuals who also have palantiri. His reliance on the Ringwraiths also demonstrates his imperfect gaze.

Sauron needs the Ringwraiths to capture Frodo and the Ring, but they are remarkably ineffectual in this capacity. The Ringwraiths' chief weapon is fear. They inspire terror amongst their opponents because they are a symbol of Sauron's tyranny, yet they avoid any engagement in which they are not assured victory. We see the Ringwraiths in physical combat twice. After attacking the Hobbits when they are alone on Weathertop, the Ringwraiths momentarily fight Aragorn before fleeing, even though they vastly outnumber him. In *RotK*, the Witch-king, mounted on a wyvern, attacks Théoden's horse before battling Éowyn. Despite the Witch-king's threat that she will "die now", Éowyn decapitates the wyvern and destroys the Witch-king with one sword thrust. Because the Ringwraiths are cowardly and easily dispatched, there seems to be little justification for the widespread fear they engender. They are such effective agents of terror mainly because they are known to act for Sauron.

Indeed, their enslavement to Sauron makes the Ringwraiths perfect examples of Foucauldian delinquents. According to Foucault, the modern prison system is interested not in torturing the body but in controlling the soul. Once criminals are punished, he argues, they are forever caught up in the prison system as part of an information-gathering network serving the dominant power. Foucault refers to this inconspicuous incorporation as "delinquency". (Foucault, 1995) Similarly, the Ringwraiths were once "Men, who above all else, desire[d] power," and as Aragorn explains to Frodo, because of their lust for power, they became "blinded by their greed[...] one by one falling into darkness. Now they are slaves to [Sauron's] will." (*FotR*) Just as the dominant power gains a wider range of surveillance through the delinquency of the criminal, the Ringwraiths hunt Frodo for Sauron because Sauron possesses their souls. The Ringwraiths are unable to capture Frodo; but as Foucault makes clear, in the modern prison system the role of delinquents is not to apprehend. Their purpose is to observe, a task that the Ringwraiths do fulfill. Yet Gollum is a far more effective tool of the Dark Lord because unlike the Ringwraiths, he locates and tracks Frodo, feigning servitude in an attempt to gain the Ring. While the Ringwraiths are purposefully sent to find the Ring, Gollum's success is motivated by his own desire for the Ring, not by instruction from Sauron.

Given the Ringwraiths' and Gollum's delinquencies, the Ring can be compared to the prison system. Once incorporated into the disciplinary system, the individual has no power but that allowed by the prison/Ring. Individuals released from the prison system tend to repeatedly return to it, just as those corrupted by the Ring have an ingrained need to seek it out. This delinquency is demonstrated not only by the Ringwraiths and Gollum, but also by Sauron himself.

While the Ring is a physical extension of Sauron, it is often identified as an independent agent: "*it betrayed* Isildur," "the Ring of Power *perceived*," "*it abandoned* Gollum," "*it wants* to return". (*FotR*, my emph.) And despite his supposed omnipotence, Sauron is disembodied and needs the Ring to assume corporeal form. Without the Ring, Sauron is not "above fear," as Gandalf puts it. He tells Aragorn, "Doubt ever gnaws at [Sauron]. The rumor has reached him [that] [t]he heir of Númenor still lives. Sauron fears you, Aragorn. He fears what you may become." (*The Two Towers*) As heir to the throne, Aragorn is assumed to possess enough power to wield the Ring and destroy Sauron. Because of this possibility, Sauron fears his own destruction and enacts a fervent search for the Ring. It is this need for the Ring that makes Sauron the ultimate delinquent of his own prison.

By searching for the Ring, Sauron forms a recognizable (if theoretically imperfect) panoptic image. In Jackson's *RotK*, as Sam and Frodo cross Mordor, they see Sauron's tower and his great eye searching his lands. This image resembles the panoptic tower, or Panopticon, except that the Panopticon theoretically can see everywhere simultaneously. Although the prisoners under the gaze of the panoptic tower are not watched at all times, observation is always possible. Because the prisoners are never aware when they are watched and when they are not, they act as if they are observed at all times, effectively making the Panopticon all-seeing.

Sauron, on the other hand, is more like a lighthouse, which can only observe one place at a time. While the observed place is seemingly random, warranting some fear of observation, the observed are aware when they are being watched and when they are not. Because of this flaw, Sauron is neither all-powerful nor all-seeing. Sauron's power, however, does produce an outcome similar to that of the Panopticon. Mordor is barren, the Orcs are tortured perversions of Elves, and Sauron's citizens are a monolithic army. As Patrick Curry states, "the non-allegorical nature of the Ring is[...] the willful exercise of power applied instrumentally to the realization of a single overarching goal." He adds, "[t]he precise nature of that power [is] homogeneity." (Curry, 2004: 146) This eschewing of diversity is also the ultimate effect of the Panopticon, which erases all individuality amongst its subjects and produces uniformity as a consequence of power.

Because of the visual basis of panopticism, it is important to reflect on the meta-filmic role of the audience. In one way it seems that the audience is indeed all-seeing: we know many things that the characters do not and usually see them through an objective medium long shot, but ultimately the audience is only privy to what Peter Jackson decides to show us. Our supposedly omniscient view is thus hampered by Jackson's ability to film only one place at a time as well as by our ability, as mortals, to see only one place at a time. In Foucault, while the Panopticon is theoretically omniscient, the guards inside the panoptic tower are not. They are able to view through only one section of the panoptic tower. But because it is the fear of observation that disciplines those who are under surveillance, Foucault famously commented that it did not matter whether the guards or convicts are in the central tower. (Foucault, 1980: 164-165) Bentham's proposal even noted that it did not matter who observed in the central tower. (cited in Foucault, 1995: 207) And as Foucault notes, "the more numerous those anonymous and temporary observers are, the greater the risk for the inmate of being surprised and the greater his anxious awareness of being observed." (Foucault, 1995: 202) Taken one step further, the tower could indeed function when empty as long as the prisoners believe that it is occupied. Far from being panoptic, then, the role of the audience most clearly parallels that of the guards or observers inside the Panopticon. In both cases it is the apparatus that has the power: the panoptic tower creates the discipline just as the camera creates the audience's interpretation of the filmic world.

Power of Surveillances

While Jackson's *LotR* seems to associate surveillance with Sauron and innate belief with the Free Peoples—Gandalf, after all, cannot see Frodo and Sam on their journey—Aragorn uses the same tools of surveillance as Sauron. Aragorn has the ability to use the palantiri and, in the novel, the surveillance of his Rangers functions in a way similar to Sauron's Ringwraiths. But Jackson iconically differentiates between Sauron and Aragorn's power. In *RotK*, when Frodo, Sam and Gollum are on their way to Mordor, they walk by a graffitied statue of an old Númenórean king. Its head has fallen off and been replaced by a giant stone in the shape of an eye overlaid with metal teeth. The eye represents Sauron, while the metal teeth signify manufactured destruction and consumption: Sauron devours nature to enhance himself. The king's head rests nearby, lying beside a tree and crowned in flowers. This is the image of Aragorn, the temporarily usurped but natural king.

Aragorn's royal legitimacy is ordained not only by his bloodline but also by the approbation of his subjects. Each culture accepts him as its sovereign, and Aragorn allows each to have autonomous rule. Aragorn demonstrates both his acceptance of diversity and his connection to nature when he uses his knowledge of herbs to heal Éowyn after the battle of Pelennor Fields—as well as Faramir and Merry in the novel. (Tolkien, 1994: 847, 850) The healing of individual subjects by the sovereign demonstrates Aragorn's regard for life, a sentiment wholly foreign to the Orcs, who decapitate one of their own over a disagreement and then proclaim, "Looks like meat's back on the menu, boys!" (*TT*) Jackson also emphasizes the difference between Sauron and Aragorn by diminishing Aragorn's confidence in his royal role. When originally offered the sword of kings, Aragorn says, "I do not want that power. I have never wanted it." (*FotR*) This reluctance is a departure from Tolkien's Aragorn, who always carries the shards of Narsil and never doubts his destiny. This change is made specifically to diminish Aragorn's superiority over the other characters and reflects the notion that power should be in the hands of those who least desire it.

A central theme of *LotR* is the rejection of power. Frodo's quest is to destroy the Ring, a symbol of ultimate power. Yet when he is standing above the lava within Mount Doom, he is unable to do so. Instead he turns to Sam, says, "The Ring is mine," and puts it on. (*RotK*) This action could have destroyed Middle-earth if it had not been for Gollum. As Sam stands by helplessly, Gollum creeps up and wrests the Ring from Frodo, falling with the Ring into the lava below.

This destruction of the Ring is only possible through the existence of a "loophole" in the panoptic structure. In her discussion of panopticism in Harriet Jacobs' *Incidents in the Life of a Slave Girl*, Michelle Burnham examines the existence of these overlooked sites of agency. As Burnham points out, according to the Oxford English Dictionary, a loophole is both "[a] narrow vertical opening[...] cut in a wall or other defence, to allow of the passage of missiles" and "[a]n outlet or means of escape." (Burnham, 2001: 282) In the physical sense, the major loophole in *LotR* is the tunnel that comprises Shelob's lair. When Frodo and Sam make it to Mordor, they come to a giant black gate guarding the entrance. Unaware of any other way in, they are about to walk through Mordor's main gate when Gollum stops them. He leads them to a tunnel through the mountains, which is also the lair of Shelob, a giant spider. This space is unobserved by Sauron because it is unknown by outsiders, and Shelob kills all who enter. Gollum also knows about Shelob and is luring Frodo to her in order to take the Ring from Frodo's corpse. This passage in the mountain creates what Burnham refers to as an "inevitable blind spot" in panopticism. (Burnham, 2001: 289) This blind spot exists "in sites that elude the gaze not because they are outside the structure[...] but because they are clearly and centrally a part of it." (Burnham, 2001: 289) Sauron is not watching the tunnel through his mountains because he does not believe anyone could pass through it. Of course, Frodo would be unable to survive Shelob without Galadriel's phial, whose light repels the dark-dwelling Shelob and becomes a method for attaining agency. Thus, to borrow Burnham's language, the loophole is created "by relocating agency [here symbolized by the phial] in the juncture between the structure [the tunnel] and the subject [Frodo]." (Burnham, 2001: 289) Frodo's access to the tunnel and repulsion of Shelob create a combination of circumstances that Sauron is unable to predict. The existence of this loophole allows Frodo and Sam to enter Mordor with the Ring, and the passage through the tunnel becomes the "outlet" of freedom for Middle-earth. Shelob's lair also has the physical properties of an actual loophole, "a narrow[...] opening[...] cut in a wall or other defence, to allow of the passage of missiles," (Burnham, 2001: 282) as the Ring passes through this loophole to become the weapon that destroys Sauron.

Sauron's destruction is enabled by his lack of foresight in other ways as well. When Aragorn confronts Sauron through the Gondorian palantír, Sauron assumes Aragorn has the Ring because, as the heir to Gondor, he would be capable of wielding it, and it would be suicidal to attack Mordor without it. This assumption backfires on Sauron, as Aragorn's challenge is only a diversion to assist Frodo and Sam by emptying Mordor of its armies. Sauron's single-mindedness is invoked by Gandalf when he says, "that we should seek to destroy [the Ring] has not yet entered [his] darkest dreams." (*TT*) In his myopia, Sauron is unable to understand that anyone could resist the Ring, much less give up their lives to destroy it. As Brian Rosebury puts it, this "inability of complete evil to understand self-renunciatory motives is consciously exploited by Sauron's antagonists in their decision to attempt the destruction of the Ring." (Rosebury, 2003: 37) Sauron's inability to understand the thoughts of others enables his destruction and proves that he is not an omnipotent, "all-seeing" Panopticon. The knowledge that creates the Panopticon's power—the knowledge of an everlasting, anonymous gaze—reinforces the control of the Panopticon. The gaze of the tower cannot be influenced because the guards are numerous and ever changing. Sauron's gaze, on the other hand, is individualized, and because he has a specific and well-known agenda, he can be easily manipulated.

Despite the many flaws inherent in Sauron's all-consuming evil, the most obvious and pervasive loophole is perhaps the least easy to recognize. This is the idea of combating despair with hope. In order for the quest to exist, there must be the belief, however small, in success against this supposedly omnipotent being. This resistance to the produced truth, manifested in differing degrees by all the good characters, also constitutes a loophole. Sauron's failure to recognize the determination of individuals supports the idea that the Panopticon "allows thought to remain hidden, even under the most intense scrutiny." (Burnham, 2001: 286) The inability to control thought leads to a deficiency in the dominant truth, which becomes the flaw that destroys the entire apparatus of authoritative power. As Burnham explains in the historical context of African-American slavery, "those seemingly monolithic methods of surveillance that ostensibly make escape from detection impossible may finally enable escape by the very fact that they make it seem so impossible." (Burnham, 2001: 288) In *LotR*, Sauron's downfall is enacted by his own seeming omnipotence, and the once powerful "all-seeing eye" falls to a Hobbit-sized flaw.

Bibliography

Burnham, Michelle (2001), "Loopholes of Resistance: Harriet Jacobs' Slave Narrative and the Critique of Agency in Foucault" in McKay, Nellie Y. and Frances Smith Foster (eds), *Incidents in the Life of a Slave Girl*, Norton, New York

Curry, Patrick (2004), *Defending Middle-Earth: Tolkien: Myth and Modernity*, Houghton Mifflin, New York

Foucault, Michael (1995), *Discipline and Punishment: The Birth of the Prison*, Vintage, New York

Foucault, Michael (1980), *Power/Knowledge: Selected Interviews and Other Writings 1972— 1977*, ed. Colin Gordon, Pantheon, New York

Kocher, Paul Harold (1972), *Master of Middle-earth: The Fiction of J.R.R. Tolkien*, Houghton Mifflin, Boston

McHoul, Alec and Wendy Grace (1993), *A Foucault Primer: Discourse, Power and the Subject*, New York University Press, New York

Rosebury, Brian (2003), *Tolkien: A Cultural Phenomenon*, Palgrave, London

Tolkien, J.R.R. (1994), *The Lord of the Rings*, Houghton Mifflin, Boston

Section V

Tale after Tale

19

EXTENDING THE TALE
An Analysis of *The Lord of the Rings* Extended Editions

Paola Voci

THE LORD OF THE RINGS extended editions released between 2002 and 2004 exhibit some peculiar traits which set them apart from other special editions. Special editions' main goal is to revive interest in films that have already circulated in movie theatres and, of course, make more money. Special editions generally claim to offer a different, longer or supposedly better version of a relatively old film (e.g., the re-mastered and re-worked versions of *Star Wars*, dir. George Lucas, 1997 and 2004).[1] Unlike most special editions, the LotR extended editions were planned and advertised at a very early stage of production and generated an interest that went beyond the making, marketing and reception of the films. This chapter argues that the extended editions played an important role in the development of two auxiliary tales. If *The Silmarillion* gave Middle-earth a history and a mythology beyond the story developed in Tolkien's LotR, the extended editions helped provide the film trilogy with a history—the tale of its making—and a mythology—the tale of New Zealand as Middle-earth.

Although most of the advertising for these expensive sets of DVDs focused on the extra minutes of film footage, the extended editions did not significantly extend

---

[1] The original *Star Wars* trilogy was screened between 1977 and 1983. The 1997 re-mastered versions were also re-released in theatres; in 2004 new high-definition special editions also included some changes intended to make the earlier trilogy better match the three episodes of the prequel (1999–2005).

the film narrative.² However, since the first extended edition was announced, an auxiliary tale about the very making of the film began to unfold, mostly on the Internet. During many interviews with both printed and online magazines, the director was often asked why certain scenes had been excluded from the original films. Fans' websites were full of speculation about what would be included in the next DVD extended edition.

The extended editions also contributed to the creation of another supplementary tale, which has the theatre's silver screen version as a reference, but mostly focuses on the making of Middle-earth. Each set of DVDs includes two additional disks containing several hours of documentaries and image galleries. This second tale helped create a new tourist Mecca (New Zealand as Middle-earth) and contributed to making remote New Zealand more familiar (though no less exotic) to the rest of the world.

The Setting: the DVD Extended Editions

Many film-lovers maintain that a film must be experienced in a movie-theatre and that home video "formatted-to-fit-your-screen" versions (whether VHS or DVD format) are poor substitutes for the cinematic experience. The argument is that viewing a film as a DVD implies a more distracting environment, the possibility of interruptions, and a different awareness of the filmic illusion. If so much is lost, what is there to gain from viewing a film on DVD? The emphasis on agency is certainly one of the key issues. A DVD allows the viewer more control over the medium. The ability to watch, stop, select, and re-watch a particular scene or frame adds yet another layer to the voyeuristic pleasure described by Laura Mulvey.³ (Mulvey, 1975)

---

[2] Thirty-two minutes of extra footage were added for the *FotR*, forty-two for *TT* and fifty for *RotK*.

[3] Mulvey's famous essay on the scopophilic pleasures of film-viewing has generated abundant discussion. While the main criticism concerns the definition of such pleasure as being mainly "masculine", Mulvey's main contribution has been in opening up the debate on "pleasure" as a main issue in the dynamics created by the interaction of a film medium and its audience.

In the past few years, DVD marketing has grown immensely. Despite initial fears that the development of this new technique could kill the film industry and its distribution system, the alliance between film and DVD has been mutually beneficial. Although home entertainment systems are increasing in popularity, theatres remain an unsurpassed location for film viewing. Over the years, rather than offering an alternative to movie-going, DVDs have increasingly marketed themselves as a complement to cinema by emphasizing their additional features. A DVD does not claim to offer the viewer an experience comparable to the silver screen, but suggests that it can provide something completely different. Some films have been re-marketed in their "director's cut" version; old films were restored to their original (or better than original) splendour; cult movies have been repackaged with additional commentaries and interviews; blockbuster films with a heavy reliance on special effects were expanded with scenes which for one reason or another had not made the final cut.

LotR seems to perfectly fit this last category. The DVD sets of the trilogy consist of additional footage, interviews, commentaries, and documentaries about the making of the film.[4] However *LotR* extended editions go one step further and set the stage for the development of much more than a corollary to the film.

Two Auxiliary Tales

What is included in the extended editions? Each set includes a longer version of the film (on two disks) plus appendices (disks three and four).[5] The first auxiliary tale originates from the longer versions of the film and expands—through Web-based ramifications—to discussions on what else is still missing. It is an open-ended tale

---

[4] Besides the material directly linked to the trilogy, a section in the extended edition of *RotK* is dedicated to a young filmmaker, Cameron Duncan, who died of cancer. His two short films (the 5-minute *DFK6498* and the 11-minute *Strike Zone*), are also included as a tribute to his memory. *Strike Zone* was directly inspired the lyrics of Annie Lennox's song "Into the West".

[5] A description with comments on the content of each DVD extended edition was posted on filmfreakcentral.net (all links were still active when retrieved on 15 January 2006). For *FotR*, see the second part of the review posted at http://filmfreakcentral.net/dvdreviews/attackrings.htm; for *TT* see http://filmfreakcentral.net/dvdreviews/twotowersee.htm; for *RotK* see http://filmfreakcentral.net/dvdreviews/returnofthekingee.htm.

about the making of a film in relation to Tolkien's original book, Jackson's own interpretation, and the expectations of the readership. As such, it is a self-reflective meta-text about both a film narrative and its reading and is therefore a project that can only be initiated but never completed. By pointing to the infinite possibilities erased by one single editing choice, the first auxiliary tale restores the film to its unfinished cut stage.

The second auxiliary tale is narrated by the various documentaries and, in particular, by the section entitled "New Zealand as Middle-earth". It is also a self-reflective meta-text which deals mostly with the definition of a mythological location for the first auxiliary tale. While the two disks of appendices can be considered a departing point, most of this tale is told elsewhere, predominantly but not exclusively on the Internet. It seeks to define a space where producers and consumers, stars and fans, fiction and reality can meet and interact. It was the tale that the tourist industry was quick to appreciate for advertising New Zealand as the ultimate exotic adventure.

In the following sections I shall analyze how both tales have developed and created a multimedia text which is both inter-reliant with and autonomous from its archetypal source. I argue that one key for the understanding of these tales is the link between the DVDs and the Internet. Nowadays, almost all films are critiqued by a variety of online magazines or privately-run sites and blogs. However, in the case of *LotR*, Web-based discussion extended to issues of pre-production, editing, and marketing.[6]

The *LotR's* Unfinished Cut: How Long Is Long Enough?

The first auxiliary tale finds its departing point in the audience-perceived deficiency of the original film. *LotR* was, from the start, defined by a sense of absence and a continuous feeling of anticipation. The first instalment of the trilogy was necessarily incomplete. At the same time, the lack of an ending was balanced by the promise of something-yet-to-come. Viewers knew that in the following months the tale was

---

[6] It is not unprecedented for fans to try to influence production choices by advocating the casting of a certain actor or the development of a sequel. However, the acknowledged exchange between the makers of *LotR* and their fans was unprecedented.

not simply going to be suspended until the release of the next film, but would continue and expand, moving from the silver screen to smaller screens.

Once the first extended edition for *The Fellowship of the Ring* was released, people were advised that there was more to expect and that not all had yet been decided. The extended version of *FotR* was released to fill the gap and keep interest in *LotR* alive. Furthermore, viewers were alerted that in the next chapter of the saga, there would be missing segments saved for the following extended edition. Fans were also aware that the final cut had not been completed and Jackson was still shooting some scenes. As a result, the debate about editing choices intensified and many Tolkien and *LotR* devotees started to advise Peter Jackson on what he could or should do through a variety of media (the Internet in particular).

The same process occurred with the two sequels, activating a cyclic mechanism of interruptions and expansions that lasted for over three years. In fact it continued long after the last extended edition for *The Return of the King* came out.[7] *LotR* extended editions did not help the film to achieve closure; rather the additional scenes, shots, and frames showed that so much more could/should have been included.

Moreover, from the author's point of view the extended editions did not reinstate a lost wholeness. The longer films are not director's cuts, but simply versions that best fit the DVD medium. Unlike what is typically implied by the idea of a "director's cut", Jackson's extended editions were not in opposition to the commercial release and did not restore the original creative project of its author.[8] They were in fact planned simultaneously with the theatre-released version by the

---

[7] Many blogs on fan websites were still actively discussing issues of loyalty to the original books, problems with casting and editing choices, even after the extended edition of *RotK* was released. The release of *King Kong* (2005, Jackson's first film in the post-*LotR* phase of his career) seems to have only partly diverted fans' attention from the *LotR*. On Theonering.net, for instance, the movie discussion section still has many active threads.

[8] For instance, Ridley Scott's *Blade Runner* (1982) was commercially released with added voice-over and a happy-ending explicit denouement. When several years later the director's cut became available (1992), only one, arguably minor, scene was added, but most importantly the explanatory voice-over and the last sequence were gone, making the film's overall message less optimistic, more cryptic and open to multiple interpretations.

director himself and did not reflect the frequent conflicts between commercial imperatives and the author's creative freedom.

Peter Jackson himself discarded the idea of a director's cut and argued that the main raison d'être for the extended editions was to allow the public to view the saga in more detail. He repeatedly defended himself from the accusation of recycling footage that had not made the final cut. The additional scenes were not added as a bonus (as often happens in other DVDs), but were inserted within the film and were supposed to create a "different movie". Jackson attended a large number of interviews with both official and unofficial media, and *LotR* fan sites, in an attempt to promote the theatrical and the DVD extended edition versions as complementary.[9] Paradoxically, the additional scenes were supposed to be at once essential (to justify the claim of a "new" film in the extended edition) and yet superfluous in the original (to preserve the theatrical release version's legitimacy).

> For the fans who want to see more detail and are not so concerned with the momentum.... We're basically putting scenes back in which we know on some level are destroying the momentum of the story, making it slow right down, which is why we took them out in the first place. But DVD seems to be a medium that allows you to do a certain amount of that. You have it in your living room, you can pause it, you can make a cup of tea, you can watch it over two nights. It's a much more forgiving environment to watch film in. (cited in Anon, 2003/2007)

According to Jackson's above description, the additional footage actually slows the momentum and can be endured only because of the different space in which DVDs are generally watched: a home environment that allows a more detached and self-aware viewing. Jackson's explanation echoes McLuhan's basic distinction between hot and cold media. (McLuhan, 1994) If the theatrical release was supposed to

---

[9] In his official site, Jackson explains: "The extended version should be a good alternative to the theatrical cut." (http://www.lordoftherings.net/film/exclusives/editorial/peterjackson_fellowship.html). Some fans and film critics disagree with Jackson and view the film and the DVD extended editions as competing products. For instance, writing for Under Ground Online, Ian W. Hill argues that "Unfortunately, *Two Towers* and *Return of the King* were more damaged in their theatrical cuts, becoming merely trailers for their better DVD editions." (Hill, 2007)

mostly absorb audiences and require a low level of participation, the DVD was a "cool medium" that engaged its viewers in a higher degree of interactivity.[10]

If the extended editions did not offer a true director's cut of the trilogy, it would be too simplistic to dismiss the project solely as a commercial enterprise to help Jackson and his production team make more money to cover the films' high costs. Although the increased revenue is by no means a marginal factor in the making of the additional expensive DVD sets, Jackson's own desire to make his gigantic endeavour more visible and memorable certainly played an important role. Jackson believed that his achievement was unprecedented and would make film history. Many other films have reached or exceeded a three-hour length. Many other films have achieved or surpassed the level of special effects of *LotR*. Many other films have become cult-movies and generated a variety of fandom responses. However, not only Jackson's trilogy was the first to be filmed simultaneously, but it expanded into its own mythology even before release.[11] Jackson not only set out to make a film, but also to create a myth about its making. The extended DVD editions were part of this larger project from the very beginning. Thus, although the film text is an important factor in the *LotR* media event, it is not the only one.

Who and How?

Scrutinizing the director and the production's intentions can overshadow the importance of the audience in the construction of *LotR* as a virtual world with a real geographical referent. In fact, the level of discussion generated by the exclusion of scenes that were later included in the DVD is clear evidence of a complex, multimedia and multiplayer interaction. Rather than focusing on effects of the

---

[10] McLuhan's problematic definition of cool (low definition and high participation) and hot (high definition and low participation) media has been the focus of on-going criticism. One of the unanswered and much debated questions in McLuhan's theory concerns the role of new media such as the Internet and DV technology that arguably imply both high-definition and high participation.

[11] When *The Matrix* (dir. Larry and Andy Wachowski, 1999) was released, it quickly became a cult-movie. While the sequels (2003) might have been imagined or even planned at the time of the first film's release, it was only at a much later stage, that they were actually produced, capitalizing on the first movie's success, together with its commercially lucrative parallel worlds (e.g., videogames, animatrix, and all sorts of other gadgets).

additional scenes on the *LotR* original film text, the real question shifts to *who* participated in the debate surrounding these additional scenes and *how* this participation took place. While the extended editions re-opened and expanded the tale by exposing its many holes and loose ends, the first auxiliary tale was mostly developed by fans on the Internet.

It is important at this point to distinguish between the general audience and fandom. In terms of *uses and gratifications* (Katz, 1974) and regarding being able to actively decode a media message, (Fiske, 1989) both movie-goers and DVD-viewers participate in the complementary dynamics of media-production and audience reception, and contribute to creating additional meanings for the original media text as well as more broadly, its cultural and social context. Active audience theories have abundantly demonstrated the necessity of viewing them as meaning-makers and not passive receivers.

Fandom constitutes a special sub-category. Not only are fans considered a part of an interpretive community, but they are also very self-aware about belonging to such a community.[12] Fans know that their pleasure is shared by many others in the same intense and possibly even obsessive way.[13] Media scholars have also noted how fans' passionate consumption of the film medium translates into a variety of behaviours that complicate their relationship with mainstream culture. While in the past they were seen as pathologically brain-washed, researchers have focused on their creative behaviours including their subversive and rebellious component.[14] (Bacon-Smith, 1991) Although each fan group should be viewed in the specificity of its context, work in this area has led to a general understanding of fan activity as multi-layered, imaginative, and conducive to the creation of alternative social

---

[12] General audiences are also interpretive communities, but they are seen as a collective either as a matter of market strategy or as contextualized groups in ethnographic analysis. However, they do not share fan communities' self-awareness of belonging to a specific community.

[13] Ross and Nightingale explore the concept of fan audiences from both semantic and ethnographic perspectives, showing how fans actively reinterpret texts through a variety of public and private practices and at the same time engage with other fans. (Ross and Nightingale, 2003)

[14] For more on the question of fan behaviour in relation to interpretive communities and popular culture, see also Jenkins (1992) and Jenkins (2002).

communities. (Jenkins, 1992) Researchers all agree that fans' engagement in cultural production is much more intense and visible than that found in general audiences.

> While all of us, simply by virtue of being members of audiences, work with the texts we read, watch, listen to, in order to produce meaning and pleasure, fans often take this engagement a step further[....] In becoming a consumer/producer, then the fan ceases to be a passive disciple but rather becomes a proactive collaborator. (Ross and Nightingale, 2003: 136-137)[15]

It is therefore the specific concept of fan audiences that can help us better understand the type of interactive discourse generated by the relationship between the extended editions and their Web-based extensions. Fans took a very active role in the development of an auxiliary tale in which the Hobbits meet Tom Bombadil, or Saruman dies in attempt to conquer the Shire.[16] This open-ended tale in which all is still possible is therefore both the result of the extended editions' remaking of the film and the creation of fans' cultural activism.

The Making of Middle-earth

The second auxiliary tale concerns the creation of Middle-earth. In many ways it overlaps with the first, but it deviates more radically from the original film and develops into many overlapping projects. In each set, disks three and four (for a total of six parts) are supposed to create a parallel trilogy. The first DVD set starts with "from book to vision" and "from vision to reality"; the second carries on with "the journey continues" and "the battle for Middle-earth begins"; the last one ends with "the war of the Ring" and "the passing of an age". The progression from part

---

[15] The literature on this topic is too large to summarize. The different behaviours developed by fan communities range from the quasi-religious position vis-à-vis their object of desire as in the case of Bruce Springsteen fans, (Cavicchi, 1998) to fan art production as in the case of women writers of *Star Trek*-inspired fanfic. (Bacon-Smith, 1991)

[16] The number of websites and blogs which deal with suggestions and comments on what should be, or should have been, included in the movies is simply too large for any meaningful selection. On TheOneRing.com, for instance one can find "The Complete List of Film Changes" which documents the many differences between the original book and the film, despite the fact that only *FotR* section has been completed. (http://www.theonering.com/landing_pages/25,3.html last accessed 13 February 2007) One of the most elaborate extensions of the tale I found was "The Optimal LotR Prequel Movie" (Fauskanger, 2007).

one to part six is not linear as it was artificially crafted to regroup a large amount of material that did not necessarily have a common topic. However, some main thematic developments are followed throughout the three sets and the appendices do achieve a remarkable unity, although their overall structure resembles the fragmented and hyperlinked organization of a website.

In *FotR*, the first introduction is made by Jackson and the second by Elijah Wood (Frodo). The content of the DVDs is broadly introduced as extra "good" stuff; the tone is friendly but relatively neutral. In *The Two Towers*, the level of familiarity is increased as Jackson implicitly addresses fans by noting that after shooting under high security he is finally able to reveal production secrets. The final introductions for *RotK* are those most clearly directed to fans. It is assumed that if you are watching the last instalment of the extended editions, you have seen all the others and you are more likely to be a fan than an occasional viewer. As was the case in the first two sets, Jackson presents the first disk, but in the second disk Elijah Wood is joined by Billy Boyd and Dominic Monaghan (who play respectively the Hobbits Pippin and Merry). They address the viewers individually but editing renders each little monologue fragmented and alternated. The tone now resembles an old friends' farewell, both witty and nostalgic. For instance, Jackson says, "I'm sure we will probably see each other again. You know, next time you'll see me in this chair, I'll be a grey-haired old man for the twenty-fifth anniversary edition…" On the same lines, Wood concludes: "Hopefully we will see each other again in some fashion. Just remember: the fellowship carries on," while Billy Boyd jokes "And do get out of the house… occasionally."

The appendices are designed to expand the tale even further by bringing the book and its adaptation to screen, using "behind-the-scenes" sections to illustrate why and how certain cinematic choices were made, and showcasing New Zealand as the perfect setting for Middle-earth.

According to the introductory booklet in *RotK* extended edition DVD package, *RotK* contains several hours of commentaries and interviews with director Peter Jackson, the co-writers, the cast, and the production and design teams about everything from adapting the book into a screenplay to *magically* turning New Zealand into Middle-earth.

Each of these threads is also part of an on-going dialogue between the filmmaker and his audience and, in particular, his fans: "this is certain to excite newcomers to *The Return of the King* as well as satisfy devoted fans of the film trilogy." (introductory booklet in *RotK*)

The appendices were produced in "close collaboration with the filmmakers and artists", (introductory booklet in *TT*) but they also have a life of their own, especially when it comes to their link with New Zealand and the promotion of "Kiwiness" as the real-world equivalent of the heroic quality of Middle-earth's characters. New Zealand becomes the land where imagination and courage can still be found, and is presented as an ideal balance between natural environment and high technology. It is a place where one can find the best real world and the most sophisticated computer-generated reality. In summary, the documentaries in the appendices constitute a rather self-conscious project to promote New Zealand, not only as an ideal location to shoot epic films ("Aotearoawood"), but more broadly as an ideal business partner and a supreme tourist destination.

The appendices are evidence of Peter Jackson's self-appointed role of ambassador for New Zealand's beauty and talent. They are clearly designed to commemorate the accomplishments of a Kiwi director who worked with a Kiwi team in his homeland. The non-Kiwis are equally celebrated, but they are so deeply interconnected with the physical reality of New Zealand that, even though they might speak with a different accent, they easily blend into the making of Middle-earth as a Kiwi experience.

The point, however, is not whether or not Jackson consciously set out to market New Zealand as Middle-earth, which is a fact not only stated in all the documentaries included in the appendices, but also openly acknowledged by all those involved in the film production. From the start it was clear that the making of New Zealand as Middle-earth was not just a by-product of the film but an essential part of Jackson's endeavour. The most interesting issue then becomes *how* and with *whose* help this was achieved.

For instance, actors contribute to the identification between Middle-earth and New Zealand on two different levels. In a more direct way, during the interviews, they repeatedly mention their own astonishment at New Zealand's amazing landscapes and their love and admiration for its people's warmth and ingenuity. The message is reinforced by the fact that they are often interviewed in a semi-fictional environment. Fragments of different interviews are often combined so that actors appear as the characters they interpret (in make-up and costume) and as themselves.

Many strategies are employed to bind the documentaries to the fantasy world. The most basic feature common to all documentaries is the use of parallel editing to frame the real into the fictional. Shots of Jackson describing what will happen in a location, or pointing to where the characters will interact, are invariably intercut with the scenes just evoked by the director. Other frequent techniques involve the use of soundtrack, the shifting of characters from the fantasy to the real world, and the superimposition of images from both the book and the movie onto the New Zealand landscape.

While many other direct and indirect references to New Zealand are made throughout all the documentaries, New Zealand becomes the declared focus in "New Zealand as Middle-earth". In each of the three extended edition DVD packages, this section (on disk three) includes seven short documentaries (approx. three minutes each).

The identification between the two worlds is made visually obvious from the start as the DVD menu displays a map of New Zealand which easily resembles the Middle-earth maps in both the books and the films (same colours, drawing style and fonts). Each documentary focuses on a specific *LotR* location and, after selecting the title, the map zooms onto the corresponding New Zealand location. In the documentaries, Jackson himself, as well as other producers and actors, enthusiastically explains why New Zealand was the perfect place to shoot Tolkien's saga.

The use of music scores from the movies is one of the most recurrent and self-conscious attempts to invest New Zealand with the magic of the fantasy world. For instance, in one of the documentaries included in the extended edition of *FotR*, a long shot of a seated Peter Jackson gazing at the location for Hobbiton is allied with the familiar sound track that in the film introduces the Shire and its inhabitants. ("Hobbiton" in The Appendices, Part 1, *FotR*)

While discussing the building of the locations for the films (either as CGI or as small-scale models), producers and art-directors redundantly reiterate that whenever possible they have chosen to rely on New Zealand's natural beauty rather than re-create Middle-earth as a virtual or staged setting. In one of the documentaries, Andrew Lesnie (director of photography), Dan Hennah (supervising art director), Rick Porras (co-producer) and Peter Jackson all comment on the area chosen for the setting of Emyn Muil, i.e., Mt. Ruapehu (north of Wellington, the main volcano in the North Island) with passionate adjectives: "amazing volcano formations", "it feels like a very forbidden place", "fantastic landscape", "it kind of feels like you are on another planet", "it's incredibly stark and powerful environment", "we just felt this is pretty atmospheric, it's fantastic". ("Emyn Muil" in The Appendices, Part 3, *TT*)

New Zealand remains the perfect location even when it admittedly lacks some of the features of Middle-earth. For instance, when Jackson introduces the location for Rohan (Poolburn, Alexandra, South Island), he begins by saying: "In the book, the plains of Rohan are described as prairie land. We actually don't have that in New Zealand. There is nothing in New Zealand that matches that. The best we could find for Rohan is a slightly more dramatic landscape." However, as the short documentary progresses, Poolburn is shown and commented upon as in fact an ideal place to capture Rohan's open horizons. Poolburn is described as a beautiful setting, with a "unique look", an "epic-John Ford landscape", in fact a location that captures and magnifies the very soul of Rohan culture. ("Rohan" in The Appendices, Part 3, *TT*)

The identification between Middle-earth and New Zealand was not simply constructed through the appendices. Just like the first auxiliary tale, the construction of Middle-earth was developed well beyond the extended editions. The fans, once again, played an important role. In their websites, while they celebrated Middle-earth as the object of their attachment, fans still mostly reproduced it as a fantasy that engaged them in their activism as both consumers and producers of culture. However, as the extension of this fantasy, they also began their journey to the *real* New Zealand.

Overall, fans on the TheOneRing.net and their alter-ego (often sarcastic and desecrating) Tbhl.theonering.net (The Bastards Have Landed, Home of Peter Jackson's official fanclub) all endorsed the idea of New Zealand as Middle-earth.[17] Among the most extensive elaborations on this topic, is an e-book written by Tehanu (a Kiwi member of TheOneRing.net): *The Search for Middle Earth*. In this "insider" exploration of New Zealand, the author follows Jackson's tracks while he is still shooting the film and tries to capture the latest news on the crew while offering to the other fans descriptions and pictures of New Zealand.[18] Here is an excerpt from her book:

> More boulders choked the space where the stair would have been, and a whole pinetree lay across it like a carelessly-dropped straw. [picture link of the Kawarau set Upriver] "...the country.... sloped away up away from the river, a tumbled waste of grey limestone-boulders, with many hidden holes shrouded with weeks and bushes...."—that's Tolkien's description of the country around where the Fellowship portages their boats around Sarn Gebir. This is it exactly! (except for the limestone. There's always a purist out there ready to be upset.) (Tehanu, 2000)

By connecting the landscape to the LotR tale through a combination of autobiographical narratives and fictional references, *The Search for Middle Earth* helps to advertise New Zealand as a fantasy-land and prefigures the project later developed by the extended edition's documentary features.

The tale of Middle-earth was extended not only by *LotR* fans, but more extensively by pragmatic supporters with specific invested interests. They can be considered the executive fans of Middle-earth. From the adoption of *LotR* icons on Air New Zealand aeroplanes, to the climatic celebration of the premier of *RotK* in Wellington (a.k.a., The Return of King Peter to New Zealand) it was no secret that there was official endorsement of Jackson's trilogy as a national project. When *RotK* was awarded eleven Oscars, the BBC reported Prime Minister Helen Clark's comments:

---

[17] I base my analysis mostly on the archives of discussions included in both Theonering.net (which, it should be noted, is not associated with Theonering.com) and Tbhl.theonering.net.

[18] Similar autobiographical accounts of New Zealand written by non-Kiwi fans can also be found on TheOneRing.net and on all sorts of privately-run websites.

"It's just blowing everybody away." She said the result was an "unbelievable" advertisement for New Zealand. "It's an incredibly proud day to be a New Zealander, to see Lord of the Rings sweep the field... it was simply amazing," she said. (Anon, 2004/2007)

The New Zealand film industry also embraced Jackson's success. On their website's main page there is a link to "New Zealand Home of Middle Earth" (http://www.filmnz.com/middleearth/index.html) which extensively displays shooting locations with a large amount of images, video and audio clips.[19] Last but not least, this endeavour in making New Zealand a real Middle-earth was fully embraced by the tourist industry. For instance, New Zealand Tourism Online maintains a page dedicated to *LotR* and proudly states:

> New Zealand is known as Middle Earth for its Lord of the Rings trilogy. New Zealand born Peter Jackson filmed the entire three films in various locations around NZ. This Academy Award winning trilogy of films (4 Oscars for *The Fellowship of the Ring*, 2 Oscars for *The Two Towers* and 11 Oscars for *The Return of the King*—including Best Film and Best Director awards) showcased the skills of the cast and crew. One of the big winners however is New Zealand. It took two years to film the LOTR trilogy but millions of years to build the sets. (Anon, 2007)

Although three years have elapsed since the release of the final chapter in the saga, many tourist companies still capitalize on the connection between Middle-earth and New Zealand. Some offer "the ultimate Lord of the Rings day tour"; (http://www.lordoftheringstours.co.nz/) others provide a more in depth experience of Middle-earth in "your ACTIVE NEW ZEALAND trip" (sic). (http://www.activenewzealand.com/lord_of_the_rings.php) The fellowship carries on.

Conclusion

The extended editions are less an extension of the films and more part of a multi-media space surrounding the films. They need to be framed in the larger public discourse on *LotR* and understood from a reception analysis perspective. Active audience theories have long made clear that the added meanings that naturally result from the interaction between the media text and its audience should be taken

---

[19] Besides the many documentaries include in the appendices, in 2004 Jim Hickey also produced a sixty-minute documentary called *DNZ: The Real Middle Earth*.

into account. Furthermore, new media's interactive nature certainly favours a more decentred view of media production and reception. While the higher interactive capacity of new media should not be overestimated and its effects are still being evaluated and debated by media theorists, most agree that watching a DVD, or browsing/posting on the Internet are media uses that radically differ from theatre or TV viewing.[20]

In particular, the case of the two auxiliary tales shows that the message conveyed by the DVD extended editions necessarily refers to a much larger negotiation of meanings that involves both producers and audiences (in particular, fans). While the Internet was not the only place where these tales were developed, websites have been the most traceable and visible public spaces where these meanings were created and debated.

The issue is not to what extent fans might have influenced the making of the film. The fans might not have affected the final cut of either the theatrical release or the extended edition versions. Neither did they invent or initiate the connection between Middle-earth and New Zealand. However, by pointing out the fans' contributions, my analysis shows that the process through which these tales were created was a circular one, rather than one initiated by Peter Jackson's production and simply reacted to by the fans.[21] In such a circular process, a de-facto alliance can originate and develop among film producers, fans of the book, fans of Peter Jackson and other players (such as NZ film and tourist industry).

Thus, a very heterogeneous social/virtual community is created by the tales. It is not an abstract theorisation, but rather an occasional fellowship of partners who, while not necessarily always directly communicating, are aware of the others. Their

---

[20] Studies focused on new media and/or alternative media have reconfirmed the inadequacy of the effects/hypodermic model, and fully (although also critically) embraced reception analysis by Fiske and de Certau as essential to understanding media texts and their meanings beyond the semiotic analytical frame (Morley 1980). Janet Steiger has published an insightful revision of media reception analysis framed into its historical development. (Steiger, 2005) For an in-depth overview on the developments of reception analysis in the context of alternative media see Atton (2002) and Couldry and Curran (2003); in the context of new media see Lievrouw and Linvingstone (2002).

[21] For instance, the case of *The Search for Middle Earth* shows how the rhetoric of the construction of Middle-earth had already been addressed by fans at a very early stage, before it became one of the main features of either the launch of the films or the DVD editions.

interdependence is noticeable. The two main fan websites (TheOneRing.net and Tbhl.TheOneRing.net) established on-going dialogue via a direct link on their home page, members' cross-over and commonality of topics. The official film site of Thelordoftherings.net also communicates with fans' sites at different levels. On the main page there is a link to the conventions organized by TheOneRing.net and an update about the annual convention is the latest item still posted on the news page.[22] Thelordoftherings.net also includes a selection of fans' questions and commentaries taken directly from the fan websites (http://www.lordoftherings.net/film/filmmakers/fi_pjack_qanda.html). Because of all these recognized connections, I suggest that in the last extended edition, when Peter Jackson and Elijah Wood say "we will see each other again", they are not just addressing their audience in a rhetorical way, but are truly acknowledging the fans who have supported and debated the project since its inception.

Similarly, Peter Jackson's semi-official mission as New Zealand's ambassador to the world interrelates with those fans' experiences who have shared their Middle-earth trips via the Internet. They all have acted as testimonials for the New Zealand tourist industry and—with different degrees of self-awareness—have contributed to the promotion of New Zealand as a land of business opportunity.

Such a heterogeneous community remained together as long as the tales still mattered. Once the One Ring that bound them together was gone (i.e., after the last DVD edition was released), each group of players departed down separate paths. Peter Jackson engaged in making another tale (*King Kong*) partly followed by his devoted fans on Tbhl.TheOneRing.net. *LotR* movie fans continued to remember the films (the 2006 convention still attracted a large number of people including several cast members), but they have begun to withdraw from the public space. Some of the most active websites, like Ringbearer.org or Tolkien-movie.com, are now inactive.[23]

---

[22] In the 2006 convention, guest stars from the *LotR* films included Elijah Wood, Sean Astin, Billy Boyd, Miranda Otto, Daniel Reeve and John Noble. The 2007 convention occurred at the Burbank Airport Marriott Hotel in Burbank, California on 9-11 March and invited Billy Boyd (Pippin), David Wenham (Faramir) and Andy Serkis (Gollum) to be guests of honour. (http://www.creationent.com/cal/one_ring.htm)

[23] Other *LotR* fan sites still online are Ringquest.com and Ringzone.net (both still retrievable on 13 February 2007). The largest and most widely known website for Tolkien fans remains TheOneRing.com. Although TheOneRing.com also includes links to the

New Zealand incorporated Middle-earth as one of the defining moments of its history (rather than *the* main defining moment). Only on the Internet are the tales that brought them together still visible. At least until the last of the film websites disappear too, into the Grey Havens of cyber space.

Bibliography

Anon (2003/2007), "The Man Behind 'Rings' Says Goodbye" *CNN.com*: http://www.cnn.com/2003/SHOWBIZ/Movies/12/15/film.rings.jackson.ap/index.html

Anon (2004/2007), "Jackson Celebrates Oscar Glory" *BBC News* website: http://news.bbc.co.uk/1/hi/entertainment/film/3506871.stm

Anon (2007), "Lord of the Rings New Zealand" *New Zealand Tourism Online*: http://www.tourism.net.nz/lord-of-the-rings.html

Atton, Chris (2002), *Alternative Media*, Sage, London

Bacon-Smith, Camille (1991), *Enterprising Women: Television Fandom and the Creation of Popular Myth*, University of Pennsylvania Press, Philadelphia, Pennsylvania.

Cavicchi, Daniel (1998), *Tramps Like Us: Music and Meaning Among Springsteen Fans*, Oxford University Press, New York

Couldry, Nick and James Curran (2003), *Contesting Media Power: Alternative Media in a Networked World*, Rowman & Littlefield Publishers, Lanham, Maryland

Fauskanger, Helge Kåre (2007), "The Optimal LotR Prequel Movie": http://www.uib.no/People/hnohf/num-intro.htm

Fiske, John (1992), "The Cultural Economy of Fandom" in Lisa Lewis (ed.), *The Adoring Audience: Fan Culture and Popular Media*, Routledge, New York, pp. 30-49

Fiske, John (1989), *Understanding Popular Culture*, Unwin Hyman, Boston

Hill, Ian W. (2007), "The Lord of the Rings: *The Return of the King* Extended Edition DVD Review" Under Ground Online: http://www.ugo.com/channels/filmtv/features/lotrweek/review.asp

Hills, Matt (2002), *Fan Cultures*, Routledge, London

Jenkins, Henry (1992), *Textual Poachers: Television Fans & Participatory Culture*, Routledge, New York

---

movies' official and fan sites, the links are not obvious on the homepage, but more discreetly listed in "links" as part of the "movie" subcategory (the other two link categories are "reference" and "official sites").

Jenkins, Henry, Tara McPherson and Jane Shuttuck (eds) (2002), *Hop on Pop: The Politics and Pleasures of Popular Culture*, Duke University Press, Durham

Katz, Elihu, Jay Blumler and Michael Gurevitch (1974), *The Use of Mass Communication*, Sage, Beverly Hills, California

Lievrouw, L. and S. Livingstone (eds) (2002), *Handbook of New Media: Social Shaping and Social Consequences*, Sage, London

McLuhan, Marshall (1994), *Understanding Media: the Extension of Man*, MIT Press, Cambridge, Mass.

McQuai, Denis (1994), *Mass Communication Theory: An Introduction* 3rd ed., Sage, London

Morley, David (1980), *The Nationwide Audience: Structure and Decoding*, British Film Institute, London

Mulvey, Laura (1975), "Visual Pleasure and Narrative Cinema" *Screen* 16 (3), pp. 6-18

Ross, Karen and Virginia Nightingale (2003), *Media and Audiences: New Perspective*, Open University Press, Maidenhead, Berkshire, England

Staiger, Janet (2005), *Media Reception Studies*, New York University Press, New York

Tehanu (2000), *In Search of Middle-earth*: http://www.theonering.net/features/exclusives/thesearch/chapter03.html

The party is over and the Hobbits are gone; sheep return to their "lawful" land and are feasting under *the* Tree.
(photo by Bill J. Jerome)

20

BREAKING OF THE FELLOWSHIP
Competing Discourses of Archives and Canons in *The Lord of the Rings* Internet Fandom

Robin Anne Reid

HENRY JENKINS is probably best known to fandom and the growing community of scholars who study fan culture for his argument that fan fiction is creative poaching. He also makes a number of arguments about the relationship between fandom and the academy as interpretative communities, arguing that "[o]rganized fandom is, perhaps first and foremost, an institution of theory and criticism, a semistructured space where competing interpretations and evaluations of common texts are proposed, debated, and negotiated." (Jenkins, 1992: 86) Arguing against the stereotype of fans as mindless consumers of texts, Jenkins constructs them as actively engaged in a process traditionally assigned to reviewers and academics: interpretation. This interpretation takes place in part through fan fictions, but Jenkins' analysis of a *Twin Peaks* computer discussion group (involving no fan fiction) shows that fans produce non-fiction texts as well as fiction. (Jenkins, 1992: 109-112) Jenkins' consideration of non-fiction texts within the context of the fan interpretation opens the possibility of focusing analysis upon a range of fan-produced texts.[1] This chapter focuses on one of the structures which exist to house,

---

[1] See Brobeck (2004). Most scholarship focuses on fandom as a culture, the gender issues of fans writing fiction, especially slash fiction, the genre that has attracted the most academic attention. Brobeck's is the only article I am aware of that focuses on an archive, and she focuses more on fans' feelings and attitudes about the Henneth Annûn Story Archive (HASA), than on the writing styles or discourse issues. I am also working with HASA, which is, as far as I know, the largest archive dedicated to *LotR* fan fiction, as well as being one of the more controversial.

organize, select, value, critique and, on occasion, award fan fiction: specifically, selective archives on the Internet. I analyze text from two archives within *The Lord of the Rings* fandom which, unlike many media fandoms, has conflicting groups who define themselves as fans of J.R.R. Tolkien's novel, or as fans of Peter Jackson's film, or as fans of both.[2] The existence of competing source texts, either of which may be disdained as inferior by fans of the other, leads to conflicts between fans, performed in individual and communal settings.[3]

Archives are websites built by and maintained by fans (usually volunteers, although many who do the actual programming do so professionally) for the purpose of storing writers' work such as fiction, poems, or essays. Archives can offer a variety of other resources to fans, ranging from links to other sites and writing resources, but one of their most important functions is to provide a site where writers can post their stories and receive feedback from others. Some archives have associated discussion lists. Archives can house thousands of stories, or just a handful relating to an obscure area of a small fandom, or be any size in between. Archives can be open and multi-fandom (such as fanfiction.net) which means any writer can post their own work (although some content restrictions may apply). Other archives are selective, meaning authors must submit work for evaluation by volunteers, who can accept or reject it. Given the extent to which many fans see writing fan fiction as a hobby done for fun and for socializing with friends, the debates that occur over the concept of selective archives should not be surprising. Areas of conflict include: debates over authority within the fandom, especially to what extent volunteers should have to meet certain criteria to evaluate fan fiction; and arguments over what the canon texts are or should be.[4]

---

[2] There are other fandoms, most notably the Harry Potter fandom, where the original books and the film adaptations lead to similar divisions within fandom. How much of my observations of *LotR* fans might apply to the other book/film fandoms would have to be the subject of a separate study.

[3] This research was reviewed and determined to be exempt by the Institutional Review Board at Texas A&M University-Commerce.

[4] The term "canon text" carries a different meaning in fandom than in literary studies where the "canon" is that body of work defined as the most excellent and most worthy of study and teaching. In fandom, a canon text is the source text, the primary authority. Canon information is that information given in the source text. One of the more serious criticisms for a fan fiction writer is that her character is not "canonical". Debates over

Such debates arguably occur in all areas of fandom, both historically and contemporaneously, no matter the medium (hard copy fanzine, conference discussions, electronic listservs, or weblogs). The issues range from structural/aesthetic (plots, characterization, grammar and mechanics) to extra-textual (the nature of feedback for fanfiction writers; how authors should receive and respond to reader criticism or feedback; how readers should give feedback). Debates often occur in public communities, such as the wide variety dedicated to mocking badly-written work. The debates over canon and fan fiction in *LotR* fandom are complicated by the complex history of publication of Tolkien's Legendarium. Fans do not agree upon which of Tolkien's published works are included in the canon and should thus be considered necessary reading for fan writers. The twelve volumes of early drafts of the novels, together with commentary by Christopher Tolkien published after Tolkien's death, are considered canonical by some fans, but not by others. The edited volume of Tolkien's letters is also debated, given that Tolkien both explains and contradicts himself in letters from different years. As the material was not approved for publication by Tolkien, and because some information in early drafts and published letters may provide different stories and characters or contradictory information about the author's intentions, some fans choose to ignore that material while others draw on it, especially for "Alternate Universe" stories. In recent years, live action films by Peter Jackson have to a greater extent complicated the nature of "canonicity" in this fandom. These debates, all unresolved, thread throughout *LotR* fandom and sub-fandoms which are similar to all fandoms in being "competitive, argumentative, and factional". (Hills, 2002: 1)[5] Some of the most heated debates arise over the merits of book compared to film. Much of the factionalism exhibited by *LotR* fans mirrors similar divides in other fandoms: for example, the split between writers producing general (stories with no sexual content), het (stories with heterosexual erotic or sexual content) and slash

---

cannon interpretations show that the boundary between canon information and reader interpretation is fluid.

[5] While different fandoms share many similarities, the extent to which media (television, film, gaming) fandoms may differ from fandoms based on books (which may then be made into films) requires further consideration. Certainly Tolkien's stature as a "literary" author may add fuel to the debates about the quality of fan fiction written based on his works.

(stories with homoerotic or homosexual content, including both male/male and female/female stories). Other controversies are specific to *LotR*, relating to Tolkien's characters and plot. Fans tend to divide into communities or groups depending on their interest in specific groups of characters: Elf fans are the largest group, with Hobbit fans a clear second, and Man (Gondor, Rohan) fans a distant third.[6] Fans who write stories with erotic or sexual content can split not only along the het/slash lines, but also argue pairings and species issues; the different species in Middle-earth are often read as "races". Interspecies writers (who pair a Hobbit, usually Frodo, with a Man, usually Aragorn) are marginalized because the size differential between the fictional characters offends some other fans. Finally, a number of tragic stories defined as Alternate Universe (AU) stories often revolve around a character taking the Ring and Middle-earth falling into darkness and may be seen as problematic by fans who prefer a stronger adherence to Tolkien's concept of eucatastrophe. While, as Hills notes, argument and controversy may be the nature of fandom, so is the fans' declared love for their source text; in the case of *LotR* fandom, the extent of the controversy which flares between fans who read and write fanfiction may be seen as ironic given the themes of fellowship and diversity many admire within the novel and the film.

In *Fan Cultures*, Matt Hills argues that much academic scholarship on fan culture has been shaped by academics' disciplinary biases. (Hills, 2002) As a result, scholars tend to valorize in fandom what they recognize as most akin to their academic culture, with other aspects of fandom regarded as less useful. Since there is no way to step completely outside one's culture, I attempt to complicate Hills' argument by noting that this tendency could be a greater problem if academics were not conscious of the extent to which their disciplinary attitudes shape their perspectives. An alternate approach in scholarship is to acknowledge how our academic lenses equip us to analyze certain specific aspects of a broad and complex sub-culture and that any one academic analysis must by definition be partial. I was a fan for some years before completing my academic work although I decided in grade school to be a writer. I joined a *Star Trek* group, Outpost 13 of the Puget Sound Star Trekkers, as an undergraduate, edited its newsletter, and watched the show

---

[6] Barbara Lucas, personal communication and unpublished presentation, ICFA 2003.

and the films, debating their meanings with friends (male and female), with whom I often disagreed about gender constructions on the show. As an academic, I have earned degrees in creative writing and literature. As a teacher, I have edited newsletters and journals, and I assign television shows and films in my English classes to teach students how to analyze and debate meanings, often around issues of gender and ethnicity. Now, returning to fandom via the Internet, I participate as a fan in a *LotR* online community (book and film) while performing scholarship on the book/film adaptation and, in recent years, on fan writing.

As a creative writing and literature teacher, my academic bias is toward the text, not the culture, although as a feminist/cultural critic, I know texts are always embedded in a culture and are read within and against that culture. However, knowledge about that culture is often accessed through other texts: those not considered "literary". As a creative writing/critical theory teacher, one of my fields is the excluded/marginalized literatures that were denied canonical status in past years: multiethnic American literatures, literature by women writers, and science fiction/fantasy. Since I have been involved in the U.S. debate on "culture wars" since the 1980s, I tend to be aware of issues of canon, the existence of multiple canons, and how ideologies drive canon formation. As a fan and an academic, I have several contexts against which to read discursive practices in fandom that involve debates around "literary" terminology and discourse and assumptions about values and standards. As a result of my academic background, I am well aware of the extent to which Tolkien's novel has been ignored by the academic creators of canons: while a good deal of scholarship has been produced on the novel, it has, until recently, been done primarily by medieval scholars, not by modernists. Academic anthologies on Tolkien's work lament the extent to which the popularity of the novel precludes "real" academic work.[7] The disdain British intellectuals and academics have expressed for Tolkien's novel has been analyzed as class conflict by Tom Shippey in *The Author of the Century*. (Shippey, 2000: 316) While a number of college courses on Tolkien have existed in the United States since the 1970s, these courses, like similar

---

[7] For an example, see Neil D. Isaacs, "On the Possibilities of Writing Tolkien Criticism" in Isaacs (1968) where he makes a specific connection between fanzines and fan activity and the lack of serious academic attention to the novel.

classes on "science fiction" and "creative writing" exist in what some describe as academic ghettos: they are run by English departments who know these courses will generate student numbers, and thus, funding, but the classes are separate (special topics) rather than embedded in the canonical requirements courses. Thus, Tolkien's novel will be taught separately but not included in classes such as "Modern Literature", "World Novels", "British Literature". The failure of the academic world to embrace this controversial work has not deterred its fans from making it the centre of their community.

LotR fandom provides an interesting study in the extent to which some fans engage in interpretative, literary, and publishing (online as well as in hardcopy) activities around a text which is not yet fully accepted by the academy whose practices are also part of fan culture. As a fan and an academic, I am thus predisposed to see the extent to which LotR fan conflicts draw upon discursive practices that are familiar to me. These practices involve larger cultural conflicts around what is canonical literature, and how certain kinds of discourse and behaviors are gendered masculine (academic) and feminine (fan or amateur). The women who participate in this fandom do not hesitate to debate these questions, both with regard to Tolkien's work and with regard to their own writing.[8]

Henneth Annûn and Stories of Arda

I learned about these two separate archives in a debate over fan fiction awards that occurred in LotR fandom during July-August of 2004 on what is known as a "hate" thread.[9] The thread was posted in a community set up to allow anonymous postings about genres, authors, or individual stories that fans disliked or felt were over-rated. The discussion (which soon grew to nearly 1400 posts) gave way to debates over a recent fanfiction award which had raised far-reaching issues. In the context of the debate, a number of posts discussed the merits of two selective archives: the Henneth Annûn Story Archive (HASA) (http://www.henneth-annun.net) and

---

[8] While little concrete demographic information exists on any fandom, my experience and the consensus of fan studies scholars is that the clear majority of fan fiction writers are women, with slash writers being nearly 100% female.

[9] Thread on *The Lord of the Rings FPS* has 1399 posts on 2 July 2004. (Anon, 2004a)

Stories of Arda (SOA) (http://www.storiesofarda.com/index.asp). These two were described as competitors by some of the fans posting despite disclaimers by the moderator of SOA who was posting under the names she used in fandom on the thread. Both archives had critics and supporters, but few fans posting supported both equally.[10] Both archives require writers to submit their work for evaluation which means some authors/stories are rejected.[11] As a result, the sites must provide information on the processes by which writers/authors may submit their work for consideration, along with some sense of the criteria used in evaluating the work.

The texts I chose for my analysis are from the public information posted on each website for authors, readers, and potential members. Each site lists the sort of information found on most websites: "About Us", "Contact Information", and "Submission Guidelines", material standardized in content if not style for which the purpose is communication rather than literary effect.[12] I analyzed the text from the "About Us" section, arguably the first or one of the first pages examined by a reader who is new to the site. The "About Us" sections provide an early introduction to the style of the site.

I use M.A.K. Halliday's linguistic methodology to analyze the "About Us" sections. (Halliday, 1994) Halliday's methodology provides a systemic means of analyzing English clauses, focusing on the functional aspects. The system uses some traditional prescriptive grammar terms but relies primarily upon its own extensive terminology. The analysis provides data regarding the extent to which different discourse styles support hierarchies of fans as well as patterns of exclusion or

---

[10] I should note here that other than an early fic I posted at an open archive, the Library of Moria, I do not store any fan fiction in any archive. I have never submitted my fan fiction to selective archives or been accepted or rejected by any archive. I publish my fan fiction solely on my own LJ and post links to it in several LJ communities that are not selective.

[11] One difference between the two archives is that HASA requires that individual stories be submitted for consideration on a case by case basis, and SOA reviews work by authors and then grants them posting approval, although if the moderator believes an author is going against the site guidelines, she may intervene.

[12] As is often the case, no individual identification of authorship is given for such standardized text. An individual associated with the site, or a group of individuals will have written, reviewed, and edited it, but, unlike fiction (which may be collaboratively written with credit given to multiple authors), such workaday text is rarely claimed as the product of a single writer/author. Because of that, although this project was reviewed by my university Institutional Review Board, I did not believe it necessary to request permission to analyze such anonymous text.

inclusion. Since the style of one archive can best be described as "academic/formal/masculine" and the other as "nurturing/informal/feminine", the differences can be mapped along traditional constructions of gender difference although arguably most, if not all, of the site maintainers/moderators are female.

Linguists such as Halliday approach language descriptively rather than prescriptively, viewing language as a set of systems without evaluating any one as inherently superior. At the same time they acknowledge that those perceptions exist among users. This approach is not well known among literary scholars, who nonetheless speak often and evaluatively of "style", especially in the privileging of "literary" style based on a perception of aesthetics which is rarely perceived as requiring justification. Yet the prescriptive set of grammatical terms which attempts to force English into a Latin mould does not provide sufficient terminology to analyze discourse in any depth or consistency. Halliday, for example, presents six different categories of verbs. Halliday's method can be applied to any text, spoken or written, and provides quantitative evidence to support the use of terms such as "academic style".

In analyzing the "About Us" sections, I first examined how agency is constructed through the grammatical Subjects of the independent clauses. In English the majority of clauses are Subject/Verb/Object (SVO), with the grammatical Subject having agency or authority in the majority of clauses.[13] Second, I examined how inclusion/exclusion in the group or communities of fandom is constructed on both sites through pronoun usage. Pronouns play an important function in showing how speakers or writers perceive their relationship with their audiences in English, and yet analysis of style often overlooks pronouns.[14] Appendix

---

[13] Identification of agency can vary depending on the class of verb and structure of the clause, but I do not analyze that deeply here. I will not discuss the technical/web/programming aspects of the two sites, which would have to be included in a full semiotic analysis, other than to say that both would probably be considered good sites by programming and Web reading evaluative criteria.

[14] Although pronouns often serve the same grammatical function as nouns, pronouns differ from nouns in two respects. The first is that pronouns are a closed set. New nouns are coined regularly as needed, but it is rare for the pronouns to be increased or diminished, as has been shown by the difficult task of coining a gender-neutral pronoun in recent years. The other feature that distinguishes pronouns from nouns is that pronouns are rarely if ever preceded by determiners. There are two examples of the extent to which

A and Appendix B contain the full text I have analyzed, with each clause numbered, and explanatory notes identifying the Subject/Theme of each clause and the references of each Pronoun. My analysis is tabulated below, preceded by a discussion.

Subject/Theme Analysis

The grammatical Subject of a clause in English is usually the noun or word group at the beginning of the clause; however, at times, the word group at the beginning of a clause—the "Theme" in Halliday's terminology—can be a phrase that is not the subject. My Subject/Theme analysis identifies the Subjects and Themes of the clauses in the HASA "About Us", and considers how agency is constructed. The Subject may also be the Actor (that element which has agency) in the clause. A review of the Subjects in the HASA text reveals that a good deal of agency in HASA's text is given to non-human Subjects. The site itself and the Yahoo discussion list, along with other fan fiction sites, are given the most agency in terms of occupying the largest number of Subject positions. Humans program and run the sites; humans participate in the discussion list. But the Subjects of nine clauses are "HASA", or "the site", or "the list", or "other sites"; thus, 50% of the total Subjects are non-human. Humans as Subjects appear in five clauses, or 28% of the time, all as referents of the first person plural pronoun "we", which can refer to either HASA administrators or Discussion list members. Neither personal names nor informal/singular pronouns ("I" or "you") appear in this text. The agency on this site is overwhelmingly constructed as belonging to the site, its administrators, and the list; "members" occurs only once as a subject, considerably modified, as does another non-human subject, "membership". Finally, the fan fiction which is the main reason for the site's existence appears only once as a Subject. If the academic style tends to privilege a formal, objective, distanced, "non-human" stance (shown by the traditional formal choice to avoid pronouns, especially the first-person, and to use

---

pronouns set up patterns of inclusion and exclusion. One is the controversy ignited by Ross Perot's reference to his African-American audience when running for president; he addressed them as "you people". Another is the large amounts of energy and ink expended over the "generic masculine" debate in the U.S. over the years.

the passive voice), then I would argue that HASA's style in regard to Subject/Theme choices and the construction of Agency fits that definition.[15]

Henneth-Annûn Story Archive "Who We Are" Subject Table[16]

Category	No.	%	Subjects
site	5	28	*HASA/this site/the site/its (HASA)*
admin.	4	22	*we/our goal/we/[unstated we]*
Yahoo List	3	17	*we/we*
other sites	3	17	*excellent smaller sites/these sites/a number of these smaller sites*
members	2	11	*even our own site members*
story	1	5	*every story that is recommended or submitted*
Total	18	100	

The style of discourse at SOA, in choices of Subject/Theme, constructs agency in a markedly different way than does HASA. The agency is shared, with more attributed to potential site members than claimed by the site maintainers/moderators. Thirteen, or 34%, of the Subjects of clauses are a nominal group relating to "writers/readers/site members", and eight of those Subjects are the second person informal pronoun "you", stated and unstated. This page gives immediate details of how to become a member and author (on both sites people can be members without being authors, but HASA's membership information is not immediately apparent; I found it only after multiple "clicks" and finally going in frustration to the site map). The information on how to become a member is the second largest source of Subjects, still focusing on the reader, with eight "you" subjects totalling 21% of the total. As the table shows, agency is grammatically given to members, authors, and even potential members and authors. The site is the Subject of five clauses, but the next largest category is stories (three) and then reviews of those stories (two), for a

---

[15] When I first began this project, HASA required prospective site members to join the Yahoo discussion list. That policy changed on 8 June 2005, and is noted in an announcement on the site.

[16] The full analyzed text may be found in Appendix A. Halladay identifies the "unstated" subjects of imperative clauses which are counted along with the stated subjects of declarative clauses. So the phrase "Unstated You" which is in bold italics in the tables and the text shows my recovery of those unstated elements which function in the clauses.

total of five or 13% Subject positions. On SOA, the user names of both the site administrator and site programmer are available as well as email addresses, despite the existence of spam bots, the reason HASA gives for not making such information available.[17] Most fans do not put their real names on their Internet sites, but fan "pseudonyms" are used in all fandoms and are not considered dishonest so much as protective. The people who run this site are the grammatical Subjects of only two clauses. The largest single category of Subjects is not related to the site or its administration at all.

Stories of Arda "About Us" Subject Table[18]

Category	No.	%	Subject
writers/readers/site members	13	34	*we*/[unstated *you*] (8)/*authors; two existing members/you/they*
process/membership/author	8	21	[unstated *you*] (5)/*you* (3)
site	5	13	*this website/the goals of this site/this site/one of the goals of this site/his site*
stories	3	8	*fanfiction stories set in the universe..../entertaining... stories/stories*
reviews	2	5	*a review/any valid complaints against a story*
admin.	2	5	*we/a group of individuals who...*
Tolkien	1	3	*Tolkien*
interrogative	4	11	*who/how/what/who*
Total	38	100	

Pronoun Analysis

Pronouns reflect and create boundaries and hierarchies. Since few people consciously notice or think about pronoun usage, except in the most formal writing, the patterns can be revealing. In the case of HASA, the pronouns, along with the Theme/Subject choice, support the hierarchy of administrators over members or

---

[17] There is an anonymous admin email address which people can use to communicate with the HASA moderators/maintainers.

[18] The full analyzed text may be found in Appendix B.

prospective members. "We/our" referring to the site administrators and the Yahoo Discussion List are fourteen of the twenty-one pronouns, or 67%. The referent of "we" can slip from the group of people who administer the site to the large discussion list of members, all active to some extent, past or present, in the fandom. I doubt that a singular and consistent collective position could be held by that many people, so the usage in this text gives HASA's pronoun usage a scope similar to the royal "we". In contemporary terms, this pronoun usage is familiar to anyone writing in an institutional context. It is one I often used when performing an administrative role at my university and writing memos on behalf of my department.

Henneth-Annûn Story Archive "Who We Are" Pronoun Table[19]

Pronoun	Referent	No.	%
we/our	site admin.	11	52
their	HASA members	3	14
we	Yahoo Henneth-Annûn Discussion List	3	14
it	story/fiction	2	10
you	reader of site	1	5
its	HASA's	1	5
Total		21	100

In real life terms, the programmer and administrator on SOA have the same power as the administrators who run HASA or any website. However, SOA has constructed a discourse that seems more attuned to sharing agency with members and writers than the discourse of HASA. That agency is shared through a process of inclusion which is created by the pronoun choices in the text: thirty-five of the pronouns are "you/your", referring to the site readers/members (current and potential). In terms of agency, a look at the five pronouns referring to "Tolkien" supports an impression that Tolkien is given more focus on this site than on HASA's site where he is somewhat dismissively referred to as "JRRT". "Tolkien" is the Subject of only one clause, but that clause is in the second sentence on the page which quotes "Letter 131", in which Tolkien speaks of his hope that his created world would leave "scope for other minds and hands" to create. (Tolkien, 2000: 143-

---

[19] See note 16.

161) This sentence, by a fan who cites Tolkien's authority for writing fan fiction (a complex subject in today's world of copyrights, intellectual property, and "Cease and Desist" letters feared by fans) is a sophisticated rhetorical choice. Superficially, it can be read as a standard/academic/masculine appeal to an outside (in this case, canonical) authority. Yet the third sentence begins with the most inclusive "we" of all: in this clause, the pronoun is the all-inclusive fannish "we": all those who create within Tolkien's world. Site creators and writers are part of that collective group, yet the group is subordinated to Tolkien: we take what he created and "weave in our own creativity." The fan site's programmer and administrator include themselves in the group referred to by that "we", placing themselves within the fan community rather than set apart/above the writers/members of the site.

Stories of Arda Archive "About Us" Pronoun Table[20]

Pronoun	Referent	No.	%
you (or unstated *you*)/*yours*	readers of site	35	61
they/their	writers	6	10
he/his	Tolkien	5	9
it	story/fiction	3	5.5
we/our	site admin.	3	5.5
we	all who create	1	2
I	potential members (interrogative)	2	3.5
her	Rorrah	2	3.5
Total		57	100

Comparison of Styles

Many would describe the style of the HASA text as formal and distanced/objective. These characteristics are often strongly associated with academic writing and, as Jenkins notes, with a traditionally defined masculine style. It is impossible to discover the names of the administrators of HASA by reading the publicly available information; they do not post email addresses for fear of bots, and provide an

---

[20] See note 18.

anonymous contact form. However, during the Summer 2004 conflicts, a number of people posting in their own weblogs or communicating with fellow fans in a variety of weblog communities identified themselves as administrators or volunteers of HASA, and mostly identified as women (admittedly, some could have been men masquerading as women). The one self-identified man who was involved with HASA and participated in the discussions is now running another Tolkien fanfic archive. It is impossible to know who wrote the text posted on HASA's "Who We Are" page. Their language style, here and elsewhere, implies collective decision-making and review processes. However, this page is the public face that HASA chooses to present to potential members of their site.

In contrast, an analysis of SOA's "About Us" page, which is signed by the site moderator, Nilmandra, with "Hugs to all", reveals a style that can be described as occupying the opposite end of the spectrum from HASA. If HASA's style is academic, professional, masculine, objective, SOA's is informal, amateur (defined as doing what you enjoy for love not money), feminine, emotional, nurturing. Whether or not these descriptors are the most appropriate for the two styles is debatable. I believe most "mainstream" speakers/readers of U.S. Standard English (a term implying a homogenous group that does not exist given class, gender and ethnic differences) would regard the two texts as differing in style. Many trained in academic writing would use the same descriptors as I do. Even readers who lack a specialized vocabulary would detect differences in tone.[21]

I am not arguing that either style is inherently more welcoming or distancing to any reader/readers. We evaluate communication styles and discourse as welcoming or forbidding depending, to a large extent, on our familiarity with a style, not with its inherent qualities. Those readers/fans who are trained in and comfortable with the academic/professional/masculine styles that HASA uses will find that site as welcoming as do fans who find SOA welcoming because it reflects a style that is more traditionally fannish and communal—the style many perceive as feminine. Given standard expectations of a gender binary, it is possible that many who identify one or the other style as most appropriate would dislike the opposing

---

[21] Fans who dislike HASA often describe it as "elitist" in tone or nature, a standard term used of academics. (Brobeck, 2004)

style. Thus, clear stylistic differences between the two discourses may partly explain why some strong supporters of HASA express dislike for SOA and vice versa. It would be interesting, although extremely difficult, to discover how many fans are active on both sites, presumably finding both styles welcoming or being able to navigate between the two styles without discomfort. Some fans no doubt house their fics at both with the pragmatic goal of attracting more readers. And yet, women are heavily involved in running both sites as well as posting, reading and interacting with each other on both.

The two sites represent very different styles. These styles could be called traditionally masculine and feminine styles although both are constructed by women. The extent to which the styles on different archives operate in a primarily female fandom which is centred around a male-written text suggest that gendered discourses in mainstream are more complex than many are prepared to admit. Another binary that could be applied to the two styles is that of "formal/informal". As Tom Shippey has argued, Tolkien's novel works with a large range of styles and language, ranging from formal and archaic (Elrond's) to informal and vernacular (the Hobbits'). (Shippey, 2000: 68-77) That same range of styles can be found in the fandom, but seldom within the same space, if these two archives represent two ends of a spectrum.

Bibliography

Anon (2004a), Fanfic_Hate Live Journal Community website: http://www.livejournal.com/community/fanfic_hate

Anon (2004b), Henneth Annûn Story Archive website: http://www.henneth-annun.net/

Anon (2004c), Stories of Arda website: http://www.storiesofarda.com/index.asp

Brobeck, Kristi Lee (2004), "Under the Waterfall: A Fanfiction Community's Analysis of Their Self-Representation and Peer Review" *Ractory: A Journal of Entertaining Media* 2004.5: http://www.refractory.unimelb.edu.au/journalissues/vol5/brobeck.htm

Halliday, M.A.K. (1994), *An Introduction to Functional Grammar* 2nd ed., Oxford University Press, Oxford

Hills, Matt (2002), *Fan Cultures*, Routledge, New York

Isaacs, Neil David and Rose A. Zimbardo (eds) (1968), *Tolkien and the Critics: Essays on J.R.R. Tolkien's* The Lord of the Rings, University of Notre Dame Press, Notre Dame

Jenkins, Henry (1992), *Textual Poachers: Television Fans and Participatory Culture*, Routledge, London and New York

Shippey, Tom (2000), *J.R.R. Tolkien: Author of the Century*, Houghton Mifflin, Boston

Tolkien, J.R.R. (1986-1996), *The History of Middle-earth Series* 12 vols, ed. Christopher Tolkien, Houghton Mifflin, Boston and New York

Tolkien, J.R.R. (2000), *The Letters of J.R.R. Tolkien*, ed. Humphrey Carpenter, Houghton Mifflin, Boston and New York

Appendix A:

Analysis of the "About Home/Who We Are" on Henneth Annûn Story Archive
Text source: http://www.henneth-annun.net/ as on 6 October 2004

Serial	"About Home/Who We Are"	Subject/Theme	Pronoun
1	*Henneth Annûn Story Archive* is a Web site supported and run by an all-volunteer staff.	S/T: Henneth Annûn Story Archive	
2	*This site* was the result of a discussion on the Henneth Annûn discussion list, which can be found at: Yahoo Groups-Henneth Annun.	S/T: This site	
3	*We* came up with the idea for this site after the list had been in existence for about a month.	S/T: We	We=Yahoo discussion list members
4	*We* were wishing that there was one location on the Web where we could find well-written, imaginative, engaging JRRT fan fiction without encountering large amounts of frivolous material and distracting advertising found at commercial fiction posting sites.		We (twice)= Yahoo discussion list members
5	*There* are *a number of excellent smaller sites* with marvelous material.	S: a number of excellent smaller sites T: There [empty subject]	
6	*However, these sites* are often: Single genre—only humor, only slash, etc. Single main character - only Sam, only Legolas, etc. Maintained by hand by one person, who cannot dedicate time and resources to supporting a large archive site	S: these sites T: However [empty subject]	
7	*A number of these smaller sites* are operated by HASA members.	S/T: A number of these smaller sites (passive construction)	

Serial	"About Home/Who We Are"	Subject/Theme	Pronoun
8	*The consensus of the list* was to create a site that would accept a story of any genre or rating and with any combination of main characters as long as <u>it</u> was a quality work of fiction.	S/T: The consensus of the list	it=story
9	And not just fiction!	Fragment but meant to build on last clause: *The consensus of the list* was to create a site that would accept quality work in genres other than fiction	
10	<u>We</u> are also pleased to post critical essays about JRRT's works and about JRRT oriented fan fiction.	S/T: We	We=HASA administrators
11	*The site* is set up to accept recommendations from site members, and to allow for non-member author self-submissions.	S/T: This site	
12	*Every story that is recommended or submitted* is reviewed through a standard process, and either accepted or declined based on <u>our</u> review criteria.	S/T: Every story that is recommended or submitted	our=HASA administrators
13	*Even <u>our</u> own site members* must submit <u>their</u> work through this process.	S/T: Even our own site members	our=HASA administrators their=HASA members
14	*As HASA has grown, <u>its</u> mission* has broadened.	S: its mission. T: (dependent clause) As HASA has grown	its=HASA

Serial	"About Home/Who We Are"	Subject/Theme	Pronoun
15	*While <u>we</u> still review and post stories, the emphasis of the site* has shifted to writing.	S: the emphasis of the site T: (dependent clause) While we still review and post stories	we=HASA administrators
16	*In <u>our</u> Members area, <u>we</u>* have an extensive Forum where <u>our</u> members discuss <u>their</u> work, a growing Research Library of information and citations drawn from *LotR, The Hobbit, The Silmarillion, and HoMe*, and a Challenges section to encourage authors to expand <u>their</u> writing interests.	S: we T: (dependent clause) In our Members area	we; our=HASA administrators their (twice)= HASA members
17	<u>*Membership*</u> is free and is open to all JRRT enthusiasts, not just authors.	S/T: Membership	
18	<u>*Our goal*</u> is to provide <u>our</u> readers with a selection of the best JRRT fan fiction <u>we</u> possibly can, and to inspire other authors to write more of <u>it</u>!	S/T: Our goal	Our (twice); we= HASA administrators it=best JRRT fan fiction
19	Thank <u>you</u> for visiting our site,	S/T: Unstated [we]	We=HASA administrator
20	Henneth-Annun.net		

Appendix B:

Analysis of the "About Us" on *Stories of Arda*
Text source: http://www.storiesofarda.com/index.asp as on 6 October 2004

Serial	"About Us"	*Subject/Theme*	Pronoun
1	*This website* contains stories that were written because the authors have a deep love and respect for the world created by J.R.R. Tolkien.	S/T: This website	
2	*Tolkien*, in <u>his</u> letters (The Letters of JRR Tolkien, Letter 131) spoke to <u>his</u> original (rather grandiose, in <u>his</u> own words) attempt to create a world that "would leave scope for other minds and hands, wielding paint and music and drama", that <u>he</u> was creating a world, a mythology, for other to come and add to.	S/T: Tolkien	his; he=Tolkien
3	*We* take the cultures, races, histories, geography and languages <u>he</u> created and weave in <u>our</u> own creativity.	S/T: We	We; our=all writers, Tolkien's "others" who will add to his world and mythology he=Tolkien
4	What kinds of stories are found on this site?	Interrogative not counted in this analysis	
5	*Fanfiction stories set in the universe of JRR Tolkien*, with respect for <u>his</u> original work Rated G-R, non-slash	S/T: Fanfiction stories set in the universe of J.R.R. Tolkien	his=Tolkien
6	*entertaining and well-written stories* created by people who take pride in <u>their</u> work	S/T: Entertaining and well-written stories	his=Tolkien their=authors of stories on site
7	*The goals of this site* are:	S/T: The goals of this site	

Breaking of the Fellowship

Serial	"About Us"	*Subject/Theme*	Pronoun
8	*We* hope that *our* members will: Enjoy *themselves*. Be good readers. Aim to be entertaining writers. Tell a good tale that will amuse or stir or even teach *your* readers something.	S/T: We	We; our=site administrators themselves=members your=the writer's
9	*This* is site where people who love reading and writing LOTR fan fiction can indulge *their* hobby and have fun.	S: This site T: This [empty subject]	their=people who love reading and writing LOTR fan fiction as a hobby
10	*If you read a story you like*, send the writer a review.	S: [unstated you] T: (dependent clause) If you read a story you like	you; [understood you]=good readers (may be members of site or may just be readers)
11	*One of the goals of this site* is to encourage writers, and *nothing* is more encouraging than *a review from a reader*.	S: One of the goals of this site T: nothing [empty subject] S: (in revised clause) a review from a reader [is the most encouraging thing for a writer to receive]	
12	Who may post their stories here?	Interrogative	
13	*Stories* will not be judged on individual merit, but *authors* will be screened to ensure that growth is controlled and to ensure that authors will be posting stories that fit within *our* guidelines.	S/T: Stories S/T: Authors	our=site administrators
14	How do I become a member?	Interrogative	

Serial	"About Us"	Subject/Theme	Pronoun
15	Click on the link on the home page called "Become a Member".	S/T: [understood you]	[understood you]= prospective members
16	Fill out the basic information and <u>you</u> will receive an email confirming <u>your</u> login name and password.	S/T: [understood you]	[understood you]; your= prospective members
17	*As a member, <u>you</u>* will be able to receive author alerts whenever an author on <u>your</u> list updates a story or begins a new one.	S: you T: (dependent clause) As a member	you; your= member
18	<u>*You*</u> will also be able to keep track of <u>your</u> reviews.	S/T: You	you; your= writers who are members
19	How do I become an author?	Interrogative	[understood you]= prospective members
20	*If you are not a member*, please sign up as a member first.	S: [understood you] T: (dependent clause) if you are not a member	
21	Review the guidelines to ensure your story is appropriate for site.	S/T: [understood you]	[understood you]= prospective members/ authors
22	*If you believe it is*, then follow the instructions at the bottom of the register page.	S: [understood you] T: (dependent clause) if you believe it is	[understood you]= prospective members/ authors

Serial	"About Us"	Subject/Theme	Pronoun
23	*Two existing members* will review *your* work to ensure *it* is of the type that is appropriate for this site.	S/T: Two existing members	your=prospective members it=work of prospective members
24	*You* will be notified by email that *you* either have author privileges or that *your* work does not match the type normally posted at storiesofarda.com.	S/T: Your	you; your= prospective members
25	What are some benefits of being an author?	Interrogative	
26	Update and add new stories to the site	S/T: [understood you]	[understood you]= authors
27	Receive copies of all reviews by email	S/T: [understood you]	[understood you]= authors
28	Have alerts sent out to *your* readers when *you* update	S/T: [understood you]	[understood you]; you; your= authors
29	Maintain a list of favorite authors, favorite stories, and links	S/T: [understood you]	[understood you]= authors
30	*You* may link to *your* own site, other websites *you* enjoy, and any stories *you* have written that are not on this site (e.g. slash and/or NC-17).	S/T: You	You; your=authors
31	Who will be screening authors?	Interrogative	
32	*A group of individuals who have volunteered their time to assist with the site* will help screen new readers, review changes in guidelines and review stories for which complaints have been received.	S/T: A group of individuals who have volunteered their time	their=volunteers who screen

Serial	"About Us"	Subject/Theme	Pronoun
33	*Any valid complaints against a story (such as plagiarism or inappropriate content)* will be forwarded to the author and *they* will be asked to either edit their story or remove it from the site	S/T: Any valid complaints against a story (such as plagiarism of inappropriate content) S/T: They	they; their=author (singular referent; casual and non-sexist usage of plural); it=story
34	*Any general questions, suggestions or comments* may be directed to Nilmandra@comcast.net.	S: (passive voice) agent=[understood you] T: Any general questions, suggestions or comments	[understood you]=anyone with a question, suggestion, or comment
35	*Please* report any bugs or problems to Nilmandra or to Rorrah at Rora@mindspring.com	S: [understood you] T: Please	[understood you]=anyone who finds a bug or problem
36	*This site* has been programmed by Rorrah with the same dedication and concern for quality as the authors who post their stories here.	S/T: This site (passive voice; agent=Rorrah)	their=authors
37	*Please* be sure to leave her a "review" too, if you like the site, at her email address.	S: [understood you] T: Please	[understood you]= anyone who likes the site
38	Hugs to all, Nilmandra		

SECTION VI

The Lord of the Games

21

LORD OF THE GAMES?
Father and Son Review *The Lord of the Rings* Video Games

Kenneth and Simon Henshall

SON SIMON'S TALE

Hi, I'M THIRTEEN and live in Christchurch, New Zealand. Computer science is my best subject, and Dad said I should "establish my credentials" by mentioning that I recently came top in the country for my age group with 100% in the New South Wales Computer Science Test, and that I have certificates in game programming. I play a lot of video games on various platforms, and spend so much time on them that I've been able to set a few records. So, my dad asked me to write about what I think of *The Lord of the Rings* games. I'll make some general comments about these first, then review each of the games, and reply to some questions from my dad. Then I'll hand over to him.

General Comments about *LotR* Games

I have played six games associated with *LotR* and Middle-earth series, on three different platforms. These were *The Hobbit* (PS2, Vivendi), *The Fellowship of the Ring* (Xbox, Vivendi, also on PC), *The Two Towers* (Xbox, EA), *The Return of the King* (PS2, EA), *The Third Age* (Xbox, EA), and *The Battle for Middle Earth* (PC, EA). The games produced by Vivendi are based on the books, and those by Electronic Arts (EA) are based on the movies (at least those in the Trilogy) and have scenes, music and voices from them. A number of the EA games also have interviews with the actors from the movies, such as Ian McKellen (Gandalf) and Elijah Wood (Frodo). You can pick up some personal background about each of the actors, how they felt about the movies, and how well they think each game relates to them. Elijah Wood, for example, along with his Hobbit friends, really enjoyed playing the games, and Ian McKellen would like to play but lacks the finger skills to do so. He also thinks the "samurai" aspect of Gandalf has been brought out. Although I cannot recall the books in exact detail, I'm sure they were more focused on Frodo's adventures, while the movies had more action. The games have even more action, and apart from a few quests are almost entirely fighting—or more exactly, moving from one fight to another. The only real exception is *The Hobbit*, which strictly speaking isn't part of the Trilogy anyway. It is also interesting to find that while most of the games have an M15+ rating, there are also ratings of 11, Teen, and 7+, meaning that you can definitely find something to buy to suit your age, or something you like.

Review of the Games

The Hobbit (PS2, Vivendi, 7+, 2003)

This is quite an original game in two senses. First, it is the prelude to the Trilogy, and therefore the original starting point for the sequence of events in the series. Second, and probably more importantly, it is also original in that it seems to be a more "family orientated" game than the others. There is very limited violence, and no really gory spilling of blood. This makes it quite distinctive and "precious", to use Gollum's term. The age requirement is only 7+, no doubt because of this limited violence. Unfortunately the graphics are poor in quality, and you can't easily tell who Gollum is. Still, the game is fun to play, and is very interactive. You can interact with characters that appear in the book but do not appear in the films or other games. You can also do mini-quests like retrieving items for people, usually for some reward that enables you to progress. There is inevitably some fighting, but as I said, it is limited and not very gory.

Overall, though it's fun, I consider it to be an average game. It is a good buy if you are looking to purchase it for young children. I recommend it to anyone who is heavily into RPGs (Role-Playing Games), and not into excessive violence. In fact, you don't even have to like *LotR* to enjoy this game.

I should add that I remember this game partly because Bilbo looks like images I've seen of a red-haired Irish leprechaun!

The Fellowship of the Ring (Xbox, Vivendi, M15+, 2002, also PC, Teen, 2002)

The Fellowship comes with a few interesting twists. It's the only *LotR* game where you can play as Aragorn or Frodo or Gandalf but not as Gimli or Legolas. The characters in fact alternate. The two versions of the game come with different age requirements (Xbox being M15+ and PC being Teen), even though you'd expect the games to be basically the same, since they're produced by the same company. I must admit I haven't played the computer version very much, but it does seem the Xbox version is a little fuller with more moves and weapons and so on. The main way to play the game is to use the power of the Ring as Frodo, except this drains your health, meaning it can be quite difficult to kill enemies. Playing as Aragorn and Gandalf later in the game is a lot better. It is interesting but rather disappointing that you do not seem able to advance any of your characters, in the sense of giving them new skills. You also must play more defensively, as your main objective seems to be avoiding Ringwraiths. One plus is that this game features Tom Bombadil, a character from the book who does not appear in the film. The same is true of the Barrow-wights.

However, though I hate to be a put-down, in my view this is the poorest game of the series. I just can't seem to get into this one. Maybe I just haven't played it for long enough, or there is something I'm missing. Personally, I wouldn't recommend this game.

The Two Towers (Xbox, EA, 11, 2003)

The Towers seems to be a very good game. The storyline is maintained, and involves a lot of action—ok, fighting—to keep you entertained. You can play as Aragorn, Legolas or Gimli, plus a secret unlockable character that I'll keep secret, and advance them as you journey through Middle-earth. There are four levels of skill in killing: fair, good, excellent, and perfect. This is exponential, in that the better you kill, the stronger your character becomes, which means you can kill even better. It does have one major let-down though. As far as I am aware, you cannot replay levels. I may be wrong, but if you want a perfect score, you're going to have to be prepared to start a few new games.

I recommend this game strongly to *LotR* fans, but not to anyone who loves to fully complete games (i.e. finishing with a perfect score), as this one is very difficult. You might be disappointed.

The Return of the King (PS2, EA, M15+, 2003)

The Return has excellent graphics, with cut-scenes that lead into actual scenes from the movie. You can (eventually) play as all nine of the major characters, and even with a friend in "Co-operative Play" mode. This is truly interactive play, as you topple rubble to destroy Orcs, or fire catapults. It also has excellent combat modes, similar to the four kill/skill levels of *The Two Towers*. You simply encounter enemies as you journey ahead, providing you with new challenges, and—if you dispose of them—you get new skills that you can use to defeat other enemies. The levels that you progress through are similar to those of the movies, and it really builds up a story. This is great, as it allows you to get truly involved in the game. There are even two bonus dungeons you can access (and of course fight in) once you have completed the game. These sites are not in the film.

One puzzling thing about the game—or more exactly its promotional blurb—is that the information on the box says it is the only game with scenes and music from the film. In fact it seems to me that some other games have those features (unless those other games have some subtle technical differences from the actual films). Another point to note is that it is *extremely* difficult. I am an experienced game-player, yet I found it very difficult to pass this game even on "easy" level. I even had to use cheats to pass the bonus dungeon in "Co-operative" mode! That's what makes the game a challenge though, and challenges are major factors in making a game appealing. The only other thing is that you have to play as certain characters. For example, on the first mission you must be Gandalf. However, once you have completed the game, you can choose to play any level as any character, even if it is a little repetitive. (When you play as some characters "out of scene", say as Gandalf in an Aragorn scene, it can sometimes lead to strange effects like swords with no-one holding them, but this adds to the fun.)

I think it's a great game, and it's my personal favourite from the series. I really recommend it to anyone who wants to experience the *LotR* journey, and is also heavily into combat.

The Third Age (Xbox, EA, M15+, 2004)

This is a very interesting game in that it spans all three movies of the *LotR* trilogy. You also get six new playable characters to choose from, two of them female, and all of them "peripheral" characters such as Berethor (Captain of the Citadel Guard) and Idrial (a woman who serves Lady Galadriel). There is also a distinctive battle mode in which three characters fight together, with set Health Points and Magic Points, taking turns to attack—the only game in the series with this feature. There is also a combat meter, which indicates how likely you are to have a battle. Not only that, but you also get a distinctive style of menu, which is a mixed blessing. You get more options, but you must manually (as opposed to it happening automatically) use items to restore health, and also customize your character with different weapons and armour. You must also explore the areas to find hidden chests or switches. This is a welcome change from the other games as you can play through the game at your own pace. There are a total of 109 different scenes from the movies, and it takes a long time to watch them all. In fact, you could just about watch all of these in succession instead of the movies! The only let-down is the "Co-operative" mode. Because the game is RPG-centred, the second player simply controls half of the players in combat. Player One controls everything else.

Once you have progressed a little you can also choose to play as Evil characters using the Evil Mode—I blitzed Gandalf very quickly as the Balrog—though these characters are not as developed and personalized as the Good guys and do not for example have "pen pictures" in the accompanying booklet. Interestingly, but perhaps not surprisingly, even if you kill named Good characters in one scene they still return in the next (just as Gandalf does in the tale).

I highly recommend this to anyone who is really into *LotR* and is also a major RPG fan. The combat system will probably annoy anyone who dislikes RPG's, but the gameplay is excellent if you can put up with the combat.

The Battle for Middle Earth (PC, EA, M15+, 2004)

This game has a completely different style to the rest of the series. It has a storyline like the others, but is also almost a second version of *LotR*, a Real-Time Strategy (RTS) game similar to *The Age of Empires* (Ensemble Studios, from 1997) or *Warcraft* (Blizzard Entertainment, 2004) series. Here you must create your own *LotR* empire, such as by creating buildings and troop units, which gives the player much more interface and scope than the other *LotR* games. You can choose named characters to include in your unit, but it is not an RPG and there are limits on character advancement. The graphics are generally quite disappointing, mainly because the game is viewed from far behind the characters, meaning it does not need much detail. However, some of the film scenes help to make up for this, together with scenic shots with good 3-D effects. The game certainly makes up for its graphics with its campaigns. It is my personal favourite type of gameplay (war and strategy), and is highly addictive. It also has multiplayer functions that allow the game to be played over the Internet, which can be very useful for playing with friends.

As with *The Third Age*, you can choose to represent either Good or Evil. You can also introduce variations into the storyline.

This game is very different to the other *LotR* computer game I tried (*The Fellowship of the Ring*) as its complexity requires an enormous amount of memory— both your own and the computer's! You need at least 3 gigabytes of free space to run the game, and it is very slow if you have less than 512 megabytes of RAM. With my 256 MB RAM desktop computer (which admittedly might need defragging), it takes 5 minutes just to save the game, whereas on my 512 MB laptop it takes only about 5 seconds.

I really recommend this game if you like computer games more than console games, and if you have the right equipment to play the game the way it should be played. If you have a slower computer, I really do not recommend buying the game.

Ten Questions (and Lots of Sub-questions) from Dad

1) Why do you like video games? Is it empowerment? Escapism? Or what?

I really like the interaction. I feel like I'm actually part of a story and not just reading it or watching it. And I like a good storyline. The empowerment thing doesn't really matter. I guess I do like the escapism, but that's not the main thing, which is interaction. I like to be active and involved.

2) What's your preferred genre? Your favourite game? Favourite platform?

I like war games, especially FPS (First-Person Shooter) and ones that involve strategy. In that genre *Halo* (Xbox) is my favourite at the moment. It gives me lots of opportunity for sniping, which I really like, and the graphics are very good. I also like RPGs (Role Playing Games), and my favourite would have to be the *Final Fantasy* series (PS2). I use sword-play in that, which I also like. Recently I'm also getting very much into MMORPGs (Massive Multiplayer Online Role Playing Games), especially *Runescape*. There can be up to 150,000 people worldwide playing it at the same time, including sometimes up to a dozen of my school friends. We search for each other's player-names and link up with each other, and then share tasks or exchange things. With platforms, I prefer the Xbox as it has so much you can do to control things with the console. It's hard at first but it soon becomes part of you and you do things instinctively. The PS is also good like that. But computers are too fiddly and you never get to feel the keyboard is part of you, like you do with a console. They also break down and give problems too often, like the slow speed of *The Battle for Middle Earth* if you run low on RAM.

3) How do the *LotR* games stack up for you personally and in general?

Personally I think they're okay but nothing particularly special, yet my friends really rave about them. I guess that means I'm the odd one out, but I just can't see what all the fuss is about, either with the games or the movies. When it comes down to it, my friends seem mostly to like the idea of fighting and killing in a variety of roles and ways—as opposed to something like *Halo*, where you have limited choice and fairly anonymous characters.

4) What sort of roles do you prefer—in *LotR* and in general—and why?

It depends on the game but in general I like warrior roles, as well as mages. In *LotR* that means I prefer Gandalf if possible, as he's both a mage and a fighter, but if he's not available I go for Aragorn because I like sword-fighting. My friend H likes Legolas, because he's an effective fighter with ranged weapons, and H also identifies with him at a personal level. Come to think of it, most of my friends—especially the girls—seem to like Legolas. Perhaps it's because of the actor (Orlando Bloom) in the movies.

5) Do you like quests? And how does *LotR* stack up in that regard?

Yes, I really do like quests, especially when they're bonuses as opposed to being a necessary part of the game in order to advance. The Vivendi games are good with quests, but most of the other *LotR* games are pretty restricted, and mostly just involve battles. *The Battle for Middle Earth* is more interesting though.

6) What do you think of the violence in video games, both in general and in *LotR*? Could it influence some people into committing real-life violence?

Yes, majorly, especially because of the interaction. Players can actually do violence in video games rather than just reading or watching about it—a sort of training-ground for real-life violence. In fact, people prone to violence probably never read books and so don't get any influence from the written word at all! What's scary is that the graphics are so good nowadays—especially when they bring in photographic stuff like from the *LotR* movies—that it's getting easier and easier to blur reality and virtual reality. Another scary thing is that it's not just targeted enemies who can get killed but also bystanders and other innocent people, such as all the pedestrians who get literally splattered in a game like *Grand Theft Auto*. It doesn't mean anything to the player if he can save a few seconds by running over a pedestrian, since they're not real people, but I think that's sending dangerous messages to some weaker-minded players. Actually, I know of some who even go out of their way just to splatter a pedestrian over the pavement! The *LotR* games aren't too bad, with a pretty standard level of violence and not too much gore. My friend H thinks it's pretty standard too. If you want to see really bad violence, and generally disgusting behaviour, check out *Max Payne* or *The Getaway*.

7) What do your friends think about video games in general and the *LotR* games in particular? Is there a different attitude between boys and girls?

As I said earlier, most of my friends really like the *LotR* games, and they also like video games in general. But I have friends in the chess club who aren't into video games. They tend to be more into books. I mostly mix with boys and don't know for sure but I don't think the girls I know are quite as much into games as the boys are. But I do know one who's really into "X-rated" games. And the girls do seem to like Legolas. Come to think of it, I know the figures show that worldwide girls are keen players—something like a third of all players—so I guess I couldn't really say my answer was accurate.

8) What do you see happening in the future in video game development?

More RPGs and FPSs, and definitely more MMORPGs and use of online technology in general. More 3-dimensionality, and eventually holographs. Probably also more haptic sensation, like in vibrator consoles, but with holographs.

9) With *LotR*, which do you rate most, the books, the movies, or the games?

Definitely the games, because of the interaction. Books have no real interaction unless perhaps—unlike me—you've got a very vivid imagination. The *LotR* books in particular seem too wordy and long and boring. The movies are better because they have sound and vision, and of course scenes from New Zealand that I have actually visited, but they still lack interaction. Also I personally dislike the "actor cult", which I know helps sell the films and give them an appeal for a lot of people, but for me it detracts from the content and story.

10) How important is video game knowledge for making and keeping friends?

Quite important for boys, maybe not so much for girls. It's a means of getting acceptance and respect. Those who don't play, even if they're chess champions or top musicians or whatever, are seen by the players—that's to say most boys—as "losers". The same goes for those who really want to play but can't because their parents won't let them—they're still losers. Even computer whizzkids are seen as nerds and losers if they don't actually play games. My friends talk a lot about games so it really is important to be able to get involved and know about them. At the same time, if you're good at games you can get bothered a helluva lot by novices—flattering at first, but it can wear you down when you get a dozen phone-calls a day asking for help!

FATHER KEN'S TALE

THEY SAY THAT the generation gap gets bigger with each generation, owing in large part to the accelerating pace of technological innovation and the flow-on effect on expectations, attitudes, behaviours, and ultimately values. In fact, my wife and I were both born in 1950, and had our son in 1991, so with this forty-one year gap we're effectively two generations removed from his worldview, not merely one. And we were born and raised in England, not New Zealand. It was a time and place where fat people were called fat, where Britons pointed with pride not shame at all the pink bits in the atlas, where there was respect for authority and for older people, where molly-coddling was at a minimum, and where it was—with a few exceptions—safe to walk the city streets at night without fearing gratuitous mugging or even murder.

I'm a working-class lad, but when I was Simon's age I was fortunate enough to be studying—thanks to a rare day when my brain cells actually worked and got me a scholarship—at England's top academic school, King Edward's in Birmingham. At Assembly the Chief Master would frequently exhort us to ever greater achievements—exhortations that generally fell on deaf ears, especially when he was talking in Latin—and reminding us of the School's great heritage. Notable Old Edwardian achievers forming part of that heritage included Field Marshal Viscount William Slim ("Slim of Burma", later Governor-General of Australia), the Right

Honourable Enoch Powell (a brilliant scholar, one-time professor of languages, and youngest ever brigadier in the British Army, facts often overlooked after his controversial "Rivers of Blood" speech in 1968), and arguably even the Great Bard "Stratford Billy" Shakespeare (through a tenuous and not absolutely proven link with a junior school, but widely treated as an Old Edwardian nonetheless). And another, of course, was John Ronald Reuel Tolkien—another scholarship boy.

I mention these other three figures because they go together with Tolkien in my mind. J.R.R. Tolkien was actually at King Edward's at the same time as Slim, in the first decade of the twentieth century, and they were only a year apart in their ages so would almost certainly have known each other, though I don't know whether anything about their possible friendship has ever been researched or written. Certainly Tolkien, having served briefly in the army himself before being invalided out, would have been aware of his fellow Edwardian's later meteoric rise to dizzying military heights. Enoch Powell came along some twenty years later, but again Tolkien would surely have noted at some point (possibly after Powell achieved prominence in politics) the career of a similar top scholar and professor of languages, and may possibly also have noted Powell's military achievements. And the link with Shakespeare is obviously because Tolkien was also to achieve fame as a major English writer.

Of course, in what we might term a case of "*l'école oblige*"—yes, all Edwardians learned French to very advanced levels!—I read his *LotR*. However, I have to say that I found it, as my son Simon did, wordy, too long, and often confusing. It came across to me very much as the creation of an incredibly fertile and constructive imagination, which I admired, but at the same time as just too *précieux* and pedantic in detail, "over-written", overdone, and in such regards consistent with my stereotype (at that time) of a scholar of dead languages. The combination of scale and detail seemed to suggest a major disillusionment with the real world—not surprising given the depressing events of the first half of the twentieth century—and an almost God-like wish to create another world, yet one puzzlingly even fuller of fighting than the real world. The ultimate triumph of Good over Evil did not strike me as particularly impactive or inspiring, and in general I found the whole work somewhat depressing.

I heartily applaud Peter Jackson for having the vision and courage to take on this mighty opus and convert it from the medium of text to that of cinematic picture. This adaptation, this visual transformation, has given it a new impact and appeal for a much wider public. In English we have a saying that "A picture paints a thousand words," in Chinese and Japanese there is a similar saying that "Even a hundred hearings is not as good as one look," and likewise in Russian there is a saying "It's better to see once than to hear a thousand times"—evidence that acknowledgement of the efficacy of the pictorial relative to the verbal/textual is universal. On the negative side, it could be argued that a dimension of free imagination permitted to the reader, in visualizing in their mind's eye their own individualized scenic interpretation of Tolkien's books, has been lost. Through film the scene has been set for one and all viewers, and free imagination has been replaced by real-world scenes from somewhere in New Zealand. But hey, it's a beautiful country, and in my view the loss of personally imagined visualization is a small price to pay for the greater impact and clarity of the pictorialized story. (I will not raise here the baser merit of boosting New Zealand's economy!)

Just as the films have given Tolkien a new life—a Second Coming, as it were—so too in my view have the *LotR* video games given him a still further lease of life, and spread the appeal of *LotR* even more widely.

In his noted study of Tolkien, Brian Rosebury lists four forms of "cultural afterlives": relabelling, assimilation, imitation, and adaptation. He understandably assigns the films to the adaptation category. However, though he admits it is not clear-cut, he assigns the *LotR* video games to the relabelling category, on the grounds that the basic elements of gameplay (button-pushing, character movements, regaining health points, obtaining rewards, performing tasks, etc.) remain the same as in numerous other video games, and that the *LotR* elements are just an overlay, with obvious implications of commercial capitalizing upon the success of the films. (Rosebury, 2003: 194-195) I take his point and would not deny that there is some degree of relabelling, and it would be naive to deny the commercialization, but I also think that the categories may not be mutually exclusive, and that the video games could also in part be legitimately seen as adaptations. In my view, and certainly my son's, they adapt *LotR* to a new medium, which one of my students has described as "like an electronic novel in which you can actually take part".[1] As Simon too has said (yes, "Simon says..."), you can get actively involved and interact in a way that is not possible in either the book or the film versions. Simon's reviews above also make it clear that the video games contain considerable variety and diversity, with a number of original elements. Not the least of these is that you can choose to fight for Evil, which would very probably not have been to the liking of the converted Catholic Tolkien, who once said that the entire *LotR* opus was a religious statement.[2]

Basically, while the films represent a cinematic version of *LotR*, the video games provide a virtual reality version. Given that the games are based far more on the films than the original books, Baudrillard and friends would no doubt have a field day at the hyperreality represented by these "copies of copies", especially since the original "real" was itself an escape from actual reality into fantasy. (See for example Baudrillard, 1994) But I'm not an authority on Baudrillard so I won't make any further reference to him.

I myself do not hold necessarily negative views about the hyperreal, or virtually real, or simulation, or simulacra, or what have you. On the positive side, think of the benefits of flight simulators in training pilots. And if you wonder why Michael Schumacher is such a successful Formula One driver, apparently it's partly because he practices not just on the actual tracks but also on the *Grand Prix* video game, which has an extraordinarily accurate representation of the various courses and variables such as weather and tyre-types. Much better to find out "virtually" rather than "really" that if you take the third bend on the Monaco circuit in wet weather tyres at 175 kph you'll crash, but not if you take it at 170. And what about the "virtual reconstructions" of bodies in medical science, not just the famed "Adam" but one's own MRI and CT scans? And so on.

---

[1] Tze-On Oh, personal communication, 17 October 2005.

[2] In a letter written in 1953 to Robert Murray, a Jesuit priest, Tolkien wrote: "The Lord of the Rings is of course a fundamentally religious and Catholic work; unconsciously at first, but consciously in the revision. That is why I have not put in, or have cut out practically all references to anything like 'religion', to cults or practices, in the imaginary world. For the religious element is absorbed into the story and symbolism." (cited in Anon, 2007b)

In fact, though I won't go too far into this, the question of virtual reality is to my mind tied in with the question of constructs. Much scholarship over the last few decades has been concerned with deconstruction, which is fine when it represents dissection and analysis. But I do take issue with those scholars who go a step further and deny the value of the construct. In my area of Japanese Studies, probably one of the most obvious constructs is that of the pre-war propaganda-driven idea of the emperor as divine. Yes, it's a construct, but literally millions died for it, and their deaths were not constructs, but very real. (And we could no doubt raise the whole question of religion as a construct, but I won't go there, even though it seemingly underlies much of Tolkien's writing of *LotR*.)

The point I'm making is that there is often a blurring between the "constructed" or "virtual" and the actual. Simon gets actual enjoyment from his virtual reality games, and he gets actual "street cred" and respect from his friends through his ability in playing them. The games can also teach him skills—such as resource management, strategy, and so on—which he can, at least to some extent, apply in real life. Persons with certain physical handicaps, such as dyspraxia, and those with social interaction difficulties, such as sufferers from Asperger Syndrome, have a whole new world opened to them—okay, a virtual world, but it's one they can relate to, be active in, get pleasure from, and get a sense of companionship and/or empowerment and/or identity. Of late there has also been an interesting development in which some widely despised "non-genuine gamers" called "gold pharmers" [sic] advance a character to a point where they are possessed of abundant wealth, weapons, etc. and have reached an advanced level in the game, and then sell the character on IGE or eBay or similar real-world trading sites for real money. (Reuters News, 2005b)

This last point leads on to the negative side of virtual reality. As in most things, it seems the balance between good and bad is a matter of degree and moderation and common sense, and of avoidance of abuse (such as by the "gold pharmers") where possible. I mentioned above how socially unskilled persons can benefit from game playing, but it can be a two-edged sword, and if game playing gets to the point of obsession it can become pathological. Donald Ritchie, a Japan-based specialist in popular culture, has cited a case where a young Japanese man fell hopelessly in love with a video game character. (Ritchie, 2003: 22-23) The aim of this Japanese video game, which was based on a dating show, was to do the right things to get the virtual (yet not necessarily virtuous?) young woman, Shiori—idealized of course as the embodiment of beauty and nubility—to say "I love you". Gauche in his relations with real-life females, the young game player fell head over heels with this virtual maiden, who might tell him "no" time after time, but with whom he could persist and finally get the green light. Perhaps, like Simon and his strategy games, this was useful practice for real life, but I do personally find it a bit "sick" that this grown man apparently bought every bit of commercial merchandise (a very considerable amount) based on this character. But he was evidently not alone. Virtual Shiori has now been made into a film (the reverse process to *LotR*), which attracts hordes of young men to its frequent showings! You be the judge: would you let your daughter go anywhere near these guys?

Many of us remember the Japanese tamagotchi craze of a few years ago, which reached plague proportions in the West too. This was a little creature you had to raise, giving it regular food, managing its toilet functions, etc. Neglect it at your peril, for it could get sick and even die. But if that happened, you could bury it with due pomp and ceremony in a virtual cemetery. But even Ritchie, battle-hardened to the extremes of virtual reality after living many years in VR-mad Japan, was left shaking his head over the behaviour of some supposed professionals: "On television a doctor, a grown man, said that when his [tamagotchi] passed away he was sadder than when one of his patients died." (Ritchie, 2003: 26) Well, at least the death of his virtual creature won't bring him a lawsuit for malpractice—yet! (A future video game on medical lawsuits?)

Japan is an extreme case when it comes to virtual reality, for the Japanese have been main players in developing video games as well as *animé* and *manga* (a type of extended comic). The Japanese view of virtual reality is something else I won't go into in detail here, for it is a complex issue, other than to make two points. First, Japan has traditionally been a very conformist society, and, as many Japanologists have pointed out, the role of the vicarious is much greater there than in societies permissive of greater diversity in individual behaviour.[3] In this regard it's interesting to note that the Japanese have a strong preference for RPGs in which they can

---

[3]   For example, Buruma (1985). See also Henshall (1999: 158).

customize their virtual alter ego. Second, Japanese socio-psyche includes an ambivalence towards a potentially hostile natural environment, concomitant with a fear of raw nature and a compulsion to tame it into a mere aesthetic form, and also concomitant with a respect for the artificial.[4]

The greatest potential negative in the blurring of virtual and actual reality, certainly from a parental perspective, is surely the possible encouragement of violence. Simon's comments above on this matter do not bode well, though as his father I am relieved that he can objectivize the issue and realize the potential problems. Fortunately he is actually mature beyond his years, but one does fear that less mature players might well be influenced. In fact, though I cannot recall specifics, I believe that a number of cases of definite copy-cat violence have been identified in New Zealand and elsewhere, with the model being a video game. I personally find that too many games contain too much violence, and I can only shake my head over just how popular these games seem to be.

The Japanese—sorry, a brief return to those shores—have generally argued that virtual violence functions as a catharsis and helps prevent actual violence, but one is not necessarily convinced, certainly when it comes to interactive violence as opposed to merely observed or read-about violence. One can see why a non-specialist observer might come to such a conclusion in Japan's case, with its very low level of actual violence, but it could well be a false conclusion, in that it is perhaps a case of little violence in Japan *despite*—rather than because of—the large amount of virtual violence there. A main factor in this low level of actual violence could well be the extraordinary degree of self-control most Japanese seem to possess—another consequence perhaps of a tradition of orthodoxy and restraint, at least in Japan itself.[5]

---

[4] See for example Kalland (1995: 243-259). See also Buruma (1985: 65), and Henshall (1999: 44-45).

[5] I am of course mindful of the appalling violence and atrocities carried out by Japanese in the late 1930s and early 1940s. Among other things this involves a situational ethic rather than a universal morality, a hierarchical mindset, and a division of relationship-zones into intimate, protocol-based, and anomic. Japanese treatment of foreign "others" deemed "inferior", especially outside Japan itself, has in the past sometimes been anomic to the point of brutality. The role of violence in Japanese life is a very complex issue beyond the bounds of this chapter. For further discussion please refer to my *Dimensions of Japanese Society* (Henshall, 1999: esp. 147-167).

The jury is still out in Japan, but in California, and with some degree of irony, movie bone-breaker Arnold Schwarzenegger, in his position as Governor, has very recently signed legislation banning the sale of violent video games to young children (under ten years). The legislation stated: "Exposing minors to depictions of violence in video games, including sexual and heinous violence, makes those minors more likely to experience feelings of aggression, to experience a reduction of activity in the frontal lobes of the brain, and to exhibit violent, antisocial, or aggressive behaviour." (Reuters News, 2005a)

One wonders how effective the ban will be, as there will certainly be those above the the age of ten who will get hold of the games and pass them on (or more likely sell them on) to younger children, but at least it is sending appropriate signals.

Similarly, *The Press*, the newspaper in Christchurch where I live, in a recent editorial on the gratuitous bashing to death of an innocent pedestrian by a group of young "car hoons", observed: "This attitude [that of the youths], at least in part, must be linked to the near saturation violence they are exposed to through computer games and movies, and through the music and culture of gangsta rap which glamorises violence... Common sense as well as numerous studies tell us that repeated exposure to violence has a numbing effect." (*The Press*, 2005) As *The Press* observed, it is not just video games that expose youngsters to violence, but nonetheless it is probably fair to say—based on common sense—that the interactive factor does make them leading contenders when it comes to the power of influence.

We must not overlook the fact that the *LotR* games and the *LotR* films do indeed have a lot of violence—albeit rated as merely "standard" by Simon and his friends—and more so than in the books (which themselves have quite a lot). (Rosebury, 2003: 211) One can understand this from a practical point of view, in that the battle scenes are often the most difficult and expensive to create (be it by computer graphics, scale models, or real actors in costume), so it is only natural for producers to want to get as much cost benefit out of them as possible. And the producers also know that the fight scenes go down well with the average viewer/player.

I don't know the answer to this. One would really have to go back to that old question as to whether violence and the aggression that underlies it come about through learned behaviours or through genetic heredity. In my student days I remember reading Konrad Lorenz on the argument that aggression and violence were part of the human make-up, and reading rather less convincing arguments to the contrary by Ashley Montagu et al. (see Lorenz, 1966; Montagu, 1973) Recent developments in genetic research have come down heavily on Lorenz's side of the fence, showing that genes play a huge role in predisposing our personalities.[6] The word "predispose" is important, for it does not mean "determine" (except perhaps as a default), and therefore admits the potential of environmental and circumstantial influence on our behaviour. Certainly, as I implied in my opening comments, England has become a much more violent place than in my youth, and something other than genes must be responsible for that—perhaps a lack of self-control with regard to keeping a genetically violent predisposition in check, and/or perhaps an excessive liberalism and misplaced tolerance on the part of society.

Anyway, referring to my opening comments, I am pleased that despite a double generation gap between my son and myself, I am able to share my son's interest in video games and experience something of his world. I am not alone in this, for the data suggests that quite a lot of people in their fifties play. Mathematically, the average age of players is not in the teens, but late twenties. Though this does not mean that teenagers don't form the bulk of the players, it does suggest that the average is pushed up by quite a few "high agers". (see e.g. Anon, 2007a) I prefer the sports and racing games, and Simon prefers the war strategies and battle games. Truth to tell, each of us finds the other's interests boring and repetitive, but we do have a strong bond in our high estimation of video games in general, and we both talk the same language. My son also knows and shares my concerns about possible violent influence, and he is aware that any act of violence

---

[6] See for example, Ahuja (2003). The article includes the comment: "It is now thought that genes account for 40% to 70% of an individual's personality, and some researchers wonder if this is an underestimate." Very recent research shows that even our feelings towards our mother are basically down to genes. (see Anon, 2005) The recent situation in post-hurricane New Orleans also suggests a widespread predisposition to violence.

Lord of the Games? 391

on his part will result in a ban on his playing games. I have confidence and trust in him.

When I was his age, I was familiar with Tolkien and his books, but I never dreamt that they would be adapted into video games. Computers in those days were cumbersome, room-sized Heath Robinson contraptions of storage cabinets and reels, portrayed occasionally in sci-fi programmes such as *Dr Who* (which first aired in 1963). None of us could even conceive of personal desktop computers, let alone computer-derivates such as game consoles (in themselves vastly more powerful than the early computers), and of course the games that would accompany them. "Virtual reality" —and indeed "video"—were simply not in our vocabulary.

Similarly, I never dreamt of the New Zealand connection. My only "contact" with New Zealand was the tales of the All Blacks that our rugby coach—a former England player—frightened us with. That all three—*LotR*, computers, and New Zealand—should come together was totally unimagined, but I'm pleased it's happened. Such are the turnings of Fate.

In conclusion to this verbose chapter—put it down to Tolkien's wordy influence—just as I congratulated Peter Jackson on adapting the *LotR* books into film, I do the same to Vivendi and Electronic Arts for carrying the adaptation a stage further into video games and giving my son and me and many others a source of entertainment and fun. Try them out for yourself. Or wait for the holographic version!

P.S. There is bound to be a video game version of the *Chronicles of Narnia*, by Tolkien's friend C.S. Lewis. Like *LotR*, the new film version features scenes shot in New Zealand. And will we perchance eventually see games based on all the classics, including Shakespeare's works? (And in his original English?)

Bibliography

Ahuja, A. (2003), "Luck of the Draw: Personality, Health, Even Political Beliefs may be Largely Inherited" *The Times* (England), reproduced in *The Press* 22 December, Christchurch

Anon (2005), "Scientists Find Gene that Makes You Love Mother" *The Times* (England), reproduced in *The Press* 26 June, Christchurch

Anon (2007a), "Video Game" in *Wikipedia*: http://en.wikipedia.org/wiki/Video_game

Anon (2007b), "Tolkienet" website: http://www.tolkienet.com/lothlorien/theman.asp

Baudrillard, Jean (1994) [1981], *Simulacra and Simulation*, University of Michigan, Ann Arbour

Buruma, Ian (1985), *A Japanese Mirror: Heroes and Villains of Japanese Culture*, Penguin, Harmondsworth

Henshall, Kenneth (1999), *Dimensions of Japanese Society: Gender, Margins and Mainstream*, Macmillan, London

Kalland, Arne (1995), "Culture in Japanese Nature" in O. Bruun and A. Kalland (eds), *Asian Perceptions of Nature: A Critical Approach*, Curzon Press, London

Lorenz, Konrad (1966), *On Aggression*, Methuen, London

Montagu, Ashley (ed.) (1973) [1968], *Man and Aggression*, Oxford University Press, New York

Ritchie, Donald (2003), *The Image Factory: Fads and Fashions in Japan*, Reaktion Books, London

Rosebury, Brian (2003), *Tolkien: A Cultural Phenomenon*, Palgrave Macmillan, London

Reuters News (2005a), "Ban on Violent Games" cited in *The Press* 11 October, Christchurch

Reuters News (2005b), "Virtual Trading So Hot" cited in *The Press* 11 October, Christchurch

The Press (2005), "Editorial" *The Press* 20 October, Christchurch

22

WILL AN ONLINE VIRTUAL MIDDLE-EARTH STAND A CHANCE?

Bill J. Jerome

THE CREATION of worlds and realities separate from our own is an art form that has been with us from our earliest imaginings. Sharing those worlds with others has been with us as long as we have known how to communicate. As time marches on, newer ways of sharing those worlds have become possible; from painted canvas, printed words, and recorded sound, to movies, stage performances and (more recently) computer software that can present people with virtual environments in a completely different way. Computer power has been behind music mixing and digital film effects for some time, but personal computers have become powerful enough to present detailed worlds directly at home in an interactive way. These worlds are best known when applied to games such as *EverQuest* (Sony Online Entertainment, 1999) and *World of Warcraft* (hereafter *Warcraft*, Blizzard Entertainment, 2004), although there is no inherent reason why these virtual *worlds* should be games.

Over the course of two years, I was involved with a research project (Project Massive, which continues today at www.projectmassive.com) that looked into the communities and behaviours of people who play these massive multiplayer online role-playing games (MMORPGs).

There are always new games in development appearing on the radar of people who play such games. One such is *Middle Earth Online.* (Anon, 2005g) Could such a venture succeed? The mere thought of making a computer game—any computer game—of the world Tolkien created is regarded as blasphemous by many devoted readers. Since the dawn of computer gaming, however, there have been computer games based in Middle-earth. As far back as the early 1980s a game called *The Hobbit Software Adventure* (Addison-Wesley, 1982) was released for the Apple II computers. Hence, the basic concept of creating a computer game based on Tolkien's works is *not* new. What *is* new is attempting to create a totally virtual Middle-earth which allows gamers the freedom to move around in the world and interact with it, together with many others.

A Virtual Game World

There are a number of key differences between the personal computer game medium and any of the more traditional arts; the most obvious is interactivity. The user does not usually play a passive role in a *story* but rather engages the virtual world for oneself. One creates one's own stories in that world, and engages in the creation of stories with other users (such as adventuring with someone else, or several others).

For the purposes of this chapter it is essential to separate Middle-earth the location—be it literary, filmic or virtual—from the stories that occur there. It is a foregone conclusion that not everyone will agree that this is possible. Those who do not will undoubtedly be uncomfortable with the creation of a virtual Middle-earth. A virtual Middle-earth is not an adaptation like Jackson's, but rather a *place*, or experience, inspired by the books. While players are able to progress along a path that may at times parallel the books, this adaptation is not an attempt to tell the participant the story of Frodo, Sam and other characters as it occurs in the books. It is a medium to engage participants in that environment, not tell a linear story.

The creation of these virtual environments is a massive undertaking, requiring huge resources. It costs money to create these worlds, which means the product has to sell. In contrast to only ten years ago, the market for such worlds is quite crowded, and it is all (that is commercially successful) gaming (as opposed to simple virtual environments without gaming goals). The purely social and experiential interactions have no sales track record, and nobody would invest the money to create a high quality environment without any commercial prospects. There are no doubt many who would enjoy engaging in a virtual world modelled after Middle-earth strictly for their love of the place they have read about or seen on screen, and who would be content to have that world match as closely as possible the one they have imagined. Perhaps night after night as an Elf in Imladris telling stories, listening to others' stories and wandering the woods, might be engaging or even superior to a game. Thus we arrive at a project once called *Middle Earth Online*— a licensed virtual *world* based on Tolkien's books.

From *Middle-Earth Online* to *Lord of the Rings Online*

After years of suspended development, the project was taken over by the company (Turbine) that eventually released the game, and work resumed on 22 March 2005.[1] The title was changed to *Lord of the Rings Online: Shadows of Angmar* (hereafter *Shadows*). This title change alone is interesting because it shows a shift from attempting to more fully integrate the *story* of the books to an environment based in the *world* of the books. Rather than continuing to reference the entire story, the title now limits the scope of the game. It is also worth remembering that a lot of the sustainability models for MMORPGs rely on constant additions to content called "content updates" (free to existing players) and "expansion packs" (additions that cost money even for existing players) so limiting the scope from the beginning also has a practical implications for the future development of the product.[2]

Despite the large fan base for *The Lord of the Rings* (both books and films), a self-sustaining virtual environment must not only cater to hardcore fans (many of whom would not be interested in an online "adaptation"), but also to the masses. Take this excerpt from the "Developer Diary" by Chris Pierson on the Turbine website regarding the upcoming game:

> The biggest challenge with the Old Forest is that it has to feel big, but it can't actually *be* big, because no player actually wants to have to walk for days to get

---

[1] The property was under development by Sierra Online as early as 1998. Sierra's parent company, Vivendi Universal Games took over in 2001. Finally in 2003, the rights were transferred to Turbine. (Anon, 2007e)

[2] *Warcraft* released its first paid expansion pack, *Burning Crusade*, two years after launch though approximately eleven free content updates were made in those years. *EverQuest* has released thirteen paid expansion packs since 2000. (Anon, 2007b)

from Bucklebury to Bree. (Yes, you in the back, I know *you* do, but trust me, you're an exception to the rule.) (Pierson, 2005)

Pierson goes on to describe that the Old Forest as represented in-game is essentially a labyrinth to provide the user with a "lost" experience. It serves as an example of changes made to create something that "feels like" the books. In fact, this is not the story of the books at all, to say nothing of meeting Frodo in the Old Forest, or hoping to rescue Fellowship members from Old Willow. Instead, gamers can delight in the company of Tom Bombadil; (Pierson, 2005) this is not entirely unappealing, but it is not in keeping with the plot outlined in the books.

There are certainly signs that the game developers are attempting to do everything possible to preserve the feeling and the spirit of the books, at least outwardly. In another such diary, Chris Foster writes regarding "quests" (or objectives) in the game:

> Also, the quest is bestowed by an object found in the world, and not an NPC. Both mechanics have been used in other games, but are particularly critical to LOTRO: this is a game where slaughter without cause is an unacceptable motivation for adventure; and a world where the land yields secrets to the canny explorer. (Foster, 2005)[3]

I have separated the main question of this chapter into two parts, and briefly answer the first: can *Shadows* succeed as a project? Yes. There have been many games released under the Electronic Arts banner during the production and release of the film trilogy, which were tie-ins to the movies (sometimes voiced by the films' cast, and even film clips). These were highly successful, particularly *Battle for Middle-earth* (Electronic Arts, 2004), which received critical acclaim and was followed by a sequel in March 2006. Therefore, success is certainly possible.

In the same timeframe, another company released two games which were related to the films only by the source texts. Despite its attempt to capitalize on the popularity of the films, the company secured a license merely for games based on the printed texts rather than the films, denying it access to the actors, score, etc. However, these games had the freedom to explore elements from the books that the

---

[3] Non-Player Character (NPC) is a character that appears in the game but is played by the computer or a non-player human. *Lord of the Rings Online* is commonly referred to as LOTRO.

films did not, such as Tom Bombadil. These two games are *The Hobbit* (Vivendi Universal, 2003) and *Fellowship of the Ring* (Vivendi Universal, 2002). They did not succeed in the marketplace, hence the lack of a *Two Towers* or *Return of the King* title from this license. These are recent examples of the franchise as a whole both succeeding and failing as computer games. Thus, success is not certain.

Now to the rest of the question, assuming that an MMORPG based on Middle-earth *can* succeed, we now consider whether or not it *will*.

Will the *LotR* connection help Turbine sell games? Naturally it will give them the up-front advantage of persuading people to try their game. Copies will be sold; people will sign up: some did, even before release. For these types of products, however, the game will need to have "legs" to keep people coming and staying. No amount of invoking the words "Frodo" or "Bombadil" is likely to keep fans, rabid or casual, paying each month for the privilege. For example, the *Star Wars Galaxies* game (Sony Online Entertainment, 2002) has not been able to capitalize on the quite considerable inbuilt fan base of *Star Wars* fans in any way that matches the success of *Warcraft*.[4]

Sony Online Entertainment's *EverQuest* has had a long life since its March 1999 release, continuing to run into 2007, even though the playing population of that game is currently declining. This is evidenced by their recent merging of servers, which indicates the playing population per server was getting too low. Aside from drawing on the fantasy genre, *EverQuest* had no pre-existing lore, or built-in target audience, to appeal to customers. Also, *EverQuest* had no pre-existing lore to live up to. Blizzard Entertainment's *Warcraft* is another major industry success. Although it is still too new to discuss longevity, the playing population is over two million in North America alone (Anon, 2007f) and eight million worldwide. (Anon, 2005g) *Warcraft* does, in fact, have lore to rely upon, but not with the same widespread popular awareness as LotR. Apart from a number of games previously released by

---

[4] Although current statistics are unavailable, *Galaxies* was with 2.8% market share as of June 2006, at around 175,000 subscribers paying at most US$14.99 per month compared to *Warcraft*'s over 1 million at that time (also at US$15 per month), and *Galaxies* was trending downward while *Warcraft* now claims over two million U.S. active subscriptions, and 8.5 million worldwide. (Anon, 2007d)

Blizzard, there have also been many novels based in the world that are treated as "canon" for the content of the new game. (Anon, 2007c) However, as the same company produces the lore of this game as it did the others, it has always retained the rights for revision. The fan base seems to be forgiving of changes to the game lore, just as Tolkien fans accept fixes Tolkien made himself to different editions of *The Hobbit*, etc.

One key difference *Shadows* can take advantage of (and, similarly, suffer defeat at the hands of) is the fact that everyone knows the plot. *Warcraft* may have lore that some know, but this is nothing compared to those who know the story of Frodo and the Ring. You don't even need to have seen the movies in today's popular culture to know that, basically, Frodo and some friends against all odds take and destroy an evil ring. Even that is more than would be known about the evolution and direction of existing games such as *Warcraft* by the common consumer.

As players will not be playing characters they recognize from the books, no one can be a virtual Frodo, although one can be a virtual Hobbit in the Shire, and meet some form of the characters from the book. (Anon, 2005a) This is a clear disadvantage for *Shadows* when compared to the single player games which allow direct contact with, or control over, the beloved characters such as in the Vivendi Universal titles.

Virtual Consumer Society

Commercialization is inevitable with any online Middle-earth. So far we have looked at ways that the *world* may be altered in order to promote commercial success by making the *world* a game. On average, this is to be expected and is generally acceptable to the average consumer but there is always a danger in how far the company takes such commercialization. There has been some criticism and indeed open mockery of Sony Online Entertainment's commercialization of their product, *EverQuest*. In February 2005 they formed (and publicized) a partnership with the Pizza Hut delivery and takeaway chain in the United States, providing an *in game* command "/pizza" which would allow gamers to place orders for pizza delivery without having to leave the game. (Anon 2007a) Apart from the obvious break with role-playing ideals, it was widely recognized as a money-grabbing move by the software company. Even Blizzard Entertainment scoffed at it on April Fool's Day 2005 by advertising a (phoney) addition to *Warcraft* called "/panda" which gave players access to a fictional Chinese food delivery service called "Pandaren Xpress". (Anon, 2005f) One can assume that any inclusion of this kind of commercial venture in a Middle-earth game would be equally badly received.

We cannot consider a virtual Middle-earth game without commenting on role-playing. Role-playing is a form of gaming where participants assume the roles of characters in a story and attempt as a part of the gaming experience to behave accordingly. Table-top games such as *Dungeons & Dragons* have always contained elements of role playing, with the immersion level varying from group to group. Some merely depict actions in their roles, others speak as they think their characters would speak, and some groups dress and act out entire games in what is known as Live Action Role Playing (LARPing). In some cases, gamers advance in relation to how well they act their parts, regardless of advancing game goals. In the virtual world, there would be little point (given the current state of technologies) in dressing up, but many people enjoy speaking to other players in the game by playing a role. Some games designate special "servers" where participants who are particularly interested in role-playing can gather, so as not to be pulled out of the game by those who are not interested in role-playing at the same level. A virtual Middle-earth, however, may attract a larger number of these players. Imagine speaking as an Elf and telling stories, or sitting at a table in the Green Dragon in between working on your game progress. It would be essential for Turbine to provide support for people who wish to role-play through their gaming. As of July 2007, *Warcraft* was running approximately twenty-two such dedicated servers of 225, or about 9.8% of available servers for their U.S. and Oceania customers. The lore and background of its virtual world is less well known than that of Middle-earth, which should generate a higher level of role-playing interest.

Shadows has designed a few features specifically for these players. One small but effective design element is called "titles". Some titles such as "of Gondor" are given right from the start. Others are earned through deeds or actions in the game, such as "the Wary" (earned by reaching level five without being defeated), or "Pie-eating Champion" (I will let the reader imagine how this title is earned!). At any time the player may select any of their titles as the one they display to others in the world. Secondly, there is a music playing system that enables players in the world to "play music" on virtual instruments. The first content update adds even greater functionality (more scales, more instruments, and the ability to compose offline!). These elements are a great start in supporting more casual, role-playing interactions with the game than just questing and levelling.

Success for such an endeavour as Turbine's will depend largely on the quality of their game-play (entirely invented, and unrelated to the plot of *LotR*), and how far they take steps to control commercialization. One can imagine fee structures based on extorting hardcore fans: pay more to go here, pay more to see that, buy the soundtrack (yes, games market their soundtracks), which could alienate players, regardless of their affinity for the books and/or films. There are already examples of games that charge above their regular monthly fee to provide extended community services, for example Sony Online Entertainment's *EverQuest II*. (Anon, 2005b) So far, no obvious gimmicks have arisen, and prior to release Turbine even made an offer to dedicated fans where, for a fixed price of approximately US$100, subscribers could forgo the monthly fee for the life of the game.

It would seem that based on the research of Project Massive, people who commit to play MMORPGs for a long time, play with (or against) each other, rather than the characters in the game. For example, nobody has continued to play *EverQuest* for seven years because he/she loves fighting a particular dragon over and over again. *Shadows* can rely on the following of the book to attract some people at the start, but that alone will not keep them paying monthly. It will need to rely on its novel features and its merits as a good game if it is to take its place among long-standing, or even recent, grand champions of the genre, such as *EverQuest* and *World of Warcraft*.

Crucial Elements for a Successful Online Virtual Middle-earth

Having reached these conclusions, what kinds of things *would* keep people playing? The following possibilities are strictly speculative, and should *not* be confused with information about the Turbine creation. They are concepts which centre around Tolkien's *world* and the possibilities this *world* provides, and do not include any general game features that other games could capitalize on.

One concept would be to approach the story and *world* from the side of evil. Perhaps this is a prospect for the *Shadows* game in some future expansion (allowing players to play Orcs, etc.), although the current statement rules it out. (Anon, 2005b) This allows a level of familiarity with much less "baggage", since Tolkien did not describe enemy movements in the same detail as those of the free people. This is one way to portray the world without the burden of keeping all the plot elements intact. Although the current game does allow some "control" of the monsters, it is hard to regard this as "playing evil".

A particularly daunting task could be to embrace the story in full. This could be one in a number of ways, such as allowing the story to take place in "real time" over the course of a year, where players engage indirectly (or even directly, possibly based on game skills) in assisting the plotline. There is some involvement included in *Shadows*, but the timeline is not linked to time but to player progress. (Anon, 2005i) The idea would be to start by creating the virtual world, placing all the known characters in the right locations at the right times, and allowing the rest of the world to flow around it. "World changing events" such as those that might be imagined for *Shadows*, such as the partial destruction of Helm's Deep, have only recently been included in such large-scale games as *Warcraft*. For example, the "Gates of Ahn'Qiraj" event, which will only happen once per server, is triggered by the players themselves when they achieve a certain goal. The developers of *Shadows* have apparently implemented a variant of this gaming element from the start called "layered instancing". (Anon, 2005c)

Apart from the gaming experience under development, there are other key aspects to a healthy gaming environment. Much of the work of Project Massive (including one survey that received over 1300 respondents) examined these aspects of MMORPGs. (Seay et al, 2004) A game culture has to be supported by tools. Guild creation, for example, is an essential mechanism for players coming together and working together (or competing against each other). These are called "Fellowships" in *Shadows*. (Anon, 2005d) Real-time communications, even voice communication, all need to be technically supported. Collaborative tools are not game elements *per se*, but tools to facilitate interaction among players which, hopefully, have them returning to play with their friends. Finding ways to simplify social networking is also essential in building and maintaining a community. Again, this will be the key to the success of *Shadows*, but has little or nothing to do with Tolkien.

Additionally, many current MMORPGs support Player Versus Player (PVP) gaming where human competitors may battle each other. *Warcraft*, *EverQuest II* and other games support and encourage such gaming styles which appeal to a large segment of players. *Warcraft* servers which primarily support PVP play are currently 107 of 225. Although the remaining servers also have many PVP activities, they are more controlled. The developers of *Shadows* do not intend to support that primary style of game-play. (Anon, 2005e)

The conclusion is that *Shadows* can only envisage long term commercial success based on elements totally unrelated to Tolkien. It could be the parallel of Peter Jackson's films regarded as a stunning achievement by the public, with fewer detractors than fans, or it could be the parallel of the widely panned animated cartoons. You can make a good work based on Tolkien; you can also make a bad work based on Tolkien. The rich background and fan base give an advantage to the *Shadows* creators over any new random MMORPG, similar to but greater than the advantage *Warcraft* had with gamers at the start. But in neither case is that enough to succeed.

So far there are very promising elements, such as the music system, and the fact that new players are immediately introduced to recognizable terrors (Ring Wraiths, Cave Trolls, etc., depending on their race selection) that help to draw a new player in the game. Not having major server issues on the first days of release has also helped Turbine to avoid some of the player unrest generated by *Warcraft* when their server capacity seemed unable to withstand the demand following their launch.

Having relegated Tolkien's works to a minor role in the *long term* success or failure of *Shadows*, a question remains about the final integrity of the original work when such commercialization is made from the texts. It is unlikely that there will be any lasting tarnish of the original works by *Shadows*, just as the animated films or early computer games have not tarnished the name of *LotR*.

As noble as is the thought that such expansion of the canon without commercialization can happen, it is not capitalization in and of itself that demerits the art form. I would be hard pressed to believe that Peter Jackson could be honestly or fairly criticized for "cashing in" on *LotR* just because he made a lot of money from his movies, and not because he had a genuine *vision* of the world.

Will others attempt to cash in on his and Tolkien's success? Yes! Will *Shadows* be simply a cash-in opportunity, or the result of labours by individuals dedicated to the source material as were the films? That remains to be seen.

Bibliography

Anon (2005a), "The Lord of the Rings Online FAQ" 29 September: http://lotro.turbine.com/?page_id=56#gameplayquestions20

Anon (2005b), "The Lord of the Rings Online FAQ" 29 September: http://lotro.turbine.com/?page_id=56#gameplayquestions27

Anon (2005c), "The Lord of the Rings Online FAQ" 29 September: http://lotro.turbine.com/?page_id=56#gameplayquestions38

Anon (2005d), "The Lord of the Rings Online FAQ" 29 September: http://lotro.turbine.com/?page_id=56#gameplayquestions33

Anon (2005e), "The Lord of the Rings Online FAQ" 29 September: http://lotro.turbine.com/?page_id=56#gameplayquestions30

Anon (2005f), "Too Lazy to Get up and Use the Phone? Pandaren Express" 29 September: http://www.worldofwarcraft.com/info/underdev/pandaren-xpress.html

Anon (2005g), "Turbine Acquires License from Tolkien Enterprises and Becomes the Exclusive Online Worlds Publisher" (media release) 22 March: http://lotro.turbine.com/index.php?page_id=20&pagebuilder[module]=article&pagebuilder[display_item]=4

Anon (2005h), "World of Warcraft® Surpasses Five Million Customers Worldwide" (media release) 19 December: http://www.blizzard.com/press/051219.shtml

Anon (2005i), 29 September: http://lotro.turbine.com/?page_id=56#adventuringinmiddleearth24

Anon (2007a), "EverQuest II" in *Wikipedia*:
http://en.wikipedia.org/wiki/EverQuest_II

Anon (2007b), "EverQuest" in *Wikipedia*:
http://en.wikipedia.org/wiki/Everquest#EverQuest_expansions

Anon (2007c), "History of Warcraft": http://worldofwarcraft.com/info/story/

Anon (2007d), "MMOGCHART.COM": http://www.mmogchart.com/

Anon (2007e), "The Lord of the Rings Online: Shadows of Angmar" in *Wikipedia*:
http://en.wikipedia.org/wiki/The_Lord_of_the_Rings_Online:_Shadows_of_An
gmar

Anon (2007f), "World of Warcraft Surpasses 8 Million Subscribers Worldwide" (media release) 1 July: http://www.blizzard.com/press/070111.shtml

Foster, Chris (2005), "Precious Machinery" 9 September:
http://lotro.turbine.com/index.php?page_id=101

Pierson, Chris (2005), "By Water, Wood and Hill" 29 September:
http://lotro.turbine.com/?page_id=104

Seay, A. Fleming, William J. Jerome, Kevin Sang Lee, Robert E. Kraut (2004), "Project Massive: A Study of Online Gaming Communities" in *Proceedings of Conference on Human Factors in Computing Systems, CHI 2004*, Vienna, pp. 1421-1424

CONCLUSIONS

23

A Road to Erewhon
Waiting for the King to Return

Nataliya Oryshchuk

Dear readers,

I thought it would be unforgivable to conceal from you a very interesting correspondence which I have been having over the last two years with an old acquaintance, a certain Hobbit from the Shire. I contacted him in 2005, hoping to obtain an essay from a representative of Middle-earth's indigenous population. The essay, however, has never been written. My friend[1] was a little scared by a possible association with the Dark Art of Cultural Studies (as he called it). An exciting discussion ensued, a reprint of which I now bring to your attention.

15 October 20xx (of X Age)

Dear D,

It's been a long time since I last heard from you—hope you are doing well.

I am co-editing a collection of essays entitled How We Became Middle-earth. *Don't be surprised, it is devoted to That Very Novel (very well familiar to you) and its recent film adaptation, which was shot here in New Zealand. Since this film has become very popular all around the Big World, everyone has started calling New Zealand "Middle-earth". I know this may sound ridiculous to you, but that is how things are here. And now we are putting together a collection of*

---

[1] My friend preferred to remain anonymous. He keeps an old Hobbit tradition of showing himself to the Big World as little as possible.

academic essays, taking a Cultural Studies approach. (Have you heard of Jean Baudrillard, for instance? He is French, and his books are very fashionable now.)

I just thought it would be absolutely wonderful to have your essay included in this collection. You could send me some pictures as well, if you happen to have suitable ones. (It's very difficult to get a picture for publication in the Big World—there are always some nasty copyright owners about.)

Looking forward to hearing from you.

Yours, etc.

~

23 October 20xx

Dear Nataliya,

Thank you for your letter. It was very nice to hear from you[....]

As for the collection—I don't think I can do anything useful for it. I haven't seen this thing you call a "film adaptation" and have no idea about Cultural Studies or that Frenchman you mentioned. I asked my friends and neighbours but none here have ever met or even heard of him, let alone read his books.

It's very strange that some other land wants to be the Shire—well, we are all proud, of course, but I can't imagine how there can be two identical Shires. Surely, if one of them is real, then the other one is not? Does New Zealand want to be the one that is not real? Or would they prefer that our Shire becomes a non-real Shire? Hmm, it's all very confusing.

Please tell me what you think about it all. Does New Zealand truly resemble our Hobbiton that much? I can't say for myself because, as you know, I've never been to New Zealand but you've visited the Shire so you must be able to compare.

Thank you again[....]

P.S. I'll ask my friend the painter whether he has any paintings of our Shire that we can send you for your book. I can't promise much, however, since he is working terribly slowly and concentrates on the details far too much. For instance, he spent the last two years painting a single leaf. But everyone says it looks absolutely perfect—just like a real one.

~

3 November, 20xx

Dear D,

[....] You say that you are not familiar with Cultural Studies but, essentially, it is very much about "real" and "unreal" things. Frankly speaking, it isn't that much about "real" but mainly about "unreal" or—even worse—"hyperreal" things, which are particularly nasty. (That Frenchman Baudrillard, whom I mentioned before, had lots to say about them).

If I analyze the text of your last letter using a linguistic approach (this is the way you have to name things if you want to sound like a respected academic!), in other words—if I count the occurrences of the word "real" in your letter, I would say that it is a typical piece of Cultural Studies writing. And I hope this fact will convince you that you are actually capable of contributing to a Cultural Studies collection. For instance, if you could write more about your vision of the "real" and "unreal" Shire, it would be exactly what we'd like to see. (My co-editor Adam Lam—I will introduce him to you one day! —would be especially delighted, as he loves Cultural Studies).

Best regards, [...]

--

22 November, 20xx

Dear Nataliya,

[....] What you are saying about Cultural Studies is very interesting indeed. But, still, I feel it sounds a bit like dealing with magic (and maybe even the darker side of it) and I'm neither very good at that nor much willing to do it. I imagine Cultural Studies is somehow related to seeing the unseen world behind things and lands; seeing something invisible or something so powerful and evil that only the very wise and courageous can face it. You have certainly heard about the magic of the ancient world, such as the Palantiri (nowadays many consider them to be a legend, but I believe them to be real). I think a Cultural Studies scholar plays with powers similar to those of a Palantír, seeing images of different lands and times and trying to make sense of them. But, whilst trying to solve mysteries, he could encounter deeper mysteries yet. He would be trying hard to see something-else-behind-something-else-that-is-not-there, and his road would be getting darker and darker. This is a perilous journey. That is why, despite having famous travellers amongst my ancestors, I would not like to go on it. If one is looking at a green meadow or a swift stream and wondering whether or not it is real (or how other people imagine them or for how much this image can be sold), one becomes very sad and sick at heart. I believe it is better to face a dragon (which I've never really done, I must confess!) than to embark on a quest for those unreal realities.

You also mentioned the word "hyperreal", which sounded very suspicious. Is it about the Dark Arts, which are known to be practised by some of the Big Folk? [...]

Best, [...]

~

1 December, 20xx

Dear D,

[....] I understand your concern about Dark Arts scholars but believe me there are no such people among Cultural Studies academics (well, not many of them, anyway). It's also true that the Big World nowadays has become corrupted and transformed by the Palantiri-like power which we call "the media". It keeps showing us images and telling us stories which it wants us to believe, and we are growing more and more dependent on it. Media is manipulating us in exactly the way that the Palantiri did. Sometimes it seems that the One Ring has come back to life and is trying "to bring them all and in the darkness bind them" again... As you can see, this power has already duplicated the Shire, and we have to investigate it and write a book about it—otherwise there will be even greater confusion regarding the identity of Middle-earth. So we have to deal with Cultural Studies to explore things, whether we like it or not.

The Cultural Studies people are not necessarily corrupted by these dangerous powers; they are just trying to understand them. You are right: there is a bit of wizardry in the whole thing and the Cultural Studies journey can be truly dangerous for some. It happens that some scholars can't see the green meadow any longer—they can only perceive the Unseen Powers and Illusions. Sometimes they even start to believe that the green meadow has never existed and they dwell only on the idea of the Dark Wizard whose Charms created the Illusion. They cannot see the beauty or harmony any longer, cannot laugh or sing—they just keep staring at the Emptiness they see behind every living thing.

To explain myself more clearly, I need to tell you the story of the Black Square. Once upon a time (a hundred years ago, to be precise) there was a painter called Kazimir Malevich. He created many strange and wonderful pictures, which were very much unlike everything painted before. His most famous painting was called The Black Square, and, indeed, a black square it was and nothing but that. When first exhibiting his work in one Russian city (Russia being a land somewhat similar to Rohan, as we discussed the other day), Malevich put his Square in the upper corner of the room, where the Icon (the image of God) had previously been placed. And he said thus to people of the Big World: God is dead. The Author is dead. The King will never return. What is now looking down at you from the Icon—is the blackness and nothingness of Sauron's Eye. And many people believed because they felt the growing influence of the Unseen Dark Power...

Did you like my story? I did my best to narrate it in an Epic style that is to your liking. Anyway, since the Black Square was raised, we have been living in a world where Cultural Studies is a necessary instrument for exploring our reality. Oh, here we are, coming back to the definition of "reality". I suspect it will lead us back to the nothingness of the Black Square, so we'd better move in the opposite direction. Forgive me, dear D, for upsetting you with my story. But the good news is that, now, people are trying to turn away from Sauron's Eye and they are waiting for the King to return. That is why they are becoming interested in the history of the Shire and Middle-earth. And that's why we started a collection! [....]

Yours, [...]

--

12 December, 20xx

Dear Nataliya,

Thank you for your long letter. To tell you the truth, I read it a couple of times to some of my friends and relatives—especially the story of the Black Square. T even wanted to look at that painting but we convinced him not to. Firstly, he'd have to go to the Big World for it (of course, it is possible to travel to Gondor's great Library but I don't think they'd keep such things there) and, secondly, why should he look into Sauron's Eye? It is a great temptation and many Men have fallen because of it...

No, we don't want to see Malevich's painting. I hope I'm not offending you by saying this. I'm sure you will understand our feelings—we don't want to play with dark and dangerous things again. All journeys are good, except the journey to Nowhere.

Please accept my warmest [...]

~

3 January, 20xx

Dear D,

Sorry for not replying earlier—we have just celebrated the coming of the new year, which is traditionally a very busy time for us.

I won't press you any further into writing an essay for our collection, if you don't feel like it. But it's very interesting that you mentioned the journey to Nowhere in your previous letter. Believe it or not, we have a place here in New Zealand (not very far from the city where I live) called Erewhon, which is "Nowhere" if you read it backwards. It bears this strange name in honour of one Samuel Butler, a writer who lived there more than one hundred years ago. He wrote a novel called Erewhon, meaning the strange "never-to-be" place. Actually, it was a satire of his own land and society but that doesn't really matter now. He was inspired to write the book by his travels around New Zealand, in which he saw a land of hidden realities; the "nowhere" of the "real" world.

I'm absolutely sure that the area of mountains and plains around New Zealand's Erewhon does have some special magic qualities. My dear D, if you ever travel to the Big World, I would very much like you to visit this place and give me your opinion of it. Believe or not, the Erewhon I'm talking about has now become very popular here, as... Edoras! Yes, I mean that semi-mythical Golden Hall of Rohan's lords, of which so many stories are still told in the Shire. It has happened because of that film adaptation I told you about in one of my October letters. And though I also said that the media (like the Palantiri) can be blamed for much of the confusion nowadays, I must agree that it gave people from the Big World an opportunity to escape from the Black Square of Nowhere into Erewhon. The place became part of a famous destination for tourists; a part of the thing which people in Cultural Studies (and elsewhere) call "consumerism" or "commercialization". The word itself belongs to the Dark Side of contemporary wizardry and it has a very distinctive aura of Nowhere about it. But listen to what I discovered: there is Hope, too. No matter how many gold pieces these people are giving for the chance to enter that mythical land, they are on their own quest for the Dream. This Dream is their personal and much-cherished possession which brings with it the great joy of creation—however real, non-real or hyperreal it may be. And, as long as they follow *this quest, their path will never lead to the emptiness and blackness of Nowhere. Their road to Erewhon goes ever on and on...*

Postscript

My friend Hobbit and I wish to give credit and pay our respects to the following people, for giving us food for thought and inspiration:

Baudrillard, Jean (2001), *Selected Writings* 2nd ed., ed. Mark Poster, Polity, Cambridge

Jackson, Peter (dir., 2002), *The Fellowship of the Ring: Extended Version*

Jackson, Peter (dir., 2003), *The Two Towers: Special Extended Version*

Jackson, Peter (dir., 2004), *The Return of the King: Special Extended Version*

Raby, Peter (1991), *Samuel Butler: A Biography*, Hogarth, London

Simmons, W. Sherwin (1981), *Kazimir Malevich's* Black Square *and the Genesis of Suprematism 1907-1915*, Garland Pub, New York

Tolkien, J.R.R. (1994), "On Fairy-Stories" in Christopher Tolkien (ed.), *The Monsters and the Critics and Other Essays*, Houghton Mifflin Company, Boston

Tolkien, J.R.R. (1995), *The Lord of the Rings*, HarperCollins, London

Tolstaya, Tatyana (2002), "Kvadrat" in *Izium: Otbornoe*, Podkova, Moskva

Remains of a filmic civilization.
(photo by Bill J. Jerome)

24

A Journey to Erewhon or a Journey to Nowhere?

Adam Lam

As SAMUEL BUTLER playfully claimed in his famous novel *Erewhon: Or Over the Range*, first published in 1872, the rural areas and mountain ranges in New Zealand (or perhaps one should say, New Zealand as a whole) really was Nowhere on the world map, in the nineteenth century.[1] In commemoration of Butler, the little rural village where he once lived has been named Erewhon, ever since. Contemporary New Zealand has now made a significant move by naming itself "Middle-earth", in the age of digital technology and globalization. Today's Middle-earth country is both parallel and very different from Erewhon: parallel because both identities are based on locations that originated in the literary world; very different because, whilst his rural village was the site which inspired Butler's novel, New Zealand had literally nothing to do with J.R.R. Tolkien's mythical creation. One thing both names surely share is that they each provide an identity for a place we do not otherwise know how to name; in an artistic, yet financially very rewarding, way. If there is a different title we can think of for this collection of essays, on the cultural implications of Peter Jackson's adaptation of Tolkien's *The Lord of the Rings*, it must be "How We Name Ourselves in the Age of Digital Technology and Globalization".

---

[1] Butler created the novel's title—which is also the main setting of the story *Erewhon*—by spelling "nowhere" backwards (with the exception of the "wh", which he took as a single phonetic unit and, thus, did not reverse it).

Postcolonial Fellowship of the Ring

New Zealand has a relatively short history of more or less 170 years, although the history of Aotearoa is slightly longer.[2] It was not (or, at least, not *only*) the triumphant England tour of the All Black rugby team in the early twentieth century that made New Zealand known to many in the United Kingdom and some in Europe. Rather, it was telegraph news coverage (the earliest form of transcontinental, if not yet global, mass media) that allowed a tiny nation—or, to be more precise, a territory under the British Crown's governance with relatively vast land but a very low population—to occupy an international spot. While New Zealand was very much recognized by most British and other Commonwealth citizens as a "rugby nation"—thanks, first, to telegraphic technology and, later, film newsreels and live television coverage—most of the rest of the world only discovered that New Zealand *was* a country (rather than a state of Australia) with the release of Jane Campion's 1993 film, *The Piano*.

Not long after the country became widely known as New Zealand or, to borrow Benedict Anderson's term, New Zealand was realized as an "imagined community", (Anderson, 1983) thanks to global media and Campion's film, the identity of the country experienced a second twist. At the beginning of the twenty-first century, it became a mythical, hyperreal location of the pseudo-medieval; this time, through the popularity and box office success of Peter Jackson's blockbuster adaptation of *LotR*. On one hand, the very cold reception Prince Charles received on his most recent visit to New Zealand and Australia, in March 2005, further confirmed the end of a historical era in which New Zealand had, for years, identified itself as a loyal subject of the British Empire. In the age of global economy (which triggered a series of global this and global that, including global culture), New Zealand began to feel an ever stronger urge for a national identity, with which to brand and market itself to the world, as well as to curb the postcolonial anxiety

---

[2] A Declaration of the Independence of New Zealand in 1935 and Treaty of Waitangi signed in 1840 indicated the existence of New Zealand as political entity in the modern sense of nation, whereas the first Maori settlement in Aotearoa can be dated as early as AD800-1300. I use "slightly longer" to refer Maori settlement because, compared to human history throughout the world, the roughly 1,200 year human inhabitation of Aotearoa is still relatively short.

caused by its diminishing affiliation with the British Empire. Ironically enough, though, New Zealand could not find anything better than an *imagined* world (created by an *English* writer, in the post-war era) in its keen search for a new identity, capable of keeping pace with the age of the Internet, transnational capitalism and globalization.

In the new historical era, like any other consumer goods produced for a global market, films are not only aided but also fundamentally changed by digital technology and the Internet. Indeed, many chapters in this collection discuss the way audiences and fans used Internet media to influence the making of the *LotR* films and, no doubt, shared their interpretations of the literary and cinematic versions of the tale. Nowadays, products are shipped further than ever before and the origin of manufacturing countries is progressively more confused by the operations of transnational enterprises and the trans-border division of labour. As a result, some people are upset by a (perceived) loss of their traditional national pride, whereas others use the opportunity to proclaim a more significant international status for economic, political and psychological benefits. The majority of New Zealanders seem to belong to the latter. New Zealanders were not only proud to claim Jackson's adaptations for Hollywood's New Line Cinema as "New Zealand films" but also did not hesitate to change the name of the country to "Middle-earth". In addition, the names of many other cities, towns and places in the country were "Middle-earthized", accordingly. Amongst all of this, as Lisa Wong points out in her chapter in this book, New Zealand is more than happy to be the "best supporting country" in a global film market dominated by Hollywood.

Nonetheless, the irony remains because Middle-earth is arguably an even more English *state* than England itself is, today—Shire, the core of Middle-earth is Tolkien's ideal (and idealized) England. Therefore, the making of *LotR* films was a golden opportunity for New Zealand to obtain a postmodern, postcolonial identity that aided its economic survival in a global market, on one hand, and compensated for the ("mainstream", Pakeha) psychological break from Anglo-Saxon tradition, on the other. The *LotR* thus became the stone that killed two birds and New Zealand now happily enjoys being a member of two Fellowships at once. There is, however, another important implication: one must be a team player in order to be a valuable member of any fellowship. By making the *LotR* films a successful artwork and commodity at the same time, New Zealand pays significant subscriptions for its Fellowship of Hollywood filmmaking and the Fellowship of the British history of literature and art.

While the ultimate goal of Tolkien's Fellowship of the Ring is to finally destroy the Ring, the Fellowships that New Zealand has managed to squeeze into (through the *LotR* films) really mean to rule the world. They almost rule it already, through two very powerful instruments: media (especially digital and other electronic media) and global trade—which we may nickname the Two Towers and which are both landmarks of our postmodern world; Black Riders that uproot all cultural heritages, in order to enable the full span of consumerism.

A World Consumed by Two Towers

The media and global trade consume our world in many ways, most significantly in the way they burn out natural resources (as we can see in scenes from *LotR*), but provide us with an illusion of a cleaner, greener world while the pure nature has already been irreversibly damaged by industrialization. It is all too common to see automobile companies advertising their latest models as environmentally friendly, in order to sell more cars to the ever increasing number of automobile owners. However, this requires greater consumption of natural resources to manufacture the vehicles, in the first place, and then to drive them. In the case of using *LotR* films to promote New Zealand, we see a successful story of inviting overseas visitors to consume the country as a tourist destination. Inspired by Lisa Wong's paper, while I was at Auckland International Airport waiting for my transit to Hong Kong on 30 May 2004, I took the opportunity presented by the meeting of two Air New Zealand jets. With my digital camera, I caught the "Kodak moment" (though on a Sony Memory Stick, rather than on Kodak Film) of a taxiing Boeing 747 passing a stationary 767, each painted with characters from *LotR* and the airline's slogan: "Airline to Middle-earth".

Many chapters in Section One of this book discuss consumerism and New Zealand as a tourist destination. What I would like to share with the reader is the other end of consumerism—namely, the consumption of spaces in New Zealand by postmodern images. I was very enthusiastic, from the moment I took it, to use the aforementioned photo for the cover of this collection. It was a photo taken by me in a public space, consisting of the runway, terminal and transit lounge of Auckland International Airport. While New Zealand taxpayers are, collectively, the dominant shareholder of Air New Zealand, ratepayers in the Greater Auckland Area are the airport's key owners. When this taken-for-granted personal photo of mine—featuring Air New Zealand aircrafts in a *public* New Zealand space—was sent to Air New Zealand by Walking Tree Publishers, requesting consent for it to be used, Air New Zealand agreed willingly *but* advised the publisher to double check with New Line Cinema. New Line Cinema replied with disapproval.

I am not disputing New Line Cinema's legal right to make this decision or their perfectly legitimate concern about the critical nature of an academic book. Instead of challenging New Line Cinema's legal right to do what they did, I am concerned with the impact of their *having* that right. Amongst intellectual property rights, copyright is believed to be the key legal establishment that led to today's prosperity in the capitalist, market-economic world. While this right is vigorously protected by legislation in Western countries, it is a value system which is also *forcibly* introduced to many other countries in the world, regardless of whether such a principle is, in fact, against these countries' cultural traditions. When it comes to intellectual property rights, there is no room for mutual cultural respect. In order to protect the capitalist foundational principle, multiculturalism can be mercilessly flushed down the toilet.

I do not think that a truly multicultural society has ever existed, nor do I believe that multiculturalism is ideal. As seen in the intellectual property issue, so-called multiculturalism is only feasible under the Western hegemony of capitalism. As a matter of fact, the very activity of consumption (due to which, today's market economy is able to grow consistently) has become an invitation to colonization. By consuming the image of the *LotR* from New Line Cinema, the state-owned airline of New Zealand actually forsook its authority over its own aircrafts. Even worse, the Air New Zealand aircraft became "combat jets" for the postmodern media force (under New Line Cinema's command, in this case), conquering and colonizing the world, as they passed through or landed in each place. In hindsight, I really want to celebrate the fact that I did not purchase any of the *LotR* memorabilia—especially the "jewellery" items—that so tempted me, from time to time. Had I bought and worn them, I might well have run the risk of not being able to claim my body as my own, anymore! But, hang on, what about all of those brand names the companies forcibly print onto almost all of the clothing we wear today? Do we risk being sued by transnational enterprise giants, such as DKNY or FCUK, for publishing photos of ourselves and others, wearing their T-shirts, without their prior permission? This might sound ridiculous, yet it is a real possibility, given the direction that the capitalist fundamental principle of intellectual property rights seems to be leading us in. This new form of colonization, aided by legislation to protect the fundamental capitalist principle of intellectual property rights, is not only taking our land and space but could also take our bodies (literally).

Where Does the King Return to?

LotR films created a "new" kingdom—New Zealand/Middle-earth—for the King to return to. In light of Baudrillard's elaboration of how Disneyland Parks function in postmodern hyperreal signification, Lisa Wong's chapter in this collection argues that New Zealand (and, arguably, all other contemporary tourist destinations) has not only become a giant theme park but also achieved a new identity. (Baudrillard, 1988: 166; 2003) Following this argument, be that identity called Middle-earth or Post-New Zealand, it is a "purified and simplified" cultural construct out of, and at the same time disappearing *into*, the integral "real" New Zealand.

Today the "integral truth" of New Zealand, generated by the combined power of tourism and electronic media, is both widespread and highly influential on our mindset and, thus, our perception of and approach to the contemporary world. We can see an example of this in the simulated courtroom, complete with an actor resembling Michael Jackson (for the purpose of telecasting, in 2005), which created yet another "tourist spot". This time it was a virtual location tour, which allowed millions of television audiences around the world to experience Michael Jackson's high profile paedophilia trial, in the United States.

When studying the idea of nationalism, Benedict Anderson described modern nationhood as an "imagined community". New Zealand's search (through fantasy literature) for a postmodern identity, in the age of globalization, provides a good footnote to Anderson's explanation. More importantly, while this imagined community may no longer be the power that binds together a group of people, it is *still* intended to distinguish one group of people from the rest. The case of *LotR* and New Zealand further surprises us by showing how crucial the natural environment is, in aiding people's imagination. The films turn a real nation into a *simulacrum*; the television coverage of Michael Jackson's court case, on other hand, reveals the power of *simulated* reality, both in Baudrillard's terms. (Baudrillard, 1994: passim)

Many chapters in this collection touch on the issue of the return of the King; whether this "King" is seen as a Christian symbol, a moral system, an ideal leader or a pastoral, eco-balanced environment. As in Tolkien's novel and Peter Jackson's films, the King and his heir have always been there; thus, these ideals of "King" have never disappeared from our mentality, even in the postmodern world. The question, however, is where does the King return to? When fundamental capitalist principles (including, but not limited to, intellectual property) have uprooted all of our cultural, religious and artistic traditions, the King can still be crowned but, in reality, he has been left without land or people to rule. While national borders might be clearly marked and countries like New Zealand widely known, national cultures and traditions have long since disappeared into global culture. The kingdom has become hyperreal. Likewise, the King can merely remain a *sign* of hope.

What the *LotR* films provide for audiences is not a journey to Middle-earth, to New Zealand or to Erewhon but a journey to Nowhere.

Bibliography

Anderson, Benedict (1983), *Imagined Communities: Reflections on the Origin and Spread of Nationalism*, Verso, London

Baudrillard, Jean (1988), *Selected Writings*, trans. Mark Poster, Polity Press, Oxford (UK)

Baudrillard, Jean (1994), *Simulacra and Simulation*, trans. Sheila Faria Claser, University of Michigan Press, Ann Arbor

Baudrillard, Jean (2003), "Disneyworld Company":
   http://www.uta.edu/english/apt/collab/texts/disneyworld.html

Butler, Samuel (1872), *Erewhon: Or Over the Range*, Trübner & Co., London

Mordor, where the Ring is to be destroyed.
(photo by Bill J. Jerome)

INDEX
(excluding thematic topics, and entries in the book's bibliographies)

Adamson, Andrew 5, 49, 69, 113, 169
Adventures of Priscilla viii
Age of Empires 378
Aguirre 109n
Alice's Adventures in Wonderland 294
Althusser, Louis 204
Amon Hen 162, 166
Anders, Allison 87
Anderson, Benedict 416, 420-1
Anduin River 92, 93, 156, 160, 163
Angmar 219, 230, 395 – see also *Shadows of Angmar*
Aragorn 30, 45, 54, 67-8, 79, 135, 137, 139-41, 156, 174, 192, 200, 200n, 201-2, 206-10, 223, 231-4, 236, 253, 257, 281, 285, 298, 300, 302-3, 316, 318-9, 321, 323, 350, 375, 377, 380.
Arathorn 207
Argonath 160, 162-3, 216
Aristotle 157, 260, 283
Armstrong, Gillian 142
Arnor 207
Arthur, King 14, 129, 158, 170
Arvendui 209
Arwen 91, 139-41, 160, 230, 232-4, 244-51, 253, 285, 302
Aslan 170
Astin, Sean 42, 95, 155, 343n
Attenborough, Richard 131
Austen, Jane 111

Bag End 78, 164, 176, 227
Bainbridge, Anthony, xii
Bakshi, Ralph 12, 110

Balin 216, 235
Balrog 122, 160, 235, 377
Barad Dûr 78
Barrow-wights 375
Battle for Middle Earth 373, 378-80, 396
Baudrillard, Jean x, 87-8, 90, 92-3, 101-2, 385, 408-9, 420-1
Berethor 377
Bergman, Ingmar, 263-4
Big Country 172
Bilbo Baggins 7, 23, 58, 149, 153, 164, 172, 234, 259-60, 276, 291, 297-8, 304, 375
Black Gates 200n
Blade Runner 331n
Bloom, Orlando 23, 380
Bombadil – see Tom Bombadil
Boorman, John 151-2, 157-8
Boromir 151, 231, 257, 302
Bourdieu, Pierre 130
Boyd, Billy 23, 77, 81, 81n, 85, 218, 336, 343n
Boyens, Phillippa 42, 157, 159, 284n
Braindead 49
Bram Stoker's Dracula 108
Brando, Marlon viii
Braveheart 52
Bree 151, 396
Brego 223
Brodie, Ian 69, 69n, 90, 92, 218, 218n, 223
Brophy, Jed 80
Bruinen Ford 93, 160, 160n, 247
Bucklebury 396
Butler, Samuel 412, 415, 415n

Cameron, James 108n
Campbell, Joseph 229-31, 234, 242, 300
Campbell, Martin viii
Campion, Jane vii, x, xi, xiv, xv, xvi(n), xvii, 5, 109
Camus, Albert xviii, 25, 257-61, 263-4
Capra, Frank 277-278, 278n, 279
Caradhras 75, 166, 166n
Caras Galadhon 156
Caro, Niki 49, 131
Carroll, Lewis 294
Charlie's Angels 157
Chetwood Forest 92
Chronicles of Narnia (*Lion, Witch & Wardrobe*) 5, 49, 59, 69, 152, 169-70, 180
Close Combat 165
Conan Doyle, Arthur ix
Coppola, Francis 108
Cormack, Danielle viii
Coronation Street 111
Crash 109n
Cronenberg, David 109n
Cruise, Tom 102
Cunningham, Carol xi

Dahl, Roald 295
Dante 273
Darabont, Frank 281
Deagol 81
Deleuze, Gilles xii
Denethor 76, 141, 201, 236, 302, 316
Dersu Uzala 162
DeSanto, Tom 43
Dickens, Charles 294, 296, 296n
Dimrill Stair 166n
Disneyland x, 87-8, 89n, 98, 100, 420-1
Dr Seuss 295
Dr Who 391
Dune 157-8

Dúnedain 207
Durkheim, Emile 209
Dwarves ix, 132-3, 141, 149, 166n, 170, 175, 239, 258, 282, 299

Eärendil 264
Eco, Umberto, x, 164
Edoras 47, 67, 67n, 68n, 91, 175, 221, 412
Elendil 205, 207, 302
Elessar 207
Elladan 234
Elliot, Stephan viii
Elrohir 234
Elrond (inc. Council of) 135, 140-1, 149, 159n, 207, 233-4, 249n, 251, 253, 262, 298, 302, 314, 361
Elves 4, 23-4, 37, 41, 80, 97, 133, 135-6, 141, 156, 169-70, 198, 230, 232-4, 239, 240-3, 247, 249, 252, 257, 273, 284, 312, 320, 395, 399
Elvish (language) vii, 59, 79, 230, 232
Emyn Muil 282, 339
Ents 84, 138, 175, 180-1, 190, 192, 230
Éomer 95, 207, 236
Éowyn 67, 69, 71, 139-40, 200, 208, 230, 318, 321
Erestor 80
Erewhon 220, 407, 412-3, 415, 415n, 421
Estel 232
Evenstar 232-4
Everquest 393, 395n, 397-8, 400, 402
Excalibur 157-8

Fangorn Forest 92, 161, 175, 191, 194, 230, 236
Fanon, Franz viii, 138, 140
Faramir 158, 200-1, 207-8, 236, 300, 321, 343n
Fellowship of the Ring (film) 22, 27, 35, 41, 47, 54, 71-2, 94, 98, 102, 129, 135, 141, 152, 156-7, 160, 162, 164, 166n, 175, 177-8, 215-6, 241, 249n, 257-9, 282, 286n,

302, 311-6, 318-9, 321, 328n, 331, 336, 338, 341

Fellowship of the Ring (game) 373, 375, 378, 397

Ferguson, Mark 80, 85

Field of Dreams 52

Final Fantasy 379

Fitzcarraldo 109n

Ford, John 172, 278, 278n, 339

Forest River 150

Forgotten Silver xv

Forman, Milos 281

Fornost 209

Foucault, Michel xiv, 111, 312, 315-20

Fox, Michael J. xvi

Frankenheimer, John viii

Frighteners xiv, xvi, 50, 56

Frodo 23, 25, 28, 69, 91, 95, 133-5, 137, 141, 152-3, 155, 159, 159n, 160, 162-3, 166, 171-2, 176, 192, 200, 200n, 207-8, 231, 233-5, 239-245, 245n, 246-7, 249, 249n, 250-5, 257-65, 280, 282-4, 284n, 285, 297-305, 308, 311, 313-9, 321-3, 336, 350, 374-5, 394, 396-8.

From Russia with Love (game) 154

Fuqua, Antoine 170

Galadriel 129, 133, 139, 156, 164, 176, 230-2, 235, 253, 262-4, 282, 284, 300, 312, 315, 322, 377

Gamling 80

Gandalf xvii, 7, 67, 132n, 135, 138, 140-1, 149, 150n, 158-9, 159n, 160-1, 164, 166n, 174-6, 192, 202, 206-8, 230, 233-6, 254, 257-60, 262, 264-5, 276, 297-300, 313-4, 316, 319, 321, 323, 374-7, 380

Gandhi 131

Getaway 381

Gibson, Mel viii, 52

Gildor 80

Gil-galad 80

Gimli ix, 67, 135, 141, 156, 164, 236, 257, 274n, 282, 375

Gladden Fields 93

Glamdring 217, 235

Glorfindel 160, 233

Goethe 90n

Gollum 92, 140, 159, 200, 207, 218, 225, 273, 300, 304, 319, 321-2, 343n, 374

Gondor 46, 76, 159, 173-4, 192, 200, 200n, 206-7, 209, 316, 323, 350, 399, 411

Gorbag 81

Gorgoroth 151

Gramsci, Antonio 133

Grand Prix 385

Grand Theft Auto 380

Great Expectations 296

Great River 149, 166n

Green Dragon 399

Grey Mountains 150n

Grimms' Fairy Tales 294

Grin, Alexander 6

Grishnakh 81

Guattari, Felix xii

Gwaihir 162

Hadahafang 233

Haldir 80

Halo 17, 379-80

Haradrims 139

Harding, Jonathan 80

Harry Potter / Harry Potter 99, 99n, 100, 291-3, 296-7, 303-8, 348n

Hassle-Free Tours 67, 67n, 76, 76n, 85

Heavenly Creatures xiv-xv, 56

Heidegger, Martin 175

Helm's Deep 161, 181, 237, 281, 308, 401

Hennah, Dan 339

Henneth Annûn Story Archive 347n, 352-61, 363-5

Herbert, Frank 158

Hercules vii
Herzog, Werner 109n, 134
Hitchcock, Alfred 161-2, 278, 278n
Hitler, Adolf 137
Hobbit (book / film) 4, 20, 26-7, 149, 150n, 234-5, 277, 293, 296, 307, 365, 398
Hobbit (games) 12, 149, 152, 153n, 373-4, 394, 397
Hobbiton xvii, 46-7, 52, 71, 92, 97, 111, 123, 169, 175-7, 218, 226, 235, 338, 408
Hobbits 19, 37, 41, 57, 69, 133-4, 139n, 140-1, 143, 150-1, 170, 198, 239-41, 243, 245, 254, 258-9, 262, 273, 280, 282-3, 299-301, 303, 311, 316, 318, 324, 335-6, 350, 361, 374, 398, 407, 407n, 413
Hopkins, Bruce 80-1, 81n, 85
Howe, John 68, 79, 85, 160
Hulk 157

Idrial 377
Imladris 395
Indiana Jones 142
Into the West 171
Isengard 46, 93, 138, 156, 162, 175, 176, 180-1, 223, 316
Isildur 129, 205, 207, 218, 233, 302-3, 312-3, 319
Island of Dr Moreau viii
Istari 206
Ithilien Camp 92

Jackson, Michael 420-1
Jackson, Peter ix, xi, xiv-xviii, 5, 36-7, 39, 42, 44, 49-51, 53, 56, 59, 61, 67-71, 74, 76-8, 80, 83-4, 88, 90-1, 109, 110n, 113-4, 115n, 132-6, 138-42, 144, 149, 151-3, 155-7, 159, 162, 164-6, 166n, 169-70, 172-7, 181, 185, 190-5, 210, 215, 217, 228-236, 241, 257-8, 264, 271, 275-7, 279-80, 281n, 282, 282n, 284-5, 285n, 286, 292-3, 296, 298-9, 301-4, 307-8, 311-2, 312n, 313-4, 316, 319-321, 330-1, 331n, 332, 332n, 333, 336-43, 348-9, 384, 391, 394, 402-3, 415-7, 420-1
Jameson, Frederic 175
Journey to the Centre of the Earth ix
Jung, Carl 229-30, 232
Jurassic Park ix

King Arthur 170
King Edward's School 382-3
King Kong 5, 51, 59, 69, 331n, 343
King of the Dead 80-1
Kopp, Sandro 80
Kurosawa, Akira 157, 162

Lacan, Jacques 141
Lad from Old Ireland 171
Last Samurai viii, 5, 46, 102, 194
Lawrence of Arabia 131
Lean, David 131
Lee, Alan 60, 68, 68n, 79, 85, 160
Lee, Christopher 194
Legolas 67, 135, 141, 156, 231, 236, 257, 274n, 363, 375, 380-1
Lesnie, Andrew, xi, 339
Lewis, C.S. 6, 274n, 391
Lord of the Rings Exhibition 35-7, 101, 101n, 111
Lord of the Rings Location Guidebook 69n, 90, 92, 111, 218, 218n
Lorenz, Konrad 390
Lost World ix
Lothlórien 73, 92-3, 156, 230-1, 264-5, 282
Lucas, George 60, 77, 202, 205, 279, 292, 327
Lynch, David 157-8

Mad Max viii
Malbeth 209
Maori vii, viii, x, x(n), 75n, 79, 89, 92-3, 114, 138, 142, 172-4, 179, 116n

Master and Commander 81
Matrix 333n
Max Payne 381
McCarey, Leo 278
McKellen, Ian xvii, 41, 197, 374
Meduseld 67-8, 68n, 76
Megacon 73-4
Merry xvii, 67, 135, 138, 192, 246, 257, 321, 336
Middle Earth Online 393, 395
Miller, George viii, ix
Milton 134
Minas Morgul 159
Minas Tirith 39, 59, 78, 156, 158-9
Mirkwood 149n, 150, 150n
Mirromere 166n
Misty Mountains 78, 161-2, 166, 166n, 247
Mithrandir 208
Monaghan, Dominic 23, 336
Mordor 5, 91, 132-3, 153n, 156, 159, 175, 192, 225, 235-6, 262, 273, 298-9, 314-7, 319-3
Morgul 159, 200, 234, 244
Moria 12, 27, 156, 159n, 160, 175, 235, 353n
Mortensen, Viggo 84
Mount Doom 28, 135, 155, 200n, 233, 257, 322
Murnau, Friedrich 108
Myst (game) 154, 154n

Narsil 234, 313, 321
Narya 235
Nazgûl 138, 140, 158, 160, 160n, 162, 200n, 219, 233, 243, 247, 298, 304
Neill, Sam ix, xv-xvi
Nenya 231-2
New Line Cinema / Studio 36, 39, 99, 100, 114, 123, 131, 171, 179, 185, 210, 307, 417, 419
Newell, Mike, 171, 292, 306

Nietzsche, Friedrich 25, 257
Noble, John 76-7, 77n, 78, 85, 343n
Nomad Safaris 91
Norell, Paul 81, 85
North by Northwest 278
Nosferatu 108
Noyce, Phillip ix, 142
Númenor 79, 207, 319

Olcott, Sidney 171
Old Forest 78, 395-6
Old Willow 396
Oliphaunts 138, 151, 160, 216
Oliver Twist 294, 296
Once Were Warriors xvii, 131
One Flew over the Cuckoo's Nest 281
Orc Tree 93
Orcs 80, 122, 139, 150n, 151-2, 156, 160n, 176, 181, 198, 236, 262, 276, 304, 313, 320-1, 377, 401
Orme, Stuart ix
Orthanc 61, 175-6
Osgiliath 158
Otto, Miranda 71, 343n
Outback New Zealand 98

Palantír (Palantiri) 162, 201, 315-6, 318, 321, 323, 409-10, 412
Parker, Craig 80, 85
Pelennor 57, 91, 230, 321
Pianist 87
Piano vii, xiv, xvi, xvi(n), 5, 109, 416
Pippin 74, 77, 81, 135, 158-9, 164, 192, 257, 336, 343n
Plato 137, 283
Polanski, Roman 87
Porras, Nick xvii, 339
Powell, Enoch 383
Prancing Pony 151

Quenya 284

Rabbit Proof Fence viii-xix
Radagast 207
Rangi, Shane 80
Rauros Falls 160
Red Book of Westmarch 58, 172, 301
Red Carpet Tours 47, 91, 92n, 95, 95n, 96, 96n
Redhorn Gate 166n
Reeve, Daniel 343n
Return of the King (film) 43-4, 57, 95-7, 102, 138-9, 141, 155, 158-9, 161, 173, 180, 192, 197, 219, 223, 283-4, 284n, 292, 301, 316, 318-9, 321-2, 328n, 329n, 331, 331n, 332n, 336-7, 340-1
Return of the King (game) 373, 376-7, 397
Rhys-Davies, John, ix
Ringers: Lord of the Fans 41-4, 217, 217n
Ringquest.com 343n
Rings Scenic Tours 97
Ringwraiths 12, 45, 80, 138-40, 243, 247, 249n, 250, 254, 304, 311, 315, 317-9, 321, 375, 402
Ringzone.com 343n
Riven 154, 154n
Rivendell 23, 37, 59, 69, 93, 135, 140, 149n, 175, 234-5, 239, 241-4, 245n, 247, 249, 249n, 252-4, 257, 260
Robins, Thomas 81, 85
Robinson, Phil 52
Rodenberry, Gene 205
Rodger, Tania 69, 79-80, 81n, 85
Roeg, Nicolas vii
Rohan 67-8, 68n, 76, 80, 173, 206, 276n, 339, 350, 411-2
Rohirrim 57, 68, 76, 84, 151, 156, 236
Rowling, J.K. 292-3, 296-7, 303-8
Runescape 17, 379

Sam Gamgee 28, 54, 78, 95, 137, 155, 159, 192, 246, 257, 259, 280, 282, 284, 284n, 285, 300, 301, 316, 319, 321-3, 363, 394
Saruman 122, 136, 138-40, 161-2, 175, 177, 181, 192, 194, 206, 236, 315-6, 318, 335
Sauron 122, 129, 136, 138, 155, 160n, 176, 192, 199, 200n, 201, 206, 231, 257, 302, 304, 311-3, 315-324, 411
Schindler's List 109
Scott, Ridley 331n
Searchers 172
Serkis, Andy 343n
Seven Samurai 157
Seventh Seal 263
Sex and the City 87
Shadowfax 68, 158, 192
Shadows of Angmar 395-6, 398, 401-3
Shagrat 80
Sharku 80
Shawshank Redemption 281
Shelley, Mary 295
Shelob 216, 282, 284, 322-3
Shire 41, 67, 69-73, 78, 80, 122-4, 132-4, 141, 144, 150, 155, 173, 175-6, 190, 199, 234, 241, 243, 245, 249, 252, 259-60, 262, 273, 282-3, 298-9, 301, 310, 318, 335, 338, 398, 407-412, 417
Shore, Howard 163, 191, 218n
Silmarillion 20, 172-3, 327, 365
Silverlode River 92, 166n
Sinclair, Harry vii
Slim, William 382-3
Smaug 149
Sméagol 300 – see also Gollum
Snaga 80
Sorbo, Kevin vii
Spielberg, Steven ix, 109, 142, 279
Star Trek 198, 202, 335n, 350
Star Wars 60, 77, 202, 307, 327, 327n, 397
Star Wars Galaxies (game) 397, 397n

Stevenson, Robert Louis 295
Stoker, Bram 108, 295
Stories of Arda 352-61, 366-70

Tait, Peter 80
Tamahori, Lee xvii, 131
Taylor, Richard 36, 45, 53, 69, 79-80, 81n, 85, 275
Te Papa – see LotR Exhibition
Thèoden 140, 161, 302, 318
TheOneRing.net 24, 38, 41-4, 47-9, 96, 96n, 132n, 198, 210, 286n, 331n, 335n, 340, 340n, 343, 343n
Third Age (game) 373, 377-8
Third Age 110, 205
Thorin 149
Titanic / *Titanic* 31, 36, 108n
Tol Brandir 160
Tolkien Society 19, 24, 78-80, 85
Tolkien, Christopher 159, 349
Tolkien, J.R.R. xiv, xvi-xviii, 4-8, 10-16, 19-28, 38-9, 41, 43-5, 49, 60-1, 68, 68n, 69-70, 74, 77-80, 85, 90-2, 97, 110, 115, 119-20, 123, 129, 132, 132n, 133-5, 137, 137n, 138-9, 139n, 144, 149-50, 150n, 151-6, 159-60, 162, 165-6, 166n, 169-70, 172-3, 176, 180, 182, 191, 198, 198n, 199-202, 204-10, 229-30, 232-6, 239-40, 258, 271-4, 274n, 275-82, 282n, 283-5, 285n, 291-304, 307-8, 312-6, 321, 327, 330-1, 338, 340, 343, 343n, 348-9, 349n, 350-1, 351n, 352, 357-61, 366, 383-5, 385n, 386, 391, 394-5, 398, 401-3, 415, 417-8, 421
Tom Bombadil 138, 159n, 202, 335, 375, 396-7
Topless Women vii-viii, xi-xii, xiv(n), xv
Tourism New Zealand 52, 88n, 92, 94, 94n, 95, 95n, 96, 96n, 97-8, 98n, 99, 99n, 114, 123, 171, 178-80,
Toynbee, Arnold xii
Transformers 43
Troll's Clearing 240, 243, 247-8

Trolls 12, 135, 152, 235, 258, 402
Twin Peaks 347
Two Towers (film) 71-2, 75, 84, 95, 135, 138, 140, 164, 192, 216, 225, 236, 276, 279, 282, 284, 319, 321, 323, 328n, 329n, 332n, 336, 337, 339, 341, 418
Two Towers (game) 373, 375-6, 397
Tyler Liv, 51, 84

Urban Karl 95
Ure, Stephen, 81
Uruk Lurtz 160n
Uruk-hai viii, 136, 138-9, 156, 172-3, 304

Valandil 207
Valar 207-8, 283-4
Valinor 207
Verne, Jules, ix
Vertical Limit viii

Wachowski, Larry and Andy 333n
Wagner 137
Walkabout viii
Walking with Dinosaurs ix
Walsh, Fran 42, 56, 157
Warcraft 378, 393, 395n, 397, 397n, 398-402
Warg 92, 149n
Weathertop 200, 254, 298, 318
Weber, max 201
Weir, Peter 81, 142
Welles, Orson xv
Wenders, Wim 285n
Wenham, David, 343n
Weta Worshop xiv, 45, 52-3, 59, 61, 69, 79-80, 231
Whale Rider 49, 131
White Mountains 163n
White Witch 80
Wilder, Billy 278

Wings of Desire 285n
Winter Sonata 87
Witch King 80, 200, 219, 230, 318
Wood, Elijah 95, 155, 336, 343, 343n, 374
Wyler, William 172

X2: X-Men United 43
Xena vii
X-Men 43

Yun, Seok-ho 87

Zizek, Slavoj 161-2
Zwick, Edward viii, 5, 46, 194

 Walking Tree Publishers was founded in 1997 as a forum for publication of material (books, videos, CDs, etc.) related to Tolkien and Middle-earth studies. Manuscripts and project proposals can be submitted to the board of editors (please include an SAE):

Walking Tree Publishers
CH-3052 Zollikofen
Switzerland
e-mail: info@walking-tree.org
http://www.walking-tree.org

Cormarë Series

The *Cormarë Series* has been the first series of studies dedicated exclusively to the exploration of Tolkien's work. Its focus is on papers and studies from a wide range of scholarly approaches. The series comprises monographs, thematic collections of essays, conference volumes, and reprints of important yet no longer (easily) accessible papers by leading scholars in the field. Manuscripts and project-proposals are evaluated by members of an independent board of advisors who support the series editors in their endeavour to provide the readers with qualitatively superior yet accessible studies on Tolkien and his work.

News from the Shire and Beyond—Studies on Tolkien.
　　Edited by Peter Buchs & Thomas Honegger. Zurich and Berne 2004. Reprint. First edition 1997. (Cormarë Series 1)

Root and Branch: Approaches Towards Understanding Tolkien.
　　Edited by Thomas Honegger. Zurich and Berne 2005. Reprint. First edition 1999. (Cormarë Series 2)

Richard Sturch. *Four Christian Fantasists: A Study of the Fantastic Writings of George MacDonald, Charles Williams, C. S. Lewis and J.R.R. Tolkien.* Zurich and Berne 2007. Reprint. First edition 2001. (Cormarë Series 3)

Tolkien in Translation.
　　Edited by Thomas Honegger. Zurich and Berne 2003. (Cormarë Series 4)

Mark T. Hooker. *Tolkien Through Russian Eyes.* Zurich and Berne 2003. (Cormarë Series 5)

Translating Tolkien: Text and Film.
　　Edited by Thomas Honegger. Zurich and Berne 2004. (Cormarë Series 6)

Christopher Garbowski. *Recovery and Transcendence for the Contemporary Mythmaker: The Spiritual Dimension in the Works of J.R.R. Tolkien.* Zurich and Berne 2004. Reprint. First edition by Marie Curie Sklodowska University Press, Lublin 2000. (Cormarë Series 7)

Reconsidering Tolkien.
　　Edited by Thomas Honegger. Zurich and Berne 2005. (Cormarë Series 8)

Tolkien and Modernity 1.
　　Edited by Frank Weinreich & Thomas Honegger. Zurich and Berne 2006. (Cormarë Series 9)

Tolkien and Modernity 2.
　　Edited by Thomas Honegger & Frank Weinreich. Zurich and Berne 2006. (Cormarë Series 10)

Tom Shippey. *Roots and Branches: Selected Papers on Tolkien by Tom Shippey.* Zurich and Berne 2007. (Cormarë Series 11)

Ross Smith. *Inside Language: Linguistic and Aesthetic Theory in Tolkien.*
Zurich and Berne 2007. (Cormarë Series 12)

How We Became Middle-earth: A Collection of Essays on The Lord of the Rings.
Edited by Adam Lam & Nataliya Oryshchuk. Zurich and Berne 2007. (Cormarë Series 13)

Myth and Magic: Art according to the Inklings.
Edited by Eduardo Segura & Thomas Honegger. Zurich and Berne 2007. (Cormarë Series 14)

The Silmarillion—Thirty Years On.
Edited by Allan Turner. Zurich and Berne 2007. (Cormarë Series 15)

Beyond Middle-earth: Tolkien's Shorter Works 1. Proceedings of the 4th Seminar of the Deutsche Tolkien Gesellschaft & Walking Tree Publishers Decennial Conference.
Edited by Frank Weinreich & Margaret Hiley. Zurich and Berne 2007, forthcoming.

Beyond Middle-earth: Tolkien's Shorter Works 2. Proceedings of the 4th Seminar of the Deutsche Tolkien Gesellschaft & Walking Tree Publishers Decennial Conference.
Edited by Margaret Hiley & Frank Weinreich. Zurich and Berne 2007, forthcoming.

Martin Simonson. *The Lord of the Rings and the Western Narrative Tradition.*
Zurich and Berne, forthcoming.

Constructions of Authorship in and around the Works of J.R.R. Tolkien.
Edited by Judith Klinger. Zurich and Berne, forthcoming.

Rainer Nagel. *Hobbit Place-names: A Linguistic Excursion through the Shire.*
Zurich and Berne, forthcoming.

Tales of Yore Series

The *Tales of Yore Series* grew out of the desire to share Kay Woollard's whimsical stories and drawings with a wider audience. The series aims at providing a platform for qualitatively superior fiction with a clear link to Tolkien's world.

Kay Woollard. *The Terror of Tatty Walk: A Frightener.* CD and Booklet.
Zurich and Berne 2000 (Tales of Yore 1)

Kay Woollard, *Wilmot's Very Strange Stone or What came of building "snobbits".* CD and booklet.
Zurich and Berne 2001 (Tales of Yore 2)